RICHARD GAMBINO

BLOOD OF MY BLOOD

THE DILEMMA OF THE ITALIAN-AMERICANS

T0155364

GUERNICA

TORONTO — BUFFALO — LANCASTER (U.K.)

2011

Blood of My Blood was originally published in hardcover by Doubleday &
Company, Inc. in 1974, and a later edition was published by Anchor
Books/Doubleday.

First published by Guernica Editions in the Essay Series in 1996.

Antonio D'Alfonso, Editor.

Guernica Editions Inc.

P.O. Box 117, Station P, Toronto (ON), Canada M5S 2S6
2250 Military Rd., Tonawanda, N.Y. 14150-6000 U.S.A.
Gazelle Book Services, White Cross Mill, High Town,
Lancaster, U.K. LA1 1Xs

Legal Deposit — First Quarter
National Library of Canada
Library of Congress Card Number: 99-66849
Canadian Cataloguing in Publication Data

Gambino, Richard
Blood of my blood : the dilemma of the Italian-Americans
2nd ed.
Picas series ; 7)
First ed. published New York: Doubleday, 1974.
ISBN 1-55071-101-6
ISBN 978-1-5507-1101-1

1. Italian Americans – History. I. Title. II. Series.
E184.IG35 2000 305.851073 99-901231-2

BLOOD OF MY BLOOD

THE DILEMMA OF THE ITALIAN-AMERICANS

PICAS SERIES 7

BLOOD OF MY BLOOD
The Dilemma of the Italian-Americans

Contents

Preface

This book is an interpretation of a people, Italian-Americans. Although it draws upon many historical, sociological, and other scholarly sources, it is a personal interpretation. The book represents *my* view of *my* people. I have included many personal experiences, but only those which years of study have convinced me are typical and illustrative of the Italian-American saga. By checking the objective record with my own experience, I have tried to heed the warning of an old Italian saying, *traduttore, traditore*—translator, traitor. By wedding my experience to the written records I have tried to be true both to the life of individuals I know and to the story of millions of others. Equally important, I have tried to capture not only the story but the warm, turbulent, and thriving soul of Italian-Americans, a much misunderstood and often maligned people. And I have done so as passionately as a Sicilian-American as much as a writer. In the end, I have tried to present a life, not an apology, a caricature, or an idealization.

There are four people to whom I am indebted in the writing of this book. I would like to thank Barbara Odani, a student at Queens College of the City University of New York, for helping me in research. I am grateful to Giuseppe Cardillo, Director of the Istituto Italiano di Cultura in New York City, and to Walter I. Bradbury, my editor, for reading the manuscript and making many helpful comments and corrections. Any errors contained in the work are, however, solely my responsibility.

Most of all I thank my wife, Gail, who inspired me to write this book and whose love and patience, intelligence and encouragement sustained and strengthened me in the labor.

Richard Gambino
New York City
July 1973

The Family System

During the first sixteen years of my life I lived in Red Hook, Brooklyn. Still largely Italian today, the area then was almost exclusively composed of Italian-American families, many of whose men were longshoremen on Brooklyn's large waterfront. It was typical of the many "Little Italies" in America, and, incidentally, is the area where Arthur Miller chose to set his forceful play about an Italian-American longshore family, *A View from the Bridge*. Also typical of many families in the Little Italies, I lived with my parents (my father emigrated from Palermo, Sicily, at age thirteen; my mother was born in Red Hook shortly after her parents came from Palermo), and my maternal grandparents.

One of my early memories is of an event that happened when I was perhaps seven years old. One of my closest friends was an Italian immigrant boy named Tony. One winter day, I forget why, Tony and I fought. We tumbled on the ground and hit at each other. Somehow, Tony's nose began to bleed. The sight of the blood on the dirty snow terrified both of us, and we each ran home. Because both my parents worked during the day, I went to my grandparents' basement flat rather than to my own, immediately above it. Of course I kept silent about the fight and the blood, preferring to shiver in fear next to the hot coal stove. In a few minutes, the inevitable happened. The doorbell rang, and I watched with a sense of doom as my grand-

mother walked the long corridor to the outside "gate" of
the old brownstone. I thought my fate was sealed a minute
later when I heard her call to me in the uniquely sharp,
decisive Sicilian dialect, *Veni iccà!* (come here!). My
second-generation mother had taught me that fighting was
wrong, that hurting someone was wrong, and sometimes
reinforced these and other lessons of American morality
by spankings. I was thus totally unprepared for the scene
I found at the gate. There was my grandmother, a big
woman, standing in the doorway facing Tony's mother,
totally blocking the latter's view. My grandmother stood
squarely on both feet, hands resting on hips, palms turned
outward from the body—the reverse of the American manner. In the body language of Southern Italy, the stance's
meaning was unmistakable—"Don't tread on me or mine!"
The two women were engaged in delivering ritual insults
to each other, in hissing voices, almost spitting as they
spoke. Southern Italians have a name for a game of ritualized oratory—*passatella*. The gist of my grandmother's
part of this serious passatella was that Tony was a worthless son of worthless blood and it was a *vergogna* (outrage)
to allow him to walk the streets with her *nipotino* (fine
little grandson). This was news to me—my grandmother
often saw me play with Tony and previously had spoken
to his mother with courtesy, hence as a peer. After the
confrontation, back inside the house, my grandmother
asked me what had happened. Her only comment upon
my explanation was that since I shed Tony's blood, *he*
must have committed some *infamia* (infamy)!

I was astonished. My mother, when informed by my
teacher of some misbehavior on my part in school, had
automatically taken the teacher's side and promised me a
beating when I came home—a promise kept. But my grandmother's only punishment to me was a one-sentence lec-
ture on choosing my companions more carefully. She did
not even mention the incident to my "American" parents.

My parents were embarked on the *via nuova* (new
way), and I suppose my grandmother, in accordance with
a Sicilian proverb, considered them too far down the road

to recognize what was demanded in such a family confrontation. The proverb is, *Chi lascia la via vecchia per la nuova, sa quel che perde e non sa quel che trova*—"Whoever forsakes the old way for the new knows what he is losing but not what he will find."

At least 85 per cent of the total of Italians who immigrated to the United States, and perhaps 90 per cent of those who came in the great flood of immigration from 1875 to 1920, were from areas south and east of Rome. Italians call this area the Meridone or Midi or Mezzogiorno. It is composed of the six provinces of Abruzzi, Campania, Apulia, Lucania (also known as Basilicata), Calabria, and Sicily. The name Mezzogiorno is rich in connotations. One of the most significant is, "the land that time forgot." About 25 per cent of the immigrants from the land forgotten by time came from Sicily.

Italian immigrants were overwhelmingly of the *contadino* class—peasant farmers—but also fishermen, artisans, and unskilled urban poor whose ways of life were contadino from such cities as Naples, Palermo, Bari, Messina, Catania, Reggio di Calabria, Foggia, Salerno, Cosenza, Catanzaro, Enna, Ragusa, and Agrigento. In the contadino tradition shared by these people, there was one and only one social reality, the peculiar mores of family life. *La famiglia* and the personality it nurtured were very different from the American nuclear family and the personalities that are its typical products. The famiglia was composed of all of one's blood relatives, including those relatives Americans would consider very distant cousins, aunts and uncles, an extended clan whose genealogy was traced through paternity. The clan was supplemented through an important custom known as *comparatico* or *comparaggio* (godparenthood), through which carefully selected outsiders became to an important (but incomplete) extent members of the family.

The only system to which the contadino paid attention was *l'ordine della famiglia*, the unwritten but all-demanding and complex system of rules governing one's relations within, and responsibilities to, his own family, and his pos-

ture toward those outside the family. All other social institutions were seen within a spectrum of attitudes ranging
from indifference to scorn and contempt.

One had absolute responsibilities to family superiors
and absolute rights to be demanded from subordinates in
the hierarchy. All ambiguous situations were arbitrated by
the *capo di famiglia* (head of the family), a position held
within each household by the father until it was given to—
or, in the case of the father's senility, taken away by—one
of the sons, and in the larger clan, by a male "elder"
(*anziano*). The contadino showed calculated respect
(*rispetto*) to members of other families which were powerful, and *pietà*, a mixture of pity, charity, and haughtiness
or indifference toward families less powerful than his own.
He despised as a *scomunicato* (pariah) anyone in any family who broke the *ordine della famiglia* or otherwise violated the *onore* (honor, solidarity, tradition, "face") of the
family.

Thus the people of the Mezzogiorno survived a harsh history of invasions, conquests, colonizations, and foreign
rule by a procession of tribes and nations (including
Phoenicians, Carthaginians, Greeks, Romans, Vandals,
Goths, Austrians, Byzantines, Arabs, Normans, French,
Spanish, and various Northern Italian powers) and centuries of exploitation by landowners of great estates. Although they rose in violent rebellion many times, these insurrections were always crushed, betrayed, or both. What
enabled the contadini to endure and develop their own
culture was a system of rules based solely on a phrase I
heard uttered many times by my grandparents and their
contemporaries in Brooklyn's Little Italy: *sangu du me
sangu*, Sicilian dialect for "blood of my blood." (As is
typical of Sicilian women, my grandmother's favorite and
most earnest term of endearment when addressing her children and grandchildren, and when speaking of them to
others, was *sangu miu*—literally "my blood.")

It was a norm simple and demanding, protective and
isolating, humanistic and cynical. The unique family pattern of Southern Italy constituted the real sovereignty of

that land, regardless of which governments nominally ruled it. Governments and aliens came and went over the centuries. If they brought any customs that might strengthen the family system, these were gradually absorbed. Indeed, in an important sense, all who are derived from this land are descendants of these many cultures, "indigenous" and "alien," of thousands of years. But those customs that were hostile to the family were resisted.

Although much was absorbed from many cultures, the famous Sicilian collector of his island's folklore, Dr. Giuseppe Pitre, was essentially correct when before his death in 1913 he wrote, *"Noi siamo in mezzo a un popolino che non conosce altro galateo di la dal suo, altri usi se non i suoi"*—"We are in the midst of a people who know no other life pattern than their own, no other customs than those of their ancestors."

I was once again reminded of Pitre's words when I visited my sole surviving relatives in Palermo, one great aunt, age seventy-six, and one great aunt by marriage, age eighty-five. They could not understand why my "distant" relatives in America—cousins, great-uncle, etc.—and I do not often see each other. I tried to explain the busy pace of the United States, but they kept returning to the puzzle, at one point asking me if Manhattan (where I live) is very far from Brooklyn and Long Island (where my relatives live). At the end of many attempts at explanation on my part, one of them closed the conversation by saying in a resigned voice, without a trace of irony, "You must all live far from each other."

Among those raised in it, and this to various degrees includes all Italian-Americans, it is impossible to be untouched, if not determined, by *la via vecchia*. An understanding of this pattern of family life is critical to any understanding of Italian-Americans of any generation, the most "assimilated" third- and fourth-generation young people as well as wizened old immigrants. La via vecchia, cultivated for centuries, does not die quickly and certainly not easily. Even in the life of an urbane man like Luigi Pirandello, it had remarkable stamina. The great writer,

whose works probe the philosophical implications of the
subtle line between illusion and reality and are among the
most sophisticated of our time, lived much of his life away
from his homeland. Yet when he decided to marry, he
chose to return to his native Agrigento in southwest Sicily
to marry a young woman selected for him by his father,
a woman whom the writer had never seen before!

An example analogous to Pirandello's occurred in my
own family about ten years ago. It began with a tragic loss
for a cousin of mine, then a woman twenty-four years old.
Her Italian-born husband, age twenty-eight, drowned in a
boating accident, leaving with her two very young children. Following the morality of la via vecchia, after the
proper interval of time for mourning, the dead man's parents took it upon themselves to send word back to their
relatives in the homeland to find a suitable new husband
for their widowed daughter-in-law and father for their
grandchildren. But here the parallel with Pirandello ends.
For my cousin is of the third generation of Italian-
Americans and would not accept a "match." Several other
American-born members of my family had to meet with
her parents-in-law to explain that she wished to choose her
own spouse in her own time. Although they acceded to the
via nuova, the immigrant parents regarded it with disbelief
and alarm. I doubt that they were really resigned to it until
sometime later when my cousin married again—to a man
of her own choice.

The role played in my cousin's dilemma is typical of the
second generation, a generation that forged a great compromise between la via vecchia and la via nuova. Thus, in
this example, they interceded between the two ways. Interceding on behalf of the third-generation preference for
the via nuova to be sure, but interceding in a manner
typical of la via vecchia, *the family interceded.* This pattern
of relations between second generation (now mostly
middle-aged people) and the third and fourth generations,
mostly young adults, teen-agers, and children, is common.
In my opinion, it will prove to be one of the decisive determinants in the just beginning quest for identity on the

part of the younger generations of Italian-Americans. The strengths of this pattern will be a boon to them. The weaknesses in the pattern will define some of the chief problems they will have to overcome.

There is an illuminating saying among Southern Italians that the father is the head of the family, and the mother the center. The father, as the ultimate retainer of la via vecchia, made all important decisions concerning the family. A living for the family and good marriages for its children were the primary goals toward which decisions were aimed. In this culture, young people had to re-establish in each generation the only social reality of the land, the family, by marriage. Therefore a good marriage was more than just a question of social status. It was tantamount to survival and was treated as a basic bread-and-butter necessity.

In the first aim, a living, the father played an active key role. He labored and maneuvered to gain the most produce and money. In this he acted according to true Machiavellian principles, guarding and guiding the welfare of his family in a dangerous, even treacherous world where la miseria, desperate poverty, was a constant plague. He acted as a true monarch for the good of his endangered kingdom, according to the severe rules of Realpolitik. Family security, power, status, and necessities of life were goals pursued in this microcosm of the world of sovereign states. And as in the system of nations, they were goals pursued without regard to sentimentality or other moralities that were disastrous in the amoral social world. The father exercised this responsibility without confiding its problems or details to his wife. They were simply fatti suoi, his business. He would discuss them only when necessary, and then only with close male relatives, most often the clan's elder. To a more guarded degree, he might consult his padrino (older godparent) or his compare (a close friend, a peer godparent).

In a tradition that continues to puzzle foreigners who have a simplistic stereotyped notion of the Italian man's ideal of manliness, which they mislabel with the Spanish word *machismo*, the father turned over his earnings to his wife for complete management, keeping only a small allowance for his daily needs. Except for reserving the right to intercede in the case of mismanagement or other crisis, the father did not further concern himself with the family budget. Similarly, although he retained the right of veto over any proposed match, often the father was not the one who initiated arrangements for the marriages of his children. Often he did not enter into the picture until the way for the match had been carefully and quietly arranged by the mothers, aunts, and godmothers of the prospective bride and groom. Usually it was only when a match was virtually assured that the fathers of the respective families would enter into negotiations of which the public was aware. Similarly, the father played a subdued, background role in the raising of young children, stepping in only when he thought it necessary to preserve the over-all aim of the process—to turn out children who were *ben educati*, or, in the dialect, *buon educati*. As we shall see, this notion of being well educated had nothing to do with schooling. Rather it meant being brought up to value la via vecchia in thought and feeling, and to honor it in practice.

The family was the major transmitter of its own culture, and other institutions were welcomed only if they aided this goal. Those that were perceived as neither aiding l'ordine della famiglia nor endangering it were tolerated. Hence one source of the Italian's legendary attitude of "live and let live." To be more precise, institutions not affecting la via vecchia were regarded with simple indifference as *cose senza significato*, things of no consequence. But any person or event, idea or institution that was perceived as a threat to la via vecchia or to the members of the family served by the old way was stubbornly, fiercely, and if necessary violently resisted. Not only the father, but every member of the family down to the limit of the *bambini* (roughly the age of seven) was expected to protect the established code of behavior, the onore della famiglia. For example, the sons of the family above the age of puberty were expected to defend any undermining of the welfare of the females of the family, or, worse, any insult to their reputation or status, this being synonymous with an insult to the family's onore.

Individual rights, wishes and feelings were defined by one's membership in the family. One treated a person according not so much to his individual characteristics as to the status of his family and his particular place in it. In fact, it was difficult to conceive of a "person" in any realistic sense apart from his place and role in a family. The famous book *Christ Stopped at Eboli* offers an excellent proof of this. Its author, Carlo Levi, an artist, physician, and writer from Turin, in Northern Italy, was a vociferous opponent of the Fascist regime of Mussolini. Because of this, he was exiled in 1935 to a small village in the southern province of Lucania (the "anklebone" of the Italian boot).

His book describes the life of the people there. In one passage, Levi tells of a visit to him by his sister, Luisa, and the dramatic difference it created in his status as a person among the contadini. As he tells us, until then he might just as well have been a creature from Mars in the eyes of the people of the Mezzogiorno.

Hitherto they had thought of me as a sort of man from Mars, the only one of my species, and the discovery that I had blood connections here on earth seemed somehow to fill in their picture of me in a manner that pleased them. The sight of me with my sister tapped one of their deepest feelings: that of blood relationship, which was all the more intense since they had so little attachment to either religion or the State. It was not that they venerated family relationship as a social, legal or sentimental tie, but rather that they cherished an occult and sacred sense of communality. A unifying web not only of family ties (a first cousin was often as close as a brother), but of the acquired and symbolic kinship called *comparaggio* [godparenthood], ran throughout the village . . .

Toward evening, when my sister and I walked arm in arm along the main street, the peasants beamed at us from their houses; "Blessed is the womb that bore you!" they called out to us from the doorways; "Blessed the breasts that suckled you!" Toothless old creatures looked up from their knitting to mumble proverbs: "A wife is one thing, but a sister's something more!" "Sister and brother, all to one another." Luisa, with her rational, city [Turin]-bred way of looking at things, never got over their strange enthusiasm for the simple fact that I had a sister.

All obligations, feelings, or rights of radical individuality were repressed by any good father or mother, daughter or son. For example, if a married daughter claimed she or her children were being abused by her husband—which could mean only that he was not conforming to la via vecchia—it was her brothers and, if necessary, other young male relatives who were expected to confront the culprit. Upon confirmation of the charge, the offending husband would be privately warned to mend his ways. In the Mezzogiorno, such a warning of offended onore, like everything else that touched upon the maintenance of la via vecchia, was never taken (or given) lightly.

In their tenacious will to survive inbred over centuries, the contadini paradoxically valued la via vecchia more than their very lives. For survival and the old way had been synonymous for ages.

In the United States today, much of the behavior of Italian-Americans becomes more intelligible when its roots in la via vecchia are understood. For example, as recent studies have shown, Italian-American families move their homes reluctantly. Further, they do so only when it nurtures the traditional values of their families. The persistence of Little Italy in and near New York's Greenwich Village, side by side with Jewish families in times past, Chinese families until today, and wave after wave of "bohemians," "beatnicks," and "hippies" has been cited as an illustrative example. It is only when Italian-Americans perceive (correctly or not) some other group behaving in ways that are antithetical to the life of la famiglia that they react with resistance, often merely labeled "intolerance" by the press without further attempts at analysis.

For example, a near race riot in Brooklyn a few years ago was explained by a nun very simply by citing the fact that an Italian-American girl had been whistled at and spoken to in rude terms by a Puerto Rican boy. It is a pattern of America's history that it forces the groups at the lowest rung of its social-economic ladder to compete and clash with those at the next to lowest rung. In the past, first the Irish, Germans, blacks, and Scandinavians clashed with each other and with those of British background. This was followed by strife between the Irish and Germans on one hand, and Poles, Italians, blacks and Jews on the other. Now the clash is between poor and working class Irish, Poles and Italians, those "one rung up," and blacks, Puerto Ricans, and Chicanos on the bottom of the social-economic ladder. The simple-minded explanations that Polish-Americans, Irish-Americans, and Italian-Americans are more racist than other Americans is fostered by media coverage which too often "sees all," reports it, and explains little. The fact is that for millions of Italian-Americans, the capacity to tolerate anyone is in inverse proportion to the extent that the person's life style is perceived by them as a threat to la via vecchia. No doubt the racism that has played a role in America since its founding as a nation in Lincoln's terms, half slave, half free, has been learned by some Italian-Americans. But this only complicates the question of relations between Italian-Americans and other groups. Italian-Americans fought Irish-Americans in America's past, and dozens of other white groups in the history of the Mezzogiorno who were perceived in various ways as threats to la via vecchia.

As will be seen in the chapter on attitudes toward outsiders, a solution to the problem in the United States today must be based upon an understanding of la via vecchia, which Italian-Americans maintain and defend. Mere condemnation of "racism" and moralistic lecturing about it will continue to be ineffective. In Southern Italy one sees complexions ranging from very light to very dark. One need only to walk the streets of a city like Palermo to see evident descendants of Carthaginians and Arabs, who played a part in the history of the Mezzogiorno and descendants of the blond, blue-eyed Normans, French, and other whites who are part of the history. Although the people of the Mezzogiorno have had many quarrels with many "aliens" and among themselves, there is not now, nor has there ever been, discrimination based on racial characteristics in that part of Italy.

It is instructive to note that there has been no strife between Italian and (nonwhite) Chinese-Americans in downtown New York, in spite of many years of living very close to each other, just as there was little friction between Jewish and Italian-Americans there in the past. On the other hand there is strife everywhere among Italian and black and Spanish-speaking Americans. This is because the Italian-American does not perceive the Chinese and Jewish family-oriented life styles as a threat to la via vecchia and, correctly or not, does perceive the black and Hispanic "street style life" as opposed to it. Thus, the kind of insight often given, e.g., in 1971 by Glazer and Moynihan in their famous book *Beyond the Melting Pot* (M.I.T. Press) is true, but it is really unconstructive:

> Herman Badillo [a Democrat of Puerto Rican background] explaining why he would support Mayor Lindsay [then a Republican] instead of Mario Procaccino [the candidate of the Democratic Party], was quoted in *The New York Times* (July 30, 1969): 'When he talks about crime and treating juvenile offenders as adult criminals, he's talking about black and Puerto Rican kids. Everyone knows he's not talking about Jewish and Italian kids.' Interestingly enough, when you talked about criminals and juvenile delinquents in this city until twenty-five years ago, you *did* mean Jewish and Italian kids.

The father in la via vecchia was the "official" voice of the family in its external relations, and the ultimate authority in its internal affairs. The family of the Mezzogiorno was what anthropologists might call an agnatic group, meaning its organization was defined by relationships to males. This differs from the "bilateral family" definition of

Northern European families. Yet the contadino family
was no simple patriarchy, if by this word we mean exclusive rule by the father. Except for family emergencies,
the father played his role in the everyday internal affairs of
family in a relatively passive way. He did this for two reasons. One was economic necessity. In the Mezzogiorno, the
contadino descended from his village to work his fields,
often going great distances to do so and not infrequently
having to spend several nights a week away from his home.
The villages of the Mezzogiorno date from ancient or
medieval times and were usually built high up the slopes
of the severe, stony mountains of the land for purposes of
security against invaders, brigands, and the malaria-filled
marshes of the valleys. Virtually all people lived in these
villages. There were no equivalents to the system of isolated individual farms typical of rural life in America and
elsewhere. Paradoxically, rural life in the Mezzogiorno
was town life.

Similarly, because of their vocation the many *pescatori*
(fishermen) of the Mezzogiorno were away from their
homes during much of the time. Although with relatively
little land, mainland Italy, Sicily, and Sardinia are a peninsula and two islands and have many miles of coast.

Even the artisans and the poor of the large cities, most
of whom were contadino in origin, were influenced by the
tradition to stay out of daily household affairs. Like the
fathers, the older sons of the family were at work away
from the home from the time the father decided they
should begin work and turn over their earnings to the family purse, as he did. And the father usually made this decision by following an old formula of the Mezzogiorno
that says, "When hair grows between the legs, it is time to
work."

Of course, this rule also covered daughters. Females in
some areas of the Mezzogiorno, e.g., Sicily, worked in the
home and never outside of it, while in other regions, e.g.,
Calabria, they did light work in the fields as well. (A vestige of these practices is seen in the many gardens of
Italian-Americans. These are seldom tended by the

women.) This was continued in the New World. Many daughters were sent to work by Italian immigrants, and many second-generation women work after their marriages. It is interesting to understand why this last practice changed. For the explanation serves as a model for most of the differences between the life of Italian-Americans and the life of their recent ancestors in the old land.

In general, Italian-Americans have adopted only those new ways that they perceive as compatible with the family system and its values. Others have been shunned. So, for example, Italian-American daughters, and later wives, worked because this contributed to the family welfare. Nevertheless, they were held, and held themselves, close to the home. As in the Mezzogiorno, it was unthinkable for a single woman—or man—to live away from the family. Women left the house in time to get to the job and came home immediately after work. They were found, and later sought, jobs where they could work with other Italian-American women. A network of mutual reinforcement of the traditional values was extended. Significantly, they did factory work. No matter how poor, the Italian-American woman to this day does not work as a domestic. For to work in the house of another family (sometimes an absolute economic necessity in the old land) is seen as a usurpation of family loyalty by her family *and by her*. And if one loses one's place in la via vecchia, there is no self-respect. In American history, there is no Italian counterpart of Irish, German, black, Spanish-speaking, English, Scandinavian, and French maids. In 1950, most of the second generation was into adulthood and together with the Italian-born population in New York City numbered 859,-000, according to the United States Census of Population report. The report that year listed only 1 per cent of the female Italian immigrant population as employed as private household workers, while the figure for the second-generation female population was zero per cent.

My mother's experience is illustrative. The daughter of immigrants, she was sent to work in a large garment factory as a seamstress, to work together with numbers of other Italian-American girls, including an older sister. The compulsory education law of New York State posed few problems for the younger girls. In common practice, the truant officer was simply bribed to look the other way and to turn in reports that he was "actively pursuing" a child's case until he or she became sixteen and was no longer of legal concern. A working girl was expected to spend all of her remaining time learning the domestic skills. To put it mildly, any activity outside the home was discouraged, and there was no acceptable excuse for not being home on time after work. The immigrants compromised with la via nuova only when it served la via vecchia, and only to the extent that was necessary to serve this end.

The second reason for the father's passive role in daily household affairs, and indeed the only reason it was possible, was the active role played by the mother. Her designation as the "center" of the family might be extended—she was in a crucial way the center of the culture. For it was she who not only maintained the home as the seat of l'ordine della famiglia, but also had responsibility to nurture it in her children with every word, look, and gesture. If the father was monarch in the family kingdom, the mother was the powerful minister of internal affairs.

Italian-American homes are kept immaculately clean, so much so that Americans are bemused thereby. Sometimes the bemusement turns to bigoted amusement. Thus the stereotype of the "unliberated" Italian mamma, concerned exclusively with the home, is a source of condescension and outright ridicule. How simple she seems, even covering the furniture in her working-class living room with covers of transparent plastic. As with most stereotypes, there is here a germ of truth, albeit very distorted.

Traditionally, the home was the site and the source of all that gave meaning to life. A well-kept home was the symbol of a sound family. Furniture that lasted was symbolic of family stability and hence family strength. Plentiful food in the kitchen was a sign of family well being. But ostentation was shunned. As we shall see, the unique religious attitudes of the Mezzogiorno were an amalgam of

Christian doctrines, magic, and pagan beliefs. In this morality, it was considered unwise to display signs of one's wealth. Conspicuous consumption, or anything approaching it, was a sure sign of moral madness. It was a sign of sinful hubris, inviting a punishing nemesis on the part of the forces governing the universe, powers that were believed to be immediate, palpable, and ever present. So to this day, Italian-Americans tend to live *below* their financial means. Their homes, clothes, and cars often represent less than they might afford.

In a land where conspicuous consumption, in the style dictated by class-conscious fashion, is the sign of having "made it" in society, the opposed patterns of Italian-Americans make them the objects of condescension, ridicule, or at least of misunderstanding. They are tagged as socially gauche, un-chic working-class types stigmatized in the sad American practice of ethnic jokes. Thus, the same joke I heard about Poles in St. Louis and about Italians in Philadelphia: "What is the first thing a flamingo does when it buys a home?" Answer: "It puts a Polack [Italian] out on the lawn." Or to take a case of misunderstanding, in a recent movie review published in the New York *Post* panning the film *The Godfather*, Emily Genauer noted that the Italian-American family in the film was wealthy and she found fault with the film because:

> . . . and yet there are no signs of wealth to be seen. The house Don Vito lives in is ugly and commonplace, filled with squalling kids, with women old and young who show none of the appurtenances of wealth

The reviewer's ignorance of the life style of many Italian-Americans is understandable. Yet are we so far into materialism in the United States that we must simply accept Miss Genauer's judgment that the Italian-American home is "ugly and commonplace"? Could it be that the current fascination on the part of many Americans with the Italian-American home and family reflects a discontent with the hollow, brainless, and heartless ideal of "the beautiful people" incessantly trumpeted by advertising and the media, an ideal that Miss Genauer presumably thinks more appropriate to people who have money? Perhaps we might ponder whether these Americans are attracted to the values of warmth, loyalty, sense of belonging, palpable enjoyment of everyday life, and lack of pretense they perceive in the Italian-American home. Further, perhaps we should ponder which set of values is preferable.

The stereotype of the Italian-American mother's preoccupation with food also has a kernel of truth in it, although again distorted. To all Mediterranean people, food is the symbol of life, of all that is good and nourishing. We are all familiar with the legends surrounding the importance of food to such peoples as the Italians, the Spanish, the French, the Arabs, and the Greeks. Thus, these people find the attitude of some Americans toward food worse than barbarous. This attitude, characterized in the extreme by the American food stand where one eats bland mass-prepared food on the run, is seen as sacrilegious. To the Italian-American, food is symbolic both of life and of life's chief medium for human beings, the family.

I remember the attitude conveyed to me as a child by the adults in my family, immigrants and second generation, that the waste or abuse of food was a sin. They did so not by any attempt to link waste with the Catholic religion, or by inducing guilt through invidious distinctions as in the "think of the starving children of India" approach. On the contrary, I was made to feel that food was the host of life, and not in any remote or abstract sense. It was the product of my father's (or grandfather's, or uncle's, etc.) labor, prepared for us with care by my mother (or grandmother, or aunt, etc.). It was in a very emotional sense a connection with my father and mother, an outreach by them toward me. In a very poignant way, meals were a "communion" of the family, and food was "sacred" because it was the tangible medium of that communion. To this day I cannot bear to see food wasted and tend to save even the smallest quantities of leftovers from a meal. To see edible food thrown in a garbage can has a similar emotional effect on me to seeing a trampled flower in a field, or a dead animal by the side of the highway.

Respect for food as the host of life is upheld even in the most anonymous, poor, and crowded of circumstances. While in Palermo, I spent some time wandering through the area of the city where my father lived as a boy. It is a maze of streets in the old medieval heart of the city around the Via Porta di Castro. The streets and alleys are impossibly narrow, congested with people, and squalid. The buildings are archaic. Except for the presence of electricity, the area is a kind of casbah, unchanged for centuries and as impoverished as perhaps any area in Europe. I watched life there as I had heard it described by my father. Swarms of people walking past groups of others sitting on chairs in the streets, most of which are too narrow to permit automobiles. The earnest chatter of adults animated by swift arabesques of hand gestures and punctuated by the shouts and squalls of children. The women who lower baskets by rope from their windows to accept the objects of the errands their young children run for them. The open stalls that are the counterpart of both our shops and workshops. The artisans and workmen in the latter, laboring in tiny one-room cubicles. The fantastic, elaborate, and odorous outdoor markets where every kind of meat, fish, and produce is prepared and displayed, in exactly the same way as it had been on Court Street, Smith Street, and Union Street when I was a boy in Brooklyn. The cacophony of smells of my boyhood was replayed. Salted fish (*baccalà*, *stoccafisso*), fresh fish, dried peppers, newly baked bread, the sickly smell of bloody cuts of meat, the spicy odor of sausages, the cutting smell of enormous cheeses, the tang of oranges, the allure of garlic and oregano were all blended yet distinguishable.

And here I would eat lunch, in this medieval anachronism just a short walking distance from Palermo's "Fifth Avenue," the Via Macqueda, where one finds long rows of sophisticated shops like Elizabeth Arden's flanking the headquarters of Sicily's Communist Party opposite the famous opera house, the Teatro Massimo at the Piazza

Giuseppe Verdi. (The party incessantly blasted forth propaganda from its building via an earsplitting, high-decibel PA system, to the evident disgust of the many passers-by who included sleek girls in minis and old women dressed in the traditional black. The only verbal response to the magnified exhortations for "a new Italy" coming from the large building was from a man, about twenty-five years old and dressed in mod clothing à la London's Carnaby Street. He looked up to shout *cafone*—a term meaning a vulgar, undignified person; roughly, a "slob"—at the voice from the loudspeakers and proceeded to harangue it on the subject of *buon costume*, proper behavior! I burst out laughing. It was as if John Lennon were to embark on one of my grandparents' lectures on traditional Sicilian good behavior.)

Lunch at one of the open stall restaurants consisted of typical foods, dishes I used to enjoy in the sawdust-floored longshoremen's restaurants in Brooklyn. I feasted on my favorites—*arancine* (deep-fried rice balls, each the size of a baseball, stuffed with chopped meat, peas, and spiced tomato sauce) and *panelle* (a type of flat, rectangular pancake made from chick-pea flour, deep fried and eaten with or without bread). The prices of the food reflected the poverty of the area. Lunch could be had for 125 lire, about a quarter. Being accustomed to the hot dog stand in America, the first time I ate at one of the "luncheonettes" of Palermo's poor, I began to wolf down the food at the counter while standing in the street. (The people who live in the area buy the food hot and take it home to be eaten at leisure, often at a door-side table.) The lone proprietor and cook immediately invited me to come sit inside (the sole room being the kitchen), and set a makeshift table for me on a food counter. In the midst of the hurly-burly and destitute poverty, the natural manner was one of medieval chivalry, so cherished in Southern Italy. The ceremony of eating was to be honored.

I was reminded of a conversation I had a few years ago with a retired social worker in New York City. In her career, she had visited the homes of the succeeding ethnic

waves of New York's poor. She related to me how struck
she was when she first went into Italian-American homes
during the depression of the 1930's. Nothing of any consequence could be discussed until at least some token meal
was shared. Entering into the family communion was a
prerequisite to partaking in any of its affairs, even for that
most distrusted class of people, agents of the state.

On my first, unannounced, visit to my great-aunts in
Palermo, I was greeted with great enthusiasm. Yet despite
their obvious curiosity, they would not presume to ask me
questions until I had shared some of their strong black
Italian coffee. My first sip was a cue that we could now
talk as *cristiani*. (In an unbroken medieval tradition the
term for "human being" used in the Mezzogiorno is
cristiano.)

Of course, the social worker told the story to stress how
impressed she was with Italian hospitality. This is a common feeling among Americans, who do not realize that
the Italian words for hospitality and guest (*ospitalità*,
ospite) are not used in the Southern Italian homes. Even
among second-generation Italian-Americans, "friends" is a
preferred word to "guests" and "good manners" is a term
used more than "hospitality." This derives from their immigrant parents' use of *buon costume* and *amici*, the latter
a term that means more than "guests" to the contadini but
considerably less than "friends" in any intimate sense. For
one was truly intimate only with the family.

The paradox of a legendary hospitality without use of
the word is cleared up when we understand that l'ordine
della famiglia carefully prescribes a hierarchy of categories
of people. They are, from top to bottom: 1. family members, "blood of my blood," 2. *compari* and *padrini* and
their female equivalents, *commare* and *madrine* ("godparents," a relationship that was by no means limited to those
who were godparents in the Catholic religious rites of baptism and confirmation, and which would be better translated as "intimate friends" and "venerated elders," 3.
amici or *amici di cappello* (friends to whom one tipped
one's hat or "said hello"), meaning those whose family

status demanded respect, and 4. *stranieri* (strangers), a designation for all others, including people one may speak to everyday—for example, shopkeepers or fellow-workers on the job. It is an iron rule that one has nothing to do with *stranieri*. One had to go up the hierarchy from the class of "stranger" to "friendly acquaintance" before one could even have human discourse. In a curious psychological twist of the logic, the rule was observed by permitting passage from one class to the next highest through the rite of sharing a meal (or just coffee), a symbolic entering into the ceremony of family communion.

In the tradition, each meal is significant. The noontime meal, *colazione*, was taken whenever possible by the entire family. Workers in Italy still prefer to come home for "lunch" rather than eat at work. Often this was impossible for workingmen because of distances. But even in the field, the contadini ate with family—sons, brothers, cousins, etc. Of course, it was unthinkable that young children ate anywhere but at their mother's table. Despite the well-publicized and economical (state subsidized) hot-lunch program at Public School 142 in Brooklyn, almost all of us walked home for lunch. Although it was frowned upon by Board of Education dietitians who (erroneously) considered Italian food to be of inferior nutritional value, the practice was fine with us. A good home-cooked lunch of the *paese*, for example fried eggs and potatoes on Italian bread, was indescribably delicious and much preferred to the school's institutional "balanced meals."

One of the first signs of liberation of us second- and third-generation boys was permission to eat lunch at the "candy store" (a local luncheonette serving Italian sandwiches, before they were called "heroes"). It was a hard-won privilege, the granting of which was resisted by parents and grandparents for as long as possible. It was never granted to girls, of course.

Obedience to parental authority was a strictly enforced value, exemplified in the saying that he who disobeys parents *fa la morte di un cane* (will die like a dog). Yet in a paradox Americans have never understood, boys had the boldness to disobey, to assert their developing ability to be *furbo* (foxy), because it was really expected that they should develop this ability to deal with the world outside. The ability had to be honed, so friction against the world on one side was encouraged, and friction against the family from the other side was provided and defiance allowed gradually to succeed. However, because this worldly capacity was not deemed necessary or desirable for females, any such assertive disobedience by girls was always severely punished. It was never permitted to win the day.

Pranzo, dinner, was a gathering of the entire family. The only outsiders to be sometimes invited were godparents and occasionally honored "friends" (in the Mezzogiorno someone demanding "respect," i.e., of an equal or better family). The American custom of children regularly visiting at their friends' homes for dinner was unknown in my neighborhood. Whenever one of us (influenced by the media) would broach the idea with parents, the response was always an unyielding: "You come home for dinner!"

The major meal of the week was the one at which time and circumstances permitted the most leisurely and largest gathering of la famiglia. It was the Sunday pranzo, which began in midafternoon—breakfast has never been an important meal for Southern Italians—and lasted until early evening, or even late into the evening. It is a relaxed social gathering of the clan, featuring intimate conversations as much as well-prepared courses. Often it began with an antipasto, featuring all the tasty cheeses, fishes, and salamis familiar to Americans, and others which few Americans know, such as fatty ham cold cuts known as *capocòllo* and *mortadella*. These last were often served with melons when in season. The meal always included a pasta dish, followed by one or more main dishes—meat, fish, or poultry—with side dishes of vegetables. Dessert in the old tradition meant fresh fruits and nuts, peeled and shelled by each person at the table. Desserts of sweets were introduced only as the immigrants and their children learned American ways.

Coffee was served black, with a choice of anisette, mint, or nuts.

Although the routine of American life has altered the schedule, especially of daytime weekday meals, Italian-Americans still cling to the ceremonies of the evening and Sunday *pranzi*. In addition, the favorite foods of the Mezzogiorno are as current as ever. These include not only those most Americans know from the countless Italian restaurants in the United States, all but a fraction of which serve Southern dishes, but also many that most Americans would find exotic, to say the least. As a carry-over from the "waste not" practice of the old land where meat was seldom plentiful, Italian-Americans now eat for enjoyment foods that were necessary to sustain life for their ancestors. These include dishes made from the internal organs of livestock. Special favorites are lungs (often sliced and fried and served with grossly grated cheese), kidneys, brains, and tripe. As a boy I savored tripe prepared in soup, or with tomato sauce and cheese, and loved not only the honeycomb variety (stomach), but also the bitter intestines. I understand the latter has since been banned for sale in New York by the Board of Health.

I remember my grandmother eating, along with fish bodies, fish heads, including the eyes, and commenting that it was "the best part." To this day, one can see a particular favorite of the Mezzogiorno in the windows of butcher shops on Union Street, Mulberry Street, and Arthur Avenue, three avenues which are market centers of New York City's three Little Italies, respectively in Brooklyn, Manhattan, and the Bronx. It is the heads of goats, all parts of which are eaten. The same is true of eels, also plentiful in the three markets. Snails, conch (*scungigli*), squid (*calamari*), and mussels are all favorites and conjure up childhood memories of gustatory delight for me.

Similarly, the common vegetables of the old land are now loved for their tastes by American-born Italian-Americans. These include squashes, eggplants, unbearably hot cherry peppers, and escarole. The last was eaten by contadini from all parts of the Mezzogiorno in the belief that *scarola* was needed at least once a week "to cleanse the intestines." Often repeating this credo, which I doubt he believed, my father insisted on a pattern that almost every Monday evening's meal included escarole, either made with pasta or as a side dish dripping in olive oil and spices. Chick-peas in olive oil spiked with garlic and parsley are still one of my favorites of the old dishes of *la miseria* (poverty). And the two lowliest of all meals are now enjoyed as a special treat. These are hard, even stale, pieces of Italian bread dipped in olive oil, pepper, and oregano; and the dish mildly scorned in the old land as the mark of desperation, *fave foglie*, beans mashed with greens into a paste bonded by olive oil.

Coming from a land where it was folly to eat the meat of an animal not freshly slaughtered, the immigrants shunned canned meats and hamburger meat. When I went shopping for poultry with my grandmother, we would go to a market that had live chickens, select one, and watch as it was decapitated. Succeeding generations of Italian-Americans prefer to shop in Italian markets, where even the cold cut meats are of gourmet quality not to be compared to the plastic-encased, bland specimens of the supermarket. It is quite common for Italian-American housewives to travel considerable distances for their food; for example, to drive into the center city "old neighborhood" from homes in the outlying suburbs. They return to neighborhoods like that of my childhood, for there the pushcart vendors had shouted the traditional assurance of the old *paese*. It was only years later that I understood the significance of the vendors' shouting, *Roba dalla mia*—my own goods.

As it was in the Mezzogiorno, Italian-Americans still prepare the special dishes appropriate to specific holidays. Christmas Eve has always been the chief among these. Following the tradition, my family would gather, several dozen strong, in the home of my grandparents. Tables would be set end to end, supplemented by makeshift ones arranged from planks set across chairs or wooden horses. The meal was served after midnight, and the conversations would continue sometimes until dawn. Dinner on Christmas Day, although an important family gathering, was an anticlimax for Italian-Americans, and many of them met the American tradition halfway by serving ham or turkey then—typically preceded by an Italian pasta dish. The Christmas Eve feasts featured fish dishes. Typically, at my grandparents', *purpo* (octopus served hot or cold with lemon juice, olive oil, garlic, and spices) was the main dish, usually flanked by other "holiday" fishes, sea urchins being a most treasured one. In the wee hours of the morning the group might have soft-boiled eggs—not eaten with a spoon, but "drunk" in the old-fashioned way, that is, sucked from the shell.

As is the case on all holidays, children were permitted to stay up until three or four in the morning. A second-generation friend recently reminisced about how he and the other children in his family would be picked up and carried off to bed one by one as they dozed off in the sleep of exhaustion. They would awaken on Christmas Day, lying side by side in neat rows, a half-dozen or so children on the grandparents' bed.

I remember that during a break in the meal, my grandfather would roast chestnuts on the coal stove that warmed his combination living room-dining room. He took orange peels that lay on the printed oilcloth-covered table and placed them on the stove, creating a sour-sweet room redolent of Southern Italy. He would also deep-fry in a pot that seemed to me the largest and heaviest utensil in the world, significantly called the "laundry pot," a special treat called *zeppole*. These are little balls of sweet dough, about double the size of a golf ball, dipped in white powdered sugar. We would watch anxiously to see which of us would bite into the annual practical joke—a *zeppola* stuffed with absorbent cotton. Each holiday had special dishes, e.g., the incredibly delicious, rich, and dense *pizza di grano* (grain pie) of Easter. It is a dish that bespeaks the miracle of life's springtime renewal with its grain, ricotta cheese, and diced fruit prepared to a creamy texture.

Of course, all meals were taken with wine. A traditional

saying has it that a day without wine is like a day without sun: *Un giorno senza vino è come un giorno senza sole.* The contadino custom of mixing wine with fruits was followed (fresh peach slices dipped in dark red wine is still my idea of ambrosia), and was extended in America by mixing wine with the fruity carbonated soft drinks of the new country. Wine is quite properly considered a natural food, and to the consternation of American schoolteachers, social workers, and visiting nurses, immigrants regularly gave their children small quantities of wine from the age of two on up. As a young child I never cared for beef, and I remember my grandfather dipping pieces of the meat in his wine to make it more palatable for me. Perhaps, predictably, it gave me a love of wine I have to this day, but I continue to dislike beef.

It is altogether fitting, then, that the mother would be the creator of all these meals, the daily communions, and the holiday celebrations. For her role as the family's center was celebrated by her culinary arts, and not limited to it as the stereotype would have it.

To be sure, in the Mezzogiorno a wife would never contradict her husband in public. Often she went so far as to address him in public by the formal "you" or "thou" (*lei*) rather than the informal *tu*. Yet she had her ways of expressing herself within the walls of the home. This sometimes included—as in the case of my grandmother, a volatile woman—stormy argument which my grandfather endured by blowing clouds of dense acrid smoke into the air from the appalling, wrinkled, black Di Nobili cigars that he all but chain-smoked. Finally, after she had had ample say, he would erupt with a *"basta!"* (enough!). This would be followed by about an hour of silence, while both privately meditated what form the compromise action would take. The resolution, whether it involved only them or some business with the outside world, was never spoken, but merely implemented.

In the Mezzogiorno people considered the death of the mother the ultimate in disasters, far worse than a father's dying. For a family could endure the loss of the father, but seldom the mother. A new family head could be found, but not as easily a new center. A new woman coming into the home as mother would mean more children. She would either bring them from a former marriage if a widow, or bear them if marrying for the first time as a young girl—usually a very young girl with many childbirths before her, for most girls married well before the age of twenty and the average Italian immigrant family had six children.

A father's replacement, on the other hand, if need be was accomplished quite simply by endowing the oldest son with responsibilities as family head. If he was still a child, the mother would rule as de facto "regent" until the boy reached the age, as the contadini would say, *quannu vennero i sentimenti* ("when responsibilities come"—puberty). Although she usually continued in reality to make the family decisions, a widowed mother would defer to her son in public as soon as he showed signs of puberty. Needless to say, the death rate of immigrant fathers being high, many a second-generation boy of twelve or so was absolutely bewildered by the contradictory behavior toward him of his mother. In the home she would treat him as a mere child, and in public as a superior. As one man remembers, his mother would simply slap his face if he dared to command her in the home, and rather obsequiously obey him if he did so in public! To complicate matters further, his high-school teachers knew nothing of the private relationship and considered the public side of it outrageous. If the phrase had been in vogue then, they would no doubt have cited his case as a perfect example of the "male chauvinism" of the Italian-American. Following centuries of precedent by Southern Italian women, his mother had real power but neither displayed it nor sought any public sign or recognition of it. This reality is behind the paradox of the two contrary images the outside world holds of the Southern Italian woman. These are the fiery, sensuous, outspoken, willful "Sophia Loren" image (indeed, the actress is a native of Naples) and the jolly, all-loving, naïve, rotund *mamma mia* image.

In an interview, the author Mario Puzo said that he

deliberately set out to write a sensational bestseller about violent crime in *The Godfather* after writing an award-winning but commercially unsuccessful novel of an Italian-American woman and her family, *The Fortunate Pilgrim*. The widowed Lucia Santa Angeluzzi-Corbo of this beautiful novel combines a great nourishing maternal love with the equally great shrewdness of a vixen and toughness that the contadini call *figatu* ("guts," from *fegato*, meaning liver). She is the quintessential immigrant Italian-American mother. Confrontations on the question of male-female relationships between her and her eighteen-year-old daughter Octavia are typical. Octavia is a girl lashed both with the cultural conflict of the second generation and the sexual conflicts of a virgin grown to maturity.

As the years pass, Octavia comes to realize that the most formidable human being she knows is this mother of hers with her deceptively simple verbalizations. Regarding the question of how to raise Octavia's younger siblings, the mother said to the disgust of the sophomoric daughter, "If you want a house to give orders in, get married, have children, scream when they come out of your belly. *Then* you can beat them, then you can decide when they will work and how, and who works."

Again, in contrast to the apparent patriarchal image of la famiglia, the mother's family played an important part in her life after her marriage and in the lives of her children, especially in the formative young years. The maternal relatives formed the only insurance she had against the possibility of her husband's death. In the event of her widowhood while her oldest son was still a child, the responsibility for her welfare and that of her children would be assumed by *her* family, and not by her husband's. Thus, despite the pre-eminence of the husband, the wife's role in the economics of the family was considerable, comprising both management and insurance. And her pre-eminent power to shape her family in its daily affairs was enhanced by the fact that female members of her maiden family usually were daily company to her and her children. Thus the nurturing of children was very strongly in the pattern of the maternal family, the father's dominance notwithstanding. Indeed, the father was formal chief executive of the family, but the actual power was shared with the mother in an intricate pattern of interactions in which the famous female tactic *pigghiami cu bonu* (stooping to conquer) played a major part.

Because so much was at stake, the selection of those outsiders who were to be admitted into the family relationship was done with great care. The institution of comparaggio was thus carefully systematized. These intimates or "godparents" were of two classes. In neither case were they necessarily godparents of the Church, i.e., those who had "stood up for" a child in the baptism or confirmation rites of Catholicism. The first class consisted of compari (male intimates) and commare (female intimates) who were one's peers in age and often were also the Church godparents of one's children. The second class were padrini (males) and madrine (females). These godfathers and godmothers were older people whom one treated with some of the respect accorded to parents. Their word was heeded, and due parental deference paid to them. Often they were also godparents in the Catholic institution. Sometimes these elders were called "uncle" and "aunt" (*zio, zia*). Thus, one's peer intimate was one's compare and at the same time was padrino or zio to one's children.

Godparents were consulted on important matters, treated with respectful courtesy, and their advice heeded. They were chosen for their prestige, wisdom, and power. Since to be invited to be an intimate was one of the greatest honors, and to refuse the invitation a great insult, the procedure of offering and accepting this role was ritualized. Usually the two people involved gradually became more intimate in their conversations through degrees of codified, circumspect conversation. If one accepted the gambit offered by the other, then one or the other would move to the next degree. If the gambit was refused, the relationship went no deeper and its progress stopped well short of the point of an honor offered and refused. It was typical of all social relations among the contadini, who believed so much in the power of human passions that they evolved a careful system of directing and controlling their fulfillment with a minimum of the destruction attendant to unbridled passions. Often the process of emerging intimacy between two peers or between an elder and a junior took a considerable period of time. In the Mezzogiorno, the process sometimes lasted for years. Thus each party to the relationship was permitted to try it and assess it at graduated levels before making a permanent commitment.

Although the privileges and obligations of being a compare or padrino were considerable, they fell short of those of blood relationships. The confidence and trust one extended to a compare or padrino was never complete as it was with one's brother or father. Conversely, the obligation to look after the welfare, status, and power of one's compare or figlioccio (godchild) was circumscribed. The limit was not precise. It could be best understood by saying that relationships of comparaggio could approach the absoluteness of blood connections, but they could never quite reach that point. Of course, in any conflict of interests between the blood and godparents, the blood came first.

Through comparaggio, a network of connections was spread throughout the towns of the Mezzogiorno. The network complemented and extended l'ordine della famiglia, giving it much greater vitality and making it considerably more impervious to disruptive forces—especially those from the outside. This pattern continues today among Italian-Americans. The legends of the cohesiveness of Italian-American families, friendships, associations, and communities, are well founded.

The social value played by comparaggio is considerable. It can be understood by looking at its origin in ancient history. Indeed, comparaggio is traceable to the system of "adoption" widely practiced in ancient Rome. In order to ensure their welfare and their society's, Roman families often adopted promising children or young adults, giving them full legal status within the family, sometimes entrusting the family's destiny to them in preference to natural children. For example, Julius Caesar adopted his sister's grandson, Octavius, and bequeathed to him the larger part of his personal fortune as well as his name, making him his personal and political heir. Upon the murder of Julius, the young Octavius revenged the murder and assumed power, later calling himself Augustus Caesar. The great emperor and Stoic philosopher Marcus Aelius Aurelius Antoninus (originally named Marcus Annius Verus) was the adopted son of his natural aunt's husband, the Emperor Antonius Pius. Unfortunately the great Marcus broke with the practice of adoption and insisted that his natural son, Commodus, succeed him as emperor. The rule of this stupid, despotic son (A.D. 180–92) was a calamity for the empire.

In retrospect, the evolution of comparaggio over the centuries might be viewed as an attempt to correct the dangers of loving one's own blood unwisely, as with Marcus Aurelius. Family love is a natural passion and hence is considered undeniable. Its fulfillment was protected against its own parochialism by permitting wise intimates to act as checks and balances over family policies. Comparaggio plays an important internal role, as well as a broader social role, in the ordine della famiglia.

The family system, extended by comparaggio, also meant that the old and infirm were cared for. No one went to poorhouses, orphanages, or other institutions of charity in the Mezzogiorno except those few unfortunates without any family intimates. Somewhat cruelly and without mincing words, the contadini called these unfortunates *poveri vergognosi* or "shame-laden poor."

Commenting on the social conditions of the poor in America at the turn of the century, the great social reformer and journalist Jacob Riis noted that the percentage of pauperism among the Italian-Americans was lowest of all ethnic groups. "It is curious," he said in *How the Other Half Lives*, "to find preconceived notions quite upset in a review of the nationalities that go to make up this squad of street-beggars." He went on to give figures.

The Irish lead the list with 15 per cent, and the native American is only a little behind with 12 per cent, while the Italian has less than 2 per cent. Eight per cent were German. The relative prevalence of the races [sic] in our population does not account for this showing.

Phyllis H. Williams, in her *South Italian Folkways in Europe and America* (1938), notes that during the depression of the 1930's, the percentage of Italian-Americans in institutions of charity was remarkably low. She records that in one city where one-third of the population was Italian-American, only eighteen of 348 people in the poorhouse were of Italian background.

An interesting set of statistics was published in 1901 by the State Board of Charities of New York regarding the pauperism in New York City. Three tables were included and are reprinted in *The Italian in America* (1905), by E. Lord, J. J. D. Trevor, and S. J. Barrows. The first showed the number and birthplaces of persons admitted to the almshouse in 1900. Italy was lowest on the list and disproportionately low in relation to the numbers of Italians in New York at that time. In fact the number was lower even than groups whose numbers in New York City were very few compared with Italians. The figures are: U.S. 554, Ireland 1,617, England and Wales 198, Scotland 39, France 21, Germany 374, Scandinavian countries 28, Italy 19, others 86; total 2,936. The second table shows the numbers and places of birth of those admitted to the Incurable Hospital in 1900. Again, Italy has the lowest figure, one out of a total of thirty. The last chart is of those admitted to the Blind Asylum in the same year. Italy again had the lowest figure, one out of a total of ninety-seven.

In 1902, the Associated Charities of Boston issued its annual report, which was also reprinted in *The Italian in America*. It noted that although in District 6, the Italian quarter in the North End (still Italian today), where "Italian families largely outnumber the others,"

the variation in the number of Italians applying for assistance is interesting. Fifty-four families came to us in 1891, and only 69 in the last year, though the Italian population of this city has in the meantime increased from 4,718 to 13,738

. . . The majority of the Italians are apparently fairly thrifty and those who have trouble are often helped by their countrymen. The little that we have been called upon to do has in some cases set a family at once upon their feet.

A report of the U. S. Bureau of Immigration in 1904 on the nativity of people in America's charitable institutions showed that Italians and "Hebrews" tied for the lowest figure, 8 per cent each.

It should also be noted that Italian-Americans were at this time at the very bottom of the labor picture. As shall be seen, they were then without exception the "last hired, first fired" and had an appallingly high rate of illiteracy. In short, they had only one advantage over others among the poor—l'ordine della famiglia.

These facts are cited not to make invidious comparisons with other ethnic groups, but to stress the importance of the Italian family and its value of self-care. It is in this context that we should view the discontent with today's welfare system among some Italian-Americans, discontent that is again blithely labeled "reactionary" by some in the media. In the tradition Italian-Americans learn that to be the object of public *pietà* or *carità* (charity) is a most humiliating experience. So it is that the credit ratings of even poor Italian-Americans is high, as I am told by non-Italian businessmen. Debts are paid on schedule, by oneself or one's relations. For one should never permit himself or any member of the clan to be the object of *pietà*. To do so is to admit the moral inadequacy of one's family, and hence to be truly one of the poveri vergognosi, one of the shameful poor.

The most shameful condition of all, however, was to be without a family. Except for a very low number of illegitimate babies (as we shall see the rate of illegitimacy in Italy was lowest in the South), this condition only befell one who was a *scomunicato*, one who violated l'ordine della famiglia and was excluded from all respected social intercourse by all families. Indeed, it was difficult even to survive in the Mezzogiorno as a scomunicato. Male outcasts could only become mountain hermit shepherds or, more commonly, the lowest component of the lowest economic class, *giornalieri* (day laborers). As the humblest day laborer, he would be hired only when the work demand was so great that all others before him were already employed. This was a most rare occurrence in Southern Italy. A female outcast could only become a whore or beggar. Because the sanction was so severe, excommunication from the family was applied only in cases of the most treacherous and/or scandalous violations of the *onore della famiglia*. For to be without family was to be truly a non-being, *un saccu vacante* (an empty sack) as Sicilians say, *un nuddu miscatu cu nenti* (a nobody mixed with nothing).

On the other hand, the devotion shown to loyal kin is difficult for outsiders to imagine. While in Sicily, I visited the Cappuccini Catacombs in Palermo. Unlike the ancient catacombs near Rome, these are recent. The Cappuccini Catacombs were used in the last century. The sight that greets one in them is ghastly (a woman fainted there during my visit). Row upon row of corpses line the walls, most of them tied in standing positions. Because they are relatively recent dead, they are in various states of decomposition. Corrupted flesh, staring eyes and grinning teeth are visible through ruptures in parchment skin. Each corpse is dressed in Sunday clothing, with a name plate hung around the neck giving the name, age, date of death (most were in the 1860's through the 1880's), and often also some inscription by the family. The most common of the handwritten inscriptions began, *"La sua vita fu tutta dedita alla famiglia . . ."* ("His life was dedicated entirely to his family . . ."). The corpses, perhaps several thousand of them, were arranged in this fashion *so that their surviving relatives could come and visit with them!* Usually on Sundays and holidays.

While in the catacombs, I spoke to a woman from Florence who was obviously upset and kept commenting in a voice not at all quiet that this had been a "barbarous practice . . . what savagery," etc. Although I tried to explain the basis of familial devotion, she seemed psychologically incapable of understanding such feelings. Thus the irony, an Americano of Sicilian ancestry explaining the ways of the not so distant past Mezzogiorno to an uncomprehending native Italian, even if a Northern Italian. Little wonder, then, that to most Americans the Chinese character is probably more scrutable than that of millions of their own countrymen who are Italian-Americans.

This background of the ordine della famiglia helps illuminate the confused situation of Italian-Americans today. As all of us are confronted with the conflicts of our loyalty to a sovereign state vs. our cosmopolitan aspirations, so the Italian-American has found himself in the dilemma of reconciling the psychological sovereignty of his people with the aspirations and demands of being American.

To the immigrant generation of Italians, the task was clear. Hold to the sovereignty of the old ways and thereby seal out the threats of the new "strangers," the American society that surrounded them. The complicated customs and institutions of la famiglia had been marvelously effective in neutralizing the influence of a succession of aliens in the Mezzogiorno. In the old land, the people survived and developed their own identity over centuries not so much by their periodic violent rebellions, a futile approach because of the small size, exposed location, and limited resources of Southern Italy. Instead they endured and built their culture by sealing out the influence of strangers.

The sealing medium was not military or even physical. It was at once an antisocial mentality and a supremely social psychology, for it formed the very stuff of contadino society. It constituted the foundation and hidden steel beams of a society that historically had been denied the luxury of more accessible (and vulnerable) foundations or superstructure. This is a reason for the contadino's famous pride. L'ordine della famiglia was a system of social attitudes, values, and customs that had proven to be impenetrable to the sfruttamento (exploitation) of any stranieri, no matter how powerful their weapons or clever their devices. But like all defenses, this life style had exacted costs in the old land. These were the vexing social and economic problems that Italians still lump together under the terms *problema del Mezzogiorno* or *questione meridionale*, meaning "the Southern problem." The problem became catastrophic after the founding of the Italian nation in 1860–1870. And as we shall see in the next chapter, millions of contadini were forced by the specter of starvation to immigrate to other lands.

Because it had worked for so long in the old land in providing them with stability, order, and security, the ordine della famiglia was held to tenaciously by the immigrants in the new country. Thus the immigrants were able to achieve their twofold goals. One, they found bread and work. No matter how dismal and exploitive, it was better than the starvation they fled. And, two, they resisted the encroachments of la via nuova into their own lives. In their terms, their audacious adventure has to be judged a success. But the price in the United States was very high. It included isolation from the larger society.

The immigrants' children, the second generation, faced a challenge more difficult to overcome. They could not maintain the same degree of isolation. Indeed, they had to cope with American institutions, first schools, then a variety of economic, military, and cultural environments. In so doing, what was a successful social strategy for their parents became a crisis of conflict for them. Circumstances split their personalities into conflicting halves. Despite parental attempts to shelter them from American culture, they attended the schools, learned the language, and confronted the culture.

It was a rending confrontation. The parents of the typical second-generation child ridiculed American institutions and sought to nurture in him la via vecchia. The father nurtured in his children (sons especially) a sense of mistrust and cynicism regarding the outside world. And the mother bound her children (not only daughters) to the home by making any aspirations to go beyond it seem somehow disloyal and shameful. Thus outward mobility was impeded.

The great intrinsic difference between American and Southern Italian ways was experienced as an agonized

dichotomy by the second generation in their youth. They
lived twisted between two worlds, and the strain was extreme. The school, the media, and the employer taught
them, implicitly and sometimes perhaps inadvertently, that
Italian ways were inferior, while the immigrant community
of their parents constantly sought to reinforce them.

Immigrants used "American" as a word of reproach to
their children. For example, take another incident from
my childhood. Every Wednesday afternoon, I left P.S. 142
early and went to the local parish church for religious instruction under New York State's Released Time Program.
Once I asked one of my religious teachers, an Italian-born
nun, a politely phrased but skeptical question about the
existence of hell. She flew into a rage, slapped my face, and
called me a *piccolo Americano*, a "little American." Thus
the process of acculturation for second-generation children
was an agonizing affair in which they had not only to "adjust" to two worlds, but to compromise between their
irreconcilable demands. This was achieved by a sane path
of least resistance.

Most of the second generation accepted the old heritage
of devotion to family and sought minimal involvement with
the institutions of America. This meant going to school but
remaining alienated from it. One then left school at a minimum age and got a job that was "secure" but made no
troubling demands on one's personality, or the family life
in which it was imbedded.

Another part of the second generation's compromise was
the rejection of Italian ways which were not felt vital to
the family code. They resisted learning higher Italian culture and becoming literate in the language, and were ill-
equipped to teach them to the third generation.

Small numbers of the second generation carried the dual
rebellion to one extreme or the other. Some became highly
"Americanized," giving their time, energy, and loyalty to
schools and companies and becoming estranged from the
clan. The price they paid for siding with the American culture in the culture-family conflict was an amorphous but
strong sense of guilt and a chronic identity crisis not quite

compensated for by the places won in middle-class society. At the other extreme, some rejected American culture totally in favor of lifelong immersion in the old ways, many which through time and circumstance virtually fossilized in their lifetimes, leaving them underdeveloped and forlorn.

The tortured compromise of the second-generation Italian-American left him permanently in lower-middle-class America. He remains in the minds of Americans a stereotype born of their half understanding of him and constantly reinforced by the media. Oliver Wendell Holmes said a page of history is worth a volume of logic. There are few serious studies of Italian-Americans, particularly current ones. It is easy to see why this has left accounts of their past, their present, and their future expressed almost exclusively in the dubious logic of stereotypes.

In the popular image, the second-generation Italian-American is seen as a "good employee," i.e., steady, reliable, but having little "initiative" or "dynamism." He is a good "family man," loyal to his wife, and a loving father vaguely yearning for his children to do better in their lifetimes, but not equipped to guide or push them up the social ladder. Thus, Americans glimpse the compromise solution of this generation's conflict. But the image remains superficial, devoid of depth or nuances.

We come, thus, to the compound dilemma of third- and fourth-generation Italian-Americans, who are now mostly young adults and children with parents who are well into their middle age or older. The difference between the problems of the second generation and those of the third is great—more a quantum jump than a continuity.

Perhaps a glimpse at my own life will serve as an illustration. I was raised simultaneously by my immigrant grandparents and by my parents, who were second generation, notwithstanding my father's boyhood in Italy. So I am at one time both second and third generation. I learned Italian and English from birth, but have lost the ability to speak Italian fluently. In this, my third-generation character has won out, although I remain of two generations, and thus perhaps have an advantage of double perspective.

My grandfather had a little garden in the back yard of the building in which we all lived in Brooklyn. In two senses, it was a distinctly Sicilian garden. First, it was the symbolic fulfillment of every contadino's dream to own his own land. Second, what was grown in the garden was a far cry from the typical American garden. In our garden were plum tomatoes, squash, white grapes on an overhead vine, a prolific peach tree, and a fig tree! As a child, I helped my grandfather tend the fig tree. Because of the inhospitable climate of New York, every autumn the tree had to be carefully wrapped in layers of newspaper. These in turn were covered with waterproof linoleum and tarpaulin. The tree was topped with an inverted, galvanized bucket for final protection. But the figs it produced were well worth the trouble. Picked and washed by my own hand, they were as delicious as anything I have eaten since. And perhaps the difference between second- and third-generation Italian-Americans is that members of the younger group have not tasted those figs. What they inherit from their Italian background has become so distant as to be not only devalued but quite unintelligible to them. It has been abstracted, removing the possibility of their accepting it or rebelling against it in any satisfying way.

I was struck by this recently when one of my students came to my office to talk with me. Her problems are typical of those I have heard from Italian-American college students. Her parents are second-generation Americans. Her father is a fireman and her mother a housewife. Both want her to "get an education" and "do better." Yet both constantly express fears that education will "harm her morals." She is told by her father to be proud of her Italian background, but her consciousness of being Italian is limited to the fact that her last name ends in a vowel. Although she loves her parents and believes they love her, she has no insight into their thoughts, feelings, or values. She is confused by the conflicting signals given to her by them: "Get an education, but don't change"; "go out into the larger world but don't become part of it"; "grow, but remain within the image of the 'house-plant' Sicilian girl." In short, maintain that difficult balance of conflicts which is the second generation's life style.

When the third-generation person achieves maturity, he finds himself in a peculiar situation. A member of one of the largest minority groups in the country, he feels isolated, with no affiliation with or affinity for other Italian-Americans. This young person often wants and needs to go beyond the minimum security his parents sought in the world. In a word, he is more ambitious. But he has not been given family or cultural guidance upon which this ambition can be defined and pursued. Ironically, this descendant of immigrants despised by the old WASP establishment embodies one of the latter's cherished myths. He rationalizes his identity crisis by attempting to see himself as purely American, a blank slate upon which his individual experiences in American culture will inscribe what are his personality and his destiny.

But it is a myth that is untenable psychologically and sociologically. Although he usually is diligent and highly responsible, the other elements needed for a powerful personality are paralyzed by his pervasive identity crisis. His ability for sustained action with autonomy, initiative, self-confidence and assertiveness is undermined by his yearning for ego integrity. In addition, the third generation's view of itself as a group of atomistic individuals leaves it unorganized, isolated, diffident, and thus powerless in a society of power blocs.

The dilemma of the young Italian-American is a lonely, quiet crisis, so it has escaped public attention. But it is a major ethnic group crisis. As it grows, it will be more readily recognized as such, and not merely as the personal problem of individuals. If they are to realize this sooner rather than later, these young people must learn whence they came and why they are as they are. A "page of history" will expose the logic of their problems and thus make them potentially solvable.

The page must begin with an understanding of why their immigrant grandfathers left their homes in the old land. This is not a tangential problem, as it may seem. In the

Mezzogiorno, these same people and many generations before them cherished their humble, even destitute homes and would have defended them with their lives (and often did). To this day, the typical contadino in the Mezzogiorno lives and dies where he was born. My elderly great-aunts have lived in the same building all their lives. It is the building where my grandmother was born.

A second generation Italian-American in Buffalo told me of his father's first impression of the United States. As the immigrant stood on the deck of a miserable ship that had just entered New York's harbor, an official boat pulled alongside. An immigration officer shouted up to the would-be American, asking him in Italian how he liked his new country. Looking out at the great mass of skyscrapers, the contadino responded: *"Non so come si può vivere in questo fuoco!"* ("I don't know how it is possible to live in this fire!"). It is time to look at the reasons why the immigrant Italians left the austere, beautiful land that had mingled into their blood over countless generations. And it is time to look at their experiences and those of their descendants in "the fire."

Reasons for Leaving

There is an apocryphal tale told in Italy about a meeting between Garibaldi and some contadini. It seems that on his campaign to unify Italy the great general was passing through one of the villages of the Mezzogiorno. Seeing some men sitting in the shade in the town piazza, Garibaldi reined in his horse. He called upon the men to come join him in the effort to expel the foreign rulers from Italy, in the South the Bourbon dynasty that ruled the so-called Kingdom of the Two Sicilies stretching from its capital, Naples, to Sicily. *"Avanti per Italia!"* ("Forward for Italy!") exhorted the hero on horseback. The contadini watched him impassively. Then one gave the only response the general was to receive from the group. The man looked at Garibaldi and slowly flicked the fingertips of one hand under his chin, the classic Italian gesture meaning, *Non fa niente*—It's nothing to me, I couldn't care less.

The story is spurious in that many contadini did join the fight. To be sure they did so more to get the old oppressors off their backs than because of any notion of nationalism. Nevertheless, the story has a point. For, sadly, history was to justify the attitude the men communicated to Garibaldi. The successful unification of Italy, along with a number of other events, was to mangle the life of the people of Southern Italy, who at the time of national unification constituted at least two-fifths of the population of Italy. Because of a concurrence of political and economic, social and natural disasters that defy the laws of probability, their condition was to deteriorate to fatal depths. To this day, the problema del Mezzogiorno continues to lacerate the people of that area.

After the decline of the ancient Roman Empire, Italy had gradually split into small political fragments. By the late fifteenth century these had been fused into some fifteen states by a long series of events, strategies and stratagems, including many wars. The dream of generations of enlightened Italians since Machiavelli was to unify the land and free it from various foreign and domestic suzerains. The fulfillment of the dream was to have to wait for another three and a half centuries.

When Napoleon invaded the Italian peninsula (1796–97), he was welcomed by many Northern Italians as the great prince, called for by Machiavelli in the sixteenth century, who would unify the country. Although he succeeded in redrawing the map of Italy, this emperor with an Italian name served France and not Italy. And with the downfall of the Little Corporal, the reactionary Congress of Vienna (1814–15) restored much of the old status quo. In 1816 the area of Naples down to Sicily once again became the Kingdom of the Two Sicilies, whose capital city was Naples, with a branch of the Bourbon family on the throne. Of course, as with numberless political doings before, all this affected the Southern contadini little, except periodically to expose him to "liberal" and "reactionary" governments. Their policies, especially those of taxation and conscription, usually succeeded only in making his lot more difficult.

Although the Bourbon rulers of the Mezzogiorno had either little knowledge of or taste for progress, they did try to achieve stability in their kingdom. And in the old mode of mercantile commerce, they tried to enrich their kingdom. In fairness, it must be said they met with moderate success. By 1860, Naples was the fourth largest city in Europe, larger even than Rome. (Only London, Paris, and St. Petersburg were larger.) And the merchant fleet of the kingdom was four times as large as that of Piedmont. But what commercial success there was rested upon a decadent political system and a hopelessly outmoded economy in a Europe that was fast industrializing. For the most part ignoring the Industrial Revolution, and the agitation for liberty and equality accelerated by the French Revolution, the Bourbons sought to continue an amalgamation of renaissance mercantilism with medieval feudalism.

The fact that their government was archaic, and corrupt to boot, in itself meant little to the people. Over the centuries, they had learned to expect nothing better from governments. The contadini continued la via vecchia and scratched out their meager living as in time immemorial. But the process became increasingly difficult under the strain of supporting the outmoded economic system of the Neapolitan regime. Lacking an industrial base, the mercantile system heavily taxed the population to raise the capital necessary for commerce. Once again, the age-old flash rebellions of the populace occurred, with increasing frequency.

One of the major causes of these violent insurrections was the heavy grist tax on grain, the *macinato*. This burden upon the staple of life of an impoverished people was intensely hated. Not infrequently, the king's tax collectors were greeted by gunfire or knives when they entered a town. This was one of the contadino's favorite solutions to tax problems and is still resorted to today on occasion. In *Christ Stopped at Eboli*, the author confirms that during the 1930's one of the major hazards of the *ufficiale esattoriale*, the tax officer from Rome, was to dodge bullets in the Calabrian mountains.

King Ferdinand II, who reigned from 1830–59, at first tried to placate his subjects by lowering the macinato, educating and disciplining administrators, taxing the rich, and negotiating profitable commercial treaties with other countries. These met with some success. However, his attempt at reform of the outrageously exploitive system of large feudal estates *(latifondi)* was stubbornly and successfully blunted. The result was that the Kingdom of the Two Sicilies was rapidly becoming an unviable structure, brittle and corroded beyond salvage. Any external pressure would accelerate the kingdom's process of disintegration. For it is a basic maxim of political science that any government that cannot effectively rule loses all right to rule. And there were plenty of pressures in the Kingdom of Two Sicilies that were becoming out of control, especially in the form of popular uprisings.

One of the most extreme of these took place in Sicily in 1837. Oddly enough, it was sparked by a natural calamity, an outbreak there of cholera. This disease had before this been completely unknown in Western Europe. Thousands of people died the horrible death of the disease, the slow dehydration of the body resulting from high fever and dysentery. The cause was then unknown, and the epidemic caused wild panic throughout the island. Cities and towns sealed themselves off, firing upon any outsiders who approached their limits. Authorities and even physicians fled populated areas to the uninhabited hills. All communications were severed, and food supplies did not reach cities and towns. Starvation complemented cholera, and soon the streets were covered with stinking corpses, which no one would touch for fear of contagion.

Unscrupulous anti-Bourbon partisans fanned a rumor that the disease was deliberately caused by the Bourbons by use of poison, a belief spread even by the Archbishop of Palermo. The result was general chaos among the people, and except for Palermo, where the local authorities maintained some degree of order, the island was beset by complete political, social, and economic anarchy. Mass rioting and looting occurred. Persons linked with the Bourbon government and the agents of the absentee large landowners were lynched. In Catania, a revolutionary committee was formed and Sicilian independence was declared.

But "independence" was short-lived. Bourbon collaborator politicians teamed with the middle-sized landowners (*galantuomini*) to prepare the way for Swiss mercenary troops sent by Ferdinand II. Through this loyalty to the king, the large estate owners (*latifondisti*) were able to

confiscate even more land from the few contadini who
held moderate-sized or small parcels of their own.

The Bourbon king, after the clumsy attempts at reform
already described, clamped down a strict despotism in 1848,
when revolutions were erupting all over Europe as well as
in his kingdom. In that year, the largest rebellion in the
kingdom took place, again in Sicily, and the Bourbon
troops there were killed or routed. The government retaliated in September of 1848 by landing a new army which
laid siege to the city of Messina, whose defenders fought
fiercely. The mutual hatred was so extreme that neither
side cared to take prisoners, and much of the city was destroyed by the attackers. Finally in February 1849 the
Bourbon government tried to compromise with the rebellious Sicilians, offering them a separate parliament and
viceroy. The offer was refused. Catania then met the same
fate at the hands of the Bourbon army as Messina. Resistance to the Bourbon forces became hopeless, a situation
aggravated by the usual sellout by the large landowners.
One of the greatest of Italy's political leaders and later its
premier, Francesco Crispi, himself a Sicilian, was later to
write bitterly that the latifondisti "feared the victory of the
people more than that of the Bourbon troops." The state—
all states—hated for centuries by the contadini, was now
despised with demonic black blood.

The government accelerated conscription, and, as it had
been in 1820, it was massively resisted. The result was an
almost steady guerrilla war against government forces, a
war that became more intense when the young, inept
Francis II became king in 1859. His agents assembled the
horrors of a police state, filling many prisons, the most infamous of which was on the island of Lampedusa. The
rule in the prisons was torture and beatings, starvation and
death. The new king maintained a façade of stability. Not
only was it the stability of a tyrant, it was also that of a
fool, for it was to last for only two years.

Since 1815, the unstoppable drive for unification and
modernization of Italy, the Risorgimento, had been gaining
momentum, led by the impassioned revolutionary Giuseppe

Mazzini, the brilliant diplomat Camillo Benso, Conte di Cavour, and the incomparably charismatic Giuseppe Garibaldi. The movement was to shake Italy to its roots and to culminate in a unified nation when Victor Emmanuel II was proclaimed king of all Italy in 1861, and it achieved final success when the recalcitrant Papal States were annexed by Italy in 1870.

Although the agitation of Risorgimento was led by the North and was ultimately successful under the House of Savoy, of the Northern province of Piedmont, the process of actual unification began in the South. And it was sparked by the Southern contadini, but not because of any desire on their part to unite "Italy," an empty abstraction to them. They unwittingly began it in a rebellion against the despised Bourbon oppressors.

On April 4, 1860, there was an armed attack against Bourbon police in Palermo. The Bourbon army retaliated by terrorizing the city's people into submission. The Sicilians answered in turn by attacking military installations in the countryside. Through their de facto control of the countryside, the Sicilians were able to cause panic among the troops, many of whose officers were apathetic. The sporadic rebellions spread and the island was paralyzed in a deadlock: the troops were able to suppress the Sicilian rebels but not control them.

These rebellions were ignored by most of the leaders of the Risorgimento in the North as just more bloody Sicilian revolts, more of many since the time when Sicilian slaves revolted against the Roman Empire. After all, the revolts had come to nothing, or so believed men like Cavour, who knew history well. One dissenting Risorgimento leader was Crispi. He saw in the many Sicilian revolts of history not just their futility, but also the potential in Sicilian ferocity to serve the cause of Italy. Ironically the rebellious energy of the Mezzogiorno, "the land that time forgot," was to initiate the birth of modern Italy.

The power of the South's traditional defiance may be seen by a brief recounting of three remarkable ancient revolts in the Mezzogiorno. In the days of the Roman Empire, many Sicilians spoke Greek and regarded Rome as a foreign oppressor. With good reason. Hundreds of thousands of slaves, Sicilians and others imported to the island, were employed on precursors of the very type of latifondi which still oppressed the people of Southern Italy in modern times. In the year 139 B.C., a Syrian slave named Eunus began a revolt of slaves in Sicily, killing their masters and establishing their own nation. In a few years, his following included from 60,000 to 200,000 liberated slaves, who managed to defeat several Roman legions sent to the island to repress them. Finally, the rebels fought to the death against a fresh Roman army. The slaves were finally trapped in their citadels at Enna and Tauromenium (now known as Taormina). Those wounded who were captured after their comrades' deaths were tortured and hurled from cliffs. None survived.

Today Taormina is a lovely seaside resort, as it has been since ancient times. Its jagged mountains thrust right into the sea, their huge stark rocks violating the calmness of the crystal clear azure water. Looking down from the heights of Taormina upon the beaches below, drenched in flawless sunlight and spotted with tiny dots of vacationers (most of whom today are English or Scandinavian), I found it difficult to imagine the screams of dying rebel slaves puncturing the pure air and their blood splotching the dark rocks and transparent sea. However, the image became suddenly vivid to me one evening as I was driving down the spiral road from Taormina to the area of beach known as Spisone. Following a sign clearly marked "Spisone," I turned in the darkness onto a dirt road, going downhill at an incline of about thirty or forty degrees. Without any warning, the road ended at a cliff edge, hundreds of feet above the rocks below. Thanks only to the sure brakes of my rented Fiat 127, I escaped the fate of the ancient slaves, a fate which at that moment I felt viscerally. After carefully retracing my route (itself a harrowing experience, backing my car up much of the way on the one-lane snaky road), I told the story to a Taorminian out enjoying the night air.

He listened with sympathy, then remarked quite casually that one should never pay attention to signs.

Despite the horrible end met by Eunus's rebels, and many others in smaller revolts, another massive revolt took place in Sicily in 104 B.C. Forty thousand self-liberated slaves fought off crack Roman legions for five years. Finally, when only one thousand rebels were left alive, they surrendered to the Romans upon a solemn promise that their lives would be spared. The Romans lied. The captured slaves were brought from Sicily to Rome to be armed with crude weapons and thrown into the Circus to do combat with wild animals for the amusement of the Roman mob. The captives learned of this fate only when they were in the underground corridors of the Circus. Rather than be used in such an ignoble fashion, the Sicilians chose to commit suicide en masse by turning their primitive weapons upon each other in the corridors leading to the open arena.

These examples had inspired the famous Spartacus to raise ninety thousand slaves in revolt in 72 B.C. in Southern Italy. His rebel army tried to reach Sicily, for, as Plutarch quotes him, he believed that only "a little fuel is needed to rekindle" the fire of Sicilian independence. But unable to obtain boats needed to cross the Strait of Messina, Spartacus and his group were trapped and crushed.

Two millennia later, Crispi urged Garibaldi to also seize upon the fire of the Sicilians, this time to ignite the long-desired war of Italian unification and independence. Crispi pressed his fellow-conspirators to act upon the opportunity offered by the Sicilian insurrection. But to no avail. Cavour thought that a final campaign of national liberation beginning in the South was militarily unsound. More important, he thought that it would weaken the claim of the Piedmontese monarchy to the throne of all Italy. Others felt it a matter of honor that the great war begin in the North. Garibaldi finally took matters into his own hands. Against the wishes, nay, even orders, of Cavour, Garibaldi raised an army of patriots to go South, his famous "thousand volunteers." He and his thousand Red Shirts requisitioned or stole (the term depending on one's point of view) two

boats and landed at Marsala, the westernmost city of Sicily.
Garibaldi landed on May 11, five weeks after the Sicilians
had begun their revolt, and drove the Bourbon regiments
into urban enclaves and then out of Sicily.

To the annoyance of his Northern co-leaders, Garibaldi
proclaimed himself dictator in the name of King Victor
Emmanuel of Piedmont. More importantly, he succeeded
in winning the co-operation of the Sicilians, who at first regarded him with contempt as just another straniero.

Rare among the Northern leaders, Garibaldi understood
the contadini. He abolished the macinato, and in the name
of the King in Piedmont, but without his authority, promised meaningful land reform.

As fantastic as was Garibaldi's personal magnetism, it
was not enough to win battles. He had to defeat an en-
trenched Bourbon force of twenty-five battalions of well-
armed and trained infantry, backed by several first-rate
cavalry and artillery regiments. To do this, he had only
his thousand volunteers, a rag tag and bobtail lot, untrained
and poorly armed (Cavour had refused to arm them in
the hope of frustrating their desire to go South), and the
numerous, widely scattered *squadre siciliane*, the bands of
Sicilian men in the countryside. Most of these groups were
composed of ordinary contadini, but they also included
bands of professional brigands. At first there was no co-
ordination among them. Moreover, they were untrained in
the military discipline and tactics needed for modern war.
And they were pitifully armed. While a handful had modern firearms picked from the bodies of ambushed Bourbon
troops, the great body had only the shotguns, rifles, and
pitchforks of farmers. A common weapon of these rebels
was a wooden club with a large spike driven through it. It
is easy to see why many in the North thought the venture
a folly.

Reflecting the Pope's hostility to Italian unification, the
Papal Nuncio called these contadini guerrillas "more abom-
inable than the Arab and barbarian invaders." It was a
double insult, for the people of the Mezzogiorno are descendants of both their indigenous ancestors and the many

invaders who were absorbed into the population, including Arabs.

To the astonishment of the world, Garibaldi took the offensive. Among his thousand volunteers were about one hundred Sicilians, who, of course, knew well the rough terrain of the island. He sent them to establish communication with the armed squadre. Then by brilliantly co-ordinated rapid movements of his thousand and the local squadre, he crushed the Bourbon forces, some of whose officers had little will to fight. The people supported the squadre and the thousand with information, shelter, and supplies. The Bourbon troops seeking these aids met with silent nonco-operation, alternating with armed harassment. Finally the Bourbons pulled all their forces into the cities of Milazzo and Messina in eastern Sicily, taking many casualties along the way. As had happened before, they hoped the Sicilians could not maintain a siege and would gradually disperse. But unlike in the past when the contadini had few or no experienced military leaders, they now had in Garibaldi a general whose innate martial genius had been perfected in twelve years of guerrilla warfare in Latin America. In fact, his reputation as a general was such that Abraham Lincoln offered him a command during the American Civil War, at the rank of major general. Replying with kind words for what he termed his "adoptive country"—Garibaldi had for a time lived on New York's Staten Island—the Italian declined because he had work remaining in Italy. Finally Milazzo was taken and the demoralized Bourbon forces in Messina surrendered the city on July 28, 1860.

After a period of four weeks Garibaldi invaded the mainland of Italy landing at Melito, in Calabria. Repeating the tactics of the Sicilian campaign and recruiting contadini as he went along, he liberated the land up to and including Naples. There he was stopped by order of Cavour, whose Piedmontese advisers and generals resented the successes of this irregular army heavily made up of Southern "rabble." This was an ominous portent of what was in store for the contadini under the new Italian nation controlled by Northerners.

The contadini had fought not for nationalism or any other ideology. (A Frenchman in Naples in 1860 wrote that upon hearing the cry "long live Italy," some Neapolitans turned to each other to ask what the slogan meant.) They fought to protect la famiglia from life-draining oppression by the government, and in many cases because of specific outrages and insults to l'onore della famiglia by alien agents and soldiers. Also, when Garibaldi promised to break up the latifondi, the contadini responded, for land was essential to la via vecchia, and land for centuries had been systematically denied them and stolen from them. The Bourbons driven out of power, the contadini returned to their pursuit of la via vecchia and a cautious hope of land reform to sustain that life. But it was not to be.

The Northerners who now controlled the unified Italy knew little of the Mezzogiorno. Most had never been there. Their opinions of it came mostly from reading texts describing ancient times when the South was an agriculturally rich part of the Roman Empire. The texts correctly said that the Romans had called Sicily the "granary that fed the empire." And the rulers of the new Italy mistook the contadino hostility against the Bourbons and the landowners for Italian patriotism in their own mode of nineteenth-century political romanticism. Moreover, few of the leaders of the new nation cared to find out about the realities of the South. Even the brilliant, clear-sighted Cavour refused to visit the South and remained in dangerous ignorance of it. Less capable politicians painted a portrait of the Mezzogiorno in the colors of condescension and contempt. The long-standing antipathy between Alta Italia and the Mezzogiorno rapidly boiled to active enmity. The new liberators from the Northern province of Piedmont were irked when reminded that Sardinia, which had been ruled for 150 years not by foreigners but their own government in Turin, was one of the poorest areas of the South, in fact economically in worse shape than some of the poorest areas of the old Bourbon kingdom. *Thirty years after unification,* the average Piedmontese had a standard of living twice as high as the average Sicilian.

Upon unification, the national government, in ignorance if not arrogance, imposed the legal system of more industrialized Piedmont upon the agricultural Mezzogiorno. The economic result was that the Southern contadini sent taxes north. In fact, the tax rate imposed on the Sicilians jumped at once 30 per cent over the rate under the Bourbons. Having virtually no national debt under the Bourbons, the Mezzogiorno was soon caught in a spiral of ever-increasing debts followed by higher taxes. By merely re-establishing their unholy alliance of corruption with outsiders, this time with Piedmontese politicians and bureaucrats, the latifondisti evaded the burden of taxation, and it fell squarely upon the contadini. For example, cows and horses were owned almost exclusively by the latifondisti. These were not taxed. But mules and donkeys, the animals so essential to the independent contadino farmers, were heavily taxed. Ironically enough, the system was rigged so that even the "taxes of the rich," excise taxes, were avoided by the latifondisti and paid by the contadini.

In addition, localities had to assume the complete cost of public works mandated by the North. Even the confiscation of Church properties by the anticlerical Roman government in 1871 hurt the contadini. Through their connections with corrupt politicians at the national capital, the latifondisti managed to have the Church lands transferred to them. The Church lands constituted from 5 per cent in some areas to 10 per cent in others, of the land of the Mezzogiorno. Practically none of this went to the contadini. In addition, thousands of contadini who had been displaced from the land over the decades and had found employment as workers in churches and monasteries were now thrown into unemployment. In Palermo alone they numbered fifteen thousand.

To meet impossible tax burdens, the contadini were forced to mortgage their lands and take loans. Of course, these were given by the predatory latifondisti or their "front" agents. One official report of the Italian government found that the interest on these transactions ranged from 400 per cent to 1000 per cent! Of course, as a result, even more land fell from the contadini to the latifondisti. In 1910, forty years after the birth of Italy, the Italian Parliament reported that a few hundred latifondisti owned or controlled the major part of the land of the Mezzogiorno. In Sicily, less than one-tenth of 1 per cent of the population owned outright 50 per cent of all the land on the island.

To benefit the industry of the North, protective industrial tariffs were instituted. The result was the closing of most of the factories in the Mezzogiorno, especially around Naples, which had functioned under the free trade policy of the Bourbons. Unemployment rose further. In their blind desire to turn Italy's economy to heavy industry, laws were implemented by the government in the North which ruined the old textile industry of the Mezzogiorno, particularly the large silk business of Sicily, traditionally so successful that silk had been a fabric commonly used by Sicilians almost as Americans use cotton and wool.

The fabled contadino who waved his indifference to Garibaldi's scheme of Italian grandeur was a good prophet. The grandeur meant for the people of the Mezzogiorno a worse political and economic deal than that suffered under the Bourbons. After a short time they rose once again, this time against their "fellow-Italians" of Piedmont and Rome. The earliest eruption took place in Naples in 1862, where the Italian government had immediately reversed many of the reforms Garibaldi had initiated. With a proud independence that still characterizes their Neapolitan-American descendants today, the people of the city and its surrounding region proudly proclaimed their equality to any Northerners. "Italian" at this time meant, for all practical purposes, Piedmontese. And the Neapolitans went so far as to declare in their newspapers that "we are Neapolitans first, and then Italians." Documents of the time place the number of organized rebels in Naples in 1862 at 81,000.

The response of the Turin government rivaled the harshness of the Bourbons they had just replaced. During eighteen months, the police reported having summarily executed 1,038 people, most of whom were suspect merely because they were found carrying personal weapons, a common practice in Naples. Another 3,000 were imprisoned without any semblance of due process of law. Fighting broke out in earnest. The government sent sixty battalions of Bersaglieri (crack combat soldiers) to teach a lesson to the Southerners. Garibaldi appealed to the new king of Italy to moderate the repression, telling him that the rulers from Piedmont were hated in Naples more than the Bourbons had been. In vain. The troops showed no effort at conciliation with the unyielding but poorly armed and disorganized population. In about a year, they killed some 3,000 Neapolitan rebels. This severity merely escalated hostilities, and by 1865 the national government had a virtual army of occupation, 120,000 soldiers, in the Mezzogiorno to repress the populace.

In 1863, the army under a savage Piedmontese general named Govone put down a rebellion in Sicily using bloodcurdling tactics. Whole families and even villages were held hostage and tortured. When the tactic failed to cause rebel surrender, he decimated families and villages. Next, he cut off water from towns in the burning Sicilian summer, causing madness and death by thirst. The general tried to get the women, children, and the old to give information regarding the whereabouts of their young men, who in time-honored fashion had taken to the hills, periodically coming back to visit their families at night when the Bersaglieri dared not venture out of the cities and compounds. Of course, very few contadini would betray la famiglia, even under torture. In savage frustration over this refusal to co-operate, Govone punished them by death, sometimes by burning them alive.

Returning home to find the corpses of their wives, children, and parents disemboweled, decapitated, or burned beyond recognition, the rebellious men were driven to insane fanaticism. They now fell upon Bersaglieri in suicidal attacks that struck terror in the ranks of the troops. Diaries and letters sent by the soldiers to their families in the North spoke of their fear of the wild men who came out of the

mountains and showed no concern for their own lives.
Among them were shepherds who had long ago been
driven from the lands by the cruel system of latifondo.
Years of living in the wilderness was evident in their aspect.
The sight of these men, dressed in animal skins, unkempt
hair and beards framing crazed eyes, turned cold the blood
of even the most seasoned troops. Even more frightening
was their knowledge that the contadini were now revenging
the atrocities against their families, sometimes killing captured Bersaglieri by cutting out their hearts.

My grandparents and their friends spoke of these events
with vividness, and with accuracy since confirmed by my
reading of Italian history. In fact, they were typical of contadini who, except for their expressed reverence for Garibaldi, spoke of Italian unification only in terms of the chaos
it brought and wars between desperate, enraged local men
banded together and the troops of the stranieri from the
North. As the people were steadily deprived of land and
employment, new squadre supplemented the older groups
of *banditi* of the hills. As the years went on, the numbers of
squadre of "brigands" increased, as did their boldness in
raiding the militia and police and robbing and kidnaping
for ransom the more wealthy galantuomini. Thus, the
source of the Robin Hood-like legendary fascination about
them on the part of immigrants I knew in Brooklyn. In
fact, I've found that even today tales of their bold exploits
are a favorite theme in the children's storybooks and marionette shows I've seen in the Mezzogiorno. To the contadini, the brigand is the equivalent of our folklore hero,
the cowboy. The culmination of the great Italian Risorgimento had little more significance to the contadini than to
reaffirm their distrust of outside authorities and their reliance upon l'ordine della famiglia as the only bulwark
against what Shakespeare aptly termed "the law's delay,
The insolence of office."

When General Govone was later accused in the Italian
Parliament of the atrocities his troops committed in the
Mezzogiorno, he did not deny them, or even much attempt
to justify them in military terms. He merely explained that

the people of the Mezzogiorno were uncivilized and merited no better treatment! In this reply, Govone echoed the police and soldiers of the various stranieri who ravaged Southern Italy for centuries.

From this perspective, we can understand why Italian-Americans have a reputation for reliance upon themselves rather than official authorities. As a child, I was told by my parents that if I came home crying for help because I could not handle an injustice wherein the odds were against me, I would be supported. But I was warned that if I came home crying from timidity, I would be "given something worse to cry about." Above all, I was admonished not to seek help outside the home. Like most second-generation Italian-Americans I know, my parents mouthed the American maxim to small children that "policemen and teachers are your best friends," but their behavior made it clear that only the family will take care of you. Of course, my Italian-born grandparents regarded these American sayings as foolishness not worth telling even to tiny children. They simply repeated the contadino saying that *la legge va contrai cristiani* (the law works against people). Policemen and teachers were to be respected by children to be sure, but because of their status as adults. Respect for adults was simply a part of being *ben educato*, and any sign that its children were *mal educati* would shame l'onore della famiglia.

There is a revealing scene in Puzo's *Fortunate Pilgrim* in which one of the family's children, a young boy, is caught stealing ice from freight cars in a New York train yard by a hard railroad policeman during the 1930's. As the boy is being led away, his older brother, a strapping youth of seventeen, pulls him away from the policeman, who is forced to fight the teen-ager with his fists. He dared not pull his gun against two unarmed Italian youths in plain sight of the Italian-American community. This would have made him a marked man. Mixed with the mother's anxiety while witnessing the incident is her thought that, "thank God the older son knows what it means to be a brother."

Forty years after the period of this novel, in July 1972, Congressman Mario Biaggi spoke in a newspaper interview of his Italian-American constituency in the North Bronx. Among other things he said was:

I worked here as a detective lieutenant for some time. . . . When you come here, observe their ground rules. Don't push. Don't touch their women. Don't come looking for trouble. This goes for outsiders and neighborhood boys as well.

When a local kid is found breaking into a place, they don't call the police. They hand him over to the merchants. First offenders rarely go back for another helping.

. . . The same goes for hoods who occasionally come from other neighborhoods. . . . Again the police aren't called. The section takes care of things without help from outsiders.

After 1860 in the old country, the outsiders' exploitation, stupidity, and cruelty toward the Mezzogiorno continued apace for decades. Although Sicily was the *only* area of Italy to show an export surplus, the unfair tax system made its people ever more impoverished. By 1910, the people of the Mezzogiorno owned only 27 per cent of the national wealth, but paid 32 per cent of the national taxes. Statistics, however, do not reveal the human suffering behind numbers, for almost all the wealth was owned by a few while the taxes were paid almost entirely by the destitute many.

I remember my father telling me that every morning his family would buy milk from a goatkeeper who led his animal through the streets of the city. In fact, all contadini relied upon their goats for their dairy and cheese supply, for cows were too expensive and were owned only by the rich signori. The government taxed the goats, gradually increasing the levy, forcing the sale of goats and thus depriving the malnourished contadini of an important food source. The practice continued into the 1920's, when finally it became more economical for the contadini to slaughter the goats for meat rather than meet the taxes upon them. Rickets is a bone disease caused by lack of calcium in childhood. American records show that it was a common disease, along with other diseases of malnutrition, among Italian immigrants. The mule tax, forcing the sales of plow mules, and the reinstitution of the macinato in 1868, which forced the people to sell substantial portions of the little grain they could produce, sharply reduced the food available to the contadini.

Even olives and citrus fruits were taxed. And no sooner was the new government born than it reintroduced military conscription in the early eighteen-sixties, one of the causes for the many revolts against the Bourbons. The thought of a young man leaving his family and depriving it of his labor in favor of some remote clique of stranieri was anathema to l'onore della famiglia. As had the old draft, so the new compulsory service was met with resistance. Corpses of military recruiters were found in country lanes marked by bullets or with throats cut. Local officials were bribed to change the recorded sex of individuals on official documents from "male" to "female."

Another common evasion was for the draft-eligible young men to take to the hills to join the brigands whose ranks were increasing. Thus, contadino families were further deprived by the loss of the honest labor of their strongest males, a loss hardly compensated for by the plunder the outlaw sons sometimes delivered to their families under cover of night. In their attempts to identify culprits, the authorities punished the innocent as well as the guilty, not only out of brutality, but because of their inability to sort out the names of local people. Before the Napoleonic era, last names were not commonly used in the Mezzogiorno. The French ordered the implementation of the practice, and in doing so often merely assigned to a family, or sometimes to an entire small village, the name of the village. This was further complicated by the fact that the contadino custom was to name first children for the grandparents, and later children often for godparents. As a result, hundreds of people of a village sometimes had the same last name, and even a small town might contain several dozen people who shared both the same first and second names. Thus, when the authorities sought, let us say, "Giuseppe Rosarno" in the area of the town of Rosarno in Calabria, they were confounded by the confusion of names as well as the nonco-operation of the people. Of course, the population had avoided this confusion among themselves by long ago instituting the practice of assigning nicknames to virtually everyone. These were usually given according to some physical characteristic (e.g., "Cockeyed Joe") or the occupation of the person or his father (e.g., "Johnny Goat" for John the goatkeeper). Frequently they referred to some behavioral characteristic of the person. My mother's family, following her parents' lead, called her by the nickname "Chiara" ("Bright" or "Light"). I never once heard my grandparents call my mother by the proper name they themselves had given to her, "Caterina." I recall one woman in Brooklyn who because of her unkempt appearence was ungenerously called "La Sporca," "The Dirty One." In sixteen years of living across the street from her, I never learned her real name. To us children, the poor woman was simply "La Sporca."

The practice of assigning nicknames continues among Italian-Americans, even of the third and fourth generations. Some of my boyhood friends were "Croaker" (voice characteristic), "Bubbie" (the mispronunciation by his immigrant grandmother of the American name his mother gave him, "Bobby"), "J.O." (standing for "Jerk Off," an obscene term meaning the boy was clumsy), "Giovanni Pelo" (Johnny-One-Hair, the boy's entire body was covered with dark hair). We young boys tagged a neighborhood man whom we found frightening "Gruesome." This custom of nicknaming fascinates Americans today, and they delight in reading the colorful nicknames of Italian-American criminals, scrupulously reported in the newspapers in parentheses between first and last name.

The confusion of the authorities from Alta Italia was further complicated by elaborate codes of verbal and body language developed over centuries by the Southerners, with variations from region to region, and even town to town.

For example, when people in Sicily want to communicate in confidence in the presence of an outsider, they will not only lapse into the heaviest dialect but also use codified body language. I once requested some small favor from two men with whom I was conversing in the lovely seaside town of Cefalù in Sicily. Although I spoke the Sicilian dialect and explained I was Sicilian-American, I could tell from their subtle eye movements, voice inflections, etc., remembered from my grandparents and their friends, that they were weighing my credibility. In the ancient practice of the Mezzogiorno, the words of outsiders are automatically suspect unless proven otherwise. Finally, when I made my request to them, their eyes met and after a second's pause, one man nodded "yes" to the other. I recognized from the very subtle nuance in the nod that it was in fact the traditional signal meaning "no." When I tactfully made it clear I had caught the code message, I was taken more seriously. Although still a straniero americano, perhaps after all I still retained some of my ancestral nature as a "cristiano siciliano," a status further advanced in their estimations when I explained I had but recently visited my remaining relatives in Palermo.

The government bungling and bayonets of the 1860's began a trend toward mass unemployment and famine. It was to accelerate and to receive a counterpoint of natural disasters in the next decades. The result was that life became a constant movement of exhaustion, a tarantella of death for millions. The vineyards so important to the Mezzogiorno were devastated in the 1870's by a disease known as phylloxera, which had spread south from France. Adding to the injury, the French government in the 1880's imposed a heavy tariff against Italian wine. The effect upon the wine-making industry of Calabria, Apulia, and Sicily was ruinous. The citrus fruit industry of Basilicata, Calabria, and Sicily began to suffer badly as Florida and California developed their own groves and American imports of Italian oranges and lemons fell sharply in the next decades.

As food became ever more scarce on the tables of the

contadini, Italy was experiencing an unprecedented "population explosion." In fact, the population of Italy doubled in the seventy years from 1860 to 1930, despite wars, famine, and the emigration of millions!

When you travel in the Mezzogiorno, you cannot help being struck by the beautiful but harsh terrain. The clay soil and the stony hills are in large areas bereft of trees, a legacy of thousands of years of greedy deforestation by the galantuomini and alien governments. The forests of the Mezzogiorno, recorded in the accounts of the ancient Greeks and Romans, are long since gone. (Italians still abuse the remnants of this natural resource. On May 12, 1972, the New York Times reported that 100,000 of the few remaining trees of Italy were felled in just two years, 1962–64, "to promote auto safety.") The result was that the soil deteriorated into clay and eroded in centuries of rainfall.

On an afternoon of June 1972, I watched a group of contadini work their land as has been done for generations. The men worked with picks and shovels, repairing a section of carefully terraced stony hillside on which they grew fragile citrus trees. I sat in the shade of one of the small trees as the men, half naked, leathery bodies covered with clay, labored in the scorching Sicilian sun. When they took a break to eat, I took the occasion to talk with them. Theirs was the age-old story of carefully terracing the severe hills by hand, planting in the sterile clay, replacing dead trees shriveled in the drought of the summer sirocco (hot winds coming north from the deserts of North Africa, accompanied by almost constant scorching sunshine) and repairing the stone terracing washed away in landslides caused by the rains of winter.

In a cruel natural pattern the reverse of that of North Italy, the South receives hot dry air in the spring and summer instead of the rain needed for agriculture. In The Leopard, Giuseppe di Lampedusa's famous novel set in the Sicily of the period of Italian unification, the central character speaks of "this climate which inflicts us with six feverish months at a temperature of a hundred and four.

Fire," he continues, "could be said to snow down on us as on the accursed cities of the Bible." Moreover, the arrival of the winter rains, not only useless for agriculture, caused great floods and produced malaria-breeding pools as they channeled through the treeless clay-stone hills. In an almost total neglect of the South, the Italian government concentrated almost all of its water control and irrigation projects in the North. Thus, in 1921, the Mezzogiorno, in dire need of these government projects, received only 8 per cent of them! This despite the fact that they were less needed in the Northern provinces, which, favored both by nature and the government at Rome, produced almost twice as much grain, and more grapes, than the Mezzogiorno in the years from 1909 to 1920. When I asked the contadini working the hillside what they thought of the adversities of their life, they answered philosophically with a shrug of the shoulders and a favorite saying, *"In questa vita ci vuol coraggio"* ("In this life one needs courage").

Although less eloquent than Camus's words in *The Myth of Sisyphus,* these tough people expressed the faith of the great humanist that in the struggle against the cruel indifference of nature "man will again find there the wine of the absurd and the bread of indifference on which he feeds his greatness." This Sisyphus-like, undefeatable life energy is in the marrow of the Italian-American. For reasons I hope to explain, it forms a latent but quickening reservoir of life energy that might help to revive the spirit of America, a country many of whose people have drifted so much into an exhaustion of purposelessness.

This stubborn love of life in the face of its adversities was tested anew in the severe agricultural depression of the Mezzogiorno that reached calamitous proportions by the 1880's. The price of the wheat produced by the contadini, already at a depressed low of 22 lire a quintal in 1888 (a quintal equals about 220 pounds) fell to 13.5 lire in 1894. During this same period, the national government, in a policy that could not have done more to kill the contadini if it had been purposely designed to do so, increased both the tax on grain and the price of salt, a government monop-

oly except in Sicily. (In a land without ice and before the
age of refrigerators, salt was essential to preserve meats
and fish.)

The French writer Alexandre Dumas (the elder) reported what he saw in the area of Naples in 1862. "While
the *signore* feeds his dogs on white bread, the people live
on roots and grass, eked out with an insufficient quantity
of coarse bread." Official reports show that in the Naples
of 1881, then Italy's largest city, two-thirds of the city's
population was completely without work or food! Moreover, their water supply was so unhygienic that they were
hit with a horrible epidemic of cholera in 1884.

Cholera came to the people of the South on top of decades of wide-spread malaria, a malady that was to plague
the Mezzogiorno until after World War II. According to
historians, hundreds of thousands suffered in the dread disease that slowly sucked the life out of its victims in the
period from 1860 to 1925.

In a savage coincidence, the same period brought a rash
of other natural disasters. The South of Italy rests upon
the edge of a huge geological continental "plate." Conse-
quently, it is an area of frequent earthquakes and volcanic
eruptions. Recently the Italian city of Ancona, northeast
of Rome reported 2,500 earth tremors in eighteen months!
The contadini have coexisted for all their history with these
constant threats. Despite numberless catastrophes, they return to face them anew and rebuild homes. I remember
visiting the ruins of Pompeii, the Roman city near Naples
destroyed in A.D. 79 by one of the many eruptions of Mount
Vesuvius. In the museum there I saw the bodies of victims
preserved by volcanic ash. They are twisted in postures of
agony. One teen-age girl is lying with her arm over her
face in a desperate effort to survive the inferno of molten
rain and hellish fumes. I could see Vesuvius dominating
the scene, and dominating the villages of the contadini who
still choose to live in its shadow!

Similarly, in northeast Sicily, I could see towering Mount
Etna, white smoke emerging from its cone into the dazzling
blue daylight. And a short distance away to the north, visi-

ble from the coast of Sicily, I saw the Lipari Islands, including Stromboli, with one of the world's most active volcanoes. The sights of these huge volcanoes are to me symbols of the irrepressible subterranean forces, literal and figurative, at work in the Mezzogiorno. They are symbolic of the slowly shifting, pressured plates of life that move imperceptibly for centuries, and then can destroy all in a few moments of violent rage. In the volcanic triangle of Vesuvius, Etna, and Stromboli, one can deepen the understanding of the Italian-American spirit of quiet determination, love and awe, hope and guardedness in the face of life. Above all, one can feel his fierce energy and his irrepressible will to prevail in whatever life presents, be it, in the good phrase of a recent writer, *dolce* or *amaro*, sweet or bitter.

The volcanic triangle was to be particularly amaro to my grandfather's generation. Vesuvius erupted in 1906, burying whole towns in the province of Campania (the province of Naples) and killing unknown numbers of people. Etna delivered a similar blow to the people of Eastern Sicily in 1910. And hundreds, perhaps thousands, were killed in 1905 when a series of earthquakes hit the provinces of Basilicata and Calabria.

But the worst of the disasters occurred in 1908. A major earthquake and tidal wave struck in the Strait of Messina, between Sicily and the mainland of Italy. Most of the city of Messina was destroyed, and about 100,000 of its people died. The city of Reggio di Calabria across the strait also was largely destroyed, and about 20,000 were killed there. More than three hundred other towns were leveled! Relief efforts by the Roman government were ineffective. In fact, in Messina, government troops using bayonets prevented the people from returning to the city they had fled to dig out members of their families trapped in the shattered city. Their pleas were overruled by the Roman government on the grounds that the people had to be kept out of their city "to prevent looting." The bitterness of the survivors was fueled when they learned that live people were still being freed from the rubble of the city days after the quake. To this day, when speaking of 1908, old people around the rebuilt city of Messina and their *paesani* in the United States will clench their fist and bite the knuckle of their index finger, the classic contadino expression of rage.

Complementing the geological forces pressing the contadini was the squeeze upon them by political and economic forces relentlessly applied by the rich landed gentry. As had the Bourbons, the new post-Risorgimento government made a much-ballyhooed effort to break up the *grandissimi latifondi*, the great estates, and give land to the aggrieved contadini. Such attempts had been made since the days of the Roman Republic, when the ruling Gracchi brothers were murdered by the patrician class for their efforts at genuine land reform in the second century B.C. Not only was this latest effort by the new Italian government unsuccessful, but the land of the Mezzogiorno actually fell into *fewer* hands during this attempt at reform, making the latifondisti more rich and powerful than ever!

Leonard Covello notes, in *The Social Background of the Italo-American School Child* (1944), that in Calabria there were 121 landowners per 1,000 population in 1882. In 1901, the figure had been reduced to 91 per 1,000. In Basilicata the 1882 ratio of 168 per 1,000 dropped to 159 per 1,000 in 1901. And in Sicily, the reduction over the same years was from 114 per 1,000 to 94 per 1,000. Moreover, by 1901, almost 90 per cent of the land of the South was in the hands of large estate owners. Moreover, the few small landowners could not successfully farm their lands under the prevailing conditions. The average holding of the independent contadino was 1.5 to 2.5 hectares of land (1 hectare = 2.471 acres), too little to be economically viable. Their holdings became even of smaller acreage through the custom of *frazionamento*, dividing the property among the sons upon the death of the father. Moreover, the independent contadino's efforts were made more difficult not only by the crippling tax system, but also by the fact that the galantuomini who owned the large estates had, through political intrigue with Northern politicians, a monopoly control of water rights and also owned most of the few decent roads of the land. They charged prohibitive rates both for water and for travel over these private roads. Public roads and other transportation was for all practical purposes nonexistent. In 1860, 1,621 out of 1,848 towns surveyed in the Mezzogiorno had no roads at all leading to them! The entire region had a mere hundred miles of railroad track, and even this was useless, for it was not linked to the rail system of the industrial Alta Italia, which terminated at Bologna, hundreds of miles north of Naples. The islands of Sicily and Sardinia had no rail systems at all. Of course, the dismal transportation system hurt the entire economy of the South, making the large estates also relatively unproductive.

The great landowners, as they controlled more land and power, moved into the larger cities, leaving the management of their estates to *gabelotti*. These overseers were paid by commission according to the profit of their management. They thus squeezed the most work at least wage out of the landless *contadini*. Ninety per cent of the rural population was forced to work on the *latifondi* or in the new sweatshops of the cities, owned by the same landowners. Kickbacks and more ingenious forms of extortion were common arts practiced by the *gabelotti* in the name of the absentee landlords. Although the average income of the *contadini* in Sicily actually declined from 1870 to 1890, the cost of living doubled! Moreover, through corrupt political machinery, it was the landowners who almost exclusively represented the Mezzogiorno in the Italian Parliament. Of course, they saw to it that every legitimate reform movement was stymied, and that every reform bill passed was rigged to increase their own power, wealth, and exploitation of the masses.

As the land was taken away from the *contadini*, virtually all of them were forced into being *giornalieri*, day laborers, to them the most humiliating status. Even many of the *artigiani* (artisans) were forced into this condition. Soon, the ever-greedy *latifondisti* and *gabelotti* favored a scheme even more exploitive than hiring unemployed, starving men on a per diem basis. This was clumsy, for in daywork one controlled the *miserabli* only while they were under the yoke of the hourly wage. A much more secure—and profitable—system was that of *mezzadria*, a form of sharecropping. Under this system, land was "leased" to a contadino family under the condition that a fixed ratio, commonly 50 or 60 per cent of the *expected yield, as determined by the owner*, was to be paid to the owner at the end of the year. Of course, expected yields were set with great optimism. The result was that the lessee family could never meet its share of the contract and was forced to borrow on next year's yield from the leasing landlord.

Soon thousands of contadino families owed a handful of landowners several years' worth of yield. The mezzadria thus, in effect, reintroduced a feudal system unknown in Europe since the Middle Ages, making the contadini virtual serfs and the latifondisti and some galantuomini veritable signori, "lords" in the medieval sense. Whereas the *giornaliero* (day laborer) was merely an oppressed worker, a modern proletariat, the *affittuario* (leaseholder in the mezzadria system) was in reality a bonded serf of times long ago.

In Sicily, the oppression also took the form of a type of mezzadria in the sulphur mines, where the ore, dug by men, was carried to the surface mostly by children working twelve hours a day. The wage contract, like that of the farming affittuario, was rigged so that the longer the workers labored the deeper in debt they became to the companies owned by the same small wealthy class. After a four-year study of the horrors of this system, which burned the eyes, sinuses, and lungs of all who labored in the mines, causing permanent damage and early death, a government commission achieved the passage of a reform law. It merely prohibited the employment of boys under ten years of age. *Moreover, the law was widely ignored.*

This sfruttamento (exploitation) once again raised defiance. Thousands of giornalieri took to the hills to join the brigands. This was more difficult for the affittuario, for to do so he would have to leave his family behind to meet the ever-increasing debt owed the landlord. Soon both giornalieri and affittuari began to organize and agitate for relief if not reform. The first response of the rich signori was to hire thugs, low level *mafiosi* and *camorriste* to repress their "uppity" vassals. When the contadini met this criminal violence with violence of their own, and gabelotti were garroted (the most contemptuous method of killing in the Mezzogiorno), the landowners turned to their cohorts in the Roman parliament. These politicians in their attitudes toward the South, varying from frustration and ignorance to anger, malice, and criminal complicity, were only too ready to believe the wealthy class's tales of violent, anarchic, dangerous rabble in the Mezzogiorno. The Bersaglieri were ordered to step up their repression of the troublesome, incorrigible creatures.

Occasional incidents between the poor and the Bersaglieri turned to frequent violent skirmishes. These came to a head in 1893, when a steady warfare began between them that was to rock the government at Rome and return Francesco Crispi as Prime Minister. It began in a town called Caltavuturo in Sicily. A half-Spanish absentee landlord duke had been coerced by the government into giving the local contadini six hundred acres of land as compensation for past enclosures of their land. Ever watchful to steal what they could from their wretched neighbors, the local galantuomini gained legal ownership of the land for themselves through a series of shady manipulations with governmental agencies. Upon this news, the enraged contadini squatted on the land and claimed it for themselves. This "illegal" move was answered by the military, who opened fire on the squatters, driving them off the land and killing or wounding fifty or sixty in the process. In a flash the people answered. Government buildings were burned, troops ambushed, officials shot, prisons stormed, and rebels and common criminals alike freed. The new prime minister, in his efforts to resolve the conflict, asked the latifondisti and galantuomini who represented the Mezzogiorno in the Roman government for advice. They submitted two recommendations: one was the abolition of the newly instituted compulsory education in the South! The other was the sending of a massive army. The second suggestion was taken. A large navy and thirty thousand additional soldiers were dispatched to Sicily and were soon entangled in the same type of frustrating repression of a semipermanent insurrection as had been their Bourbon predecessors. Meanwhile, exploitation, unemployment, and their monstrous children, poverty and famine, grew as the century turned, unemployment steadily increasing each year from 1895 to 1911.

While Northern Italy was in political crisis, with Florence afraid of rule from Turin, Milan longing for the old Austrian rule, and the Vatican frozen in hostility to the new government, the South was in a state of chaos. In answer to criticisms, the powers of the North joined with the Southern wealthy in a process of scapegoating. The Southerners themselves were blamed. No sooner had the North taken power in the Mezzogiorno than it began to foster the slander of the "innate inferiority of the Mezzogiorno and its people," first insidiously, then quite openly. The antipathy between North and South was an old one. Alta Italia had been influenced by major European currents. It was proud of the glorious culture it had produced during the Renaissance. It had entered the industrial age and was dreaming the nineteenth century's dreams of Progress. The South had remained unchanged and clung to its family system and its medieval codes of Byzantines, Normans, and Arabs. These were the cultures that had influenced the Mezzogiorno, even if highly filtered through l'ordine della famiglia, and not the French and German cultures that had influenced the North.

All of Italy was, and still is, divided into linguistic regions, each having its own unique dialect of the Italian language. The Venetian dialect is quite different from the Roman, and residents of these two areas find it difficult to understand the dialect of Genoa. But whereas the upper classes of Northerners had traveled throughout the North and learned each other's dialect, "one never traveled south of Rome," as their saying went. To this day, my own experience has confirmed that Northerners have difficulties understanding the dialects of the six Southern provinces.

The extraordinary regionalism of Italy, strong to this day, was particularly characteristic of the Mezzogiorno. Not only each region, but each town considers itself a self-contained, unique culture, its people feeling no kinship with those even a few miles away. The attitude is labeled *campanilismo*, from the Italian word for "bell" (*campana*), meaning that whatever "national" affinity the people feel is limited to those who live within hearing range of their village's church bell.

Italian-Americans retain the habit of friendly banter and rivalry between those derived from different regions. Sicilians and Neapolitans maintain that Calabrians have *testedure*, "hard heads," meaning that they are stubborn. Sicilians are called schemers by others, and Neapolitans rascals, etc.

The strongest expressions of regionalism, however, were those between the Northerners, who did not comprehend the Mezzogiorno and contemptuously labeled it *Africa*, and the contadini of the South, who identified the stranieri from Alta Italia with the old rulers (whose armies sent into the Mezzogiorno did indeed include Northern Italians). To the vexation of Italian nationalists from the North, the Southerners remained indifferent to dreams of Italian glory and a revival of classical Rome. The contadini guarded l'onore della famiglia and regarded all ideologies as fatuous instruments used by rogues to manipulate fools.

For example, later as fascism fired nationalistic spirits in the North, the South remained largely uncaring about it. In fact, no Fascist was elected anywhere in the Mezzogiorno to any public office until *after* Mussolini grabbed power in 1922 with his histrionically staged "March on Rome." Of course, after that all elections were rigged, following the precedent set at the birth of Italy in October 1860. No less a nationalist hero than Garibaldi directed a fraudulent plebiscite on the question of whether the people of Sicily, who had just thrown out the Bourbons, wanted a united Italy under the reign of King Victor Emmanuel of Piedmont, a figure more remote to 95 per cent

of Sicilians than the man in the moon. Balloting was public,
and the few voters who turned out marked their ballots
with Garibaldi's agents looking over their shoulders. These
same agents then received the ballots and simply discarded
those marked "no." The result of this parody of democracy
was the announcement to the world that the plebiscite
showed 99.5 per cent of the people of Sicily favored Italian unification, an announcement that "inspired" the naïve
nationalist students and bourgeoisie of Alta Italia, with
their fairy-tale notions of the Mezzogiorno. As conditions
in the South deteriorated in the decades after 1860, the
Northerners fixed upon the myth of the incorrigible inferiority of the Southerners to explain to the world and to
themselves the compound catastrophe occurring there.

Recently, I had firsthand experience of the continuing
conflict between Northern and Southern Italy. Three companions and I hired a car in Rome to drive south to the
area of Naples. Our driver and guide was a native Roman
in his thirties who claimed to be a graduate of Boston University. His sophisticated and friendly manner changed as
we drove south. He spoke rather rudely to everyone in the
South, except policemen. At a restaurant in Naples, he
found fault with everything and expressed it loudly to the
staff and other patrons. Yet, in my observation, the restaurant was as good as any I had seen in Rome, Florence, or
Venice. Our guide explained to me that Southerners are un-
cultured, brutish creatures, even as they treated me in a
warm, civilized way. He called them "not really Italian," a
phrase that evoked an incident in my childhood.

P.S. 142 in Brooklyn was a school at least 90 per cent of
whose pupils were Italian-American. One day, when I was
about nine years old, I was told by one of my teachers (a
non-Italian, like almost all the staff), "You're not *real* Italians." When I went home that day, I asked my immigrant
grandfather what the teacher meant. He sat there, looked
me level in the eye, shook his head slowly, and said simply,
"Gli Americani!" (To Italian immigrants, all other people
in this country were "Americans," whatever their ethnic
backgrounds.) The prejudice of the Northerners, experi-

enced by my grandfather in the old land, had been transplanted to his new home and visited upon his grandchild.

This prejudice came to maturity in the late nineteenth century when Northern Italians depicted the shrewd, hardworking, independence-loving, family-devoted contadini as lazy, irresponsible, violent "bedouins" who had only themselves to blame for their *povera vita* (poor life). To a world that understood virtually nothing of the Mezzogiorno and still does not, this "explanation" sufficed to cover up the bungling, ignorant, and exploitive policies of the national government and flooded the contadini in the light of "hopeless reactionary peasants." It obscured the merciless opportunism of the large Southern landowners (perhaps 5 per cent of the population), and the resultant inflamed class hatred was seen simply as evidence of the contadini's "primitive hatred of those better than them." The incessant escalation of exploitation by the archaic feudal system of latifondo, uncovered even by the more enlightened committees of the Italian Parliament, was completely overshadowed by the specter of the "recalcitrant Southern savage." This bogus account "justified" the brutal military occupation of the South and hid its cruel atrocities, while at the same time spotlighting the violence by the "unruly barbarians" who dwelled there. The contadini's plight of starvation was thus thoroughly dissociated from the political, social, and economic traumas forced upon them by the realities of Italian unification.

The spurious myth of innate inferiority, and hence guilt, of the Southern Italians even vitiated the sympathies of the world toward them in the natural disasters that befell them. The world regarded them in a perspective filtered through condescension as they suffered earthquakes, volcanic eruptions, soil depletion, landslides, agricultural blights, famine, and runaway epidemics of malaria, cholera, and diseases of malnutrition. The sudden collapse of a culture slowly evolved over centuries was shrugged off as the "price of Progress," "survival of the fittest and natural selection, you know."

The ancient marriage between the severely beautiful, remote land that time forgot and its tough, enduring people was being torn asunder. And to no surprise to the contadini, the world neither understood nor cared. As it had always been, it was up to them alone to solve their problems. The odyssey of souls suddenly thrust into the currents of time was to begin. True to fashion, it began with many decisions by many individual families at the traditional *consiglio* (council gathering) of the *famiglia*. The families made the decision to leave the lands where their ancestors had lived for tens of centuries and successfully prevailed over nature and outsider. Each family (not its individuals) decided which of its members were to leave, where they were to go, how, and for what aims.

Although not the dubious *dolce vita* of today, life itself had for ages been dolce to the contadini. Despite its hardness, life was sensuous, bright, throbbing with the joys of everyday life, pleasures made sweeter by their constant juxtaposition with life's hard and lethal side. The contadino mirrored his land. He reflected the brilliant, unnaturally lucid Mediterranean light that makes life so much more clear and sharply defined; the scorching sun and the refreshing shade; and stony hills and mountains, exhausting to climb, yet affording dazzling panoramas when walked. As in the creative technique of contrast invented centuries ago by Italian artists known as *chiaroscuro* (light-dark), the universal contrasts made everything more alive, infinitely more visible and valuable in the Mezzogiorno.

I shall never forget my first landing in Sicily. As the plane banked steeply to approach the runway at Palermo's Punta Raisi Airport, my vista changed from the blue-green ocean whose gentle waves were bejeweled by the white hot sun, and I found myself looking *up* at the sheer, rough hewn cliffs of mountains to one side, with their corkscrew roads visible in the brilliant sunshine.

A native Sicilian man sat across the aisle from me. During the flight from Rome, he had been spending the time playing with an infant on his lap, caressing it and making faces that sent the baby into squealing laughter. When the stewardess of the jet gave us the usual litany about landing (seats upright, no smoking, etc.), the man paused in a paradoxical posture, cautious yet casual, hairy sundried arms about the baby in a masculine yet maternal hold. When the wheels finally touched concrete, his guardedness was suddenly dismissed with a statement made mostly to himself, quite without drama, that "We made it again."

The jet was filled to capacity, mostly with Italian-Americans visiting families in the old country. As we taxied to the terminal, I saw a small crowd jammed against a police barricade. As the plane's doors opened, the people pushed aside the barriers, the two or three policemen manning them prudently stepped aside, and the crowd spilled out onto the airport runway. The disembarkation from the aircraft and the collection of baggage were engulfed in a small pandemonium of shouts of recognition, hugs, kisses, laughter, and tears. While waiting for my baggage, I asked one of the policemen, who surveyed the human turbulence with calm benignness, if aircraft always were greeted like this. "Yes," he said, "but mostly from May through September when most of the Americani [i.e., Italian-Americans] come."

The decision by families in the Mezzogiorno to send millions of their members to other lands was as emotional as leaving for another world, for that is precisely what it was to the contadini. I heard my grandparents often lovingly speak of *bedda Sicilia* (dialect for "beautiful Sicily"). I've heard Neapolitans remember their old paese as *un pezzo di cielo caduto in terra* (a piece of heaven fallen to earth), and have heard other such longings from people from other regions of the Mezzogiorno.

On the other hand, the national government of Italy only belatedly showed any sense of loss for the millions who left. Only in 1901, more than twenty years after the emigration was in full force, did it make a first move to regulate shipping companies, which, as we shall see, transported the contadini over the seas under conditions whose baseness was exceeded only by the old African slavers.

The immigrant contadini to the United States could well have written the lines of the English poet Christina

Georgina Rossetti, daughter of the Italian poet Gabriele Rossetti, a political exile from Italy who fled to England in 1824.

> Farewell, land of love, Italy,
> Sister-land of Paradise:
> With my own feet I have trodden thee,
> Have seen with mine own eyes:
> I remember, thou forgettest me,
> I remember thee.

Ahead lay the *strano paese*, America, the strange land where it was said there was work and bread.

Receptions in the New Land:
Work, Bread, and Fire

You have navigated with raging soul far from the paternal home, passing beyond the sea's double rocks, and now you inhabit a foreign land.

Medea

When the Croton Reservoir was being built in 1895 to meet the needs of New York City, a public notice recruiting laborers for the project was circulated through newspaper advertisements and handbills. It listed a daily wage schedule of three groups:

Common labor, white $1.30 to $1.50
Common labor, colored $1.25 to $1.40
Common labor, Italian $1.15 to $1.25

At about the same time, an editorial in a New York City newspaper expressed a not untypical view of the Italian immigrants then arriving in large numbers:

The floodgates are open. The bars are down. The sally-ports are unguarded. The dam is washed away. The sewer is choked. Europe is vomiting! In other words, the scum of immigration is viscerating upon our shores. The horde of $9.60 steerage slime is being siphoned upon us from Continental mud tanks.

Also at this time, in the South of the United States, Italian laborers were being employed, as in the Northern states, at wages generally less than those paid to blacks, the people at the lowest level of the economy. A popular opinion of the Italians was given by a prominent leader of Louisiana, where the composition of Italian-Americans was 90 per cent Sicilian. He was L. H. Lancaster, Secretary of the Lafourche Progressive Union of Thibodaux, Louisiana. Wrote Mr. Lancaster:

> The class with which I have come in contact is not what would be considered desirable, being entirely of the Sicilian type . . . illiterate and tending to be unruly and used only for hard manual labor, having had no training nor education and not being adaptable for scientific pursuits nor for diversified or intensified agricultural pursuits without close attention.

In the North, the hierarchy of the Catholic Church, dominated by Irish-Americans who arrived considerably earlier (their immigration to the United States peaked in 1851, while that of Italians peaked in 1907), forbade priests serving Italian-Americans to speak Italian during church services.

In 1904, John Mitchell, president of the United Mine Workers Union, whose constituency was heavily Irish and British-American, made an interesting speech. Recall that 1904 was a time when Irish and British immigration had greatly subsided. As late as 1950, 78 per cent of all British immigrants had arrived before 1914, while about 80 per cent of Irish immigrants had arrived by that date. The peak years of Italian immigration were 1901–14, when 55 per cent of the total arrived. Said Mr. Mitchell in a speech obviously aimed at Italians:

> No matter how decent and self-respecting and hard working the aliens who are flooding this country may be, they are invading the land of Americans, and whether they know it or not, are helping to take the bread out of their mouths. America for Americans should be the motto of every citizen, whether he be a working man or a capitalist. There are al-

ready too many aliens in this country. There is not enough work for the many millions of unskilled laborers, and there is no need for the added millions who are pressing into our cities and towns to compete with the skilled American in his various trades and occupations. While the majority of the immigrants are not skilled workmen, they rapidly become so, and their competition is not of a stimulating order.

In 1901, a report by an Industrial Commission on Immigration compared the working habits of Italian and Jewish immigrants. The latter were also arriving in great numbers and their peak of immigration was reached in the years 1913–21, immediately after that of the Italians.

The commission's report said:

The Italian, like the Jew, has a very elastic character. He can easily change habits and modes of work and adapt himself to different conditions; he is energetic and thrifty, and will work hard with little regard for the number of hours. It is quite usual for an Italian cloakmaker, like the Jew, after he has worked 10 hours in the shops with his wife, to take a bundle home at night. But, unlike the Jew, he not only does the work at home himself, but he is assisted by the women in his family, and often leaves a part of the work for them to do during the day.

Let us jump half a century, to the year 1970. In that year, the United States Bureau of the Census surveyed first-generation (immigrant) and second-generation white ethnic groups. Although the median family income for Italian-Americans ($8,808) was slightly higher than that of the total U.S. population ($8,632), it was even higher than that of the earlier-arrived English-Americans ($8,324) and Irish-Americans ($8,127). This despite the fact that Italian-Americans have one of the worst records of formal education among all Americans—a fact to be analyzed in a later chapter. It is lower than that of the total U.S. population and that of English and Irish-Americans. In addition, the percentage of white-collar workers among Italian-Americans (42.7 per cent) was below that of English-Americans (46.9 per cent) and of Irish-Americans (44.4 per cent). On the other hand, the median family income of Russian Jewish-Americans, $11,-554 (probably conservatively estimated since reported together with all "Russians"), was far higher than that of all the ethnic groups which arrived before them, as was the percentage of them employed as white-collar workers (77.9 per cent).

In 1963, Glazer and Moynihan in their *Beyond the Melting Pot* showed that, although the median family income of Italian-Americans in New York City was above that of blacks, the percentage of Italian-American males employed in the professions (8.1 per cent) was below that of black males professionally employed (8.5 per cent). Moreover, the Italian-American figure was far below that of professionally employed Jewish-Americans (21.5 per cent) and Protestants (22 per cent) and only slightly above Irish-American men (7.7 per cent).

Why has the Italian-American apparently done better in terms of earnings than Irish-Americans who arrived here before him and originally were paid better? Yet, why has he done little better than blacks, who have suffered unparalleled discrimination, and Irish-Americans in white-collar and professional employment? And why has his success in earning power and white-collar work been so far below that of Jewish-Americans, who arrived here slightly later than he did?

A look at the unique Italian-American experience in the *fuoco*, the "fire" or "crucible" of America, may resolve these questions and may also explain other aspects of Italian-Americans.

In the Eastman Collection of Photography, there is a photograph that is deeply engraved in my mind. It is of an Italian family arriving at Ellis Island in 1905. A man, a woman, and a young child in her arms are staring directly into the camera from behind what appears to be a low boat railing. An older child is looking off to the left. The adults resemble my grandmother (dead since I was eighteen) and grandfather (dead since I was fifteen). They are faces of typical contadini and millions of their Italian-American descendants. The erect, proud postures, shoulders back, foreheads high. Immobile faces of fixed expressions, whose marblelike muscles are belied by full, sensuous mouths, the corners of which are ever so slightly turned down.

But most of all, I am caught by the eyes looking steadily into the camera. Liquid, fixed, and penetrating, yet so powerfully alive with contained passion, seeing all and telling nothing. Eyes formed in a land where the passing of many civilizations has been seen. Yet eyes which do not acknowledge time. They bespeak only keen passion and intelligence, contrary human qualities, yet so fused together in these eyes that the distinctions between them are no longer perceptible. These eyes and faces portray the same unyielding Italian human spirit that moved one of Galileo's legendary sayings, yet paradoxically contradict Galileo's message.

Faced with the instruments of torture, shown to him by the Inquisition to intimidate him into renouncing his heretical doctrines that the heavens change and that the earth moves about the sun, Galileo gave in to untruth. Yet at the very moment of his recantation, he is said to have said under his breath, *"Eppure si muove"* ("And yet it moves"). In the same spirit, the faces of the immigrants defy the voyage they have just taken and say the exact opposite of Galileo's words, at least as they apply to the major values and truths of life: "Yet, they do *not* change or move."

They are the faces of those descended from generations who proved they might be killed but never defeated or even changed. Their faces project the lines of Robert Browning, "Open my heart, and you will see/Graved inside of it, 'Italy.' " Yet theirs is not the tender Italy of the English Romantic. It is the Italy of the Mezzogiorno, tempered by the fire of its centuries of starkly beautiful, bittersweet history. The hearts of their people throb warm blood, but are tough as the most annealed steel. However else others have "made it" in America, Italian-Americans have prevailed by their unbreakable amalgam of determination and guts, sustained by the solidarity of la famiglia. And where they have not prevailed, it has not been because of any weakness in this spirit, but in a cruel irony, precisely because they have firmly held to this spirit in a land where some of the directions of its force has greatly limited their social and economic progress.

In the photograph of the family from Ellis Island, the man and the woman are dressed in black. With his right arm, the man is easily holding on his back the family's bundle of possessions, wrapped in what appears to be tarpaulin and tied with rope. The woman holds the younger child, perhaps two or three years old, on her left hip, which is gracefully thrust to one side. The child rests easily on this womanly hip, his own posture already reflecting the proud stance of his parents. The postures of mother and child are those of so many of the great Italian paintings of Madonna and Child, paintings for which contadino women and children often posed. The child is dressed in a coat, hood, and shoes, each at least two sizes too large—obvious hand-me-downs from the older sibling standing before them. The child is relatively fortunate in its clothing. When my father arrived at Ellis Island at age thirteen, he wore homemade shoes of cloth, for his family could not afford leather shoes, not even secondhand ones.

My father's story is representative of Italian immigration. He was the oldest boy in a family of three girls and two boys, children of a tailor in Palermo. Driven to starvation, with no work of any kind available either for my grandfather or for my father, the larger famiglia made the typical decision. The working age males would immigrate to the land where it was said there was bread and work. Leaving the others behind, father and son boarded a ship, steerage class, to New York. After a long, miserable journey they landed in New York. There, distant relatives, members of their family who had preceded them, immediately found work for them. The plan was to earn and save enough to bring over the other members of the family. To this end, my father, when he was thirteen worked in a bakery, fourteen hours per night and morning, and my grandfather took whatever work he could find. Whenever he could, he worked in his skill, first mending the clothes of the poor, then working on the apparel of New York's middle class. (Lest anyone think the story is of the dead past, let him visit the workrooms of today's large men's clothing stores in New York. They are manned by latter-day counterparts of my paternal grandfather, tailors newly arrived from the Mezzogiorno.)

The family plan succeeded—with one exception. His three sisters were sent their tickets and made it to New York. However, the youngest sibling, my uncle, age four, was too ill to meet the hardships of steerage, by this time well known to all Italian contadini from the letters of their relatives in America. The boy grew into a man, and his fate was common to those left behind: childhood illness, the starvation of the Mezzogiorno compounded by the world depression of the 1930's, and conscription into Mussolini's army for combat in Africa. My father lost track of him when World War II began.

In 1945, my paternal grandfather died as the war ended, and my father tried to find news of his brother. Official channels were blind alleys. Italy, a war-defeated nation, was in chaos. Characteristically, relief efforts were concentrated in the North and the recovery of the South was slowest of all. Black market channels were more expensive but no more successful. Years of fruitless search ended only in the news that my uncle had been a POW of the British early in the war. Finally, when my father made his first trip back to Italy in 1964, forty-four years after he left Sicily, he made inquiries in Palermo. These met with success only after he returned to New York. A letter informed him that his brother was believed to be in a hospital in Palermo, chronically ill.

My father died in 1967, and in 1972, when I made my first trip to Palermo, I took up the search. The impossible task of confronting bureaucracies was made easier by two facts. One, I was a Sicilian-American whose family came from this very city, and virtually every record keeper and

hospital official I met had relatives in the States. Did I
know *mio cugino* (my cousin) so and so, living in Philadelphia (Los Angeles, Chicago, New Orleans, etc.)? When
I responded that the United States spanned a three-
thousand-mile continent and had two hundred million people, I met with quizzical expressions. What does size have
to do with the solidarity of campanilismo. Although I was
an odd character, obviously confused by being raised in the
strange ways of America, I was nevertheless the son of a
paesano, speaking the dialect, even if poorly. Second and
most of all, I was searching for a blood relation—a sacred
quest. I was not to be denied. Boxes of files were pulled out
of storage bins, finally turning up the information. After
many stays in hospitals after his postwar repatriation, the
last one of which lasted for eleven years, my uncle died in
1968, semiparalyzed, alone, and the document said *de-
mente* (insane). The fate of my uncle is like that of many
of those left behind, confirming the decision of many in the
early years of this century that the best hope lay across the
sea.

When I was a young child, my schoolbooks told me that
Europeans immigrated to the United States "seeking democracy, religious tolerance, etc." No doubt many did. But
among Southern Italians, the motive was more vital—*pane e
lavoro* (bread and work). Immigrate or the family would
starve. Therefore, the immigration was led by those who
could work hardest—the young Italian men. In the descrip-
tive Italian word, these were the *braccianti*, a term meaning
"laborers" derived from the Italian word for "arm,"
braccia. By the strength of their arms these men were to
save themselves and their blood kin temporarily left behind.
In 1907, the peak year of Italian immigration, almost 80
per cent of Italians arriving at Ellis Island were male. And
more than 80 per cent of these were between the ages of
fourteen and forty-five. My grandfather's Sicilian friends
used to sum up their experience in America by holding
up their worker's hands and saying in dialect, *"America
è icca"* ("America is *here*—*this* is America").

American immigration officials kept separate records for

Southern Italian and Northern Italian immigrants. The latter group comprised less than 15 per cent of the total of five million Italian immigrants arriving in the United States by 1924. The Northerners, together with the Italian government, convinced American officials that there were two distinct groups of Italians, or in the word used in official American documents of the time, two different "races."

The race of Meridonali, or Southern, Italians were, among all immigrants, in many ways the poorest equipped to make it in America. In 1900, records were kept of the amounts of money (equivalents of dollars) brought by twenty-five "races" (national or ethnic groups) of immigrants to this country. The Meridonali were third from lowest, bringing $8.84 per capita—compared with the $7.96 brought by the group at the bottom (Lithuanians) and the $41.51 brought by the top group (the Scots).

In 1899, the percentage of Meridonali who were illiterate was 46.56 per cent, the highest of the eleven largest ethnic groups arriving at Ellis Island. This was to remain true through the peak years of 1900–14. In 1901, a time when the total illiteracy of Italy was 38.30 per cent, 62 per cent of the Southern Italian men landing at Ellis Island were totally lacking the ability to read or write any "recognized language or dialect," as the records put it, and 74 per cent of the women were illiterate. In 1903, the rate of illiteracy among Southern Italian immigrants was 51.4 per cent. In 1904, 54.2 per cent.

Moreover, most of the Meridonali were semiskilled workers, and the group showed the highest percentage of unskilled laborers among all immigrant groups from 1890–1914. For example, the percentage in 1901 of unskilled labor among the Italians entering the country was 34.15 per cent. (Compare this with the figures of the three immigrant groups having the next highest figures for that year: Hungarians, 32.44 per cent; Irish, 25.16 per cent; French Canadian, 16.43 per cent.) Moreover, most of the remaining number were semiskilled, e.g., "railroad workers," 10.56 per cent; miners, 8.51 per cent, etc.

The Annual Report of the Commissioner General of Immigration for 1903 catalogues the distribution of occupations and professions of Southern Italian immigrants, whose number that year totaled 196,117. Of these, there were three editors, five lawyers, twenty-four physicians, twenty-three engineers, and fifty-one teachers. On the other hand, there were 2,583 carpenters and joiners, 1,790 sailors, 2,975 masons, 3,258 tailors, 4,636 shoemakers, 2,398 seamstresses, 2,088 barbers, 262 gardeners, 58 machinists, 351 miners, 605 bakers, 913 blacksmiths, and lesser numbers in other categories of skilled and semiskilled labor. The two largest categories, comprising the great majority of the total, 118,073 out of 196,117, were unskilled laborers (85,682) and farm laborers (32,391).

The relatively low proportions of professionals and skilled workers were solely a result of economic conditions in the Mezzogiorno. For the law passed by the Italian government in 1888 permitted virtually anyone to leave, except men of military age who had not yet seen military service. This provision was violated by many Southern men who, through bribery or other means (a favorite was to become a seaman and jump ship at a foreign port), left Italy illegally. In fact, my maternal grandfather first reached New York as a merchant seaman, quickly returning to Palermo for his wife and the only child then born of the six they were eventually to have.

In addition, Southern Italians landing in 1901 had the third highest percentage of the most tragic group of all—those sent back to Europe from Ellis Island because they were suffering from, in the official phrase, "loathsome or dangerous contagious diseases," or from some physical incapacity, e.g., loss of an eye or limb.

In short, the Italian immigrant was poorly equipped for the American economy, except for his powerful motivation to work for his family. Even the report of the Industrial Commission, a document reeking with anti-Italian bigotry, conceded that:

Where an Irishman or a German demands meat, an Italian will work upon staple bread and beer, and, although his physical efficiency is not as great, he works for so much less that it is profitable to employ him.

For the word "profitable," substitute "exploitive."

In the years 1900–10, the average Italian-American family income per year was six hundred dollars. This figure is only 45 per cent of the average income of the time for American-born families. And this despite the fact that in 60 per cent of Italian-American families immediate members of the family worked in addition to the father.

To Italian immigrants and their descendants today, work involves more than questions of economics. Work is regarded as moral training for the young. And among adults, it is regarded as a matter of pride. To work is to show evidence that one has become a man or a woman, a full member of the family. So strong is this ethic that it governs behavior quite apart from considerations of monetary gain. There is a dialect saying I heard among the people of Red Hook that is indicative: *Poveri si, ma perchè lagnusi?* (Poor yes, but why lazy?). I have often since heard Italian-Americans repeat the gist of the saying, even those who no longer remember the old language or who never learned it. It is a moral wrong not to be productively occupied. Even the unemployed should find something to do, something to care for. Like all Italians, the contadino enjoyed relaxation—the feeling of *dolce far niente* internationalized by modern Italy's jet set. But relaxation only in the context of first having pulled one's weight, and preferably more.

The sense of pride for something done by oneself and for one's family, whether building a brick wall, a small business, or making a fine meal, is essential to the Italian-American psychology. It cannot be overlooked if we are to understand the kinds of work done by Italian-Americans, the kinds of work they have avoided, and the types of work in which they have not succeeded. They have avoided work where the product or result is abstracted, removed from the worker. And as a group, they have been conspicuously unsuccessful as corporation executives, as "team men." They have sought a proximate relation between the individual and the end result of his labor, whether it be digging a ditch, running a restaurant, nursing a patient, playing a musical instrument, filling a pharmaceutical prescription, or teaching a child. In short, the pride that comes from seeing and feeling one's efforts and skills mingled with some result. The Italian-American seeks to do something the result of which he can demonstrate to his family. Herein lies another important component of his pride. "With these hands I built *that* wall." "*This* is my restaurant." Etc.

The rewards of modern corporate life are abstract, ambiguous, anonymous, transcending any one individual. Indeed it is because corporate life offers so few basic human satisfactions, and in fact demands service to the company to the exclusion of other personal satisfactions such as family life, that it compensates by offering great monetary rewards. The modern executive, as the sayings go, is "wedded to his company," and his "career is his hobby."

Following their traditional values, Italian-Americans have sought work where the rewards are more palpably human. This involves their sense of dignity, and it has nothing to do with keeping one's fingernails clean or even necessarily in "pride of craftsmanship." In an America where leisure and corporate status are prime values, and where the pride of the craftsman is nostalgically remembered, the Italian-American values instead his sheer labor first and his individual share of it as much as his skills. There is satisfaction felt in swinging a longshoreman's hook, or laying bricks, and feeling the relationship between the ache in one's arms and back after a day's work and the benefits from it to one's family. In work as in all dimensions of life, pride among Italian-Americans is much more visceral and passionate than sublimated and abstract.

Because of their general distaste for abstractions and abstracted values, their ambivalent attitude toward formal schooling, and their desire to remain close to the family roots, Italian-Americans have gone into blue-collar rather than white-collar work. And when they have gone into the latter, it is in areas where the individual as such can exercise his skills or just plain labor. This explains why so many second- and even third-generation Italians fill blue-collar jobs, civil service, and low echelon white-collar jobs. Many of those in the last category are employed in more static, low-growth and hence little-changing industries. For example, public utilities, like Con Edison in New York City, where my father worked for forty years. And in New York City the ranks of the Fire Department, Police Department, and Sanitation Department are filled with Italians. The top positions in these services and in their counterpart private corporations remain conspicuously and disproportionately free of Italian-Americans. These top careers demand that one pull his time and energies away from the family, and often demand high levels of formal education as well.

In a pattern that perhaps is just now beginning to change, those few Italian-Americans who have gone into white-collar work and the professions have chosen careers again where personal accomplishment, stability, and noninterference with regular family life were perceived as possible. In the Mezzogiorno, each labored for his family. As we shall see, there was no sense of larger community or any other sentiment that could be transformed into the large team life of corporate American business. Thus, white-collar Italian-Americans favor careers in law, engineering, music for entertainment, and occasionally pharmacology and medicine for males, and teaching, nursing, clerical, and secretarial work for females. Moreover, their reputation for competence and responsibility in these areas is high.

The staying power of la via vecchia can be seen in almost no change from the pattern of occupations and careers of Italian immigrants and those of their second-generation childen. For example, in 1950, when the second generation had already established themselves in employment, the census for that year reported little change

from the ways in which second-generation Italian-American
men made their livings from those of their fathers. The
1970 Census Report includes many third-generation men
who by that time had entered the labor force. Comparing
the employment of the three groups side by side, we note
little change from generation to generation:

Category	Immigrant Italian-American Males, 1950 per cent	Second-Generation Males, 1950 per cent	All Males, 1970 per cent
Professional	3	6	13.5
Managerial	13	10	14.9
Clerical and Sales	6	17	9.1
Craftsmen	24	22	22.7
Operatives	24	29	20
Private Household Workers	0	0	0
Service Workers	14	6	7.5
Laborers	14	9	6.4

Among the second generation, 66 per cent in 1950 earned
their living as craftsmen, operatives, service workers, or
laborers, while the percentage in their father's generation
was only slightly higher, 72 per cent. In 1970 the percentage among all Italian-American males, immigrant, second,
third, and fourth generations, was still over 56 per cent.

Among Italian-American females, the same little change
is noted between the immigrant working women and their
working daughters except for a major shift, a sharp rise of
32 per cent, in clerical and sales work among the second
generation in 1950 and an almost exactly equal drop of
33 per cent among "operatives." There is little change from
1950 to 1970 except for a 21-point drop in operatives. In
other words, whereas the immigrant mothers were seamstresses, their daughters and granddaughters are salesgirls,
typists, clerks, and secretaries.

Category	Immigrant Females in 1950 per cent	Second-Generation in 1950 per cent	All Females in 1970 per cent
Professional	2	5	9
Managerial	4	2	4
Clerical and Sales	8	40	39
Craftsmen	2	2	2
Operatives	77	44	25
Private Household Workers	1	0	0
Service Workers	4	4	10
Laborers	0	0	0

In short, the economic mobility of second-generation Italian-Americans up from their parents was simply a question of doing better economically in the same categories of skilled, semiskilled, and unskilled labor. It did not involve much rising out of these to executive (managerial) or professional categories. Thus, although the wages and hence the standard of living went up between the two generations, the American dream of social and economic progress was not otherwise fulfilled. In 1970, the pattern apparently was still holding.

The Italian immigrant arrived with the conviction that noi che non abbiamo educazione bisogna avere guida nelle mani—"we who have no education must guide ourselves with our hands." Why he passed this conviction on to his children, instead of the obvious alternative—"we who have no education must become educated"—tells a substantial part of the Italian-American story. Distrust of formal schooling as a threat to la via vecchia which will be examined in another chapter, distrust of careers that took one's time and energies away from la famiglia and hence threatened its ordine, valuing personalized, concrete rather than anonymous, abstract team labor, and anti-Italian discrimination all shaped the inherited work ethic.

The work ethic of the Italian is quite different from the

Puritan ethic. The latter stressed labor as punishment for original sin, and sometimes as expiation through which one might gain God's grace and entrance into heaven in the next life. The Italian work ethic is neither religious nor negative, nor is it other-worldly in its orientation. It is wholly pragmatic. One labors for the positive well-being of those one loves here on earth, one's family. To succeed in this is a source of great pride. And the closer the relation between the work and the family, the more assured of its success. For as the contadino proverb says, *Chi martella per se martella bene*—"He who hammers for himself hammers well."

In questa vita si fa uva—literally, "In this life one produces grapes," meaning one should be fruitful. Those of us growing up in Red Hook's Little Italy did not need to hear this saying too often. The attitude it expresses was thick in the ambiance of the life we lived. Thus, although no one urged me to work as a boy, and although it was not economically necessary, at the age of eleven I took it upon myself to work when not in school. I went to work in a small shop, owned by an Italian-American, that made, installed, and repaired venetian blinds, did upholstery repair work and other miscellaneous jobs, e.g., making wood cornices. I worked three hours a day after school, plus Friday evenings and all day Saturdays, sometimes into the late evening. Starting salary was $5.00 per week, and I made $7.00 per week after two years. Moreover, I valued the feelings centered around the work more than the money. The sense of one's hands racing with those of the three other Italian-American boys employed to see who could string a venetian blind fastest. Eating meals with the young men who hung out in the workshop. These were the satisfactions nurtured by the tradition, and they were more valued than pride of accomplishment in school, community, or other arenas where Americans seek self-respect.

The pattern continued. At the ages of fifteen and sixteen, I spent summers as a carpenter's helper and bricklayer's helper, always employed by small-scale Italian-American contractors. And always employed illegally. "After all, law or no law, an Italian boy should learn to build with his hands, even if he is good in school. Books are OK, but first be a man." Although my hands are now smooth, soft, and clean, I will never forget the blisters turned to calluses on my hands and aches in my arm and back after hammering flooring or roofing into place for eight hours. Nor will I forget carrying a heavy tray of bricks or mortar on my shoulder, one hand for the tray, one for the ladder up the scaffolding, a climb that became longer each day as we progressed. The first rule taught to me as a bricklayer's helper was, "Balance yourself and you can carry anything." It is as much a rule of character of the Italian-American as a laborer's maxim. Thus, carrying two heavy cinder blocks, one in each hand, is easier than carrying only one. One alone necessarily throws you off balance however you hold it.

I shall never forget coming home after 4 P.M. covered with mortar dust caked by my own sweat, every pore and muscle crying for a hot bath. There is no romance in manual labor, except for those who have never done any. But there is dignity in those who do it, or at least there was in the Italian-Americans with whom I worked.

One of my most vivid memories is of pulling one of my employers out of an accident. He was a short, dark, gentle bricklayer, but powerfully built like a weight lifter. We had just laid the concrete foundation for a building (a nursing home) and were walking on the basic floor beams, set parallel to each other, laid on edge some sixteen inches apart. Suddenly, the man who had over the summer become a quasi-padrino to me, slipped and plunged feet first between two beams which scraped the flesh off the sides of his bare chest and the insides of his arms, and finally caught him under his armpits. I ran over to him, jumping from beam to beam, and then, straddling the space in which he was suspended unable either to fall further or lift himself out of it, I somehow lifted a man who outweighed me by the strength of my back and legs thrusting up from my balanced feet. "Always balance yourself."

The two of us spattered with his blood, I drove my

mentor home in the dump truck. He wanted no part of a hospital, and the next day showed up for a full day's work, his torn and bruised chest and arms covered in bandages.

Perhaps the men who hired me were right. Perhaps I am more of a man for the labor experience than I might otherwise have been.

Italian immigrants used to joke that they were "born with a shovel in one hand and a pickax in the other." The marriage of manual labor and life, so much a part of the Italian-American saga, was begun for many immigrants by a "wedding" that took place even before they reached American shores. For the labor contract that accompanied many of them on the voyage was as binding as any marriage certificate. The contract system was a product of collaboration between steamship carriers, American businessmen, Northern Italian bureaucrats, and Southern Italian opportunists. Dubbed the *"padrone* and *paesano* system," it was enormously profitable for those who ran it and greatly exploitive of those subjected to it.

In the system, American businesses (urban and agricultural) that needed cheap labor contacted a shipping line engaged in immigrant traffic. This traffic was of enormous proportions. By the year 1900 it had already invested $118,-000,000 in the business of carrying immigrants from Europe to the United States. Italian immigration was relatively late, the majority of the contadini coming during the years from 1900–14. By that time, the system was ready for them.

In 1904, a ticket from Naples to New York, steerage class, cost from twenty-seven to thirty-nine dollars. Although this cost seems minimal today, it was very high in relation to the contadino's income. Thirty-five dollars represented one hundred days' wages to the average man of Calabria and Basilicata, and more to the Sicilian. At a time when very few contadini worked anywhere near one hundred days a year, the price was in fact high.

The ticket entitled the immigrant to travel in a manner difficult for us to imagine. One Italian-American student at the college where I teach, never having heard the term "steerage," turned to today's Webster's New Collegiate Dictionary. It was there described as "third class—now often called *tourist class*." I promptly sent the student to more adequate sources. In steerage, crowds of immigrants of all ages were jammed below decks in every nook and cranny of the ship where cargo and equipment would normally be stored. These areas were not in any sense cabins (reserved for first- and second-class ticket holders) but merely spaces. There was an absence of adequate bedding, heating, ventilation, or sanitary facilities. When the weather permitted, the passengers spent as much time as possible out on the open deck to escape conditions below.

My father described his voyage, between steel decks, overcome with the smell of vomit, urine, and excrement and the moans and wails of the sick and seasick of all ages. To go topside and expose oneself to the cold Atlantic weather was considered a luxury. Indeed, Ellis Island records show that an inordinate number of Italians arrived suffering from pneumonia.

Steerage had been an international scandal for some years before the great flow of Italian immigration. As early as 1865, the New York State Commissioners of Emigration were moved to investigate conditions aboard a German ship which arrived in New York City, 108 of its 544 steerage passengers dead! In their report, they describe conditions that were to prevail for the next several decades, except that later voyages took shorter time than the seventy days of 1865.

As to the interior of the vessel, the upper steerage is high and wide. All the spars, beams, and planks which were used for the construction of temporary berths had been removed. Except through two hatchways and two very small ventilators, it had no ventilation, and not a single window or bull's eye was open during the voyage. In general, however, it was not worse than the steerage of other emigrant ships; but the lower steerage, the so-called orlop-deck, is a perfect pesthole, calculated to kill the healthiest man. It had been made a temporary room for the voyage by laying a tier of planks over the lower beams of the vessel, and they were so supported that they shook when walking on them. The little light this orlop-deck received came through one of the hatchways of the upper-deck. Although the latter was open when we were on board, and although the ship was lying in the open sea, free from all sides, it was impossible to see anything at a distance of two or three feet. On our enquiring how this hole had been lighted during the voyage, we were told that some lanterns had been up there, but on account of the foulness of the air, they could scarcely burn. It had, of course, much less ventilation, and was immediately over the keel, where the bilge-water collects, and adjoining part of the cargo, which consisted of wool and hides. And in this place about 120 passengers were crowded for 70 days, and for a greater part of the voyage in a tropical heat, with scanty rations and a very inadequate supply of water, and worse than all, suffering from the miasma below, above, and beside them which of itself must create fever and pestilence!

The captain himself stated to us that the passengers refused to carry the excrements on the deck, and that "the urine and ordure of the upper-steerage flowed down to the lower." As the main-deck was very difficult of access from the orlop-deck, the inmates of the latter often failed to go on deck even to attend to the calls of nature. There were only six water-closets for the accommodation of all the passengers. They have been cleansed, of course; but the smell that emanated from them was still very intense, and corroborates the statement of the above-named officers—that they must have been in an extraordinary frightful condition.

Conditions of immigrant travel were so bad that, as Terry Coleman records in his book on the subject called *Going to America* (1972), New York City at one point charged ships' captains a ten-dollar fee for each dead passenger. The device failed. Captains merely buried the dead at sea and altered passenger lists to avoid the penalty. Although the United States and Italian governments made other, sporadic efforts to control the abuse of steerage, the appalling conditions continued. The trade was simply too profitable. High profit has always had a tendency to overcome humane sentiments in international trade, witness the ante-bellum slave ships from Africa, and today's traffic in heroin.

In violation of laws, steamship lines actually solicited steerage business. One line alone had 1500 agents in Europe. In Italy these agents, paid by the carriers and/or by American businesses needing labor, would advance the contadino the money needed for his journey in "tourist class." In return, the immigrant agreed to work for some American company or padrone (boss) for a given period of time to repay the loan, plus exorbitant interest. The padrone was often an Italian opportunist who acted as foreman for gangs of Italian laborers in the United States and fronted for the American employer.

An interview that took place in 1902 with an immigrant named Rocco Corresca is reprinted in *The New Immigration* (1971), edited by P. Roberts. In it, Mr. Corresca describes his relationship with a Fagin-like padrone named Bartolo, for whom he and other young Italians picked rags, did street work, shined shoes and cleaned saloons in Newark, New Jersey. Of Bartolo, Corresca said,

> He gave us very little money, and our clothes were some of those that were found on the street. Still we had enough to eat and we had meat quite often, which we never had in Italy. Bartolo got it from the butcher—the meat was that he could not sell to the other people—but it was quite good meat. Bartolo cooked it in the pan while we all sat on our beds in the evening. Then he cut it into small bits and passed the pan around, saying: "See what I do for you and yet you are not glad. I am too kind a man, that is why I am so poor."

The padroni, a new form of the old world gabelotti, were often from the same town or region as the men the overseas agents recruited. And often letters from these Judas-goat paesani in America were instrumental in getting the contadini to agree to the contract. In any case, the starving contadini had little choice but to enter into what was in effect a form of indentured servitude. One simply had to immigrate, whatever the means. We now know that

in 1910, even an unemployed young man named Mussolini planned to immigrate to the United States. Thus, the
Italian percentage of the total immigration to the United
States jumped from 6.7 per cent in 1821–1902 to 26.9 per
cent in 1903. In the next decade, an annual average of
more than two hundred thousand Italians reached the
United States. Some eventually returned to Italy, even after
staying in America for years.

The Italian arrived at Ellis Island and faced a battery of
questions. After 1885 when the American government began an effort to eliminate contract labor, on landing the
immigrant was required to swear that he was, one, not involved in contract labor, and, two, that he could maintain
himself economically. If he would not so swear, he was
warned that his papers would be declared *non in regola*
(not in order) and he would be deported. Starving, without
money, and often in fact committed to a padrone fronting
for an employer whose name he did not know, the Italian
regarded these oaths required of him as simply one more
confirmation that officials everywhere were either *pazzi*
(crazy), *schifosi* (repugnant), or both. He wasn't far from
wrong, for the "screening" process was at first largely a
sham. America needed cheap labor, and cheap labor was
allowed to pass even if *i documenti non sono in regola* (the
papers are not in order). Often the immigrant would simply declare that he was not under contract, or indeed without any other papers. This gives rise to the hypothesis that
the derogatory term "wop" originated as an acronym of
the designation "without papers."

The Italians went to work, saved their meager wages
and brought over their relatives. In 1910, the Bureau of
Labor estimated that 95 per cent of Italian-American laborers saved twenty-eight dollars to thirty dollars per month.
At a time when they made less than forty dollars per
month, this represented an incredible sacrifice! Their reputation for hard work, self-maintenance, and frugality
made them attractive to the hard-boiled employers of the
time. Thus, they were recruited for work all over the
United States. Many became railroad workers, weaving

America's vast rail network. Railroads encouraged their Italian workers to settle in towns on land adjoining rail lines when they found that under Italian care the lands increased in value. These Italian families literally settled "on the other side of the tracks" from the beginning. Italians labored in lumber camps in Michigan and built projects like the Ashokan Dam in New York State. They became workers in shipyards—the now defunct Brooklyn Navy Yard was a large employer of Italian-Americans in my boyhood. They built canals and roads everywhere. They became iron ore miners in Michigan, Wisconsin, and Minnesota; phosphate miners in the South, and stone miners in the quarries of New England. In Florida, they manned the cigar factories of Tampa, and in the Midwest they worked the stockyards of Chicago and Kansas City, and the brickyards near "Dago Hill" in St. Louis. On both coasts, they became fishermen, the predecessors of the Italians found today in San Francisco's Fisherman's Wharf and New York's Fulton Fish Market.

The welcoming guidebooks printed in Italian on Ellis Island at one point urged the immigrants to go to farm states. This was chiefly the result of the desire of large farm and plantation owners of the South to replace black labor with Italian labor. The feelings expressed in a newspaper in 1904 by one C. L. Buck of Independence, Louisiana, are indicative of the reasons for the preference for the Italian laborer. The racism of Mr. Buck notwithstanding, the chief motive expressed is purely economic.

Twenty years ago land could be bought in and around town for $1 to $5 per acre that is now selling readily at $25 to $100 per acre. One tract here of 1,500 acres sold twenty-five years ago for $1,600 and only a few weeks ago the purchaser sold 200 acres for $10,400. The assessed value of lands in this parish has been doubled in the past four years.

One will ask what was the principal cause of the development. The answer must be the Italian immigration that has come here and improved the conditions in respect to production. The majority of farmers here have done away with negro labor. Why? Because they are a shiftless, worthless sort, whereas the Italian laborer is a success. His sole object is to make money, and he knows it must come out of the ground; therefore, he is always at work when his work is needed.

They are prompt to pay their debts at the stores, meet their paper at the banks when due, and often before. I do not think there is a case on record in this parish when the State has had to prosecute them for a crime or misdemeanor . . . I find it a great improvement and cheaper than the negro labor of today. As tenants they never take up more at the store than will be realized from the crops . . .

Italians lured to the South as agricultural laborers bought land as soon as they could with their savings. (Often they could afford only the cheapest, and therefore worst, farmland.) These were the origins of the small Italian-American farm communities that today dot Louisiana, Texas, Arkansas, Mississippi, Alabama, Tennessee, Virginia, and Maryland. Northern and Western agricultural laborers followed the same policy of going after small tracts of land, and they led to the Italian-American truck farms found today in New York's Finger Lakes region, Long Island, Staten Island, around New Haven in Connecticut, the Delaware peach belt, and in New Jersey, especially the area of Vineland. By 1897, there were already 45,925 Italian-Americans in California, some of them farm laborers who went on to establish some of the Italian farming communities found there today.

Thus, from the earliest years, Italian-Americans have been widely distributed throughout the United States. As early as 1900, the Census revealed the following distribution of Italian-Americans:

North Atlantic Division	352,000
South Atlantic Division	10,509
North Central Division	55,085
South Central Division	26,158
Western Division	40,210

However, the great majority of Italians settled in America's cities rather than in rural areas. And it is in New

York, Boston, Baltimore, Philadelphia, Chicago, St. Louis, New Haven, San Francisco, Buffalo and Rochester where most of the Italian-American saga has taken place. Italians arrived at a time when America's frontier was no longer to be found on the western plains, but in the challenge of building its huge industrial cities. As Terry Coleman tersely puts it,

> It was an old superstition, sometimes half believed by the simplest emigrants, that the streets of New York were paved with gold. When they got there they learned three things: first, that the streets were not paved with gold; second, that the streets were not paved at all; and third, that they were expected to pave them.

Italians entered construction work in large numbers, first as ditch diggers, hod carriers, mortar mixers, and in other unskilled capacities, moving quickly into the skilled jobs of the construction trades. New York City's vast subway system and many of its streets and buildings were built by Italian-American labor. In Chicago, Italians replaced the Irish as street and road builders. They labored to rebuild San Francisco after it was destroyed in the earthquake and fire of 1906. The laborers settled in North Beach and the Excelsior district.

Italians also went to work in the industrial guts and on the entertainment façades of the cities. By 1939, Italians replaced Jews as the major ethnic group employed in the garment industry and were the largest group represented in the musicians' union. They established the first of the numberless small family-run Italian restaurants and pizzerias that are today common in the United States. And they began many other one-family businesses and shops, e.g., shoe repair shops, and grocery and food stands that were nurtured into shops.

In short, Italians did find bread and work in the new land. But as my grandfather used to say in Sicilian dialect, *icca si mangia, ma non franco*—"here one eats, but not for free." Alistair Cooke ended his award-winning TV series,

"America" with a story about an old Italian immigrant who for a generation labored shining shoes outside New York's Grand Central Terminal. When asked what forty years of life in America had taught him, the man replied in one phrase: "There's no free lunch."

The cost of bread was hard and often dangerous work. One of the most powerful accounts of Italian immigrants is the novel *Christ in Concrete*, written in 1937 by Pietro Di Donato. The author describes a period in his boyhood when he began work as a bricklayer after his thirty-six-year-old immigrant father and a dozen other Italian-American construction workers died in a horrible accident. The accident was caused by the negligence of "Boss," who saved money by ignoring safety standards. The scene of the collapse of the building is among the most forceful in American literature. It records the dying thoughts of Di Donato's young father, broken body impaled on reinforcing irons, crushed by debris, suffocating in wet cement,

He paused exhausted. His genitals convulsed. The cold steel rod upon which they were impaled froze his spine. He shouted louder and louder. "Save me! I am hurt badly! I can be saved, I can—save me before it's too late!" But the cries went no farther than his own ears. The icy wet concrete reached his chin. His heart appalled. "In a few seconds I will be entombed. If I can only breathe, they will reach me. Surely, they will!" His face was quickly covered, its flesh yielding to the solid sharp-cut stones. "Air! Air!" screamed his lungs as he was completely sealed. Savagely he bit into the wooden form pressed upon his mouth. An eighth of an inch of its surface splintered off. Oh, if he could only hold out long enough to bite even the smallest hole through to the air. He must! There can be no other way! He didn't want to die! This could not be the answer to life. He had bitten halfway through when his teeth snapped off to the gums in the uneven conflict. The pressure of the concrete was such, and its effectiveness so thorough, that the wooden splinters, stumps of teeth, and blood never left the choking mouth.

The exploitive work that greeted the immigrants was accompanied by wide-scale anti-Italian hatred, and ghastly slum life. No sooner had they arrived than the Italians learned that *non ci vogliono bene*—"they don't like us much." How they responded to the scorn that greeted them may be seen in the early example of Tontitown, Arkansas.

In 1899 a group of forty Italian-American families established a farm community in Arkansas which they named after a man believed to be one of the first Europeans to explore Arkansas, Enrico Tonti. Led by a newly arrived Italian priest named Pietro Bandini, they purchased cheap land. Real estate sharps, including some Northern Italians who had immigrated much earlier, were engaged in exploiting the contadino's desire for land by selling poor lands at cut-rate prices. Often, the immigrants bought distant land, sight unseen. Still more frequently, because of their lack of knowledge about modern farming in general and American agricultural conditions in particular, they bought land that could not have been worse for farming.

The forty families had come from one such misfortune, an Italian farm colony at Sunnyside, Arkansas. The soil there was unfarmable. The only thing the marshy land nurtured was malaria-carrying mosquitoes, which took their toll among the Italians. The community left Sunnyside, fifty families going to a place called Knobville, Missouri. There they bought coarse, rocky soil sold to them by the St. Louis-San Francisco Railway for one dollar per acre. The fifty families had a total of $1,000, which they invested in the land, hopefully renaming the place Montebello. The men worked as railroad laborers in the off season to earn money for farm equipment, seeds, etc. After years of hard labor, the community became a success, producing grapes, fruits, and dairy products.

The forty families from Sunnyside who settled at Tontitown faced similar obstacles. Added to their ignorance of farming and poor soil, Tontitown was devastated by a tornado. Working as miners, the men earned enough to start again, rebuilding their houses and planting fruits and vegetables. Slowly they began to succeed, but only to face another problem. The native Americans in the area at first regarded the foreigners with curiosity. The queer habits of the immigrants, their incomprehensible lingo, their earnest farming attempts and their aloofness from the community outside were all conspicuous. Soon, the bigots of the area emerged. They began to harass the Tontitown community, first with pranks, then with vicious raids of vandalism designed to drive out the foreigners. After their schoolhouse had been burned, the men of Tontitown decided to meet the crisis. If life in the old land had taught them anything, it was how to deal with marauding stranieri. And it was not by recourse to legal authorities. For in Arkansas, the officers of law and order were no more friendly than they were in Italy. They were probably on the side of the marauders.

The men of Tontitown armed themselves and set up a schedule of twenty-four-hour-a-day patrols to guard their property. The rednecks who next came "funning" to Tontitown were met by bands of grimly determined armed men. Harassment of Tontitown promptly ended. It was a long time before the Italian-American community was to have amiable relations with their neighbors. But to the immigrants, it mattered little that no ci vogliono bene. They now had rispetto. This was all that they wanted from the outside world. It was all that was needed to work and to carry on la via vecchia.

The pattern of Tontitown is typical of Italian-American experiences in the cities as well as in the countryside. The pattern had a cycle of steps that reinforced one another:

1. Hard work, self-maintenance, and the life of la via vecchia carried on in neighborhoods or communities that were transplanted versions of those in the old country.

2. Exploitation and indifference on the part of the surrounding American society, often turning to bigotry, hatred, and persecution.

3. In the face of exploitation and hostility, a strengthening of the qualities of la via vecchia, including neighborhood solidarity and self-sufficiency, distrust of American

society, and as much aloofness from its institutions as was possible.

4. Ignorance about Italian-Americans, feeding bigoted myths, rumors, and suspicions. Finally, malice toward Italian-Americans, answered after the codes of la via vecchia, etc.

The cycle of ignorance, distrust, and malice began early with the coming of the contadini. The cycle grew as it was fed by the "explanations" of Italian-Americans from Northern Italy. Unlike the later Southern immigrants, most of the Northerners immigrated to other European countries to seek temporary employment and then returned home. But a number did go abroad and did not return. As early as 1861, 47,000 Italians, mostly Northerners, were in the United States and 18,000 in Brazil and Argentina. Italian immigration to Latin America declined by the turn of the century, largely because of a crisis in the coffee industry there.

When Americans turned to the earlier Northern Italian immigrants for understanding of the Southern contadini who were crowding into the country after 1880, they received the ignorant and malicious explanations prevalent in Northern Italy. That is, the Meridionale is culturally and/ or innately inferior. He is disposed to crime and violence. He is fatalistic, stagnant, sneaky, etc. Blinded by their own fears and hatred of foreigners, Americans swallowed the explanations. From then on, the self-confirming mechanism of bigotry was at work.

For example, many ships of Italian immigrants carried women unaccompanied by men, sent for by their husbands, fathers, or brothers laboring in America. The sailors who manned the ships, hardly a genteel lot, sometimes tried to molest the seemingly alone women in steerage. The sailors knew nothing of the ways of the Mezzogiorno. They did not dream that the stoic-looking contadino men on board noticed everything and forgot nothing. The onore of these men was outraged. What is more, they knew they would be held accountable by the women's male relatives once they landed if they did not protect them. The sailors

thought the passengers at their mercy and did not understand the warning signals given by the men of the Mezzogiorno. Thus, there were occasional incidents two or three
days after an Italian woman was abused, the offending
seaman would be found in some quiet section of the ship,
bleeding from knife wounds. It was convenient to blame
attacks on the dagos in steerage, even when they were in
fact committed by other sailors. When the ship landed,
American newspapers and the grapevine would scream still
another crime by Italians. Such incidents did not happen
often, but only a few were needed to be fanned by the
yellow journalism of the day, and the always insatiable
market for wild rumors.

By the time of the mass Italian immigration, the American Know-Nothing movement was already decades old.
The movement had three basic platforms: hatred of Roman
Catholicism; hatred of foreigners and foreign ways as un-
American; and resentment of cheap immigrant labor. The
Italians replaced the Irish as the target of anti-Catholic hatred, Americans neither knowing nor caring about the
differences in the Catholicism of the two ethnic groups, or
that the American Catholic Church was in many regards
unfriendly to the Italians. The ways of the Southern Italians
were totally incomprehensible to Americans. In the twisted
logic of bigotry, they were thus flagrantly "un-American."
And Italians replaced all the earlier immigrant groups as
targets of resentment about the competition of cheap labor.

The strain between Italians and the huge Know-Nothing
sentiment in America came to a climax in a sensationally
publicized series of incidents that took place in New Orleans
in 1891. Italians were being recruited to labor on the farms
of the American South. In particular, they worked in Mississippi and Louisiana during the sugar cane cutting season
which Italians called *la zuccarata* after the Italian word for
sugar, *zucchero*. Many of the immigrants settled in New
Orleans, some temporarily, others permanently. Because
the system of regionalism or *companilismo* was transplanted
to the New World, Italians tended to settle among other

Italians from the same regions of Italy. In New Orleans, 93 per cent of the Italians were from Sicily.

In a crime that remains unsolved to this day, New Orleans Police Superintendent David Hennessey was assassinated. Fueled by wild rumors that the clannish Sicilians belonged to a then mysterious secret criminal society called the Mafia, or, as it was then more commonly called, the Black Hand, the city's Sicilians were made scapegoats. Hundreds of them were arrested without cause. They were treated to beatings in and out of jail as will be seen later.

The die was cast. From the early days of immigration from the Mezzogiorno until today, the nativistic American mentality, born of ignorance and nurtured in malice, has offered Italian-Americans a bigoted choice of two identities somewhat paralleling two imposed on blacks. Indeed, among the oldest epithets hurled against Italian-Americans was "black guinea," or "black dago," etc. Italians were considered an inferior *race*, as were blacks. Racists insist that blacks must be either childlike, laughing, Uncle Tom figures or sullen, incorrigible, violent, knife-wielding criminals. Similarly, the nativists and their descendants, the anti-Italian bigots of today, insist that Italian-Americans be either/or creatures. They must be either spaghetti-twirling, opera-bellowing buffoons in undershirts (as in the TV commercial with its famous line, "That'sa some spicy meatball") or swarthy, sinister hoods in garish suits, shirts, and ties. The criminal image imposed on Italian-Americans is in itself a major issue, and will be discussed in another chapter. Even if the image did not exist, however, the "inferior race" slander would alone constitute a major problem for Italian-Americans.

The disposition toward insularity among Italian-Americans was ingrained over centuries of Mezzogiorno history. It has since been reinforced by American bigotry. However condescendingly euphemistic and polite the language of some bigots today, they still regard Italian-Americans as racially inferior "dagos," "wops," "guineas," and "greasers." Those who assume that such insults have disappeared, or only come from the uneducated, should read Glazer and Moynihan. They cite a comment made by a "world famous Yale professor of government." In 1969, upon hearing that an Italian-American had announced his candidacy for the office of mayor of New York City, the professor commented, "If Italians aren't actually an inferior race, they do the best imitation of one I've seen."

Also, we might recall well-known tests used to identify this prejudice. In one classic study, American college students were shown photographs of members of the opposite sex with what purported to be the name of each person on the photograph. The students were asked to evaluate the attractiveness of the person in the photograph. Then, some-time afterward, names were changed and the procedure repeated with the same students. The result was that those people who were regarded as "handsome" or "pretty" when they had names like "Smith" were found not attractive when their names were changed to Italian ones. (The same result was found using names commonly thought of as Jewish.)

As a blond, blue-eyed American who is never "spotted" as Italian, I am sometimes exposed to gibes and jokes such as the one I overheard at the University of Illinois in 1961. Question: "What sound does a pizza make when you throw it against the wall?" Answer: "Wop!" The joke was greeted with much laughter, not by rednecks, but by a roomful of graduate students, some of whom became belligerent rather than embarrassed when, as a Sicilian-American, I expressed irritation at the joke.

Or, take an experience of 1972. When I told one of my college classes that I had been asked by a newspaper to compile a list of names of living Italian-Americans who have become famous or otherwise "made it" in legitimate areas of American society, one student quipped, "Are there any?" Again much laughter, albeit good-natured rather than vicious. My response to the student was that, although there are indeed, I was not going to play a numbers game. Just as I believe a group of millions should not be judged by a handful of criminals among them, so I believe they should not be judged by the celebrities among them. For this kind of pride building is as useless as the negative stigma in giving an understanding of the life, thoughts, and values of the at least 99.98 per cent of Italian-Americans who are neither gangsters nor celebrities. Although it does provide heroes for Italian-Americans to emulate, and does in a superficial sense balance the bad press of gangsterism, reciting a litany of famous Italian-Americans in itself is poor psychological motivation for Italian-American youth if it is not accompanied by an in-depth understanding of their people. This deeper understanding is, in my opinion, woefully absent among all Americans, including young Italian-Americans. In my judgment, it should take priority over public relations gimmicks. In learning the truths of their ethnicity, young Italian-Americans will in the process also find ethnic heroes. But they cannot do vice versa. They cannot put together their identity by hero citing or pride boasting. The words of a wise black man about his people holds for all people. Kenneth Clark lighted the difference between the pseudo-identity of ethnic boasting and real identity when he said of pride, "Pride, like humanity, is destroyed by one's insistence that he possesses it."

As has often been noted, New York City sports a large collection of statues of famous Italians—Columbus, Verdi, Garibaldi, Dante, etc., erected mostly at the instigation of the immigrants from Northern Italy. On the other hand, there are few, if any, statues of famous Jews in New York. This lack has not hurt the progress of American Jews at all, for they have been successful in attuning their culture to the life of America. And conversely, all the many statues of famous Italians have not helped Italian-Americans. For reasons to be further investigated, their attunement of the old culture to meet the demands of success in a new society has been considerably less successful. And such adjustment need not mean assimilation, for American Jews have retained their ethnicity at least as much as have Italian-Americans.

Face to face with a society with which they shared mutual noncomprehension, and perpetuating the spirit of campanilismo, the large majority of Italian-Americans clustered together in big city ghettos euphemistically called Little Italies. (Incidentally, the word "ghetto" is Italian in origin. According to the Italian Tourist Agency, the word comes from the Italian word *getto,* or *ghetto* in the old Venetian dialect, meaning "to cast" and indicating a foundry. In 1516, Jews in Venice were segregated into the Ghetto Nuovo, a neighborhood at the edge of the city where a "new foundry" existed.)

Italian-Americans chose neighborhoods in which to live based on the following priorities. First, they wished to be as close as possible to members of the larger famiglia. Second, in the spirit of campanilismo, they desired to live among other people from the same paese (town or region). Third, they wanted to dwell among other people from the Mezzogiorno. Rarely, almost never, did an immigrant Italian family live among stranieri, away from other Italians. Italian-American neighborhoods were indeed clusters of transplanted towns of the Mezzogiorno, compressed together in the congested cities of the New World.

Continuance of campanilismo in the New World has been criticized by some because it led to insularity and parochialism among Italian-Americans. An evaluation of it, however, must also consider its benefits. In addition to providing environments where Italian-Americans could develop their strongest institution, the extended family, it made it possible for them to develop communities. Paradoxically, these in some ways were more in the nature of genuine commonwealths, closer to the old American "community" than had been the paese of the Mezzogiorno. The towns in Italy lacked this spirit of commonwealth.

Characteristically, Italians developed the ideal in the practical form of mutual aid societies. These were designed *to assist families* and, hence, fortify the old values of l'ordine della famiglia and comparaggio. In a sense, it was because their differences from the millions of Americans surrounding them were more noticeable and important than the differences among themselves that Italian-Americans developed the more positive aspects of campanilismo. What

is more, there was a practical necessity. Italians and their
via vecchia were not about to receive support from the
largely exploitive and wholly uncomprehending American
society.

One of the earliest of the mutual aid Italian-American
organizations was established in 1863 in New York City
and was called the Società Unione e Fratellanza Italiana.
By the turn of the century, there were hundreds of such
"social clubs" as they are rendered in the poor English
translation. Chicago's Italians had four hundred such societies by 1912. Disdaining the notion of accepting pietà
from those outside the family, the mutual aid societies,
composed of entire Italian-American families, furnished
the member families with important kinds of support. For
example, financial aid in times of unemployment, sickness,
or death. In a pattern continuing until today, Italian-
Americans ask little from American philanthropic organizations—and give little.

At least as important as material aid was the morale provided by the mutual benefit societies. The member families
came together in these societies for social and recreational
events and ceremonies. Picnics were popular among the
tenement-dwelling Italian-Americans who longed for a taste
of the countryside, a longing more easily satisfied in the
old land. Whole clubs of several, sometimes many, families
would exit en masse to the woods and fields surrounding
their city on a Sunday in a time before American cities
were surrounded by semiurban suburbs. The sight of dozens or even hundreds of these people with their strange
ways descending on a rural community for an outing at
first startled Americans. Thus, whenever possible, the clubs
would travel to city-side areas where Italian-American communities already existed. For example, in New York City,
certain sections of Queens, Staten Island, Long Island, and
New Jersey became closely associated with the city's Little
Italies, first through commercial intercourse—the Italian
truck farmers brought their produce to the Italian ghettos
for market. Then the ties were further strengthened by the
activities of the mutual aid societies. Thus, the town life

organization of the Mezzogiorno, each town consisting of overlying webs of families, was re-created in the United States, blurring the lines between city and rural life.

This was to continue to have importance when Italian-Americans began to move to the suburbs. The movement began during and after World War II. The migration to the suburbs was concurrent with that of other white Americans but had different motivations. Italian-Americans had a strong desire, imported from the Mezzogiorno, to own their own homes and land. The immigrants bought what they could in the Little Italies—old tenement buildings and shops. For example, my grandfather owned the brownstone in which we lived. It had been built during the 1880's as an elegant four-story town house for one family, the top floor being reserved for servants' quarters. Real estate interests quickly realized the profit to be had from buying the building, converting each floor into a "railroad flat" by adding to each a small kitchen and a bathroom (because of the architecture of the building, on the upper two floors the bathrooms had to be installed in the corridors outside the apartments) and renting each floor to an Italian family. Thus the second, or parlor, floor where I lived had once consisted of two large elegant rooms, a dining room and a salon or parlor. These had been divided into five rooms, each retaining the now incongruous baroque sculptured ceilings, sixteen to eighteen feet from the floor! And in the room that we used as a living room, actually a portion of the old parlor, there hung a six-foot-long chandelier, made from hundreds of glass crystals, a legacy from the days of the building's magnificence. Although for the first sixteen years of my life I did not have my own room and slept on a folding cot in the dining room of a cold-water flat, I lived with ceilings and a chandelier that were the pride of the Victorian élite. Such are the anomalies of tenement life.

Like many other immigrants, my grandfather bought the building as soon as he could from savings accumulated through considerable sacrifice. All six of his children contributed their paychecks before they married. During the great depression, my grandfather, when he found work in

Manhattan, would walk to and from work across the Brooklyn Bridge to save the five-cent fare. Ownership of the building, one's own home, fulfilled a dream impossible in the Mezzogiorno. The building was painstakingly rehabilitated over the years by my grandfather's own hands. It was the Italian-American pattern of improvement that turned squalid slums in America's cities into ordered and distinct neighborhoods. What is more, the back yard of our building provided space for one's own "field," another impossible dream. But it was only a symbolic field, and Italian-Americans dreamed of moving to "the country," as they put it, where the air is *bella fresca* as they remembered it in the old country.

Moving out of cities was not economically possible for appreciable numbers of Italian-Americans until the economic boom of World War II gave them the chance to earn enough. Many then moved to the suburbs, which were, however, rapidly losing their rural qualities. Those who moved often moved in groups, two or three generations of one family sharing a one- or two-family house on a street or a section of a suburb with other Italian-Americans. As the old paesi had been transplanted to the Little Italies of American cities, portions of these tenement communities were transplanted to the American suburbs in the 1950's and 1960's. Thus, although la via vecchia went "split level," it is still very much alive in areas many of which had been the site of the truck farms and picnic areas of the old mutual aid societies. In New York City, la via vecchia lives in a belt of Italian-American small homes that stretch from areas of New Jersey to Staten Island, and across the Narrows to neighborhoods in Brooklyn, Queens, and out into Long Island.

The movement of some Italian-Americans to suburbia has been mistakenly lumped together with the larger American exodus. No doubt some of the motivations were in common, especially where second-generation Italian-Americans are involved. But the dream of moving was one as old as their fathers and had its major basis elsewhere than the widespread desire to escape from large numbers of blacks moving into the cities of the East, Midwest, and West after 1945. And although some of the second generation made the move, they made it with the conflicted quest for identity characteristic of that generation. Their desire was to be Italian in their essential value orientation, yet they shunned the more conspicuous façades of that orientation in favor of American fashions.

The immigrant generation succeeded so well in creating transplanted paesi that many among them did not even bother to learn the English language. To them English was the language of just another group of stranieri whose ways were antithetical to la via vecchia. My grandparents were typical. Although they lived in the United States for about forty years until their deaths, my grandfather barely learned enough English to say "hello" and my grandmother learned none at all. They did not care or bother to learn, for English was not necessary. They lived and worked among people who spoke Italian. On occasion, when the outside world intruded to the point where it insisted upon English, one of their children could translate. When my grandfather studied for his citizenship papers, he studied the various facts required about American history in Italian as translated by his children. And when he took the examination for his final citizenship papers, a kindly judge permitted my mother, then a child, to translate his questions to my grandfather into Italian, and my grandfather's responses into English. Thus, my grandfather could talk at length about George Washington, but only in the dialect of Sicily. As late as 1960, and probably even today, Italian continues to be the most commonly spoken foreign language in the United States, as it had been in 1950, 1940, and 1930, as noted by Joshua A. Fishman in his book *Language Loyalty in the United States* (1965).

This nonmastery of English among Italian immigrants is correctly explained by the pragmatic reasons that, first, knowledge of English was not necessary, and, second, it certainly did not preserve la via vecchia and might possibly threaten it. That these are correct explanations rather than the libel popular among Northern Italians that "the Meri-

dionale learns languages slowly" is attested to in the fact
that Southern Italians did learn each other's greatly differ-
ing dialects when life in this country's Little Italies made
it necessary.

One of the American institutions to which Italian-
Americans have become well attuned is the trade union.
Their adoption of this institution was facilitated by a combination of their experiences—the value of solidarity inherited from l'ordine della famiglia and the mutual aid
societies of the immigrants, and their treatment at the
hands of the American employer. Italian-Americans are
strong union people, and various locals and sometimes
whole unions have become their hegemonies, as in the construction trades and among longshoremen in New York.
These unions tend to reflect the values of Italian-Americans
and are often somewhat mistakenly spoken of as "guilds"
by the media. Their guildlike character comes from the
values of la famiglia, la via vecchia, and campanilismo. The
values are those of cohesiveness, passing the values from
one generation to another, and exclusion of outsiders.

At first, the Italian-American skilled and nonskilled laborer was at the mercy of the supply for and demand of
cheap labor. Thus, the American depression of 1893 forced
many to return home to Italy. However, as became the
pattern, many came back to the United States. In fact, there
was considerable back-and-forthing, e.g., in the year 1903,
when over 214,000 Italians crossed the Atlantic to the
United States, and 78,000 crossed it back to Italy. However,
by the great economic crash of 1929, the back-and-forthing
had ceased. One reason was the new immigration laws
which made it exceedingly difficult for Italians to enter or
re-enter the United States. Second, Italian-Americans had
firmly rooted themselves in the American economy. They
had become farmers instead of farm laborers, small businessmen instead of mere street peddlers (or in the Italian's
more apt phrase "walking peddlers"—venditori ambulanti).
Most of all, they had become rooted workers rather than
day-laboring braccianti. The union movement played a
considerable role in the last change in status.

At first the labor movement resented the Italians as cheap labor threatening their uphill attempts to organize and empower the American worker. And, indeed, attempts were made by American companies to use the earlier Italian immigrants as "union busters." Thus in 1874, striking miners turned on a group of Italians imported by the Armstrong Coal Works in Pennsylvania to be unwitting scabs. Several Italians were killed. In 1907, the Dillingham Commission, established by the United States Congress, reported that "strike after strike in the Pennsylvania coalfields in the 1870's and early 1880's was smashed when employers brought in Slavic, Hungarian, and Italian labor."

Italians soon caught onto the design to use them as pawns, and turned toward pro-union activities themselves. By 1910, a survey by the Immigration Commission found that 10 per cent of Southern Italians in the United States had joined labor unions, a high percentage among workers at the time. Militant Italian-American labor leaders like Luigi Antonini could appeal to his paesani to view the union as another extension of la famiglia, a mutual aid association. The strength of such organization was quickly understood by them, and the immigrants began to agitate, often as *Italian* workers per se. In 1900, some four thousand Italians working to build New York City's Lexington Avenue Subway formed a union and went on strike, led by a twenty-one-year-old Italian immigrant. In 1904, five thousand Italian workers building the Bronx Aqueduct unionized and struck. Both these strikes were mostly successful. In 1912, however, an unsuccessful strike among textile workers, including many Italians, in Lawrence, Massachusetts, was led by three Italians. When the authorities moved to suppress the strike, they arrested the three plus three hundred others and killed an Italian-American woman in the process. The three leaders, acquitted of trumped-up charges of murder, were nonetheless kept in jail for the duration of the strike in order to break it.

One of the worst suppressions of Italian-American workers took place in 1914 in Colorado. When other attempts failed to break a strike by Italian-American miners, the state militia was called in. After some mutual sniping, the troops went berserk and attacked the homes of the miners, setting them on fire and shooting indiscriminately into them. One woman and seven children burned to death, and three men died by bullets.

The union activity of Italian-Americans aggravated the hatred against them by giving American nativists the opportunity to label them as "alien radicals." Although some Italian labor militants were socialists or anarchists, the vast majority of the transplanted contadini cared nothing for ideologies—socialist, capitalist, anarchist, or others. This was patently clear to Americans who knew the Italian immigrants and their backgrounds. But very few Americans knew them, and the fear of foreign radicalism grew to hysteria. The fear culminated in two of the worst crises of the Italian-American saga—their mass deportation (along with immigrants of other nationalities) in the infamous Palmer raids, and the vicious antiradical, anti-Italian case of Sacco and Vanzetti, an affair that rocked the world and for years overshadowed all other factors in determining the path of Italian-Americans.

Alexander Mitchell Palmer was a political hack who gained power by currying favor with Woodrow Wilson, helping him to become President. In 1919, he was appointed Attorney General of the United States. During his three-year tenure of office, he raised a red scare to mammoth proportions by prosecuting and persecuting aliens, including Italians, as suspicious and dangerous radicals. His most infamous tactic was the Palmer raid. Agents of the Department of Justice would descend upon an immigrant family, or sometimes a whole neighborhood, in the middle of the night, arresting people indiscriminately. In violation of every decent legal ethic and the due process of law itself, those who were not citizens were kept incommunicado by Palmer's witch hunters, and many were summarily deported. Years later, inquiries failed to find any links between those deported and subversion. It was cold consolation to those sent back to the Old World misery they had labored so hard to escape. This insane persecution, equating foreign birth with subversiveness, created panic among all immigrant groups. Among Italians, it strengthened their insularity from the larger society, an old inclination traceable to the maxim of the Mezzogiorno that "the law works against the people."

The shameful red scare and hatred of immigrants had roots in the xenophobia of Know-Nothingism. But it was brought to flower in the twentieth century when very prominent American leaders openly embraced its bigoted positions. In fact, it may be questioned whether it could have reached such damaging proportions if the way had not been laid by some very famous and powerful Americans. Because Italians constituted by far the largest ethnic group immigrating to the United States at the time, they bore the brunt of the outrage. For example, in October 1915, former President Theodore Roosevelt went out of his way to insult all immigrants and their children, and particularly Italian-Americans. In a speech to the Knights of Columbus assembled in New York City's Carnegie Hall and including Italian-Americans, he said, "There is no room in this country for hyphenated Americans. . . . There is no such thing as a hyphenated American who is a good American." Before he became President, he had called the 1891 mob lynching of eleven Sicilians in New Orleans "a rather good thing," and boasted that he had said so at a party where there were what he called "various dago diplomats." In 1915, Woodrow Wilson said that "hyphenated Americans . . . have poured the poison of disloyalty into the very arteries of our national life . . . such creatures of passion, disloyalty and anarchy must be crushed out."

The violent nativists got the message. In 1891, several Italians were lynched in West Virginia. In 1893, several others were murdered in Denver, Colorado. In March 1895, six Italian labor "agitators" were lynched in Colorado. In 1895, six Italians were torn from a jail by a mob in Hahnville, Louisiana. All were beaten, and three hanged. In 1899, a mob dragged three Sicilian shopkeepers from a jail in Tallulah, Louisiana, and caught two others. All five were lynched. Their offense? They had permitted

Negroes equal status with whites in their shops. In July 1901, Italians were attacked by a mob in Mississippi. In 1906, a mob in West Virginia killed several Italians and maimed several others. Italians were attacked in Tampa, Florida, in 1910. In that same year an Italian was pulled from a jail in Willisville, Illinois, and shot to death. Another Italian met the same fate in Illinois in 1911.

Perhaps the most rabid of Italian haters was Senator Henry Cabot Lodge of Massachusetts. It is not true that the "Lodges speak only to the Cabots, and the Cabots only to God." Or at least it was not true of Henry. In his five years as a member of the U. S. House of Representatives and during his thirty-one years in the U. S. Senate (1893–1924), he spoke often to the American people about his hatred for Italian-Americans. In 1891, he made a distinction between Northern Italians (whom he termed "Teutonic Italians") and Southern Italians. He labeled the latter inferior, and said the "great Republic should no longer be left unguarded from them." In March 1900, he made a speech in which he alluded to Italian-Americans:

> We have seen a murderous assault by an alien immigrant upon the Chief of Police of a great city [the 1891 incident in New Orleans], not to avenge any personal wrong, but because he represented law and order. Every day we read in the newspapers of savage murders by members of secret societies composed of alien immigrants. Can we doubt, in the presence of such horrible facts as these, the need of stringent laws and rigid enforcement, to exclude the criminals and anarchists of foreign countries from the United States?

Bigoted Americans responded to the incitement of people like Lodge. In August 1920, mobs invaded the Italian neighborhood of West Frankfort, Illinois, dragging people of all ages and both sexes from homes, beating them with weapons and burning whole rows of their homes. The attacks were repeated, and the Italians fought back, turning the small neighborhood into a battleground. It took five hundred state troopers three days to end the fighting. At its end, hundreds of Italian-Americans were left homeless and, with millions of their paesani in the United States, convinced that they were in a hostile country with only themselves to rely upon.

Anti-Italian fever was virulent when on April 15, 1920, five men held up a shoe company in Braintree, Massachusetts, killing an employee and fleeing in a car with fifteen thousand dollars. Witnesses claimed the holdup men "looked like Italian." When two Italians, Nicola Sacco, a factory worker from Puglia in South Italy, and Bartolomeo Vanzetti, a mustached fish peddler from the Northern Italian province of Piedmont, came to claim a car that police had linked with the crime, they were arrested. Circumstances linking them to the crime were questionable. But when it was discovered that they were under surveillance by Palmer's Department of Justice as political anarchists and that they carried firearms, a cry for their heads was raised all over the land. They were tried under conditions that were a mockery of the judicial process and found guilty. The prosecuting attorney appealed to the worst biases of the jury, treating Italian-American witnesses in an outrageously insulting manner. The testimony of eighteen Italian-born witnesses was dismissed out of hand by the court as unreliable. After the trial, the judge who had presided is alleged to have commented to a Dartmouth professor, "Did you see what I did to those anarchistic bastards the other day? I guess that will hold them for a while." The same judge, Webster Thayer, an old immigrant-hating pillar of Back Bay Society, one year before had presided over another trial in which Vanzetti had been accused of a holdup in Plymouth. At the time, the judge had instructed the jury that, "This man, although he may not actually have committed the crime attributed to him, is nevertheless morally culpable, because he is the enemy of our existing institutions. . . . The defendant's ideals are cognate with crime." Despite the testimony of thirty witnesses that Vanzetti was elsewhere at the time of the crime, Vanzetti was convicted of the Plymouth holdup.

During their trial, nine witnesses, including the clerk of the Italian Consulate, swore that Sacco was in Boston at the time of the Braintree robbery. Six witnesses placed Vanzetti in Plymouth making his door-to-door rounds as a peddler during the time of the crime. The two Italians were found guilty, and after seven years of protests and appeals they were executed. On the morning they were to die, Massachusetts' Governor Fuller, when asked if he would intercede to halt the execution, smiled at reporters and said only, "It's a beautiful morning boys, isn't it?"

A commission headed by Harvard University's president had found nothing wrong in Sacco and Vanzetti's trial, prompting the distinguished reporter Heywood Broun to write sarcastically in the New York *World:*

> What more can the immigrants from Italy expect? It is not every person who has a president of Harvard University throw the switch for him. If this is a lynching, at least the fish-peddler and his friend, the factory hand, may take unction to their souls that they will die at the hands of men in denim jackets or academic gowns. . . .

The last hearing held for the two Italians was presided over, as were all of their hearings, by Judge Thayer. Sacco said to him:

> I never knew, never heard, even read in history anything so cruel as this Court. After seven years prosecuting they still consider us guilty.

Both men protested their innocence until they were killed.

The guilt of the two men remains in controversy. But, guilty or innocent, they received a good deal less than a fair trial. Italian-Americans, divided on the question of their guilt, were all but unanimous about the unfairness of their trial. They felt as one with Vanzetti in the latter part of a statement he made in newly learned English when he last faced Judge Thayer. "I am suffering," he said, "because I am a radical and indeed I am a radical; I have suffered because I was an Italian, and indeed I am an Italian."

Many years later (I was born in 1939, twelve years after their execution), I remember my grandfather and his friends speak with bitterness about *il caso di Sacco-Vanzetti*. Totally indifferent to political ideologies, my grandfather was typical of Italian-Americans who were convinced the two were railroaded into the electric chair in good part because they were Italians. Countless numbers of Italian-Americans contributed to the defense fund of the two men. The outcome of the affair was simply another confirmation of the ancient belief of the Italian immigrants that justice, a very important part of their value system, had little to do with the laws and institutions of the state. The poison of the Sacco-Vanzetti affair was not to be purged from relations between Italian-Americans and the United States until years later when Italian-Americans faced a new crisis of nationality in World War II, and resolved it with resounding loyalty to the United States—a story for another chapter.

The unequivocal loyalty of Italian-Americans to their country is astonishing when one considers much of their ill treatment at the hands of America. An important element of this treatment concerned the laws of immigration, which were to become more anti-Italian over the century, until the discrimination at last ended in 1968. In 1835, that most astute observer of America, Alexis de Tocqueville, wrote, "No power on earth can close upon the immigrant that fertile wilderness which offers resources to all industry and a refuge from all want." Although correct in 1835, the Frenchman's words later were to be proven wrong.

Mass immigration to the United States had been an accepted, even welcomed phenomenon before 1840. There was no anti-immigration response—for two reasons. First, the nation was still expanding its frontiers. There was plenty of room and work for all. Second, these early immigrants were from the British Isles and Northwestern Europe. They were of the same ethnic group as most of the founders of the country—White "Anglo-Saxon" Protestants. In fact, as late as 1864, despite the already active Know-

Nothing movement, then aimed at the Irish, the official policy of the American government as written in a law passed that year was to encourage immigration. In the next decades, however, pressure to exclude immigration rose rapidly as the ethnic composition of the immigrants changed. They were no longer predominantly WASP. By 1899, when the total United States population was fifty million, Protestants were among the minority (18.5 per cent) of immigrants. The majority (52 per cent) were Roman Catholics, and 10.5 per cent were Jews. In the next eleven years 2,300,000 were to arrive from Italy alone, only 400,000 of these from Northern Italy. And by 1925, there were upwards of five million Italian-Americans, a figure the nativists found alarming.

Exclusionary pressure gathered unturnable momentum as such diverse American groups as the American Federation of Labor, the American Legion, and the American Grange lobbied for restriction on immigration. Moreover, the pressure was for selective exclusion of undesirable "races," especially Southern and Eastern Europeans. This sentiment was expressed in a very popular book by Madison Grant published during World War I, called *The Passing of the Great Race*. The great race was the WASP ethnic group, or, as Grant called it, "the Nordics." The thesis of the book was as simple as it was vicious. The immigrants of Eastern and Southern Europe were "storming the Nordic ramparts of the United States and mongrelizing the good old American stock," and threatening to destroy American institutions. Grant singled out Italians as inferiors. In his crackpot explanation, Italians are the inferior descendants of the slaves who survived when ancient Rome died. This at a time when some 10 to 12 per cent of the American Army fighting in World War I were Italian-Americans. Thousands of them died and one hundred were awarded Distinguished Service Crosses fighting for a country Grant and his fellow nativists called "Nordic."

Soon a spate of legislation was introduced in Congress

to exclude these "inferior races," and others, i.e., Latin Americans and Asians. In 1896, a bill was introduced by Representative Samuel W. McCall of Massachusetts. Prepared by Boston's Immigration Restriction League, it would have excluded illiterates and, as McCall put it, those "radically different from us in education, habits of life and institutions of government." The bill would have obviously hit hard against Italian immigrants, who had the highest rate of illiteracy among European immigrant groups. Precisely this anti-Italian effect was achieved when Congress passed a literacy test law over President Wilson's veto in 1917.

In 1921, President Wilson vetoed another congressional bill. However, it was signed into law several months later by President Harding. It established a quota system for immigrants coming to the United States. That is, the equivalent of 3 per cent of each ethnic European group population in the United States in 1910 was to be admitted annually. The bill obviously discriminated against Eastern and Southern Europeans and favored WASP groups.

The law was changed in 1924 and made more discriminatory. It established a total for immigrants, not to exceed 150,000 per year. And it established a quota of one-sixth of 1 per cent of the ethnic populations living in the United States in 1920. Thus, although it cut the quota from Northwestern Europe by 29 per cent, it cut the quota from Southern and Eastern Europe by 87 per cent. The so-called Emergency Quota Law, or National Origins Act, of 1924 reduced the Italian quota from 42,057 to 3,845 per year. In 1952, President Truman vetoed a still more discriminatory quota law, saying it reflected the bias that "Americans with English or Irish names were better people and better citizens than Americans with Greek or Polish names." In vain. Congress passed the law over Truman's veto by a majority of more than two to one. This law set the Italian quota at 5,645, or about one-seventh of what it had been in the law of 1921. Finally, the indignity of quotas of national origin was eliminated by President Johnson when he signed a law in 1965. First introduced by President Kennedy, the law abolished quotas as of 1968. Entrance priorities would be based mostly on two criteria: work skills and relationship to people already living in the United States. The latter criterion is especially favorable to Italians because they have maintained ties with their extended families in the U.S. Since the law went into effect, immigration has accounted for 20 per cent of the population growth of the United States. As the New York *Times* reported on June 14, 1971, the pattern of immigration changed radically with the new law. Italians had the third largest group of immigrants to the U.S. in 1965 (10,344 compared to 29,747 British immigrants and 40,013 Canadians). But in 1970, Italians made up the second largest group coming to America, 24,397, just behind Filipinos with 25,417. The saga of Italian migration to America continues, and a whole new group of first-generation Italian-Americans is in the making as some 25,000 Italians come to the United States each year.

After the initial thrust into the crucible, Italian-Americans later became a group whose life style for the most part set a "low profile" in the United States. For reasons to be seen, the group did not develop a large number of writers and other media people to keep its story before the eyes of America. Italian-Americans as a group are also largely neglected by scholars. Thus, even their number is unknown for certain. Beginning with the figure of five million during the immigration up to 1924, it has been estimated at upwards of twenty million. These include more than five million of the second generation and more than ten million of the third and fourth generations. Until recently, these descendants of people from the land that time forgot have themselves become forgotten in their new land. The insularity of the immigrant generation, followed by the culture-conflicted desire of the second generation to appear Americanized in the eyes of the larger society gave the impression that Italian ethnicity had dissipated. As one man put it in response to a newspaper article of mine on the current resurgence of interest in Italian-Americans as a distinct ethnic group:

> The English, Scotch, Poles, Germans and yes, even the Irish have lost their identity. Why not the Italians. The second and third generation are no longer Italians and should act and think of themselves as Americans. Isn't that why their forefathers migrated to these United States?

Americans were shocked in the late 1960's when Italian-Americans suddenly emerged as a large group whose ethnic consciousness is very much alive. In fact their identity had never been lost. Like all other aspects of Italian-American life, it (and its dilemmas) was kept among the group itself, among la famiglia so to speak. The circumstances of life today, especially the influences of the media, have pulled the Italian-American saga back into the light of the larger society. The always present question of what it means to be an Italian-American is once again becoming public. Any attempt to answer it must include a look at what it means to be an Italian-American man, woman, or child. It must include further explorations of the Italian-American attitudes toward education, sex, politics, religion, and the "outside world." For these are included in the warp and woof, the possibilities and probabilities, of the future for Italian-Americans—and for their country upon which their continuous impact is certain to increase.

In an article with the intriguing title, "The Blueing of America," Peter L. and Brigitte Berger write:

> As the newly greened sons of the affluent deny the power of work, blue-collar class youth quietly prepare to assume power within the technocracy.

As should be evident from this chapter, no group of young people surpasses Italian-American youth in the sense of the power of work it has inherited. Although derived from the old notion of labor for the family, it is now, in the third generation, independent of it. It now remains for young

Italian-Americans to weave their sense of work into an identity woven with the other threads of the warp and woof of Italian-American life. As they do so, they cannot help but gain their proportionate share of what America has to offer, and make their unique contribution to what America will yet become.

L'Uomo di Pazienza—
The Ideal of Manliness

Seldom has a stereotype contained so many contrary pictures as that of the Italian-American male. Granted that all stereotypes are superficial and biased in the selection of their truths. Granted that stereotypes produce more misunderstanding than reliable knowledge. Granted these qualifications, the stereotype of the Italian-American male is extraordinary in its distortions and self-contradictions.

The Italian-American male is seen as good-natured and sunny in disposition. The picture of the simple, happy-go-lucky, sentimental Italian is familiar to Americans. A child-like boy-man, a likable semi-simpleton. The man in the Alka-Seltzer commercial, the man on the movie screen played by Chico Marx. Yet at the same time he is viewed as cynical, calculating, hard-bitten, vengeful, and violent.

On the one hand, one thinks of the Italian-American man as a volatile hot-blooded Latin type. On the other hand, the stereotype also pictures him as possessing what the French call *sang froid*. Italians themselves term this characteristic *sangue freddo*—"cold blood." The Italian-American man is famous for his expressiveness. His gestures and his words are so expressive as to seem operatic. In the stereotype, he works in the expressive vocations of artist and artisan, and is colorful even as a laborer. Yet his impassivity and his dead-pan stoicism are also legendary.

The male is caricatured as both inordinately stubborn

and as slyly "flexible." He is believed to be intensely proud, the swaggering *mascalzone* (scoundrel), yet humble in every way from the work he does to his shy and even obsequious aspect. In the popular image, he is at once hard working and placidly unambitious, transparently simple yet enigmatic and mysterious. Americans see him fatalistically resigned to life and, also, in contradiction, with an unholy determination to have his own way.

"Don't mess with his women," of whom he is thought to be very protective and jealous. Yet he shows little public affection for them; he is not at all a dashing romantic type. In another contradiction his individualism is fabled, but so is his need to be close to and highly dependent upon family and paesani. He is repeatedly presented as having a fiery sense of honor, and constantly depicted as having no ideals at all. A hot-blooded lover, a square family man. A proud, chivalrous, anachronistic Don Quixote, a worldly, shrewd wheeler-dealer. Americans insist on his being either Marcello Mastroianni, Machiavelli, a "wop"—or all three.

Despite the treacherous quality of stereotypes, they sometimes reflect realities, in a distorted funhouse-mirror way. Perhaps if we sort out the paradoxical images in the stereotype of the Italian-American male, we might begin to get a true picture of him.

The word *omertà* is familiar to many Americans. The American media often use it in connection with Italian-American gangsters. The meaning they give to it is the same as the meaning found in my Italian-English dictionary: "the criminal code of silence." This is a corruption of the ideal of manliness, or at least one of its elements, for criminal purposes. In the old value scheme of Southern Italy, the ideal of manliness did include nonco-operation with authorities and silence in the face of inquiries by stranieri, especially official inquiries. In a land where outsiders and authorities were for centuries synonymous with spoliation, exploitation, and oppression, the code of silence was necessary, sane, moral, and wise. The ideal was the *uomo di panza*, literally a man of belly, meaning a man who knew how to keep things to himself—in his guts, as it were. He was also known as *uomo segreto* ("secret" meaning private man) and *uomo che sa pensare alla sua casa* (a man who knows how to think after his home). Above all a man strove to be an *uomo di pazienza*—a man of patience in a special sense of the term.

The origins of the ideal go back to medieval times. It is a rich concept of what it means to be a man of which no one word is adequate. The ideal includes qualities far beyond surface *maschio* or masculine qualities. A man who possessed only these, only a show of manhood, was regarded as ridiculous by Southern Italians. To this day, the "proud peacock" and the "cock of the walk" are favorite butts of jokes among the Meridionali and their Italian-American brethren. They have little respect for the type of man connoted by the Spanish term *machismo*. In my boyhood, I remember the immigrants saying of this type with mocking contempt, *"Che malandrino"* ("What a tough one"). In their late years my grandparents watched John Wayne and James Cagney on television and found them laughable.

The familiar elements of Southern Italian manliness—nonco-operation and insubordination with regard to authorities, and distrust of and aloofness from outsiders—are rooted in the much more substantial but less familiar part of the ideal. This includes a man's cultivation and control of his own capacities and special skills—self-reliance and self-control. Hard work and self-denial are also essential components of the ideal, as are firmness of spirit, determination, and the seriousness and probity characteristic of maturity. In his authoritative *Conversazioni Contadino* (Contadino Conversations, 1962), Danilo Dolci quotes a response of a Southern Italian woman to the question of what is necessary to be a real man. She answered, *"la parola ferma, di essere durevole con la famiglia, di essere durevole dello vicinato e di tutte cose"*—a firm word, to be constant with his family, with his neighbor, and in all things.

These qualities were spoken of together in Southern

Italy. One who had them possessed pazienza—"patience." The idea is *not* equivalent to fatalism. Nor is it stoicism.

A fatalist is resigned to whatever fortune will bring. And in the stoic model one goes further. The stoic learns to love and actively embrace what destiny brings. In stoicism, one learns to play his determined role in life happily and without complaint. In contradistinction to fatalists and stoics, the contadino of the Mezzogiorno was determined *not* to be resigned to a life that presented itself without pity and with only little hope. Far from seeking a harmony with this grim life, he was doggedly rebellious against it. If life meant rolling boulders uphill while the gods mocked one's efforts, then, damn it, he was going to prevail despite it. He was going to do it on *his* terms. The ideal of pazienza is an ideal of control of life. First and foremost, it is an ideal of inner control, of reserve.

In the scheme one is taught to reserve his resources. One is taught to wait and plan for the moment when he may express his stronger emotions and expend his most pressing energies. Pazienza does not involve a repression of the forces of life. Instead it calls for careful nurture of them so that their eventual expression, paradoxically, is even more forceful than that of an impulsive man who lacks self-control. The code of reserve, of patience, of waiting for the moment, of planning for the event, and then of decisive impassioned action, serves life. It was the manly way of life in the Mezzogiorno because it well served the conditions of life there, whereas impetuous, ill-controlled behavior meant disaster.

The reserve that was to become the core of the masculine ideal was behind the observation of the ancient Romans that Southern Italians were a *genus acutum et suspiciosum*—a people combative and suspicious. It is easy to see why the Roman view of the Meridionale's reserve—the point of view of alien oppressors—has continued throughout history. In their reserve, the Southern men showed no emotions or passions. They seemed to see nothing, hear nothing, feel nothing, and think nothing. Yet as countless generations of outsiders since the Romans have discovered, the Southerners' periodic bursts of determined and impassioned action were obvious indications that this was not the case. The Meridionale in fact noted and remembered everything, storing and cultivating passions until a time when he could act upon them with best chance of success.

Pazienza accounts for the paradox of the Italian-American man being seemingly resigned to life yet also fiercely determined to have his way. To those who live the old life, periodic bursts of passionate activity are inevitable and essential. They provide a catharsis, a purging of restrained, fortified emotions. And they also make possible their fulfillment. To those who ponder the "dormant ethnic consciousness" of Italian-Americans and their apparent general quietude, the broad implication should be obvious.

In the Sicily of my grandfather the fishermen of the island engaged in a ritual known as *mattanza*. It was a Dionysian practice growing out of the distinct life style. Once a year the methodically hard-working men of one or more fishing villages would skillfully and carefully maneuver a school of tuna into a bay, patiently herding the fish with nets closer and closer to shore. When the fish were firmly entrapped in shallow water, the normally quiet, self-contained fishermen suddenly exploded into frenzied violence. The men would plunge into the water, flashing sharp knives. The large fish were slaughtered by hand. Men and fish writhed, tumbled, gasped, and struggled in a bloody froth. Foreigners watched the spectacle with horror. But they also recorded an inescapable fascination with it. Eighteenth-century paintings depict European aristocrats turned out in the exaggerated refinements of the time to watch the primitive killing in red water.

In Italian-American men we see a reflection of the demeanor of their ancestors, a controlled demeanor held until the moment of mattanza and easily assumed again when the blood was washed off. It is the demeanor inherited from medieval chivalry and preserved in the land that time forgot. The posture of Mezzogiorno men is a revealing anachronism. Body erect, back straight, shoulders back, even when sitting. Their faces are impassive. They are silent until spoken to. Then they respond with great courtesy. Yet they volunteer little. Though seemingly apathetic, they are alert and poised, as quickly becomes evident. When a visitor presses them too hard, they will advise him to have *un poco di pazienza*. They are doing more than asking for a little patience. They are offering a reminder that for a man, the ever-present obligation is *agire da maschio*, to act in a manly fashion. In the Mezzogiorno, the adjective "maschio" (male) is also used to mean "grand" and "fine." However, it takes more than mere demeanor or posture to be *un buon maschio, un bel pezzo d'uomo*, a good specimen of a man. Severe and demanding qualities of character are needed. The Italian-American born in the United States has made a compromise typical of him. He has dropped the courtly posture, and although he tends to keep his body more tensed than other American men, he has adopted the more casual American bearing. But the compromise tapers off when we leave the superficialities of posture and consider the essential character traits.

The essence of the manly ideal often goes by the name of honor, onore. The code of chivalry which gave birth to honor was imported into the Mezzogiorno from Northern Europe during the Middle Ages. Typically, it became altered by the life into which it was introduced. Many words have different meanings in the Mezzogiorno than they do elsewhere. "Honor" is one of them.

In Southern Italy, the medieval mode did not develop into the ideal of *noblesse oblige*, a value that Americans typically associate with honor. This chivalrous honor did not become part of the life of any class of people in the Mezzogiorno, except for the courteous manners associated with it. And these were adopted by the contadini as much as the landed rich. Given the harsh realities there, behavior after the honor of noblesse oblige was regarded as *pazzia*—craziness, foolishness. Life was stark, hard, without mercy. Its margins were set very tightly. It did not offer many chances and seldom offered second chances.

In fact, the notion of honor was the very antithesis of noblesse oblige. Onore meant protecting one's blood and advancing family security and power. One did this not by being noble, but by being clever, foxy, shrewd. In the ideal onore was synonymous with *furberia* (cleverness, cunning) and *scaltrezza* (sharpness, worldly artfulness). Boys were trained in these qualities by lessons reinforced with such material rewards as food and such penalties as beatings. The moral constantly enforced was that only the *furbo* and *scaltro* and their families would survive and flourish. The opposite, the *fesso* (fool) and his family would come to a disastrous end. And what it was to be a fesso was made quite clear. To be *troppo buono* (too good) was to be a fesso. To be too good was to be a fool. To be too good would bring about one's personal destruction and bring calamity to his family.

Few works in American literature which have been written by non-Southern Italians capture the Italian masculine spirit. One that admirably does is Arthur Miller's play, *A View from the Bridge*. The central character of the play is Eddie Carbone, a second-generation Italian-American longshoreman. Eddie has raised a niece as his daughter, showering love on her to an excessive degree. The girl is about to leave school for work. She is about to enter the real world for the first time. Eddie's advice to his treasured adopted daughter is telling. The words of the American-born man echo the view that life is perilous and that the qualities that make for survival are in direct contrast to being too good. Eddie begins a conversation with his niece (Catherine) and his wife (Beatrice):

> I only ask you one thing—don't trust nobody. You got a good aunt but she's got too big a heart, you learned bad from her. Believe me.
>
> BEATRICE: Be the way you are, Katie, don't listen to him.
>
> *Eddie, to Beatrice—strangely and quickly resentful:*
>
> You lived in a house all your life, what do you know about it. You never worked in your life.
>
> BEATRICE: She likes people. What's wrong with that?

EDDIE: Because most people ain't people. She's goin' to
work; plumbers; they'll chew her to pieces if she don't
watch out. *To Catherine:* Believe me, Katie, the less you
trust, the less you be sorry.

Eddie Carbone sounds the concern of Italian-American
fathers and their Italian fathers before them that children
need to be taught the cardinal lesson of avoiding being
pigliato per fesso, being taken for a fool.

A View from the Bridge is a human tragedy. But it is
also a specifically Italian-American tragedy. At the heart
of the tragedy of Eddie Carbone is his difference from his
ancestors in the Mezzogiorno. In a cultural conflict typical
of the second generation, Eddie is pulled in conflicting directions. He is torn between the harsh philosophy of the
old land and the philosophy of the new land given voice
in the play by his wife. This conflict is added to the conflict
that makes Eddie a universal tragedy—his sexual love for
his niece that the old code of onore della famiglia will not
permit to surface in his consciousness. The traditional ideal
evolved as a design that was to leave as little as possible
to chance. Of course, nothing is so chancy as human emotions. Setting aside the repressed emotion of sexual desire
for his niece that makes Eddie a universal tragic figure,
Eddie is an Italian-American tragic figure in his conflict
between the contadino and American ideals.

The American trust in decent emotions, in the essential
goodness of people as expressed by Beatrice, is set against
Eddie's attempt to fulfill the role of a man in the tradition.
Eddie senses this. And he senses that his effort on behalf
of the old way in the dialogue just quoted was ineffective.
So he resorts to telling the women a story whose effect
is to reinforce that most familiar part of contadino manliness, the code of silence. Thus, the entire code might gain
supremacy in its struggle against la via nuova. Eddie and
his family are about to house his wife's cousins, illegal immigrants from Sicily, two brothers escaping desperate poverty to work in America. They are to arrive this very eve-

ning, and the women are nervous. Catherine says of the men:

> Eddie, suppose somebody asks if they're living here. *He looks at her as though already she had divulged something publicly. Defensively:* I mean if they ask.

EDDIE: Now look, Baby, I can see we're gettin' mixed up again here.

CATHERINE: No, I just mean . . . people'll see them goin' in and out.

EDDIE: I don't care who sees them goin' in and out. And this goes for you too, B. You don't see nothin' and you don't know nothin'.

BEATRICE: What do you mean? I understand.

EDDIE: You don't understand; you still think you can talk about this to somebody just a little bit. Now lemme say it once and for all, because you're makin' me nervous again, both of you. I don't care if somebody comes in the house and sees them sleepin' on the floor, it never comes out of your mouth who they are or what they're doing here. *To Beatrice:* Tell her about Vinny . . . *To Catherine:* You was a baby then. There was a family lived next door to her mother, he was about sixteen—

BEATRICE: No, he was no more than fourteen, cause I was to his confirmation in Saint Agnes. But the family had an uncle that they were hidin' in the house, and he snitched to the Immigration.

CATHERINE: The kid snitched?

EDDIE: On his own uncle!

CATHERINE: What, was he crazy?

EDDIE: He was crazy after, I tell you that, boy.

BEATRICE: Oh, it was terrible. He had five brothers and the old father. And they grabbed him in kitchen and pulled him down the stairs—three flights his head was bouncin' like a coconut. And they spit on him in the street, his

> own father and his brothers. The whole neighborhood was cryin'.
>
> CATHERINE: Ts! So what happened to him?
>
> BEATRICE: I think he went away. I never seen him again.

As an Italian-American lawyer says at the end of *A View from the Bridge*, Italian-Americans now "settle for half" and perhaps it is better that way. Although the old code is no longer enforced, nor is enforceable, in the absolute terms of the old land, it is still operative. It is still taught one generation to the next. Conditions of life in the United States are not as starkly outlined as those of the Mezzogiorno, but they are essentially the same. The basic conditions of human life are universal. At least, nothing has convinced Italian-Americans otherwise.

There is an ancient Roman saying that the mind becomes dyed by the color of its thoughts. Part of the Italian-American mentality has become colored by American myths of human decency, progress, and hope. And the material rewards achieved by working in America cast a seductive face on those myths. Yet the realistic limits of the myths constantly pull Italian-Americans back toward their inherited view of life, a view that deeply colors their psychology. Events in America have not erased two thousand years of experience. Indeed, many of the experiences in America reinforce the lesson of the disastrous end of the imprudent man.

The moral is clear in many of the legends of the Mezzogiorno. One of the earliest of these goes back to the dawn of recorded history in the Western world. In the sixth century B.C., the Sicilian region of Agrigentum was ruled by a tyrant named Phalaris, who earned a widespread reputation by his cruelty. His particular delight was to discover new ways to cause pain and death. One of the tyrant's subjects was a brilliant and ambitious man named Perillus. When Perillus learned that the despot wanted a new instrument of torture and death to satisfy his sadism, he used his ingenuity in the hope of advancing himself. He invented an elaborate machine shaped like a bull and made of a special bronze. The contrivance was designed slowly to roast a man to death inside it. When the tyrant saw the thing, he was pleased. But to Perillus' final chagrin, the tyrant rewarded him by ordering that he be the first one burned in the device he had invented.

Although the Italian-American has inherited a distinctive sense of humor from his forebears, one of the dominant characteristics of a real man is a serious attitude toward life. One of the sayings drilled into young boys in the Mezzogiorno and Italian-American neighborhoods is *Tratta con quelli che sono meglio di te e fagli le spese*—Associate with those better than you and pay the expenses. This practice puts powerful people in your debt, an invaluable asset in the code with its design of reciprocity of debts and favors, loyalties and injuries. As a schoolboy, I remember that my classmates regarded as soft-headed nonsense attempts by our non-Italian teachers to instruct us in the virtues of altruism. Two of the favorite biblical readings at weekly school assemblies were the ones about turning the other cheek and the meek inheriting the earth. Other moralisms preached to us in class were not to envy the rich and powerful and to be sensitive to the poor and disadvantaged. These were attempts by well-meaning teachers to deal with the behavior of their Italian-American charges, behavior which seemed to them to be overly hard, cynical, and perhaps cruel. The intentions were good, but nothing could have been more quixotic than these efforts based on a poor understanding of the cultural roots of their pupils. When we did not fear the teachers, we would openly laugh at these moralisms. When we were afraid of them, we gave lip service and laughed inwardly.

The second maxim that was incessantly impressed upon us was *Impara a spesa d'altri*—Learn at the expense of others. The rule intended no idea of human exploitation. Learning at the expense of others meant learning by close study of their behavior. Our elders constantly held models of behavior before us. We were expected to learn by imitating sound behavior and avoiding what was foolish or worse. "Look what happened to so and so," I was told. "See what happens when . . ." my father or grandfather would say, pointing to something taking place before us or recounted in a newspaper. Incidentally, *Il Progresso*, the Italian-language paper read by my grandfather, was full of stories deliberately pitched in the direction of such object lessons. The attitude was supremely pragmatic, and its practical bent was always in the direction of the old ideal. Men were expected to be keen observers of what worked in life and to act upon this vision. But the vision was always filtered through the lenses of the traditional outlook.

Social scientists have demonstrated that certain laws are at work in all societies regardless of their differences. These are the laws of Realpolitik, the system wherein power is the essential determinant. In other words, whatever the sincerely believed or merely professed ideals of a society, the actual behavior of people is governed by rules that are more realistic (or cynical, depending on one's moral point of view). These rules center about the pursuit and possession, protection and exercise of power. Of course this generality takes varied specific forms in different societies. The ingredients of power differ from culture to culture. In the Mezzogiorno the name of the game was family power. The lessons of associating with betters, accruing their obligations, and learning at the expense of others served the power of the family. Debts were owed to the family of the benefactor, and owed by the family of the debtor. And learning at the expense of others meant marking the misfortunes that fell upon the family of the fesso.

Learn at the expense of others. Among a people who had great respect for the potential for serious consequences that exists in all behavior, cultivating a posture of lying low made eminent sense. A real man does not seek confrontations. In fact, he tends to avoid them. In the old land this was accomplished by an elaborate system of social conventions and rituals which made life orderly and predictable. Misunderstanding and uncontrolled situations were thus kept to a minimum. It was only when the very practical honor of the code was at stake, thus threatening the basic existence of individual and family, that a man initiated a confrontation or accepted a gambit offered by another.

This is at the root of the stereotype of Italian-American men as docile yet volatile. They will tolerate a great deal as long as it is not viewed as a threat to l'ordine della famiglia. When anything deemed necessary to this system is undermined, they will respond forcefully. Thus, the Italian-American man is predominantly reactive rather than active. Or so he is seen. The inherited code prescribes that he lie low. Therefore, he does not become a representative or a symbol or a spokesman, not even of or for other Italian-Americans. In today's jargon, he desires to maintain a low profile in all social situations.

In the United States where the potential of groups is measured by their public relations endeavors and other attention-attracting behavior, the true feelings of Italian-Americans are poorly perceived, and possibilities of their behavior tend to be underestimated. Americans are accustomed to reality by visibility, and to them Italian-Americans seem content merely to cultivate their own gardens. Conversely, the Italian-American regards others' lack of understanding as confirmation of the old truth that outsiders don't care. The view of life completes a self-perpetuating cycle, barely touched in the saga of Italian-Americans that stretches back some fifty years for most and in some cases for as long as a century.

The metaphor of one's own garden is especially apt. It raises connotations of property, particularly of ownership of a home on a plot of land, so central to the Italian-American mentality. In the Mezzogiorno land was an essential part of power, for it was the key to all economic might and security. A legacy of this is the Italian-American's obsession with owning his own home, no matter how humble, on his own piece of *terra*, no matter how small. (Remember that it was the earliest Italians who gave us a synonym for security: *terra firma*.)

Just after the death of my maternal grandfather when I was sixteen, I moved to a suburban home with my parents and grandmother. We joined other Italian-American families, settling in a particular area of a Long Island town, turning it overnight into an example of a much-overlooked recent occurrence, suburban Little Italies. No sooner had we moved into a modest secondhand split-level than we began completely to churn up the little plots of land in front and behind the house. We rented equipment each weekend, including one power-driven whirling machine that bit a foot into the soil, broke it, and heaved it up. Everything literally was turned upside down. We planted new grass, new shrubs, new trees on the two bits of earth. Of course my father set aside a corner, neatly marked off by stakes, exclusively for tomato and strawberry plants. I was puzzled and only later understood that we were completely redoing the land, making it ours by giving it a look completely of our family. Everything symbolic of another family was buried. And yes, we did put a lawn statue in place, a bearded lamp holder we named "Mr. Allegro," the cheerful one. Happiness was a working-class home on a plot of land sixty by one hundred fifty feet bought with the savings from two generations of labor.

In the Brooklyn building from which we moved, one of the four resident families consisted of a couple of my grandparents' generation. They had lived there for years, raising children who had since married and established their own homes. Mr. and Mrs. Pita lived on the top floor, one of my favorite places as a young child. Mrs. Pita's grandmotherly doting on me and the magnificent view from their windows of New York's harbor with its green Statue of Liberty made their apartment a very pleasant place. Mr. Pita and my grandfather had known each other for twenty or thirty years. By American standards they would be termed friends. But the two immigrant families were not living by American standards. Although they referred to each other as *amici*, they were not *compari*. I remember quite vividly that when the Pitas would visit my grandparents, the ritualized behavior of buon costume was strictly observed. Mr. Pita would knock on the door. Upon my grandfather's response to come in, he would open the door about six inches without looking in and ask, *"E permesso?,"* a colloquial phrase meaning "Is there permission to come in?" The manners observed between these friends who had lived in the same building since long before my birth were the same as they had been when the men first met. The conversations between them were held over refreshments and only after each had made elaborate inquiries and responses about each other's relatives, including sisters, brothers, cousins, etc. And the order of inquiry was always the same. Mr. Pita would inquire about my grandfather's kin. Then my grandfather about Mr. Pita's family. Then Mrs. Pita about my grandmother's relatives and vice-versa.

The conversation between them proceeded in elaborately polite terms and all references to any business at hand were made in as oblique and offhand fashion as possible, mere incidentals to the primary business of family talk. Yet meanings in the business at hand were clearly understood. Only people who were mal educati needed to resort to direct, explicit language in the house of friends who were not compari. Such language was for peddlers in the market place.

Despite their long association in America, the two men always addressed each other after the fashion of the Old World. And herein lies the clue to their relationship. My grandfather always addressed the other man and spoke of him as "Signor Pita." In fact, my grandparents never used the Pitas' first names. To this day I do not know them. In turn, Mr. Pita always addressed my grandfather as "Don Giuseppe." The term "don" is derived from the Latin word dominus meaning "sir," "master," or "lord." In the custom of the Mezzogiorno it is used when addressing or speaking of any man who commands more than usual respect. Of course, a man of property qualified. Because my grandfather owned the building in which Signor Pita lived he was a don in the eyes of the tenant. Never mind that the don owned no other property than an old brownstone divided into four flats. The people of the land that time forgot retained the full meaning which we have dropped from the English word landlord.

My grandfather had achieved his social status according

to the dynamics of social mobility in the old country. He worked at long, hard labor, regularly saving a portion of his small wages which supported a wife and six children. He invested this meager savings in property. The pattern of work and savings channeled into home and property, which might include a family business, remains strong in Italian-Americans. The mind behind this economic structure thinks of secure but gradual low-growth returns rather than the lucrative and faster but more risky possibilities of speculative investment.

One of the results of this psychology is that, although Italian-Americans have achieved social mobility relative to the scheme inherited from Southern Italy, they have achieved less social mobility by American standards. In social terms they remain largely within the lower echelons of the American middle class. Entrance into the higher social classes is dependent upon a degree of wealth that can be obtained only through audacious business and financial dealings, aggressive high-powered performance as an organization man within the executive corps of corporate America, or entrance into one of the high-paying professions. The first avenue has been traveled by only few Italian-Americans because of the inherited work ethic and scheme of social mobility through small property ownership. The other two avenues have been entered by even fewer Italian-Americans. For the same reasons, complicated by an ambivalent attitude toward education, few Italian-Americans are in the moneyed professions. All these reasons, together with the peculiar brand of contadino individualism, have made Italian-Americans rare among the top executives of American corporations.

The preference for economic security over economic adventure explains why so many Italian-American men are found in civil service jobs. Paradoxically, many second- and third-generation men have sought economic security in two occupations where there is a real risk to physical security. They have become policemen and firemen. To one familiar with the old masculine values this is understandable. Within a week two Italian-American law officers were

subjects of separate feature articles in New York City. On
October 23, 1972, *New York* magazine ran an article describing Ralph Mannetta, the policeman who won a shoot-
out with fugitive H. Rap Brown. A product of a Brooklyn
Italian neighborhood, the twenty-six-year-old patrolman
chased Brown and two others into a building. The three
were heavily armed (pistols, shotguns, automatic rifles) and
had already shot two policemen who had interrupted a
holdup. Mannetta stepped out onto the dark roof of the
building to confront what he had been told were three
heavily armed men and came upon Brown, lying in am-
bush, who traded shots with the cop from a .357 Magnum.
Brown was seriously wounded; Mannetta miraculously escaped the fusillade. The next day Mannetta was shy and ill
at ease facing a gang of reporters. Invited by the police
commissioner to tell the press what happened, he could
only say a few matter-of-fact words. Finally a reporter
asked directly if he had shot Brown. His answer was to
look up into the reporter's eyes and say quietly, "Yes, sir."
The father of three children, Mannetta later explained he
had joined the force when he was twenty-one because it
represented security.

The New York *Times* on October 27, 1972, printed a
feature story on Frank Trummillo, a twenty-five-year-old
federal agent killed in a gun battle with two narcotics dealers that left another agent with his legs permanently paralyzed and the two dealers shot by a third agent. The slightly
built, 5-feet-6-inch tall Trummillo had been a star policeman for four years, several times facing drawn weapons.
His courage had earned him five promotions in rank, more
than one per year. Interviews with his family, fiancée, and
fellow-agents produced a unanimous response. Trummillo
was "quiet," "attentive," "soft-spoken," "considerate,"
hard-working, and studious. On the job he was cool and restrained in the face of deadly danger. He had once arrested
without firing a shot a man carrying five pistols. His fellow-
agents remarked on how extraordinary was his sympathy
for prisoners. He was said to have treated even criminals
who had shot at him with compassion and "dignity." Like

Patrolman Mannetta, Trummillo cherished the economic security of his dangerous career which enabled him to contribute to the support of his parents, a younger sister in college, and save for his upcoming wedding to his childhood sweetheart, Carla Storita. Frank Trummillo sought economic security by living the traditional manly values. He earned a top salary which was less than half of what most New York dentists and many lawyers earn in their first year of practice.

Again we see examples of the irony of the Italian-American saga. The limited aims that crossed the ocean with the immigrants have been to a large extent achieved. Yet economic progress among Italian-Americans, most of whom earn only weekly wages and many of whom are still poor, and their social progress by American standards have just begun. In the criteria of success in the New World, the Italian-American saga has just started. Its major chapters are yet to be written.

From the point of view of American society, the behavior of the Italian-American man toward wife and children confirms the image of him as a lower-middle-class individual. The code commands that he be protective. In the American judgment, he is overly protective of women without being publicly affectionate enough. The paradox of protectiveness together with lack of a public romantic attitude is rooted in the sexual codes of the Mezzogiorno, codes that will be discussed in a later chapter. Here we need only note that the stance toward women in the old ideal is part of the over-all seriousness of the ideal. Displays of romantic attention to females undermine this seriousness. Romantic behavior is an indication that the man has lost control, has been overcome by his feelings. Such unmanly behavior is tolerated within limits among young single men. But in a married man, a family man, it is a sign of foolishness.

The relationship between a man and his children is governed by definite responsibilities and not by any adult chauvinism. These responsibilities all serve l'ordine della famiglia. As already indicated, a father or older brother is usually content to let the maintenance of the system proceed by its normal everyday course, which is the control of young children by the mother and other adult females of the family. When it becomes evident that his children are straying from the traditional training, the man will act directly. Italian-American fathers are noted for sudden bursts of discipline upon their children. These episodes of forceful and even apparently excessive action are interspersed with long periods wherein the family head is seemingly oblivious of his children's behavior. In reality he is quietly watchful. The role played by the Italian-American father is in marked contrast to the popular American notion of a father as a "buddy" to his children. The conflict between the cultural norms is stressful for all members of the Italian-American family, just as is the contrast between the inherited notion of public marital behavior and the American ideal which is more open and romantic.

In addition to a man's fulfilling his role in the cultivation of the next generation, the model demands that he submit his own behavior to the scrutiny of the older men of his clan. The ideal is supported by an unbroken continuity of generations. In the severe demands of living in Southern Italy, generation gaps would not have been the vexations they are in today's America—they would have been fatal. One result of this strong age-old conditioning is that it produces still another way the Italian-American man is considered out of step in our youth-oriented society. Nothing could be more opposite than the tendency to give top status to young men, the chief producers in American society, except, of course, the fashion of not trusting anybody over thirty. To the Italian-American these aspects of a youth-centered society are pure pazzia.

In the picture so far presented, I have possibly overstressed the somberness of the Italian-American man. For he also demonstrates a sense of humor and he values recreational activities and the chance to relax. The ability to laugh at the ridiculous aspects of everyday life is a direct inheritance from the Old World. The Italian-American especially sees the humorous side of pompous, fatuous, or vain behavior. He delights in making jokes at the expense of pretentiousness. In Palermo I was with a group of young men who pointed out the building on the Via Vittorio Emanuele from whose balcony Mussolini used to make his speeches when he visited the city. One of the men gave a funny pantomime caricature of the dictator's bombastic mannerisms, much to the amusement of his companions. And by no means is ridicule aimed only at remote people. The cultivation of pazienza is well served by turning this humor on the closest relatives, friends, and on oneself. Anyone who has observed Italian-American males knows that they delight in constant mutual joking and bantering. They mimic each other's mannerisms and playfully mock what they view as odd or pretentious. They regard the man who can mock his own foibles as having the greatest sense of humor. In the fashion of the medieval jester, the group clown often is the man who mixes darts aimed at others with subtle gibes at his own personality.

Even in their playful banter Italian-American men display the need for closeness typical of the entire ethnic group. One sees this most clearly in the physical quality of the interplay among the *giovanotti*, the boys and young men. There is a great deal of touching in the form of jabbing, leaning on, poking, ruffling of hair, and playful slaps on shoulders and faces. Among mature men intimacy of relationship is expressed by language that becomes more incisive and more insightful of each other's personalities. Of course Americans know well the converse of this, the Italian man's sensitivity to outsiders being too familiar. From the perspective of the old view the immediate back-slapping casual buddiness affected by American men is regarded as effrontery. Playing is a respected part of intimacy. Play-acting at intimacy is regarded as contempt. And to be treated as the object of contempt is the greatest insult sufferable. The contadino's entire constellation of values centers about the feeling that easy familiarity does indeed breed contempt. It is little wonder then that so few Italian-American men have made it in the world of American salesmanship where hail-fellow-well-met is the life style.

Once I eavesdropped on a conversation among a group of men relaxing in the square of a small town in Southern Italy. They were gibing at each other in good-natured sarcasm. From the personal and detailed nature of their comments it was clear that they knew each other well. When I entered their conversation, the playing stopped and I had to draw it out again. But now the telling personal nature of the kidding changed. The level became one of jokes that were impersonal, abstract, even stereotyped. For example, one of the men was from Calabria. What he said was discounted by the others with the taunt that all Calabrians have *teste dure*, hard heads, a stereotype of obstinate Calabrians familiar to anyone raised in one of America's Little Italies.

Wine is the drink of play, and if we are to believe the old maxim *in vino veritas*, it is also the drink that brings out truth. It is, of course, the drink of all of Italy. In the Mezzogiorno it plays a role in social relaxation even as much as it is used as a basic food. Although my grandmother learned in America to enjoy what she termed *un bel bicchiere d'acqua fresca* (a nice glass of fresh water) from the tap, something not possible in the old land where water was drawn from the local well, I never saw my grandfather touch a drop of water and I doubt that he ever did. Wine was a staple of life, taken with every meal. Following a tradition going back to a custom of the ancient Greeks of mixing wine with water, wine is often mixed with fruit juice to form a drink known as *vinello*, literally "light wine." One of the chief pleasures enjoyed by the men of Southern Italy is an evening of wine, fruit, and conversation, an evening known in some places as a *schiticciu*.

As much as the pleasant effect of wine is valued, drunkenness is greatly scorned among the men of the Mezzogiorno and their American descendants. A man who exceeds his ability to handle alcohol is regarded as unmanly. There is no romance about alcohol. A rhyme in Sicilian dialect is expressive and to the point. *La biviri non misuratu fa l'uomo asinatu*—Uncontrolled drinking makes a man an ass. The rule requires that a man remain in control. As with all pleasures, the pleasures of alcohol are valued but enjoyed under control. The stress of the tradition is greater on Italian-Americans than upon their Old World ancestors. As Giorgio Lolli pointed out in *Alcohol in Italian Culture* (1958), while only 2 per cent of Italian men drink alcoholic beverages other than wine, 48 per cent of Italian-American men have adopted the American usage of beer and the stronger apéritifs and distilled spirits.

The ancient Mediterranean principle that the French call *mesure* survived well in the Mezzogiorno and is essential to manhood. Its origin goes back to ancient Greece, where Aristotle described it as his famous golden mean (not to be confused with the golden rule of religion). It is deemed good that a man fulfill his desires, passions, and his natural tendencies toward pleasures. But in the fulfillment a real man is to shun the vices of vulnerability that result from thoughtless and excessive indulgence just as he is to avoid the thin-blooded life of abstinence wherein the natural passions and pleasures are repressed. Both the playboy and the Puritan are regarded as fools. Although Puritanism and debauchery are at opposite ends of the spectrum of attitudes toward pleasure, both are equidistant from the contadino ideal.

The golden mean is also seen in the attitude toward games. Italian immigrants enjoyed their games of *bocce, morra, passatella,* and card games such as *scopa*. In addition to their recreational values games like these also permitted enjoyment of the competitive spirit among men. Yet the competition was kept within bounds, avoiding the excess that has become so much a part of modern life not only in games and sports but in business, professional and social life. Ours is a society in which the competitive spirit runs amuck. Despite his notorious "ferocity," the typical Italian-American man is aghast at the fierce, frenzied, serious competitiveness displayed in what he regards as trivial areas of life—for example, the mad combat frequently seen on the tennis courts where the American upper classes like to spend their leisure time. The traditional Italian-American's first response when exposed to this kind of behavior is that it is pazzia. To be sure Italian-Americans are just as interested in spectator sports as is the rest of the population. This interest is the lighthearted enjoyment of a spectacle. But it is madness to become emotionally controlled by a sport, a game or a career, as are so many Americans. To invest one's ego and emotions in the kitty of such activities is to lose the perspective of sane manliness. Manhood is too important to be staked on games.

I remember conflicts resulting around this point of view when I was growing up in Brooklyn. There was tension between the immigrant generation and their children over the values to be attached to such things as sports. Of course American-born boys had considerable interest in following American sports, especially baseball, which was then the rage just as professional football is today. Among my friends, all interest was focused on that most spectacular of all ball clubs, the Brooklyn Dodgers. The pragmatic men of the old country judged this interest of their sons and grandsons by the old standards. Could this mania be productive in terms of the welfare of the giovanotti and their families? True, those who actually played professional baseball might gain wealth, social position, and hence power. In these terms, the examples of Italian-American players of my childhood like Carl Furillo and those of earlier times like Joe DiMaggio were noted and pondered. But beyond this, baseball and all other games and sports were regarded by the immigrants strictly from the perspective of whether or not they could provide examples of true manliness to be observed, recorded, and imitated by their offspring. Excitement over competition for its own sake and exuberance in winning a competition that did not have direct bearing on the real life of the family were regarded with disapproval. Life was harsh and competitive enough in daily reality. Only a madman or fool would make it more so by indulging directly or vicariously in frivolous competition or mere contests of ego.

The Catskill Mountains in New York State are known as

the Borscht Belt because of the high number of predominantly Jewish resort hotels found there. What is less known, except among Italian-Americans, is that a good number of smaller Italian resorts are also located in the Catskills. Every August I would go to one of these hotels with my parents during my father's vacation. Often we were joined by relatives or close friends. I loved these holidays, which combined a chance to get into the country with the customs, food, and general social atmosphere of the old neighborhood in the city. I played baseball, with a glove my father had bought me only after a search for a left-handed glove that had taken us outside of the Italian neighborhood, whose stores had a meager supply of baseball equipment. And I learned to play bocce in the Catskills. In bocce, played on a long rectangular earth court, the object of the game is to bowl hard balls closer to a target ball than your opponent or opponents can. The skills of the game include knocking the other side's balls out of position, and the game could be keenly competitive especially when played by teams of two men each. As I grew I became aware of differences and similarities in the way we children played our games and in the way our immigrant elders played bocce. We boys played with all the rough-and-tumble noisy exuberance of Ebbets Field. The men played bocce with the dignity of posture and behavior that is the outward sign of genuine manhood. How different it was from the casualness of American bowling. Yet I learned early that the men played bocce with an intensity that easily matched baseball games or bowling, or tennis matches. Moreover, they played bocce with at least as much *gusto* (an Italian word that has become part of the English language). Although I have not played bocce in twenty years, I can vividly recall the taste of the dry earth dust in the hot sun, the lightheadedness from sips of vinello, and the joy in skill imparted to me by the men who taught me the game. And I remember the lesson that these pleasures were to be enjoyed in a dignified manner. No matter what happened in the game, the aspect of manliness was always to be maintained.

The supremacy of the rules of pazienza was especially impressed upon me once while I was learning another of the games of the Mezzogiorno, a game of cards called scopa, which means "sweep." I was about ten years old, and both to indulge me and teach me the men of my family let me sit in on one of their games. Somehow at a certain point during one of the hands, I managed successfully to bluff my grandfather, sweeping the cards from the table while expressing great glee. There was a general embarrassment among all who were present, both immigrant and second generations. It was not in the scheme for a boy to outfox an *anziano*, and particularly not his grandfather. My card playing was quickly ended for the time being. I was, in effect, told to get lost. No doubt the men thought themselves quite foolish in lapsing from one of the principles of la via vecchia, that of peers among peers. Later when alone with my father, he lectured me sternly on the subject of respect for one's elders and proper behavior within the family.

Another of the favorite games of the Mezzogiorno that I learned as a child is perhaps the most fitting of all. It is the game of *morra*, or throwing fingers. The game originated among the ancient Romans, who called it *miscare digitis*. At a given signal each of two men shoots a hand forward, extending one to five fingers. Each player simultaneously calls out a number guessing the total of fingers extended by both. The one who approximates closest the correct total wins. The players are usually surrounded by a group of spectators. The game has a strangely hypnotic effect on all present. And all seem to emerge from a series of matches with a feeling of relaxation that usually comes from engaging in a strenuous sport. The game is well suited to the pattern of pazienza. No equipment is needed to play it but one's own wits and hands. It doesn't stress either competition as such or mere chance. It stresses cleverness in the context of chance situations, a mini-model of life. The good player is one who learns to read his opponents' patterns and to "psyche him out" by playing tricky patterns. It is the perfect game of the ideal for it stresses the ability to cope by one's quick wits in a world where chance and the cleverness of others combine to produce the everyday situations with which we are confronted.

The capacity to be furbo, or worldly clever, was also cultivated in the Mezzogiorno by the sport of hunting. Hunting continues to be popular today in Italy. In fact a controversy is now raging in Europe because of the very popularity of the sport in Italy. Conservationists in countries to the north of Italy are making vigorous protests about the practice of Italian sportsmen of shooting migratory birds which in winter seek the warmer climate of Italy. Until recently many of the species of birds were protected by laws of the Italian government. But in a recent reform designed to achieve greater local self-government, the various regions of Italy had returned to them the authority to legislate their own hunting laws. A number of the local governments immediately abolished the laws protecting species of migratory birds.

Hunting cultivates pazienza combined with quick, timely, decisive action. It is no surprise that the sport long popular in all of Italy remains especially popular in the South. In the old Mezzogiorno hunting was linked to another component of manly status, the possession of firearms. In the Mezzogiorno of my grandfather a young man in a small town did not achieve manhood in his own eyes until he owned a hunting gun. In the days of my grandfather's father and grandfather the weapon also served as a symbol that the giovanotto was now ready to protect a family and was thus eligible to marry. We have evidence that the desire for a gun was linked more to the protection of the home and the practice of hunting than to aggression, in that pistols, which are more useful for aggressive purposes, have never been popular among the contadini. A young man bought a silver-barreled rifle or a shotgun. In Sicily a weapon often owned was the famous short shotgun of the island, popularly called a wolf gun (lupara).

Although it is difficult to establish one-to-one relationships when dealing with psychological nuances, perhaps it

is not farfetched to suggest that the inclination of many
second- and third-generation Italian-Americans to become
policemen derives from the inherited tradition. The qualities of the old ideal seem serviceable in police work. Again
we see another paradox of the Italian-American saga.
These policemen are the descendants of people who held
feelings ranging from distrust to hatred of all governments
and their agents, including, of course, the various types of
polizia of the Mezzogiorno. But it must be remembered
that being furbo meant that if the chance occurred you
became allied with power regardless of your feelings about
it. Therefore many immigrants approved of their sons and
grandsons joining the police force because of motives beyond those of the American-born sons who liked the work
because it fitted the inherited life style.

No discussion of recreation among Italian-American
men would be complete without a mention of dancing. The
pattern of dancing inherited from the old land also served
the life of pazienza. It provided a catharsis of personal
energies and emotions in a controlled setting. In the Mezzogiorno dancing took several forms, sometimes solo,
sometimes a man and woman alone, and also in small
groups and large dances in the round. Dancing was both
coed and also with people of the same sex. To be more
precise, men had no inhibitions about dancing solo or with
one or more men. Men and women commonly danced
together in large groups, but coed duets were often limited
to married or courting couples.

The most popular and typical of the traditional dances
of the Mezzogiorno is the tarantella, a high-spirited dance
perfectly suited to release controlled energies. Legend has
it that the dance originated as a superstitious ritual to cure
the poisonous bite of large spiders called *tarantule*. The
typical style of the dance, wherein the arms are held high
and feet kick vigorously, seems to corroborate the legend.
The dancer seems to be kicking at large aggressive spiders.
The more accepted etymology of the name is that it derives
from Taranto (Tarantum) in Southeast Italy.

The tarantella varied from region to region, even from

town to town in the Mezzogiorno. Moreover, it is characteristically Southern Italian in that it calls for individual im-
provisation within its set patterns. The standard form prescribes that the dancer's posture maintain a dignified aspect
by keeping the shoulders and hips fixed. Within this restriction almost any individual variation is welcomed. In the
mode of the Mezzogiorno, the dance is both fixed and flexible. When danced solo, it permits individual expression.
When danced by two men or two women, it permits them
to interplay their personalities. When danced by a young
man and woman it is often openly sexual in its connotations.

I once watched a young couple, accomplished dancers,
dance a long tarantella in which a large repertoire of male-
female attitudes and relationships was depicted: seduction,
aggression, bravado, coquettishness, taunting and teasing,
anger and jealousy, feigned indifference, flirting, cruelty,
surrender, and tenderness each in turn by the man and the
woman. Of course, this was an exhibition. But it had its
roots in an old practice. A married or courting couple
would dance, each acting out feelings toward the other, to
the shouts of approval, disapproval, and pointed comments
and advice voiced by their relatives. It was a significant
form of catharsis which has been lost and not replaced
among American-born Italian-Americans.

Among the most important recreations in the Mezzogiorno were the marionette theater and the public story-
tellers known as *contastorie*. The stories of the contastorie
and the plays of marionette theater were attended by
adults as well as children. Among a largely illiterate population these two media kept alive traditional tales and folklore going back to medieval times. The stories told and the
dramas and comedies presented emphasized the ideals of
pazienza, l'ordine della famiglia, and other important patterns of life, including what we shall see is the unique religion of the Mezzogiorno, a mixture of Christian, Moslem,
and pagan folklore. I once attended a performance in a
marionette theater in Sicily of a drama that depicted the
life of a minor saint. The saint's exploits were *illustrative*.

He defended womanhood, protected helpless children, and pursued other such chivalrous ends. But he succeeded in these efforts not by any show of what we would think of as sacred behavior. He succeeded by his ability to be clever, shrewd, and canny. This was a saint clearly after the distinct Mezzogiorno style.

While visiting the Mezzogiorno I have been struck by how popular television is among the contadini. For example, the home of my great-aunts has remained virtually unchanged since the day some sixty years ago when my grandmother left it—except for one important addition, a television set. It is a large screen portable on a TV rack sitting smack in the middle of the living room, a room that to me seemed like a museum illustration of nineteenth-century Sicily. Incongruous? Yes and no.

More than any other medium television is closest to the traditional forms of the marionette theater and the public storyteller. The TV screen is easily accepted as an updated version of the small marionette stage, more so than the large screen of the movies. Television has only recently become popular in Southern Italy, and one can only guess about the effects it might produce. So far in the case of my great-aunts their responses have been similar to those I've observed in older Italian-Americans, including my grandparents, who were avid TV fans in their last years despite the fact that they did not understand English. Television merely serves to reinforce old beliefs. For example, my great-aunts told me of a news program they had seen which covered the aftermath of the crash of an airliner in Europe. I encouraged them to talk about the program, which obviously had made a great impression on them. The moral they drew from the mishap? To them it demonstrated once again the wisdom of the traditional belief that it is unwise to travel very far from home and family.

Movies were cautiously accepted by Italian immigrants and eagerly by their American-born children. With my friends I attended children's matinees on Saturday afternoons in Brooklyn in the late forties and the fifties, and our responses were typically American. We cheered the heroes and booed the villains, a reversal of the behavior of the previous generation when they were children. As late as the early 1940's a study of second-generation Italian-American children reports that they sometimes cheered triumphs by screen villains, especially when they won out over some official.

The ideal of pazienza has developed in the United States much the same as other inheritances of Italian-Americans. The immigrants strove to maintain it in their own behavior and inculcate it into the lives of their sons. In the first effort they were highly successful. However, their efforts to nurture it in their sons was one of the major causes of the intense cultural conflict to which the second generation was exposed. As in the other areas of the great compromise achieved by that generation, the now middle-aged Italian-American maintains the essentials of the ideal. He sees himself as the sanction for family authority, paramount over all else. Like his father, he values owning his own home, his own property, and his own business, or at least a sense of possession regarding his labor union. He continues the style of lying low and remaining aloof from the outside society. He especially shuns the facets of the larger society which contradict the ideal or are meaningless in terms of it. And he works to pass on the ideal to the third generation. Here tension is generated, for the young males of the third generation regard the ideals of pazienza as confusing and confused, obscure in their origins and their reasons for being. Third- and fourth-generation males tend strongly to reject parts of the outward style of the ideal while at the same time living its essential patterns, values into which they have little insight. In their conscious search for identity they are greatly bewildered by the incongruities between their ill-understood gut values and many of the values they perceive in the larger society. The result is a widespread paralysis. Ironically, the very values of pazienza which live in them serve to conceal the inner trouble by curtailing any expression of it. Thus the young male sees his problem as a matter of something vaguely but greatly wrong with him as an individual per se. Aliena-

tion, guilt, and confusion alternate with rejection of the
outward signs of being Italian and immersion in some
current American life style. Although their second-
generation fathers when young also perceived their identity crisis in personal terms, the cultural roots of the crises
were more evident to them. They had grown up in clearly
Italian homes. The third and fourth generations grow up
in homes which are American in their surface aspects, and
it is very difficult for young minds to probe beneath. The
Italian foundation of their crises is not at all evident to
them.

Ultimately the youngest generation must resolve its quest
for identity in its own terms. But whatever the resolution,
it would be accelerated by placing the crisis back in the
cultural context in which it lives—underground but very
strong. Whereas the second generation repressed all too
much consciousness of the old culture because it was so
strong as to seem a real obstacle to the forming of an identity that was American as well as Italian, it is just as necessary that the culture re-emerge for the younger generation
to synthesize its identity. In fact, there are signs of a regen-
eration of ethnicity among the third and fourth generations
expressed in some of the very areas submerged by their
parents. For example, the study of Italian language and
culture.

Although in general the study of foreign languages in
American high schools and colleges is declining, enrollment
in courses of study of two languages shows an absolute
increase. These are Spanish and Italian. The interest in
Spanish is easily explained, given the enormous government and private programs designed to aid impoverished
Spanish-speaking communities in the United States. No
such explanation covers the interest in Italian. Government
agencies and other institutions, including schools, continue
to be unaware of or unresponsive to the special needs of
Italian-Americans. This neglect includes a lack of efforts
even to collect information about Italian-Americans, so we
do not know how many of the students now enrolled in
Italian studies are Italian-Americans.

The culture of the old country had to be screened by the second generation, the first that had the formidable challenge of establishing a native-born American identity. But the elements of Italian culture which were screened out may prove to be an asset to the third and fourth generations, whose challenge is to root their inherited American identity in something older, deeper, and affording greater wholeness and meaning. In this the young Italian-American male would do well to understand the original ideals of pazienza and their modified forms which constitute so much of his fiber.

La Serietà—
The Ideal of Womanliness

The Italian-American woman is the center of the life of
the entire ethnic group. The privileges transmitted to her
give her a status which evokes the special position of
women in the legend of chivalry. At the same time the
responsibilities, demands, and expectations placed upon her
present her with problems which make the grievances of
today's women's liberation movement seem simple and
trivial in comparison. The stresses on her that result are
staggering. While all Italian-Americans feel the poignancy
of their inherited sensitivity to the essential hardness of life,
the woman experiences it deeply, almost physically, in ways
which the male is spared.

The Italian-American woman inherits a status partially
symbolized in a Mezzogiorno custom of her mother or
grandmother. During a wedding feast the groom would cut
the choicest part of the nuptial meal and ceremoniously
serve it to his bride. This was a token vow on the part
of the husband to place his family's needs above his own.
Outsiders mistakenly thought this gesture was a romantic
one made simply to the supremacy of the wife's needs. Not
so. Implicit in it was the understanding that the bride's
needs would also be subordinated to those of the new family established by the wedding. The bride received the
tribute as the symbolic center of the new family. She did
not receive it as a wife per se and certainly not as a mere
romantic object.

The equivocal status of the woman as both the core of the family, and hence of life, and in service to l'ordine della famiglia is illustrated in other ways. In the old land, the obligation of carrying on the famous practice of the vendetta fell upon the sons of a family and seldom upon the father, whose only role therein was to berate his sons if they were negligent in this responsibility. In a throwback to the medieval custom of a knight's seeking a woman's blessing before battle and carrying her colors into the fight, sons would go to their mother (not to their father) and declare their love to her at the onset of a vendetta. Like the groom's tribute at the wedding feast, this gesture represented a statement of devotion to the family made to the symbolic center of the family, the woman.

Anyone who witnesses an Italian or Italian-American funeral cannot help being struck by the different behavior of men and women. While men mourn, they do so in the fashion of pazienza. Their constant, silent, and expressionless presence is their only act of public mourning. On the other hand the women mourn dramatically, even histrionically. They mourn for the whole family. It falls upon them to express the bereavement of the entire clan. They do not merely weep. They rage against death for the harm it has done to the family. The more mature the women, the more extreme their behavior. Under other conditions of adversity these same women respond by steeling themselves. When necessary to the preservation of l'ordine della famiglia, they can press back tears and emotions and present a stony determination to the world that can even outdo the stoic aspect of their men. Yet at funerals these women weep, wail, and rage against death, berating its shamefulness in taking a member of the family and its cowardliness in the insidious way it acts. The women often will challenge death to show itself and confront their fury or to take them instead of the deceased. Their behavior seems excessive, first, because it is for the entire clan and needs to be proportionately powerful, and, second, because the more extreme it is the greater the vicarious catharsis for the other family members. The woman screams *their* screams of loss, frustration, and rage.

Early in college I came across Dylan Thomas's great poem *Do Not Go Gentle into That Good Night.* Its effect upon me was instant and complete. It expresses in the language of poetic genius the emotions I learned to feel at death and which I have purged at funerals through the medium of my female relatives. Children are taught their roles in the life of la via vecchia by direct apprenticeship. Following the usual custom I attended family wakes for as long back as I can remember. My earliest memory of a family funeral is of one that occurred when I was five and one half years old. Since at least that time I have been taught to bear, and let my female kin express, the feelings Thomas so eloquently drafted—"rage against the dying of the light." At my father's wake seven years ago I spent three days silently suffering feelings recorded by the poet. Like other Italian-American men with whom I have spoken, although I felt cheated at not being able to express my emotions more openly, I was grateful that others—the women of my family—could vent them for me.

We begin to understand the ideal of *serietà,* seriousness, the ideal of a fine woman. In Northern Italy the term *mala femmina* means a "naughty woman," one who is sexually wicked—delightfully or destructively. In Southern Italy it also has another meaning. In the Mezzogiorno words for such a woman are not minced. She is bluntly called a *puttana,* a whore, or, more strongly, a *puttana del diavolo,* devil's whore. "Mala femmina" means something else. It means a useless woman, a woman who cannot or does not fulfill her complicated role as the center of la famiglia. This woman is sometimes called a *disgraziata,* an "unfortunate one" as the dictionary renders it. As used in the South it means one whose existence is useless to herself and her family. As used in the Mezzogiorno, "mala femmina" and "disgraziata" are strong condemnatory terms, the male counterpart of which is disgraziato, one who is vile. Calling someone a disgraziato is a strong insult indicating great scorn, and not mere pity as the dictionary definition suggests. The connotations of the word are those surrounding our use of the insults "bastard" and "son of a bitch."

A mala femmina is one with no competence as a woman. To be sure she is not a good wife, mother, or godmother. But most of all she is found lacking in comparison with the ideal of what it means to be a woman. Although the ideal includes the ability to bear children and household skills, it goes much further. It includes life-supporting qualities which must run deep into the being of a person. In lacking these serious qualities the mala femmina lacks the competence to be the cohesive force which binds a family together and thus makes all life possible. She is truly a base, unfortunate creature.

Everything pertaining to womanhood in the Mezzogiorno is either anchored in the vital qualities of una buona femmina or is an ornament to them. Anything not related to them is at best cautiously tolerated in a woman by herself and others, and anything understood to undermine serietà is not tolerated at all. In the Mezzogiorno a woman was either una buona femmina or a disgraziata. There was little margin between the two because to be an incompetent woman was to court the ruin of self and family. Because of the high stakes involved, failure was more condemned as immoral than pitied as personal shortcoming. Thus the term "unfortunate one" became synonymous with a base insult.

As has been noted the institution of the contadino family developed in response to the hardships of natural conditions and political and economic oppression in the Mezzogiorno. For centuries people have indulged in abstract speculation about what the life of humans would be like if all social institutions were to disappear. Those who embrace the romantic tradition have welcomed the possibilities in this projection for a liberated life free from the restraints of the family and other social fetters. Wiser minds have agreed with the conclusion of Thomas Hobbes in the seventeenth century, that a life apart from social structures would be "solitary, poor, nasty, brutish and short."

Until recently the debate about the necessity of social

structures to truly human life has taken place mostly in terms of reasonable guesses, each side of the debate lacking concrete evidence to make its case. However, in 1972 a book was published entitled *The Mountain People*. It was written by an anthropologist named Colin Turnbull and tells an astonishing story. It is a record of a small tribe of people called the Ik living in Africa's Northern Uganda. Some years ago the tribe was forced to live under conditions in which survival became a crisis. Forbidden by law to hunt and unable to farm the poor soil where they were forced to live, the Ik were beset by mass starvation. Under these extreme conditions all of the social institutions of the tribe slowly disintegrated until at last even the family collapsed.

Turnbull's record of the life of the Ik today chills the blood. They are utterly selfish, loveless individuals, each plotting against and betraying the others. The result exceeds even the warning of Hobbes. Parents turn their children out completely at age three or four to run in packs foraging for food. The children attack and deceive each other and are killed if they try to return to the security of the home. No person acts with loyalty or concern toward others, not husband or wife, parent or child, relative or friend. Everything of culture and civilization among the tribe has disappeared. Those few individuals that survive their monstrous life are worn out hags ready to die by the age of thirty or forty.

Fortunately the people of the Mezzogiorno evolved a different answer over the centuries to severe natural, economic, and political conditions. They developed their elaborate family system as their basic institution. And they went further and developed a full culture upon this foundation. Because it is so critical to life, civilization, and culture, the family places demanding expectations upon its members. The role of women was no less than to anchor the family in the power of their own beings and warm l'ordine della famiglia by their emotions and love. This status of the woman stands behind the much-noted practice of Italians of calling upon female figures in time of stress.

For example, it explains the fact that the two most common invocations of both male and females when they are in any way troubled or upset are "mamma mia" and "Madonna mia." This is in contrast to the American habit of calling upon "God."

The position of the female as symbolic of all that is human and supportive of life also finds its expression in the great status accorded to the primary female figure in Italian Catholicism, the Virgin Mary. Although strong in all Catholic countries, the cult of the Madonna is especially powerful in Italy. In the Mezzogiorno it is honored even by the anticlerical contadino male, legendarily free-minded with regard to the Church. In the 1940's and '50's when Pope Pius XII wanted to strengthen the role of the family among Catholics the world over, not surprisingly he attempted to do so by cultivating the Marianist tradition.

In the Mezzogiorno young girls were trained in their responsibilities throughout their childhood. Their apprenticeship in serietà was so rigorous that by the age of seven they were permitted little time or approval for play. By that age they were earnestly engaged throughout their waking hours in learning skills and developing qualities of womanhood by constant supervised practice. The maxim from la via vecchia that I heard echoed to girls in the Italian neighborhood of my childhood was *Non ti far vedere senza far niente*—"Don't be caught doing nothing." And in the life of a girl over seven, play was traditionally regarded as idleness.

The family's ultimate aim for a girl was to see her *sistemata*, settled and competent in her role as a woman. The goal was abetted by the girl's father and brothers, even those younger than she. These male relatives were constantly vigilant monitors ready to bring the sanctions of la famiglia down upon her for any deviation from the life of correct apprenticeship. Although the males provided the sanction for the training, it was the girl's mother, her madrina, and her zie (aunts) who actually sculpted the realities of the ideal into a girl's personality on a day-by-day basis. Each girl had a team of older mentors and confidantes, as was true of each boy.

Perhaps the chief precept to be learned was to live as a sharp practical woman, a *scaltra*. For in the old country the necessity always to be clever was felt more keenly by the women even than by the men. Although the men lived in towns and carefully tendered their social relations according to the worldly hierarchy of values of la furberia, they worked either in the fields, on the sea, or at the artisan's post. Thus each day they were afforded some solitude wherein they could relax and enjoy the luxury of struggling only with nature, the ocean, or raw materials. The women did not have this emotional space. They lived and functioned all day, each day, in the village or city, all but constantly in the presence and under the scrutiny of their neighbors. They constantly engaged these stranieri in the competition of living according to the severe rules of la furberia. Artfulness was always required and could never be relaxed. Not in the market place, around the local fountain or stream, or in the courteously guarded socialization with local women in the piazza. Each woman together with her relatives and commare confronted every other woman and her clan in a setting where no moral obligations were owed to those outside the family except what was earned as respect. And in the interfamily competition rispetto was accorded only to actual or potential power. In a humorous anecdote Mario Puzo wrote of his elderly Neapolitan mother's response to the news that he had contracted with Paramount Pictures for a large sum of money to screenwrite *The Godfather*. "Don't tell nobody," she said.

Women learned to work ceaselessly for the welfare of la famiglia and always in competition with other clans. Thus they took great pride in their ability to bargain advantages for the clan, whether it was in arranging a wedding match for a son or daughter, gaining a good price at the market, or cleverly eliciting some valuable secret or clue from some stranieri in genial gossip. Chatting was in fact mutual probing packaged in the agreeable manners of buon costume.

In my shopping expeditions in the Mezzogiorno I have bargained fairly well, winning the compliment from the contadini of being smarter than most foreigners. I had a good teacher. My grandmother could bargain better than anyone I have since met. Because my mother worked, I spent my childhood weekdays with my grandmother. I often went shopping with her. The experience is unforgettable. My grandmother would walk into a store or shop, ignore the proprietor—in our area virtually always Italian —and peruse the store's merchandise with the most casual, haphazard manner she could affect. In the custom of the old land it was her role not to seem terribly interested in buying and certainly not to tip what she was after. And it was the merchant's role to guess exactly what she wanted. After a while my grandmother would begin to ask the prices of items she fingered suspiciously, indicating they were obviously inferior. In response to each reply she would immediately unhand the item in question, her every facial and bodily nuance saying that it was repulsive in quality and its price a moral outrage. After these unhurried preliminaries, bargaining would begin in earnest over the real object of her interest. She, of course, pretended to select it only because it was the least offensive article in the store's shoddy inventory. Starting at outlandish extremes, she and the merchant would bark out final prices. Each non-negotiable price uttered in the firmest of voices by the merchant was met by my grandmother's coldly pointing out the excessive defects in the Godforsaken item. In turn the merchant would praise his ware as being fit for royalty at least and would feign physical shock at the prices demanded by my grandmother. Often at a critical point my grandmother would abruptly call to me, *"Andiamo!"* We would head rapidly for the door as if totally affronted and turned off. More often than not when we were in the process of closing the door behind us the merchant would call out to my grandmother's expectant but seemingly aloof ears, saying that circumstances forced him to acquiesce by lowering the price far beneath the obvious worth of the

item. After a bit more of the game a sale would finally
be made.

It was a very serious game of a poor contadina on behalf
of her needy family. My grandmother very early impressed
upon me the fact that merchants, like all stranieri, would
try any trick and use any gambit and that I must be impervious to all. Sometimes a merchant would try to enlist
me on his side against my grandmother's efforts for la famiglia by tricking me into revealing an honest opinion or reaction. My grandmother taught me never to respond to
these ploys, to remain completely impassive and be ready
to move toward the door with the unhesitant stride of uncompromising conviction. I was never in any way to undermine her efforts by some thoughtless word or unguarded
gesture.

I remember one confrontation with a hapless door-to-
door salesman, a non-Italian who evidently had come into
the neighborhood not knowing the game. He was selling
linens and towels. From the moment my grandmother
opened the door to him she sized him up as a patsy, un
fesso perfetto. The man, who spoke no Italian, was ushered
into the house with exaggerated graciousness and carefully
settled into a comfortable chair. I was enlisted to act as
translator and solicitously to offer him coffee or a cold
drink. Playing the uncomprehending guileless peasant
woman, my grandmother confused the man into a corner
by expressing undiscriminating great interest in his samples
and a total lack of understanding prices. Her instructions
to me were put in precise and crisp language that completely belied her bewildered face and tone of voice, telling
me exactly what to say and how to say it. She drove the
salesman to distraction, at one point insisting that he stay
when he got up to leave in exasperation and telling him
through me how great her interest was in buying so much
of what he had shown. In the end the salesman let her
have just what she wanted and at the price she had proposed—a deliciously satisfying bargain by her lights. The
world was made up of foxes and their prey, and una
buona femmina was a vixen par excellence.

Today's women's liberation movement strongly objects to historic patterns in which women could define and fulfill themselves only in terms of their relations to men. The complaint is well taken. Many of these relations were directed to the fulfillment of men and served to fulfill women only secondarily, if at all. The myth of the woman behind the man is all too familiar to us. It is woven into much of our culture and we tend automatically to impose this model on the roles of women in other cultures. In the case of Southern Italian society this would be a great error. By the very logic of fulfillment a person can shape self-definition and achieve fulfillment only in relations with other people, institutions, work, events, etc. The Mezzogiorno woman had far more relations to her world than the unliberated American woman, and the relations engaged more of the essentials of her culture. She related to almost every crucial facet of her society, whereas unliberated women are excluded from significant relations with many critical centers of their culture, in the United States especially political and economic ones. Power in the United States is economic and political. The status of American families flows from the political and/or economic success of their members, almost always their male members. In the Mezzogiorno power usually flowed from family. The political or economic success of a person most often was dependent on the power and status of his or her family. And the family was at least as dependent upon the talents and efforts of its women as upon those of its men.

The Italian-American woman today has not attained the cloying comforts, leisure time, and privileges of the upper middle class. Her liberation efforts are still cast more at relieving her of responsibilities. Those who work outside the home do so from economic need and not for personal fulfillment. As is true of millions of working-class women, much of the definition of the women's liberation movement is considerably off their tack. The right to use "Ms." before their names, or to drink at all male clubs, or to enter executive suites as peers are not yet burning issues for them. Their pressing concerns are with their own education and working out new relations with their parents, husbands, and children.

In the classic mode of contadino life, the mother, godmother, and aunts had maximum daily influence on children of both sexes. Boys, however, began to reach beyond the female environment at the age of seven and were active in predominantly male work and social life from the onset of puberty. On the other hand girls remained in an environment dominated by females until they married. At marriage they were expected to assume the full burden of womanhood. Old studies of Italian immigrants stress that a female's life career was fulfilled as she went from her father's household to that of her husband, to that of her sons. A more accurate rendering of the pattern would be: from her mother's household to that of her own to those of her daughters-in-law. As a female moved through the stages, she was first as a child an apprentice in womanhood. Upon her marriage she was a responsible woman who fulfilled economic, cultural, and more strictly family roles. In her motherhood and her old age she became progressively more a teacher of womanhood to her daughters, daughters-in-law, nieces, goddaughters, and grandchildren.

The female learned and then taught serietà, which included not only the crucial economic and social roles of womanhood, but also the manner and style of the fine woman as interpreted in her culture. From the age of seven a female cultivated precise ways of behavior until they formed the true and visible exterior of her personality. She developed a manner of dressing, grooming, posture, walking, and talking—in short all of the obvious elements of social behavior.

While still children girls learned a code of careful grooming. In this code a girl brushed her hair daily and carefully combed and pinned it. Neatness and cleanliness were always the rule. But the deeper aim was to develop the natural beauty of health as distinct from the glamour of cosmetics. Young girls wore modest jewelry on holidays, mainly gold ring earrings (their ears were pierced at age three or four) and thin gold bracelets. But make-up was shunned by females of all ages. The use of cosmetics was regarded as subterfuge. The wearing of cosmetics was considered to be a sure sign that the wearer had more than surface imperfections to hide. It raised the suspicion that deeper blemishes of character were also present. A slovenly or careless woman was despised, and the more make-up worn the more proof that personal carelessness or slovenliness was being camouflaged.

At the graduation ceremonies of my eighth-grade class, almost all Italian-American, our principal complimented our parents on what she termed the wholesome look of the girls in the class. The principal was a product of the American feminist movement of the early years of the twentieth century. A stern, no-nonsense Irish-American spinster who fought her way up in her career, she presented a spartan image. In one of the odd accidents of American life, the wholesome contadino look of the young girls dovetailed nicely with her own values.

The principal did not express her opinion of the rest of the code that the girls had already mastered to a considerable extent. We can only guess what she thought of the sensuality that Italian-American girls projected. It was a paradoxical sensuality, at one time controlled and yet easy and fluid. It was the same ideal of dignified sexiness that made immigrant women scornful of young American women who wore business suits or slacks. What kind of a girl, I would hear them say, would hide her bosom in a jacket? Or her legs in slacks? Obviously only one seeking to conceal something symbolic of a deep flaw of feminine character. A good female was proud of her body. As a child she was taught to be proud of its vitality and fluidity. Young girls learned to stand straight. Slouching was for people ashamed of themselves. Young women were proud of the luster of their hair, the warmth of their eyes, the radiance of their skin, the slenderness of their waists and arms, the thrilling voluptuousness of their bosoms and hips. Even today on the more prosperous avenues of traditional cities like Palermo one is struck by the graceful, natural sensuality of the young women as they walk by. The young

women are at ease with the sensual insinuations of their
bodies. They are neither innocent of them nor blatant in
their consciousness of them. They are at home with their
bodies, neither bold nor shameful, cool nor obvious.

Middle-aged contadino women did not try to conceal
their age with make-up. Nor did they feel shame at their
no longer girlish figures. They were proud of the same
carefully groomed, clean, neat, and natural look. And they
took pride in the maturity of their figures, the silhouette
of the adult woman at the center of her family and, hence,
of her culture. Their pride did not conform to the cult
of youth in America, so Americans—including sometimes
their own children—were amused or embarrassed by such
simplicity.

In the tradition women of all ages can be seen walking
arm in arm in the cities of Southern Italy. Young women
who are relatives or close friends startle foreign observers
by kissing each other on the lips when they meet in public. Such greeting is part of an elaborate pattern of relations
with other women which includes medieval courtesy in all
but overtly hostile situations. The pattern also dictates
highly ritualized verbal sparring in competitive, tense, or
hostile situations between women, never to be confused
with the earnest and if need be violent combat involved
when vital family interest is at stake.

This distinctive pattern of sensuality, dignity, pride, affection, protectiveness, cunning, and anger is the truth behind the distortion of the "Sophia Loren" and "mamma
mia" stereotypes held by Americans. Equally significant,
the clash of the ideal of serietà with American ways forms
a major part of the dilemma of Italian-Americans. Understanding the background of the tradition only poorly,
and highly sensitive to American patterns, American-born
Italian-American women tend often to regard the old way
as oppressive and embarrassing. When they were young,
the daughters of immigrants chafed under the system of
constant tutelage by older female mentors. The second-
generation girls were once removed from Old World roots
and thus regarded the constant attention as nothing but re-

strictive chaperonage. Their mothers insisted on training them in the traditional skills and character traits. The daughters perceived this effort as an oppression that stifled their enjoyment of life, their dating and their self-fulfillment in the American terms of education and the pursuit of individual interests.

There was no escape from the conflict for the girls. First because, following the tradition, their mothers continued to insist upon supervising their lives even after they were adult women, wives and mothers on their own. Second, the girls had adopted too well the values of the via vecchia. Their conflict was only partially with the older generation. It was also a conflict with themselves, sparking all the special guilt and agony of self-conflict.

Being out of touch with the Old World mode in its completeness, the second-generation girls reconstructed it as well as they could using what was available to them. This included a one-dimensional view of their mothers which they endowed with perspective by placing it in a model that dominated the American scene during the 1930's and '40's, the model of "momism." At the center of this image was the neurosis-producing, overbearing woman we have since come to call the "Jewish mother." But viewing the immigrant Italian women in these terms has been a major mistake. It has left second-generation females with only straw women to battle against in their struggle to resolve their identities. Thus much of their struggle for identity has been a grappling with a bogus foil, a fight doomed to futility. The pseudo image of the Italian mother provided no real handholds, no points of leverage to use in the struggle.

The phony picture of the Italian "Jewish mother" ogress could not give insight into the conflict between mothers and daughters even in trivial matters like styles of dress. Again grasping a prevalent model of their generation, this time a watered-down version of progressivism or modernism, the daughters regarded their mothers simply as old-fashioned. Of course, this label gave no insight at all, nothing useful in building an identity.

"Old-fashionedness" could hardly explain these women preferring figure revealing dresses for their young girls over the more loose fitting garments of teen-agers in those days. It could not explain why the supposedly puritanical immigrant women put gold jewelry on their young daughters, nor why among themselves these "Puritan" women delighted in sexual talk and humor.

In the Mezzogiorno, patched clothing worn by children was a sign that the mother was caring and industrious. To the American-born girls it was only embarrassing, again tagged as old-fashioned. But the label "old-fashioned" could not even adequately explain why Italian women would wear only scarves, never hats, and why they forbade their daughters wearing hats, and this in the 1930's and '40's, a heyday of outlandish women's hats. For in the Mezzogiorno the wearing of hats was the affectation of two despised classes of women. The women of the landed gentry wore hats in their pretension to be better than the good women of the contadino class. And as a beacon of their outcast status, the whores of the big cities sported hats. A real woman wore only scarves.

The lack of mutual understanding between Italian immigrant women and their daughters was appalling. It marked a generation gap that has left the now mature daughters locked in perpetual self-conflict.

The great struggle at cross-purposes between immigrant women and their American daughters can be illustrated by the relation of my grandmother to one of her daughters. As a child and teen-ager this daughter (my aunt) was exceptionally headstrong and insubordinate. I remember my grandmother years later telling of her concern with her daughter's behavior. My aunt perceived my grandmother's attempt to cultivate in her the ideal of womanliness as an effort to impose a female-as-house-plant life upon her. She began to rebel as a child. Despite my grandmother's attempts to repress it, the resulting conflict reached a climax during my aunt's teen-age years. Although she was punished and even beaten, the girl's spirit remained unbreakable.

My grandmother faced a dilemma. She was proud of her daughter's tough willfulness. She did not want to break the girl's spirit. She saw in her courage and determination —great material out of which to shape una buona femmina. To crush the girl's élan would turn her into a dullish functionary instead of a vital woman of the tradition. The contadini did not like washed-out womanhood any more than wayward women. My grandmother set herself the task of channeling her daughter's rebelliousness rather than erasing it. But she confessed that she was uncertain of her success until years later when she saw my aunt a grown woman, settled and worldly wise—sistemata e scaltra.

Immigrant women viewed the patterns of American girls with alarm. Quite simply they regarded such behavior as living outside the parents' home, going out on dates, informality in public settings, and open quarreling with family elders as the ways of puttane. They warned their young daughters venite subito a casa dopo la scuola, to come right home after school. And they fought the Americanization of the girls to a draw. The girls succeeded in becoming American in form but remained Italian in substance. Theirs is a conflicted personality, and one which in turn now causes tension between them and their daughters.

Third-generation females are bewildered by the behavior of their mothers, who in one breath encourage them to develop their individual talents and enjoy a richer life but also insist that they remain true to the old-fashioned values. Lacking insight into the compromise of cultures that shaped their mothers and ignorant of the rationale of the old culture, the young women of today are stunned by the seeming contradictions in their mothers' attitudes. The second-generation mothers encourage their daughters to pursue a higher education than they achieved, to widen their economic role by entering better careers, and to take pride in their individuality, their personal talents and intelligence. Nevertheless, they constantly press their daughters to maintain the square values of womanhood revolving around family solidarity, practical wisdom, and self-contained sexual pride. The split is extremely puzzling,

and the efforts of the older women to explain themselves
are unsatisfactory.

Inevitably the new generation employs its own timely
frameworks of explanation to make sense of the conflict.
And among those now handiest is the ideology of women's
liberation. To be sure the third generation has been formed
too well in the traditional values to become bra-burning
activists. Instead some of them use the pat explanations
of women's lib as superficial rationalizations of their conflict with their families. As already indicated, most see the
women's lib account of the problem as incongruous with
their own experience. The image of the woman enslaved
to her careerist husband is a caricature of WASP culture.
It doesn't have deep impact upon Italian-American girls
who intuit their problem as something quite different. They
keep to the old values. And like their few Italian-American
sisters who raucously rebel against them, they go through
the fruitless agony of ill-understood anger against their
families alternating with confusing guilt and anger against
themselves. It is the old pattern of a search for identity
that is crippled by a lack of knowledge of cultural roots
and a resulting absence of appreciation of the unique dynamics of one's own psychology.

Some striking facts about Italian-American women
emerge from the 1970 census. For example, of women
from ages fifteen to forty-four of eleven major ethnic
groups reported, Italian-American women had the smallest
percentage as heads of households. Their mates had one
of the lowest percentages of husbands unemployed. Among
white females sixteen years old and over in the labor force,
Italian-American women have the second highest percentage of clerical workers (39.4 per cent); the highest percentage employed as operatives (25.3 per cent), the lowest
percentage of those in professional or technical careers
(9.7 per cent), and the third highest rate of unemployment.
Of white women in the labor force only Italian-Americans
and Polish-Americans showed as many women working
part time as those working full time.

In sharp contrast to their immigrant ancestors, second-

and third-generation Italian-American women have fewer babies and have them in numbers proportional to their family incomes. The large majority (65.5 per cent) between the ages of thirty-five and forty-four have given birth to two to four children. The next largest group (20.5 per cent) has had *less* than two children born to them per woman. Moreover, Italian-American women have the second *lowest* percentage (13.9 per cent) among the white ethnic groups of women with five or more children born to them. Among Italian-American women those whose families are in the third highest income bracket ($9,349–12,787 per year) have had more babies per woman than their less affluent sisters. Italian-American women who have graduated from high school have more children per woman than *both* their less educated and more educated sisters.

The poorly educated, impoverished Italian immigrant women of 1910 had more than twice as many children as their descendants in 1970. The typical American image of Italian-American women is a vestige left from 1910. Today's figures show that the image is completely outdated. There is a sixty-year gap between the reality of Italian-American women and the stereotype of them. Today's Italian-American woman is not the children-laden mamma of the stereotype. The fact is that the rate of birth by Italian-American women is considerably lower than the national average in the United States. Furthermore, it is lower than those of all other major white ethnic groups except Jewish women, whose rate is only slightly lower. Whereas in 1910 Italian-American women were the second most reproductive among the groups specified in the census of that year, they were the second *least* reproductive group in the 1960 census and again in the 1970 census.

In the stereotype poorer Italian-American women are supposed to have more babies than those who are wealthier. When Italian-American women between thirty-five and forty-four years of age are divided into four groups according to their family income, we see data that negate the stereotype. The birth rate increases as the incomes of the

first three groups rise! The following table lists the annual
family income and the number of children born per 1,000
women of each of the first three groups of Italian-
American women.

	Family Income	Number of Children Per 1,000 Women
Group 1	$0–7,074	2,031
Group 2	$7,075–9,349	2,217
Group 3	$9,350–12,787	2,265

Moreover, in the fourth group, those women whose family incomes exceed $12,787 per year, there is only a small
drop in the number of children born per 1,000 women,
to 2,203.

The stereotype of Italian-American women holds that
the less educated give birth to the most children. This, too,
is false. Less than 50 per cent of Italian-American women
between the ages of fifteen and forty-four had graduated
from high school in 1970. Yet they had given birth to
about 80 per cent more children per woman than the majority who had less than a high school education. To be
sure, the birth rate among the 6.5 per cent who graduated
from college drops to about half of those with only high
school educations. It will be helpful to continue the profile
presented here of today's Italian-American women before
attempting to interpret this fact.

The stereotype of the Italian-American woman depicts
her as a Roman Catholic who slavishly follows her church's
prohibition against birth control and is thus the mother of
a large brood. The truth is that Italian-American women
thirty-five to forty-four years old have the second lowest
percentage among them (13.9 per cent) of women with
five or more children. This figure is lower than that of the
national average for whites (18.5 per cent). It is also substantially lower than that of the staunchly Catholic Irish-
Americans who have the highest percentage of all white
groups (22.9 per cent). In addition, it is lower than that
of English-Americans (16.7 per cent) and German-

Americans (20.9 per cent), both whose numbers include many Protestants.

This statistical picture of second-generation and some third-generation Italian-American women corroborates the interpretation of them I have formed as American in outward form and contadina in essence. They have adapted American ways to serve the ideal of the buona femmina. Thus many work outside the home. Yet they take work which will cause minimal disruption of family life—part-time work and types of work whose demands are left behind at the end of the work day. They continue to rely upon their males, who more than any other group of men fulfill their traditional responsibilities as heads of households.

Italian-American women follow their very misunderstood traditional pattern regarding numbers of children. Large families were found in the Mezzogiorno not because the contadini confused womanhood with high fertility. Nor did they have large families to satisfy any religious views. They had large families for two reasons. First, they lacked effective birth control technology. Second, a large number of children was an asset to a family in the economic system of old Southern Italy. Incidentally, it is only because in the old scheme males could earn more than females that the contadini thought it essential to have many sons. A favorite toast among the contadini was *felicità e figli maschi*, happiness and male children. This wish reflected economic values rather than male chauvinism. Although the old ideal was to have many sons it was also to have daughters. Just as a family without sons was thought to be doomed, a family without daughters was thought to be unfortunate. Children of both sexes were vital to the family system.

Italian-American women of the second generation had means of birth control available to them. They were free to exercise only the traditional criterion regarding children—the economic well-being of the family. As we have seen, they had children in proportion to their family incomes in America, where economic realities punished families with many children. They and their husbands decided it was better for the family to limit its number of children. And they did so. They were not deterred by religious dictates against birth control because they inherited the contadino value hierarchy which subordinates religion along with all else to the well-being of the family. They were not governed either by male chauvinist desire to prove machismo by repeatedly impregnating their wives, or the desire of unliberated women to fulfill themselves by having many babies. Stereotypes notwithstanding, the first of these desires was not part of their cultural heritage and the second one has been exaggerated.

Thus, following the pragmatic bent of la via vecchia, the least educated and poorest had the fewest babies of all. The small exception to this rule—the handful of college-educated women—can also be explained in the same interpretation.

Very few Italian-American girls of the second generation went to college, because of economic need and the inherited contadino distrust of formal education, a part of the cultural attitude of la via vecchia. Those few women who did were usually driven by a determination to break with the entire structure of la via vecchia. By acts of strong personal will these women opted for a life style deliberately departing from the old way. It was this determination that caused them to choose college, fewer children than other Italian-Americans, and in many cases more demanding careers than their less educated sisters. It was not a case of a college education liberating them, but the resolve to attempt a sweeping break with tradition that drove them in the first place to college and careers.

Interestingly, college-educated Italian-American women have the same percentage of marriages as their sisters. In the absence of any other studies of the college graduates we are left to speculate about how sweeping a break with the values of la via vecchia they have in fact achieved, and how different an identity they have forged.

In my experience college-educated Italian-American women have in fact mainly limited their break with tradition to but the two areas of attending college and pursuing careers. In my observation they continue to take quite seriously their roles as centers of households. Most of them, even the small number who are verbally critical of la via vecchia, continue to reflect its other critical values in their actual behavior.

What about the latest generation of Italian-American females? How will the women and girls who are now less than thirty years old build their identity, and how much of the serietà ideal will it include? A higher percentage of them are seeking college educations than their predecessors. The many I meet as students have left me convinced that they have been nurtured in the tradition so well that it is the very fabric of their personalities. Yet although perplexed by their identity problem, they appear to be freer, less filled with guilt or paralyzed by it. They inspire hope, for they are potentially women in whom we will see an unprecedented union of the best of the old ideal with the wider self-fulfillment of the American dream.

Historically one of the most popular figures in the Mezzogiorno has been the female Christian martyr, St. Lucy. She died at the beginning of the fourth century, murdered during cruel persecutions under the rule of the Roman emperor Diocletian. Pictures of Santa Lucia are found everywhere in the South of Italy, and a reproduction of an old painting of her hung in my grandparents' home. I remember my grandmother's explanation of the exotic picture of the young girl with such beautiful skin and a graceful figure. My grandmother's account mixed Lucia's serietà attributes with her Christian virtues, a practice I have found to be common today in the Mezzogiorno. In the picture the barefoot Lucia was advancing with a bold yet feminine stride through a background of dark, somber hues. My grandmother explained this simply. Santa Lucia taught us we must have coraggio regardless of fear. She held a lamp in one hand which my grandmother explained was to help her see clearly and avoid being confusa, confused and confounded. In her other hand she held at the ready an unsheathed, wide, double-bladed sword. My grandmother said this meant we were to be always prepared to protect those we love from dangers coming from any direction. And Lucy bled from the face and neck, but seemed serenely unconcerned about it. She was demonstrating, my grandmother said, the willingness we all must have to sacrifice *nostru sangu per il nostru sangu*, in dialect meaning blood for our blood.

Looking at the picture as a child, I remember feeling both its power and its quaintness. It was archaic yet strangely real and irresistible. The myth of Lucia is a symbol of the ideal given to Italian-American women. Although no longer adequate to the lives of the young women, the myth's qualities of determination, courage, clear-headedness, and willingness to sacrifice will perhaps provide them with values for constructing their own meaning and destiny.

In any case the young Italian-American woman facing the question of her identity should heed the old injunction to contadino *signorine*—keep moving and don't be seen idle.

Sex

Italian-Americans enjoy a contradictory reputation concerning sex. Influenced by postwar Italian movies, Americans see Italian sexuality either as frank and earthy or as wanton in the fashion of la dolce vita. Because Americans associate Italian-Americans with their brethren in the old country, they sometimes also view Italian-Americans in the frame, especially in terms of the earthy picture. But more often Americans see them as very conservative in their values. Italian-American prohibitions about premarital sex for girls, double standards for men and women, fiery passions, and unrestrainable jealousy are American legends.

As is true of every aspect of Italian-American life, the legends exist largely unexamined. Serious studies of Italian-Americans are infrequent. When they are undertaken, sometimes they provide surprising information. Andrew M. Greeley, an inexhaustible researcher, provides us with a scarce look at Italian-American attitudes toward sex in his *Why Can't They Be Like Us?* (1971). Although his study was limited to feelings about premarital sex, it confirms one of the legends while impeaching another.

Despite our being accustomed to traditional Italian-American old-fashionedness, their actual conservatism regarding sex among unmarried people exceeds expectation. Greeley questioned members of five ethnic groups. First he asked them whether certain forms of sexual behavior were acceptable for a female if she is engaged to be married. Almost all people in each group felt that kissing was acceptable—the percentages ranged from 92 to 95. Then Greeley asked whether petting was acceptable. Wide differences emerged among the ethnic groups in response to this question, with Italian-Americans giving the most restrictive response. Only 41 per cent regarded petting as acceptable. Percentages among other groups were WASPS (57 per cent), Irish (53 per cent), Polish (63 per cent), and Jewish (63 per cent).

When asked whether sexual intercourse was acceptable for betrothed girls, the Italian-American response was overwhelmingly negative. Only 5 per cent said yes, while 14 per cent of WASPS, 14 per cent of Irish, 8 per cent of Poles, and 45 per cent of Jews answered affirmatively.

Legends about Italian protectiveness of young girls were demonstrated as accurate in Greeley's study. Yet the supposed Italian double standard for the two sexes did not emerge. On the contrary, Italian-American responses to questions about acceptable behavior for engaged males were almost identical to those about females. Only 5 per cent thought it acceptable for an engaged man to have intercourse; only 42 per cent approved petting; while 94 per cent sanctioned kissing.

The study brings to mind a story told me by my mother's family. One summer evening when she and her two sisters were young women in their twenties, they strolled with their mother on the boardwalk of Coney Island. In the traditional fashion, the four women walked arm in arm. By chance they spied at some distance the oldest of their brothers, then a boy in his late teens. He was headed in their direction with a girl, hand in hand. My grandmother was outraged at his brazen public behavior and started toward him. To prevent her making a scene, her three daughters surrounded and blocked her. Meanwhile my uncle had seen them and prudently and quickly steered his unknowing date away from his family. Frustrated by her restraining daughters, my grandmother watched her son retreat with a girl that by her standard could only be *svergognata* (shameless), *sfacciata* (brazen), and perhaps even a *put-*

tana (whore). She would settle accounts later that evening
with her son. In the meantime she stood hands on hips, re-
hearsing the accusations she would hurl at him. *"Beddu
spicchiu,"* she mocked, Sicilian dialect for *bello spicchio,*
meaning "fine outstanding one."

Greeley's findings, my grandmother's reaction, and
Italian-American sexual attitudes in general become com-
prehensible if we look at the basic contadino opinion of
sex. The contadini regarded sexual energy as a natural
and powerful force. While they dealt with it matter-of-
factly (the basis for the earthy image), they also respected
its enormous power. Its energy was inexorable. Like volcanoes, earthquakes, storms at sea, and other natural
forces, sex was relentless and irrepressible. It was passionately delightful, even ecstatic, yet the Dionysian energy
could also be very destructive. No one alone was strong
enough to control its impulses. It had to be governed—not
repressed—by la famiglia. L'ordine della famiglia had to
harness sexual energy in ways that permitted fulfillment of
the irresistible drive for pleasure while at the same time
preventing it from wrecking la via vecchia. In the fashion
of their ancient Greek ancestors, the contadini sought to
celebrate Dionysius, the god of pleasure, without being
consumed by him. Today's Italian films notwithstanding,
the old ideal of Italian contadini could better be described
as *la buona vita* (the good life) rather than la dolce vita.

Puritan attitudes toward sex were not part of contadino
culture. To the pragmatic people of the Mezzogiorno, puritanism never came to mind because it was totally imprac-
tical. It was absent from the culture also because puritanism is an antilife attitude. To oppose life and its natural
rhythms was unthinkable. To try to destroy the ebb and
flow of life was regarded by the contadini as being *pazzo,*
crazy. To try to ignore them was *scemo,* silly.

The contadino had no guilt about sex per se. Neurotic
sexual guilt developed later among Italian-Americans only
as they lost touch with the roots of their sexual attitudes.
After their values were torn from their traditional cultural
soil they appeared merely restrictive, prohibitive, and in-

hibiting. In the severed cultural consciousness of second-generation Italian-Americans, their own values seemed to them without rationale. A good part of the natural, generally more unself-conscious and relaxed contadino relationship to sex evaporated as its source became remote.

Contrary to popular prejudice, American culture served more to distort Italian-American sexuality rather than liberate it. American hang-ups about sex were absorbed as the healthy contadino sexual *modus vivendi* slipped away. Many second-generation people lost the ease, joy, and humor with which their parents dealt with sex. These were replaced by anxieties and uncertainties, doubts and guilt born from culture conflict. In terms of sex, the culture conflict was especially severe because it was emotionally highly charged.

Third and fourth generations experience confusion concerning sex, as they do generally about their identity. Their restless sexual energy foils itself against unrecognized cultural outlines in the dimly perceived psychological space of their inherited attitudes.

Second-generation conflict and third-generation confusion have muffled the lyric quality of the old contadino sexuality. Today's Italian-Americans cannot sing as freely the frankly sexual and sensuous songs traditional of their recent ancestors. For example, one of the most famous Sicilian folk songs is openly and humorously sexual. Americans heard it sung in the wedding feast scene of the movie *The Godfather*, a traditionally accurate setting for the song. Of course, few Americans understand Sicilian dialect, and the spirit of *"La Luna Mezzu O Mari"* by-passed them. In this song, an ardent daughter repeatedly reminds her mother of her urgent desire to marry. "Mamma mia," she pleads, "the moon is over the sea, it is time for you to marry me [off]." The mother answers, "My daughter, to whom shall I give thee?" Whereupon the girl answers, "Mamma mia, think of someone." In each verse after this introduction, the mother answers by speculating about the girl's future with one of the town's eligible young men and finds it unsuitable. Each case is more bawdily suggestive than the last. For example, the mother sings of her life with a fisherman, who "would go and come, his fish always in hand."

I remember people singing this song in the traditional manner during my childhood. They invented verses as they went along, laughingly competing with each other in ribaldry before us children without the slightest self-consciousness or hesitation. I also recall hearing burning love songs, some tender, others lusty, still others of both passions. For example, a famous Neapolitan love song is called "*Comme Facette Mammeta?*" "How Has Your Mother Created You?" The song is sung by a young man to a young woman he lovingly desires. In it he praises in direct and sensual language the girl's physical charms. As he puts it, "when your mother created you, she knew what she was doing." Another famous old Neapolitan song is "'*O Surdato 'Nnammurato*." It is sung by a soldier to his beloved who is passionately proclaimed as "life, oh my life."

Traditional contadino society encouraged passionate courtship feelings, yet greatly restricted courtship behavior. The latter practice is still desired by Italian-Americans, as Greeley indicates. The pragmatic origin of the value placed on premarital chastity for both sexes is easily understood when we remember that contadino society knew no contraceptive means except abstinence. The life of a bastard child and of its mother would be pitiful. The child would belong to no family. Its presence would prohibit its mother from entering into a family by marriage, an eventual necessity as her parents aged and died. Existing apart from the Mezzogiorno's vital institution, unwed mothers and their children found survival difficult and life bitter.

The only departure from premarital chastity even surreptitiously permitted was young men's relations with the town whore, or in larger towns and cities their visits to the local government-supervised whorehouse, called by the familiar Italian word *bordello*. Usually the town or region whore was a woman who because of premarital pregnancy or some other calamity was without a family. In a vicious cycle, her outcast status made prostitution an economic necessity, and her prostitution reinforced her outcast status.

Although a mother would attempt to keep her son away

from the local puttana or bordello from fear of disreputable company and venereal disease, mature men sometimes encouraged younger men to indulge. In a society where single women were closely chaperoned, for most young men the prostitute presented the only accessible sexual experience.

The standard was not relaxed for single women for obvious reasons. The moralistic prohibition against their having sexual intercourse was strictly enforced because they could become pregnant. Evidence of the prohibition's success is found in the rate of illegitimate births in the old Mezzogiorno compared with the rest of Italy, whose society was also sexually conservative. In her excellent *South Italian Folkways in Europe and America* (1938), Phyllis H. Williams reproduced official statistics of the Italian government on illegitimacy during the years 1906 to 1909, years during which birth control was unknown. First the rate per one hundred live births in each of the six districts of the Mezzogiorno:

Abruzzi	2.7
Apulia (containing the city of Bari)	3.1
Basilicata (Lucania)	2.3
Calabria	5.4
Campania (the region of Naples)	3.2
Sicily	4.3

Then the Northern Italian provinces:

Emilia	10.3
Lazio (the region of Rome)	15.7
Liguria	4.9
Lombardy	2.7
Marches	7.9
Piedmont	2.8
Tuscany	6.3
Umbria	9.6
Veneto	5.6

The lives of young people were closely supervised in general as well as in sexual matters. Family control of the sexuality of young people was part of the rule rather than a special case. In l'ordine della famiglia it was impossible to think of a person fulfilling his sexual nature apart from his family's interests any more than he could independently fulfill his vocational interests or personal ambitions. The family was in all regards the medium of the individual's life, almost as absolutely needed an atmosphere as air itself.

The family arranged marriages for its young people. The right of a young man or woman to refuse a match was respected or not by different families according to the autocratic or libertarian inclination of the parents and the circumstances of a particular match. From all accounts the happiness of people married by their families' judgments rather than their independent wishes varied. But as there is no evidence to prove they were more happily married than today's couples who marry out of their own romantic, sexual, or other motives, so there is no evidence to prove the contadini were as a group less happy. Viewed from the perspective of the zooming rate of divorce among American marriages, we are in much too brittle a glass house to throw stones at another culture's marital institution.

In my own experience, I have found that the old Italians had about the same amount of marital joy and sadness among them as Americans have today. Recently a middle-aged woman told me of her parents' marriage. They were contadini whose match was made for them by their families shortly after they arrived in the United States. The woman's mother in her last years of life confessed a general unhappiness to her daughter about her marriage. Her father professed an apathetic attitude toward his long marriage.

In contrast we have the record of Rosa and Leonardo DePaola as told in a 1972 issue of *L. I.*, the magazine of Long Island's large newspaper, *Newsday*. The DePaolas' marriage was arranged by their families in 1924. Rosa had come to the United States five years before at the age of nineteen from Bari, also Leonardo's home city. The two young people did not know each other. Their match was made solely upon the wishes of their families.

Today in their advanced age, the DePaolas have seen their grandchildren grow to maturity. They declare themselves happily married and grateful for their life together.

One of their four children, Mary, finds it hard to accept the traditional manner in which they were wed. Her mother's response leaves her daughter happy for her but puzzled. "I knew he was a good man," the old woman says. "And he *is* a good man. He always gave me food to eat, he helped my children to grow up. What more would I want? What would kissing have to do with that?"

Mrs. DePaola's words reveal an important traditional expectation concerning marriage. The contadini did not expect as much emotional gratification from marriage as we do today. In la via vecchia much of one's emotional life was nourished by other members of the extended family. In contrast we today have isolated the married couple from the extended family. In the smaller nuclear family, only the spouse is available to gratify emotional needs. Husband and wife expect or demand much more from each other than they did in the old culture. Perhaps the increased expectation creates a greater potential for the fulfillment of husband and wife, as is often claimed. But we should note first that there was nothing in la via vecchia which prevented a close emotional relationship between married people. Second, we cannot avoid looking at the other side of increased potential. Our greater expectations make possible greater disappointments. If the expectations of emotional fulfillment are unrealistic, as many critics of modern marriage maintain, then they actively contribute to failure's unhappiness.

The experience of the second-generation DePaola family is also typical of its group. Mary DePaola explains how she compromised with the tradition when she married. Although she chose the man she would marry, she carefully sought the approval of her parents. Asked if she rebelled in any other way, Mary replies that she broke tradition only in naming her first-born son after her favorite uncle instead of the baby's paternal grandfather.

That son is now engaged to a third-generation young woman of Sicilian background named Kathy Strollo. Although the young couple are as assimilated in American culture as most Italian-Americans, their families are very involved in their wedding plans. The families approve the match the young people have made for themselves. In the spirit of campanilismo, the DePaolas carefully point out that the Strollos are not Italian but Sicilian. And the Strollos note that the DePaolas are Italian but to their misfortune not Sicilian. The two families celebrated the engagement in the old manner. They gave a party for the engaged couple. Family and friends contributed cash gifts to the engaged pair at the celebration. As the immigrant grandparents gave their blessing to the third-generation couple, it was clear that la via vecchia had been modified but was still current.

The continuity of the old way is not as clearly visible to other third-generation young people as it is in the DePaola family. Many have been raised without sexual guidance by their parents, whose second-generation conflict makes it difficult for them to discuss sex. Deprived of useful parental guidance, these young people often follow the lead of less diffident youngsters of other ethnic groups in sexual behavior in the increasingly ethnically mixed neighborhoods where they live. By their necessarily tension-filled cultural compromise, the second generation has hobbled the force of la via vecchia.

It is passed on to the third and fourth generations in crippled form, causing them paralyzing feelings of confusion and embarrassment. The effect of la via vecchia's influence on them in sexual matters as in all other regards is the very opposite of the traditional goal of well-equipping young people for life. In the Mezzogiorno the conventions of la via vecchia gave young people guidance and supervision in the direction of clearly presented expectations. The third generation is handed amorphous expectations and perceives them as groundless. Their parents' attempts to supervise their lives seem to them efforts at pointless restriction. The second generation gives the third little guidance effective in coping with the day-to-day challenges of sexual maturation in today's environment. The breakdown represents the all-pervasive dilemma of Italian-Americans. The powerful via vecchia gives them great strength yet at the same time blocks effective use of that force in American culture. La via vecchia at one time provides power, but in the foundationless, unconscious way it has been transmitted to the American-born it shackles the very power it provides.

As I grew up in a Brooklyn Little Italy, the public school was the only place where I saw girls other than my female blood relatives. Boys and girls were segregated by the community, mostly by closeting the girls. Everything I have learned about the second generation confirms that this was typical of their upbringing. Needless to say, the result was an enormous mutual ignorance between the sexes. While the stunting effects were great on the females, boys, too, were hurt. We knew nothing about the real characteristics of girls and relied upon callow street talk for our knowledge of sex. Unlike the children of the Mezzogiorno, we did not live in a culture that compensated for sexual segregation by providing other sources of information.

In the Mezzogiorno, daily close contact with members of the extended family provided companionship with the other sex among children. As they reached puberty, they were segregated. But teen-age girls continued to receive guidance and information from the daily company with their mothers, grandmothers, aunts, female cousins, and the numerous commare of their older female relatives.

There is no denying that this system of communications had its flaws. The information and guidance given the girls reflected the biases and other limitations of their mentors. In particular contadino women tended to romanticize the wedding ceremony in the fashion of the Mezzogiorno's medieval chivalric heritage. This was done often at the expense of not emphasizing enough the long marriage after the bright wedding, and not preparing a girl for it emo-

tionally. Realistic sexual counseling in particular suffered
as a result of romanticization. But despite its limitations,
communication on sexual and marital questions was carried on between older and younger generations both before and after the wedding of young girls.

Boys were afforded a similar system of communication
with older males in the family social structure—for some
later to be supplemented by experiences in the bordello.
Boys too suffered from the defects in this system of communication. In it a groom was expected to teach his bride
in sexual matters. His ability to lead their sexual relationship to mutual satisfaction was dependent on the counsel
he received. If it was insensitive, bitter, or otherwise faulty,
the young man and his bride began their union handicapped. Experience with prostitutes might provide some
knowledge about the mechanics of sex, but it gave only
very distorted exposure to female emotions about sex. Because prostitutes at most feign passion and avoid real emotional ties with their clients, a young man's encounters with
them gave him doubtful knowledge about female passion
and none at all about the emotions of a young woman entering a marriage.

In addition both sexes were hampered by other practices
in the old culture. Sexual information was not given to
children until they reached puberty. And inhibitions about
genital nakedness were sown in children after they reached
the age of five. These had some rationale in building a sense
of privacy in a close family structure. The price for some
was shame and doubt about their sexuality which over-
came the pride in their bodies they were taught as children.

In contadino society, male and female roles were distinctly separated. Warmth and tenderness were classified
entirely as feminine roles. Aggression and impassiveness
were masculine characteristics. Contadini believed that the
mother (i.e., the female) was all-giving. Even conception
and genetics were misunderstood in accord with this bias.
The belief was that a father merely activated the child-
bearing potential of the mother. If they viewed conception
as essentially a female affair, they saw genetic inheritance

almost entirely as a female contribution. One believed that
the mother supplied most of the important physical and
personality characteristics to her offspring. Of course, the
mother later cemented this supposed influence. She was
responsible for the raising of children and their character
formation. It is not surprising that girls identified themselves overwhelmingly by their potential for motherhood.
Boys, on the other hand, saw the criteria of social status
and power rather than fatherhood as the essentials of mas-
culinity, as already indicated in the discussion of manhood.

Young couples began marriage with great obstacles to
verbal and emotional communication. To us living in the
United States today, the phrase "failure to communicate"
is a cliché because it is so frequently used to explain failures in human relations. As a consequence we should not
find it difficult to imagine the painful problems in many
Mezzogiorno marriages and may easily empathize with
those who suffered in that exotic land.

The emotional force of childhood ignorance, miscon-
ceptions, confusions, and fears often carried itself into the
mature years. Deep-seated childhood wounds are difficult
to overcome. Healing takes place slowly, if it happens at
all, and scars are commonly carried for life. The emotional
lesions produced by childhood ignorance and confusion aggravated by too abrupt societal initiation into maturity
during turbulent puberty became basic conditions of many
contadino marriages.

Although actual sexual experience of young adults was
limited and their personalities often warped to various degrees by socially produced neuroses, people about to marry
at least had a great deal of knowledge from their elders, no
matter how biased. In addition they enjoyed an invaluable
sense of support from this source of knowledge and expectations.

Caught by their rebellion against their parents' culture
in their drive to establish their American identity, second-
generation children psychologically cut themselves loose
from what they needed. The information and advice of-

fered by their elders was emotionally rejected as old-fashioned, Moustache Pete nonsense. School pulled them away from the elders of the same sex during the major portion of the day, while the elders' jobs pulled them away from the children. The children's rebelliousness in an environment perceived by their parents as American immorality caused the parents to intensify their restrictions on their offsprings, especially after puberty. In short, the classic system of sexual education and support was severely disrupted. The second generation entered its maturity full of anxieties, doubts, and conflicts. These were of a much more troublesome extremity than those of their parents. Alienated from the vitality of its inherited culture by American society and their own rebelliousness, second-generation children were vulnerable to much more damage from the traditional practices of keeping young children sexually ignorant and inducing inhibitions about nakedness and bodily functions. They are also much more vulnerable to the damaging aspects of their tradition's strictly defined roles for each sex, damage which is pervasive because the old social rationale for these sex roles had been greatly altered in America. All these problems were heightened by conditions of loneliness and isolation experienced by the second generation in Little Italies. These feelings were a mystery to the immigrants who grew up in the Mezzogiorno. The conditions that cause loneliness and senses of isolation and emotional deprivation were all but unknown in the Old World. The immigrants could only respond with bafflement when their growing children used expressions like "I want to be fulfilled." Corresponding idiomatic expressions did not exist in the Southern Italian dialects.

Perhaps the most damaging result for second-generation youth was the sense of shame imposed upon them about sex. Unfortunately, immigrants who did not suffer sexual guilt in their own young lifetime imposed it on their American-born children. As the chaperone system was difficult to enforce in the United States, the older generation instilled a broad sense of sexual guilt in their children to

preserve premarital chastity. Mothers promoted sexual
shame in both their sons and daughters, and in addition deliberately sowed fear of sex and men in their daughters.
To be sure, some sexual shame and guilt were part of the
child-rearing practices in the Mezzogiorno. But they were
muted there by the social design which did not require
their service in the interest of premarital chastity and prevention of premarital pregnancy. In the United States the
attitudes were fully mobilized in the emergency of perpetuating old values in the midst of a new culture. The dis-
tressing effect was great among the second generation and
now repeats itself as the same attitudes are passed on to
third- and fourth-generation youth.

These are the sources of the stereotyped, notoriously
square mentality of second-generation Italian-Americans in
sexual matters. As this group now tries to pass its inhibitions, shame, guilt, and inflexible masculine and feminine
roles onto its own children as moralistic standards of right
and wrong, a new generational conflict is produced. The
conflict is serious, for the emotional health of young people is at stake. Because the conflict is acted out still in an
unreflective manner, giving neither generation insights into
its own or the other's psychology, the prognosis for the
emotional health of youngsters is greatly in doubt. Caught
as they are between forcefully assertive sexual values derived from the Mezzogiorno but distorted by their parents'
experience on one side, and a popular aggressive American
sexual revolution on the other, and prevented by inadequate education and lack of maturity to cope with either,
young Italian-Americans are in a desperate quandary.

The second generation fulfilled its sexual nature by living out the values of la via vecchia with marriage partners
of its own choosing. But it never resolved its conflict in a
manner enabling it openly to articulate la via vecchia or its
own coming to terms with it. As it deals with its own children, a new break in communication is evident. Whereas
the second generation regarded the sexual values of la via
vecchia as outdated but nevertheless adapted many of them
to their American marriages, third-generation people are

simply bewildered by the seemingly meaningless values of their parents.

Young people in the Mezzogiorno expected their families to marry them off according to age, older children first. Girls usually married in their middle or late teens. The husbands were usually one to ten years older. Engaged couples met under heavy chaperonage, with members of both families represented. The longer a couple was engaged the greater its temptation to give in to passions. Therefore the number of chaperons assigned to them was increased.

In the early time of engagement, the couple spoke to each other mostly through their chaperons. Later they were permitted to address each other directly, but only within earshot of chaperons. Still later they were permitted to talk privately, but always within constant sight of all chaperons. Within these boundaries, expressions of love between the couple were approved by the families. This was a license extended to engaged people. A man who declared his love or passions without this license would seriously offend the woman's family. A woman who approached a man without the license would disgrace herself and her family.

It was always desirable to have nature fortify and not contradict family interest. In fact it was a rare family that would insist that one of its children fulfill its wedding plans if he or she developed a strong aversion to the fiancé. Therefore, engaged couples were positively encouraged to use their license and speak love to each other. They were encouraged to woo each other. Love, although not necessary in a marriage, was desirable, but hatred and resentment were poisons to be avoided if at all possible.

In the Mezzogiorno, people of opposite sexes, unmarried and married, who were not blood relatives did not touch each other in public, not even to shake hands in greeting. The taboo was strictly enforced in engagements. Couples were not permitted to hold hands and definitely not permitted to kiss. I recall my grandparents and their friends openly laughing at the romances they saw depicted on American television. They regarded as absurd presentations of single young people meeting alone, touching and kissing. One of my mother's uncles had a standard comment he would utter the moment of first intimate embrace on the TV screen: *"E finito a schifio,"* he would joke, "It has ended nastily." His response came despite many years of exposure to the more liberal American sexual customs.

In the Mezzogiorno, marriages were regarded primarily as alliances of families and only secondarily as unions of individuals. Each family was expected to contribute equally to the compact. Each marriage partner had to bring an equal trousseau to the marriage, giving rise to expressions that a particular marriage was a *dodici e dodici* (twelve and twelve) or *venti e venti* (twenty and twenty) union, meaning each partner brought twelve or twenty outfits of clothing.

The bride's family had to contribute a dowry, an obligation that fell not only upon her parents but also, if required, upon her brothers, be they single or married. In most areas of Southern Italy, the dowry remained the personal possession of the bride after marriage. All other property, including the couple's home, was by custom regarded as joint property because it was originally contributed equally by both families. If, as was the case, a married woman had no legal or customary right to sell the family home, neither could she be cast out of it.

The contributions of each family, and all other details of a match, were arranged between two families by an outside intermediary, usually a mature woman known as an *ambasciatrice*, an emissary. All of a young person's status and most of his or her reputation were derived from his family's status and reputation. "As a cat, so its kittens," went a popular saying. To a family seeking to marry one of its children up in social status, or a family trying to marry off an offspring with outstanding personal defects, the diplomatic skill of the ambasciatrice was critical. Such women were greatly in demand and well rewarded in the more populated towns and villages. The ambasciatrice worked in close consultation with each family, conferences cautiously initiated usually by a ranking female in one or both clans. The families did not meet until and unless mutually satisfactory arrangements were made. If they could not be made, negotiations were broken. A good ambasciatrice kept all in confidence, so neither family lost face. If terms were agreed upon, the fathers of both families would meet to publicly seal and announce the pact in the presence of a full turnout of both clans.

The ambasciatrice's last function sometimes was to accompany the groom's mother to inspect the linen on the bridal bed on the morning after the nuptial was consummated. A bloodstained bed sheet was occasionally even hung over a balcony or window for public inspection. In a system where divorce was impossible and the only two grounds for annulment recognized by custom and locally respected by the church were the nonvirginity of the bride or the impotence of the groom, the bloodied bed sheet was significant. It proved both female virginity and male potency. Bride and groom then spent some period of time in total seclusion, usually in their new home but on occasion in a different place provided by family or close friends. The period was equivalent to a honeymoon. Because it typically lasted one week and a groom was expected to pamper his bride, it was called *settimana della zita* (the bride's week).

Attempts by Italian immigrants to impose this system of courtship and wedding upon their American-born children were strongly rejected and led to great conflict between generations. The second generation sought parental approval but insisted on free dating and personal selection of spouses in the American manner. The second generation usually won its way, but at a cost of breaking contact with the cultural wellsprings of its own values. Even the valuable opportunity to discuss marital problems with one's family was denied to many second-generation people. Having broken with their parents' wishes, they later hid marriage problems from them. An isolated generation further weakened itself by depriving itself of the advice and counsel of parents and culture.

Second-generation Italian-Americans met members of

the opposite sex in school and at work. Natural attractions formed. America's more open customs were invoked as a rationale against parents' attempts at restrictions. Rebellion against restraints became intense. The circumstances of life in American cities made enforcement of parents' wishes difficult. For example, one of my aunts succeeded in dating the man she later married despite her parents' attempts to stop her. Life in Brooklyn was not life in Sicily, and she was able to lose the younger brother designated to chaperon her, a young boy who took his parents' assignment seriously. Finally, after a period during which my aunt answered her parents' punishments with ever more determined defiance, my grandparents had no choice but to meet her young man and publicly endorse her wish to be engaged to him. They adopted her wedding wish as their own. Although immigrant parents expressed strong disapproval of the breaking of la via vecchia and did their best to enforce its courtship rules, most finally chose to compromise by accepting their children's engagement choices rather than cutting the young people adrift. In the end, blood could not be denied.

In my aunt's case her struggle was made easier by the fact that her beau was Italian-American, the most common case among second-generation Italian-Americans. Immigrant responses to their children's desires to marry non-Italians were extreme, sometimes completely unyielding. The notion of permitting one's child to form a union with a person and family who did not know or live la via vecchia was abhorrent. Such people were not merely stranieri. They were considered living little better than *una vita selvaggia*, a savage or barbarous life. While immigrants could accept the fact that people, to their misfortune, lived such a life, they became horrified at the thought of a family alliance with them through marriage.

An Italian-American in Lancaster, Pennsylvania, wrote to tell me that his Calabrian immigrant grandmother "was taken sick in bed for a week when my father announced he was going to marry an 'American' girl."

Some young men and women were locked in their homes

or forcibly sent off to live with faraway relatives to prevent marriages to non-Italian Americans. Forced prevention of a disapproved wedding was age-old custom in the Mezzogiorno. In a case where a young person was *stonato* or out of his wits from being *colpito dal fulmine* (hit by a lightning bolt of love or passion), he had to be protected from his own folly. Being overcome with passion was normal for a young person. It was even regarded as a sign of the youth's healthy, spirited nature. But as the Meridionali saw it, it would have been irresponsible to permit someone to make a lifetime commitment motivated by such irrationality, unless, of course, it happened coincidentally to satisfy family interest.

No less a historical figure than St. Thomas Aquinas suffered similar treatment to prevent his becoming wed to a particular religious order. As his Latin name indicates, Thomas was raised in Aquino. In the year 1244, the twenty-year-old Thomas entered a Dominican convent in Naples to become a member of the order. He had come under the influence of Dominicans and fervently wished to share their life. This choice was disapproved by his family, who preferred an alliance with another religious order which would be more to its benefit. Upon instructions from their father, Thomas's brothers kidnaped him. His family kept him a prisoner at Aquino for a year before finally acquiescing to his wish to become a Dominican.

Luckily, conflicts about second-generation people marrying outside the group arose in only a minority of instances. Most second-generation Italian-Americans selected people of their own ethnic background when they chose to marry. Living, going to school, and socializing almost exclusively in Italian neighborhoods weighted the odds on the side of meeting a mate of Italian origin. A 1969 Census report showed the rate of endogamous (in group) and exogamous (out of group) marriages among seven ethnic groups, English, German, Polish (including Jewish), Russian (including Jewish), Spanish (including Puerto Ricans, Mexican-Americans, and other Latin Americans), and Italian. Unlike other census surveys, in this one a person was

classified in an ethnic group by his own self-identification.
Those surveyed included people of all generations. Assuming that more third- and fourth-generation people marry
outside their group than second-generation members, the
survey no doubt gives too low an estimate of the second
generation's in-group marriage choices. Nevertheless, the
Italian-American group had the second highest rate of endogamous marriages, 52.7 per cent. The rate of in-group
marriages among other nationalities was English (45.3 per
cent), German (34 per cent), Irish (31.8 per cent), Polish
(40.9 per cent), Russian (46.6 per cent), Spanish (76.1
per cent).

In another study, Greeley found the rate of endogamy
among second-generation Italian-Americans to be 66 per
cent, by far one of the highest among nine ethnic groups he
surveyed. (It was exceeded only by the French-Canadian
rate of 68 per cent and the rate among Spanish-speaking
Americans of 88 per cent.) The Italian group reported that
the rate of endogamous marriage in their parents' generation had been 93 per cent.

Greeley found that, when Italian-Americans married
outside their group, they most commonly chose a mate of
either German or Irish background. The pattern varies
somewhat probably only in the New York City area, where
impressions indicate Italians and Jews intermarry. The
trend began long ago. In his study of rare relations *Jew
and Italian* (1971) in the period from 1881 to 1924, Rudolf Glanz reports that in 1916 significant intermarriage
was already occurring between the two groups. In that year
the Italian interpreter at the Marriage License Bureau estimated that one hundred such marriages occurred annually.
The Yiddish interpreter put the number at twenty-five per
year.

There are two likely explanations of New York's Italian
and Jewish intermarriage. First is the obvious fact that both
groups have very large populations in the same relatively
small geographic area. Second, both groups have traditions
of strong family orientation. Although life patterns are sig-

nificantly different in both groups, their parallel family matrices serve to overcome each group's aversion to exogamous marriage.

Having won their right to select their own mates, most second-generation people conformed to customary engagement and wedding practices. Families met each other in large formal gatherings to solemnize plans. Time and care were given to ensure that each engaged person was properly integrated into his peer circle in his fiancée's family as well as thoroughly cultivated by his prospective parents-in-law. The future bride's father and his daughter's fiancé established between them a mentor relationship. The destined bride and her future mother-in-law took pains to develop the analogous relationship of female serietà.

Weddings were large events planned and carried out by family design. The entire social web of clans and their alliances turned out to witness and celebrate marriages. These celebrations provided me with the largest social events of my boyhood. One or two hundred people of all ages gathered in a hired hall. Children played along the edges of the room filled with tables as adults talked, ate, and danced to live music. The music was usually divided equally between American pop tunes and traditional Italian numbers. I vividly remember how the wooden floor would bounce almost in trampolin fashion during a tarantella as dozens of feet stamped in unison. Immigrant matrons used to hold their breasts after a fast round trying to catch their breath. During American fox trots and waltzes, it was almost as common for two women to dance together as it was for a man and woman. The practice was more popular among second-generation women than among their mothers. Dancing in an embrace, American style, was not popular among the older Italians, who especially disapproved the mode between a man and woman not married to each other. The second-generation women who danced with each other no doubt did so either out of deference to their parents' attitude or because they themselves had absorbed it.

Traditional food was in plentiful supply at the wedding feasts. Sometimes it was served at a sitdown affair. More often we ate buffet style. The log jams at the buffet tables led us to call these events "football weddings." It took the driving, pushing, and weaving skills of a running back to get to the table piled high with food trays.

Each table had a liberal supply of party favors. These always contained white sugar-coated almonds, the traditional Old World symbol of fertility. They were one of my favorite candies. Together with other young children I used to fill my pockets with as large a hoard as I could. Because candy was a rare treat in the Mezzogiorno, the older immigrants were very indulgent of our insatiable appetite for sweets. Unlike the second-generation adults who would admonish us about stomach-aches and ruining our teeth, the immigrants smilingly sneaked candied almonds into our hands when no one was looking, with a wink and an Italian blessing.

During the course of the evening, each guest would go to the table where bride and groom sat and present their best wishes and a gift. Although some second-generation people gave objects—toasters and the like—most joined the older generation in the traditional custom of giving cash. This was handed to the groom in a sealed white envelope. He in turn handed it to his bride, who put it in a special purse she carried for the purpose. The ritual symbolized the husband's role as provider of his family's budget and the wife's role as its custodian and manager. Each envelope would contain a card or other written message which would afterward be shared with the couple's parents in recognition that it represented a tribute to the families as much as to the bridal couple.

It is difficult to guess at details of intimacies between husband and wife in the Mezzogiorno. The contadini did not write of their lives, and certainly not of their private sex lives. They were loath to discuss these details with anyone except on occasions with a close relative, compare or commare.

On the other hand we know the codes that prevailed in public. Public displays of conjugal affection were not common. Among mature people such behavior would have indicated that the ideals of masculine maturity and feminine serietà had not yet controlled youthful passions as they should. A married person did not talk to a peer of the opposite sex who was not his or her blood relative except in the presence of a spouse. Adultery was taboo. The prohibition was strictly enforced for both sexes. An offense was considered to injure the entire family of the aggrieved spouse, a sanction that required great discretion when infidelity occurred. Because such behavior was viewed as an insult to his wife and her family, which could provoke their hostility and even a vendetta, such stepping out even by a husband in an unhappy marriage was done as inconspicuously as possible. There were no equivalents of whores and bordellos for women, and married women who desired extramarital activity needed to take a lover, something social circumstances made very difficult unless her husband was so estranged from her as to be quiescent. Homes were filled with numerous members of la famiglia, so trysts that did occur often took place in the fields. Raymond De Capite set such a scene in *The Coming of Fabrizze*. Augustine has returned to his village from eight years in America and makes a pass at his neighbor's wife.

Augustine sipped the hot black winy coffee. Presently he was reaching over to pinch her cheek and chin and thigh.

"You mustn't, Augustine, you mustn't."

"I was a fool," said Augustine. "I thought the mountains shut the world out. Now I see they may shut a world in."

"Augustine!"

"A little fun," said Augustine.

"It isn't right."

"A little play," said Augustine.

"But we're getting beyond that age."

"Where do you get this information?" said Augustine.

"Come down the mountain later. I'll be hiding in the forest. Hunt me down, my dear . . ."

Whatever the sexual satisfactions or dissatisfactions of a married couple, they were expected always to support each other in public. Ideally the loyalty was sincere and not merely *pro forma*. De Capite's novel presents us with such a relationship, between Fabrizze and his wife Grace. Struggling with financial difficulties, Fabrizze expresses the hope that the economy will improve. To which Grace adds the encouragement, "The strength is in you, and not there." It is in this context that we should understand the legendary contadino jealousy inherited by Italian-Americans. Tremendous loyalties were invested in all family relations and *comparatico* friendships. Betrayals provoked wrath and violent emotions generally. Because sex was the aspect which made marriage (or engagement) distinct from other binding relationships, betrayal of sexual loyalty was one of a number of hurts which could provoke extreme feelings and behavior. The fact is a contadino could be provoked to fight by a betrayal of close friendship or blood kinship as well as by sexual jealousy. Thus, the legend that attributes the start of the violent Sicilian Vespers uprising in 1282 to a French officer's offending a Sicilian girl in the presence of her male relatives, carries overtones of political and other values as well as sexual jealousy in the Mezzogiorno. And the fact that to this day the brash flirting characteristic of Rome (or New York, Atlanta, or Los Angeles) is rare in the Mezzogiorno points to social authority which transcends mere psychological jealousy.

This tempers but does not deny the one-dimensional protectiveness of contadino men toward their women. Male-female jealousies normal to most civilizations were heightened in the Mezzogiorno by the already discussed female role as the center of society as well as the provider of warm life-sustaining care. The Meridionale's exaltation of females has been scored as a male chauvinist residue of medieval times. The ancient chivalry introduced into the Mezzogiorno took hold, no doubt because it nourished l'ordine della famiglia. There are signs of this everywhere in the Mezzogiorno, where one can still see chivalric plays, hear courtly stories, and see paintings similar to those so popular in the homes of those who migrated to America. But it is also true that the appropriated chivalric code was fleshed out by the socially functional ways of contadino life. It was not honored in any shallow sense, either romantic or sexist. Only the moral dogmatist, the absolutist with no sense of moral evolution, cultural nuances or their survival value, can judge a past age by recently evolved standards.

Second-generation couples sought to fulfill the ideal of mutual loyalty they inherited. Studies of their marriages are lacking. We do not know how many people of this generation consider themselves happily married or the contrary. We do not have data on separation and divorce among them. We do not know how many of this generation have availed themselves of these escapes from bad marriages impossible in their parents' milieu. As is the case with every aspect of Italian-American life today, scholarly attention is needed. At present, we have only personal impressions. These indicate that the rate of divorce is lower among second-generation Italian-Americans than among their peers in general. Whether this indicates their marriages are more successful remains a moot question.

The American way of marriage fitted the social and economic needs of a rapidly expanding industrial society. The isolated nuclear family that resulted by wrenching the marriage choice away from the extended family and giving it play within the romantic myth also served the same needs. Unlike the Mezzogiorno family, the American nuclear family bound one to fewer people and released one's time and energy for labor and other responsibilities characteristic of industrial civilization. The American family was more flexible and mobile. It could change location and even its style to meet the demands of the job market much more readily than could the old clan.

The flexibility and mobility of the American family have since become so extreme that the viability of marriage is today greatly in question. But the years from 1900 to 1950 were its heyday. All the organs of American society propagandized and legitimized its superiority. The second-generation Italian-American found great encouragement to cast aside the Italian marriage scheme. In the end these people stayed afloat in the new American wave and also clung to the old Italian rock against which it beat. The second generation formed nuclear families that nevertheless sought continued contact with the extended clan. Conflicts between authorities of two cultures in this compromise demanded constant energy-consuming accommodation. The second generation also maintained in the new framework the male and female attitudes and roles engrained in the old famiglia. To some these seemed curious and arbitrary apart from their roots. They were honored more because of the old way's strong but nebulous hold over the emotions rather than any clearly understood sense of function. The tradition was maintained without its reasons for being, leaving the second generation's energies typically vitiated and its relations with the rest of American society typically reactive, aloof, and deferential.

The quiet second-generation conflict was acutely felt in the early years of its marriages. In these years the tension between the pragmatic functions of marriage inherited from the Italian tradition and the romantic expectations of marriage absorbed from American culture was pronounced. The old marital reasons for being—economic division of labor, reproduction and perpetuation of the family —contrasted with the emotional promises of romantic love. The joys and sorrows, strengths and weaknesses of each cultural influence spun out marital life that was demanding and absorbing. Heady passions overthrew traditional forms only to be once again stabilized by satisfactions of old ways in a ceaseless cycle. Insofar as it locked into its own motion, the cycle of cultural tensions held marriages together in a balance of forces. The dynamism of the forces shaped the happiness and unhappiness of married couples. In the fulfillment of marriages, the balance leaned more toward happiness for some, more toward pain for others. For most, marriage was bittersweet.

The dizzying pull and counterpull of two cultural traditions for years consumed most of the time and energy within second-generation marriages. The result finally was middle-aged people relieved of the conflict more by age than by purposeful resolution. The second generation gained marital peace by the grace of maturity which leads one to accept what cannot be reconciled. The peace is now disturbed anew at second hand as the second generation concerns itself with the sexual behavior and marriages of its youthful third-generation children.

The newest generation is not cognizant of the cultural definition of their parents' life style and wishes. Nor can its members remember the poignancy of their parents' struggle with emotions and cultural ties. In its comparative immaturity and self-preoccupation, it cannot appreciate its parents' marital successes or savor the emotional rewards gained in their adventure. The third generation sees its parent generation only as hopelessly out of step with the times (except for the part of the second-generation compromise which is visibly American and modern). It views its parents' advice, counsel, and guidance as well intentioned (their love is self-evident) but also as irrelevant to their needs and concerns. Tossed about on the seas of a much heralded American sexual revolution, single young people are awash in confused trouble. The old-fashioned values offered by their parents are not serviceable handholds. Adolescent turmoil and the problems of young adulthood are faced without benefit of older experience and perspective. Chances of successfully meeting these crises are reduced for young Italian-Americans. They enter marriage often directionless or with merely vague, unconnected orientations.

Drawing upon an earlier essay by Paul J. Campisi, Lydio F. Tomasi in a monograph entitled *The Italian-American Family* (1972) schematized the movement of some key values through three generations of Italian-Americans. If we use part of this scheme, alter it, and add to it, we can chart points of this chapter.

Characteristics of Contadino Life	Characteristics of Second Generation	Characteristics of Third Generation
1. Mutually dependent but sharply defined male and female roles.	1. Old sex roles maintained but their roots obscured.	1. Questioning of traditional sex roles which are seen as groundless.
2. No public display of conjugal affection.	2. Cautious, self-conscious public display of conjugal affection.	2. Confusion about public behavior, torn between self-consciousness and superficial adoption of American teenage bravado.
3. Selection of mate by parents.	3. Selection of mate by individual with parental consent.	3. Selection of mate by individual often without parental consent.
4. Marriage of someone from same class and village.	4. Most marriage within same ethnic group and class.	4. Discarding ethnicity and class as conscious marriage choice criteria.
5. No birth control.	5. Birth control, often introduced years after wedding.	5. Birth control used from beginning of marriage.
6. Sex matters discussed in family within traditional terms.	6. Sex not discussed in family.	6. Sex increasingly discussed in family, but to futile cross-purposes.
7. No divorce.	7. Divorce limited in practice.	7. Divorce openly accepted.
8. Desertion of spouse rare.	8. Desertion of spouse rare.	8. Desertion of spouse rare.
9. La via vecchia intact.	9. Life styles in conflict; sexual values intact.	9. Family intact; life style and sexual values confused.

10. Premarital sex and adultery absolutely forbidden.	10. Premarital sex greatly restricted; adultery a severe taboo.	10. External restrictions on premarital sex weakened but internal inhibitions strong. Adultery seen as wrong but sometimes excusable.

Young Italian-Americans urgently need to integrate their thoughts, feelings, and behavior. By putting themselves in touch with their cultural history, they can compose their sexual identities. Secure upon this basis, they would then be much more competent to make conscious, sound responses to options of sexual values, marriage choices, and marriage styles.

Religion, Magic, and the Church

My parents were married in 1936 in one of Brooklyn's more historic Roman Catholic churches. The Church of the Sacred Hearts of Jesus and Mary was in the midst of South Brooklyn's Italian community on Hicks Street. The old church has since been torn down and its mission of saying Masses in Italian was taken over by St. Stephen's.

Following Catholic custom, all who were to participate in my parents' ceremony made confession in the church during the week before the scheduled wedding. Of course this included my father, who was then thirty years old. Typical of males of contadino origin, my father had been an infrequent churchgoer, attending Mass only on major holidays like Christmas and on those traditional occasions when family loyalty made presence compulsory—weddings and funerals. This conduct meant that my father had neglected the most solemn of obligations the Church requires of Catholics, that of making regular confessions. In fact he had not been to a confessional for years. When he confided this to a priest it triggered a paroxysm. I remember my father telling me of the priest's reaction heard through the screen of the confession booth. First he gasped and sputtered, trying to find his voice. Then he shouted imprecations in hysterical tones that bounced around the walls of the tranquil church. My father asked the man to calm himself, a request the excited priest probably didn't even hear, let alone heed. My father then did the only thing to do in the tradition when faced with such uncontrolled behavior. He sighed, got up, and calmly walked out of the church. However, my father and the parish clergy were soon reconciled—no doubt through the mediation of his family—and the wedding took place as planned.

The pattern was an old one. For centuries the Church has had to accommodate itself to the Meridionale's attitude toward religion. Years later, at my father's funeral, a young well-meaning priest pleaded almost in desperation the necessity of good Catholics to participate in the Church according to *its* rules. As far as I know none of the Italian-Americans present then, virtually all of whom consider themselves to be Catholic, have changed their attitudes or behavior because of the sermon. By the lights of their tradition, they are religious. The stubborn persistence of this attitude in 1971 prompted Father Andrew M. Greeley to write in his study of America's ethnic groups, *Why Can't They Be Like Us?*, that "the Irish Catholic would be well advised not to hold his breath before the Italians become as religiously somber as the Irish even if they are going to parochial schools in increasing numbers."

Italian-American religious attitudes are unique. They are rooted in a fantastic amalgam of pagan customs, magical beliefs, Mohammedan practices, Christian doctrines, and, most of all, contadino pragmatism. And the old religious attitudes have evolved in a distinct way in the United States because of the Italian experience here, especially the experience with the American Church, that is to say, the Irish-American Church. Whoever thinks he understands Italian-American religion because he knows American Catholicism, or Catholicism in Rome, is deluding himself.

The special isolating conditions of the Mezzogiorno preserved old customs intact until the period of mass immigration to the United States. In fact, many of the beliefs are still held in many parts of the old country today. Life was precarious to the contadini. Evils abounded. What is more, disasters struck without warning, felling the young and the old, the innocent and the corrupt. The dynamics of natural troubles like diseases, droughts, and earthquakes were not understood. More significantly the religious or philosophical question of why they and worse man-made evils happened, why evil and undeserved suffering afflict people, is a dilemma as old as humanity. It weighed heavily upon the Meridionali. Our knowledge gained from modern sciences and disciplines has not provided any satisfactory answers to these religious imponderables.

The workings of nature and the benefits and calamities caused by them were attributed variously to saints who resembled pagan gods, to witches, ghosts, and demons, to the Christian God, to Satan, and to any and all possible combinations, alliances, oppositions and juntas of these. The sum total of all these agents was given one generic name, a practice that disturbs our sense of reason, which would have the irrational be organized as reasonably as possible. Any occult agent or collection of agents or their powers was known as *il mal occhio*, the evil eye, also called *occhio cattivo* (bad eye), *occhio morto* (eye of death), and *occhio tristo* (wicked eye). The term "evil eye" has its roots in ancient Greece, whose inhabitants introduced it into Southern Italy with their colonies. (Today's tourists to Greece often return with a jeweled representation of an eye on a charm bracelet or key chain.)

In ancient times people did not make strict distinctions between animate and inanimate things, or between symbols and their referents. Among the many animistic ideas widely believed in Greece was that springs and pools of water were the eyes of powerful subterranean forces or monsters. The Greek term for this many-eyed power was *drakon*, from which we get the English word "dragon" and the Italian *drago*. The Greek origin of the Mezzogiorno belief in the evil eye is indicated by the fact that to this day in some parts of Southern Italy the openings of springs and the pools of water that surround them are commonly called *occhi*, eyes.

Thus the ancient ancestors of the contadini attempted to make sense of a senseless and dangerous world. Events were caused by forces and powers which were in turn controlled by agents. One had to find which agent was behind a certain force and then to marshal a counterforce by soliciting a more powerful agent in opposition to it.

At first the agents were the pagan gods of Greece and Rome. In the Mezzogiorno of my grandfather it was widely thought that anyone born in January was immune from the spells of the evil eye, spells called *iettature*. This confidence has been attributed to the fact that the month of January was named in honor of one of the major Roman gods, Janus. His over-all role was no less than to guard the universe, and his particular responsibility was to guard all gates and doors, especially those of sacred temples. Thus, he was depicted as having two faces back to back, as having eyes in the back of his head. Small wonder that people born under his protection were believed to be invulnerable to the insidious ways of il mal occhio.

With the coming of Christianity, many of the pagan customs were joined to those of the new religion. This cumulative process continued for centuries, eventually also incorporating many ideas from the various Christian and Moslem sects that later influenced the area. At the same time the working religion of the people developed magical and demonic strains to complicate further the rich mixture of beliefs and practices.

The old pagan polytheism became Christianized as a whole panoply of saints was pressed into service to fulfill the functions of the gods they supplanted. As was true of the ancient gods, each saint was seen as having domain over a specific area of life and often to be in competition or rivalry not only with other saints but with Satan and other demons, with witches, and even on occasion with God. Thus the worship and appeasement of saints became a complicated affair.

Santa Lucia was among other things the protector of eyesight, a role that led to her often being pictured holding a platter of disembodied human eyes. The pictures sent chills up my spine when I was a child. Sant' Anna was the special guardian of pregnant women and of the babies they carried. Statues and pictures of her in the homes and churches of my neighborhood were heavily surrounded by

lighted candles and other votive offerings placed there by
expectant women and their relatives. Representations of
other saints were similarly adorned. Santa Lucia had small
replicas of eyes placed at her feet as tokens of supplication
by sufferers of eye ailments and as tokens of gratitude by
those cured from such afflictions. Santa Bologna was the
protector of healthy teeth, and statues of her were appropriately outfitted. San Antonio was the patron saint of animals, a very important position in the contadino farm society of the Mezzogiorno but one which declined as those
who crossed the sea became urban workers.

No human activity or possible harm went uncovered.
San Vito protected against the bites of animals, especially
rabid dogs, and Santa Barbara shielded her supplicants
against the devastations of lightning. Even gamblers had
their patron saint: San Pantaleone. In addition, each region, town, family, and even individual had special saints,
a custom which dated back to the Roman household gods,
or lares. Each saint had his day in the calendar on which
he was to be specially celebrated, worshiped, or placated.
For example, Neapolitans thought that the husband of a
pregnant woman risked harm to his wife and unborn child
if he worked on St. Aniello's day.

The influence on the Mezzogiorno of Moslem beliefs has
been obscured over the centuries, particularly because of
intensive efforts by crusading Christians to wipe out hated
Moslem influences. Nevertheless some are clearly traceable.
Even today people in the more isolated regions of Sicily
bury their dead without shoes and place food in the coffins.
These practices follow the Moslem custom of shedding
one's shoes when entering into the presence of Allah and
of Moslem belief in an afterlife in which such bodily pleasures as eating await the faithful. Statues of saints and Madonnas with black skin are found throughout the Mezzogiorno as remnants of Arab influence. The influence is also
reflected by the dialects of the South, which commonly substitute the Arabic *u* sound for vowels and sometimes for
whole syllables. Thus, the traditional Sicilian says *figghiu*
for *figlio* (son) and the title of a famous Neapolitan song

is rendered "*'Nu Surdatu 'Nnammuratu*" instead of "*'O Surdato 'Nnammorato*" (A Soldier in Love). The *u* sound also dates from the period before the Arab influence in the Mezzogiorno in the ninth, tenth, and eleventh centuries. As Robert Di Pietro and George Dimietri Selim discuss in "The Language Situation in Arab Sicily" (*Linguistic Studies in Memory of Richard S. Harrell*, D. G. Stuart, ed., Georgetown University Press, 1967), Greek and a Latin-based vernacular were spoken prior to the Arab period. The Latin vernacular also stressed the *u* sound and, greatly affected by Greek and Arabic, evolved into the modern dialects of the Mezzogiorno.

The contadino folklore of magic and witchcraft is vast and also has its oldest roots in pagan Greece and Rome. Numerical symbols, some simple, others elaborate, were painted on or carved into doors, walls, carts, bells, shepherds' staves, tools, and weapons. This was done in the belief that certain numbers (especially odd numbers), numerical combinations, and geometric forms had magical significance. The credence in numbers magic is traceable to ancient cults, the most famous of which was the Pythagoreans, a secret society of ancient Greeks who lived in Southern Italy and whose members developed an elaborate system of arithmetic magic and mathematical formulas. The latter included the Pythagorean theorem of triangles studied in high school geometry classes.

The ancients were aware of the remarkable usefulness of mathematics when applied to many practical problems, no doubt nurturing the belief in the magic of numbers among the ancestors of the contadini. For example, when in the year 214 B.C. a Roman army laid siege to Syracuse, the Greek city in Sicily, the Greek and native Sicilian inhabitants resisted for three years, thanks largely to the scholar Archimedes, who applied his knowledge of mathematics to design defense positions and engines of war. These included well-engineered catapults whose deadly accuracy splintered the siege turrets, scaling platforms and quinqueremes (warships with five rowers per bench) of the Romans. There was indeed magic in numbers. But it was limited, and when the Romans finally captured the city they killed the seventy-five-year-old Archimedes. (According to legend a Roman soldier found Archimedes in his study bent over a sandbox, which was used as a writing apparatus, working out mathematical problems. The great mathematician brushed the intruder aside with a wave of his hand, whereupon the infuriated soldier turned his sword upon the old man and killed him.) Knowledge, magic, and all other human powers are wonderful but definitely limited, a lesson which the Meridionale never forgot.

Belief in the magical attributes of numbers was linked to other superstitions, and these continue to be important in the very popular *lotto*, the numbers lottery which is now four hundred years old in Italy. Although the lottery was played throughout the South, it has always been most popular in Naples, where a study by the Italian government in 1972 showed that virtually everyone there plays. Thus when the contadini of other parts of the Mezzogiorno would dream about a priest in his church they interpreted it as an omen of good luck to them. But to Neapolitans it also indicated that the good luck should be employed by playing certain odd numbers. A dream of a priest in one's home meant bad luck, an obvious connotation in a land when priests enter homes mostly at times of family troubles such as severe illness. Neapolitans, however, tried to press even this portent into service by playing in the lotto unlucky even numbers. All bets, whether on good-luck or bad-luck numbers, were buttressed by pleas to relevant saints, especially to San Pantaleone.

Common items in the Mezzogiorno were decorated also with serpents, following both ancient pagan and medieval Christian uses of serpents as magical symbols. The ancient symbol of Sicily is the Trinacria (which was also an ancient name of the island) and today is still found in that land almost as commonly as the cross. It is a perfect representation of the themes mentioned so far. It is formed by the winged head of a pagan god or goddess at the center of three human legs (representing the three geographical points of the island, which is roughly shaped like a triangle) running at directions quasi-perpendicular to each other and entwined in the coils of two serpents.

The powers of the occult were not limited to the saints. In fact certain humans were believed to have immediate and potent access to magical powers. These were the *maghi* and *maghe* (male and female witches), people who were believed to be granted various degrees of black magic power by birth. A man or woman with more limited powers was often called *un' uomo* (*una donna*) *di fuori,* a different man or woman, literally a man or woman "outside." A powerful sorcerer was called *mago, stregone,* and even *lupo mannaro* (literally a werewolf). These extraordinary people were thought to possess or influence the evil eye. They had the power to cast spells, cause or cure ailments, change events by using their own force (even their gaze was thought to be potent), or more effectively by summoning the force of saints and especially of spirits of the dead and of demons. The contadini who believe in them cultivated their friendship. In any case it was imperative not to incur their enmity.

But normal people also could learn to protect themselves from the evil eye by employing magical symbols and by learning the incantations and rituals of the maghi and maghe. A rich store of protective devices and practices was part of the personal equipment of even the most ordinary person. Amulets were worn. These were often miniature representations of natural or man-made weapons to fight off the evil eye. Teeth, claws, and, most commonly, replicas of animal horns were worn on necklaces or bracelets, held in pockets or, safest of all, sewn into one's clothing. The little red horns (*cornicelli*) can still be purchased in America's Little Italies as good-luck charms.

As was common practice, the entrance to my grandparents' home was adorned with a protective device. Over the door hung a pair of real bull's horns, painted bright red as a warning to all malignant forces that might threaten, whether human, natural, or supernatural. I remember my grandparents taking special note of the fact that in the cowboy movies they saw on television the

ranch homes often had steer horns ornamenting a wall or
fireplace. They once asked me why it was that cowboys attended to the evil eye when other Americani did not.

My fellows at P.S. 142 had a typical assortment of pagan
and Christian amulets hanging side by side or in little sacks
from necklaces worn under their clothing or attached to
their undershirts with safety pins. In addition to those already mentioned, I saw pictures of saints, little fish (the
ancient Christian symbol for Christ), and tiny scissors
and daggers to cut or impale powers of evil. My grandmother was uneasy about the lightness of the protection
I enjoyed as a small child. It came from a gold crucifix I
wore on a chain under my shirt—the only amulet my
mother would use. At times when I was ill, my grandmother placed little sacks next to the crucifix and replaced
them almost as soon as my mother removed them. The
sacks were sewn tightly closed, and to this day I don't know
what they contained except that I could tell from feeling
them that their contents included paper and solid objects.
In the generation preceding mine some Italian-American
children were sent to school wearing toothlike cloves of
garlic under their garments. I leave the reactions of their
teachers to the reader's imagination.

Typical of contadini, my grandmother believed in as
much protection from the evil eye as possible. The red
horns over her door were supplemented by an array of
pictures and statues of Madonnas and saints liberally distributed throughout her home. In fact each room had what
was in effect a little shrine set up around a favorite picture
which was lit by religious candles and adorned with the
dried palms from Masses of the last several Easters. One of
the pictures particularly fascinated me. It was a large print
framed in glass of a full-length Madonna. She wore a long
flowing garment from her head down to the ground. The
garment was composed of hundreds of small items each
of which was depicted in detail. I remember often staring
at the huge picture on the wall, transfixed by the variety
of things that formed the Lady's clothing. There were different types of fish. Because they hung by their mouths my

guess is that they represented votive offerings of fishermen rather than symbols of Christ. Eyes and small human limbs hung side by side with different species of animals and birds and whole human figures, some of whom appeared to be saints while others looked like ordinary humans of all ages. The sheer volume and variety of objects and their explicitness overwhelmed me. This was no remote religious figure of abstract meaning. She was a superhuman individual who easily wore this world as her personal property. To the pragmatic contadini, God, the Holy Family, and the saints were personal, worldly powers in direct everyday intercourse with them.

The religion of the contadini was above all pragmatic, if by that word we refer to its classic uncorrupted meaning, going back to the Greek *pragmatikos,* something accomplished, something that works. In modern times the American philosopher Charles Sanders Peirce reformulated the ancient meaning. In what has become known as his "pragmatic maxim" Peirce said that we know what is real from the effects real things produce. "Reality," he wrote, "like every other quality, consists in the peculiar, sensible effects which things taking of it produce. The only effect which real things have is to cause belief . . ." From the ancient view and perhaps also from Peirce's restatement, it is easily concluded that we believe something to be real because we are impressed with the effects it produces, and then to the notion that something is real if our belief in it produces discernible effects. To put it crudely, if a belief works, then it is valid and its object is true. If a belief doesn't work, it is invalid and its object untrue, or at least not important. These attitudes sum up the contadino view of religion. Anything and everything was tried until the desired results were obtained. Niceties of Catholic orthodoxy and enlightened learning were employed together with pagan and satanic practices, and the lessons of common sense and science were freely mingled with those of magic and superstition.

I have had pneumonia three times, the first bout occurring when I was a young boy. A doctor was called to treat me. My grandmother of course approved. She believed in modern medicine, having seen that it frequently worked. But she also believed in the saints and Jesus and addressed prayers to them promising to do specific things to honor and please them if I were to regain health. After all she had also seen such prayers answered. In the contadino mind there was no contradiction in adding magic to science and religion. My grandmother called in one of our neighbors, a woman of her generation, to perform a cupping on me. This was just one of the myriad practices of the Mezzogiorno to exorcise malevolent spirits from the body. An empty cuplike receptacle was turned upside down and a match lighted within it, the match held in place by a homemade device. The inverted cup with its burning match was placed on the afflicted part of the person's body—in my case several cups were put on my back. As the flame consumed the oxygen in the cup the pressure in it would be reduced, creating a suction which would pull the patient's flesh into the cup. The point was to have the cup draw the sickness out of the body. I will never forget the burning hot sucking sensations on my back and the faces of the old people who watched, expecting these to draw the pneumonia out of my lungs. This could have been in the Europe of the Middle Ages. In fact it happened in New York City in the late 1940's, probably without my parents' knowledge.

As a matter of common practice contadino men would leave a few drops in their wineglasses to throw onto the bare ground, returning the produce of the earth to the earth as a gesture of thanks. All life-sustaining things of the earth were always given special respect. But particular plants or crops were thought to have special magical attributes. A crown of lemon leaves was thought to be a cure for headaches. Salt was sprinkled under and around the bed of a newly married couple to make them fertile. Grain sprouts, in some parts of the Mezzogiorno especially those grown in the dark or in the consecrated ground of a churchyard or crypt, were thought to be protection against Satan and the forces of chaos. Such sprouts were often put into coffins to protect the souls of the dead.

Just as the contadini had a pragmatic approach in the choosing of witches and saints, doctors and priests, so they selected and used whichever spells, incantations, and magic potions seemed likely to work. As a result the variety of these devices and rituals was innumerable and stregoni and gente di fuori were believed capable of inventing new ones. In *The Coming of Fabrizze,* the novel by Raymond De Capite set among the Italian community of Cleveland in the 1920's, one of the characters, Vivolo, pokes gentle fun at the credulity of his neighbor Cardino. Cardino and his wife desire to have children and the husband asks Vivolo if there is any magic ritual that will make his wife conceive:

"Listen then," said Vivolo. "It will take three days and two nights. She mustn't work during that time. Every six hours a hot bath. And then she rests. She saves herself. A bit of music."

"Music, music," said Cardino. "This is good."

"A glass or two of red wine," said Vivolo.

"Red wine!"

"It's the end of the third day," said Vivolo. "She'll take a glass of hot wine. A spoonful of sugar for the blood. She'll take another glass. And then another. And then another."

"Four glasses?"

"Or more," said Vivolo.

"And then? But don't I know? Bravo, Cardino!"

"Why are you squeezing my leg?" said Vivolo.

"Tell the rest, tell the rest."

"Send for me," said Vivolo. "Send for me."

The spells of the evil eye were deflected or broken by ritualistic precautions and countermeasures. For example, a woman with child would not look upon ugly or mutilated creatures for fear that the deformity would enter the mother's body through her eyes and impress itself on the fetus. I am told that my grandmother was furious when she learned that my mother had gone to see a horror movie while pregnant with me. When I was born, my grandmother inspected me closely to make certain that I was a normal baby. Only then was she assured that the movie had had no effect. I am sure she attributed the fortune to preventive measures she must have taken.

Precautionary measures were employed in any situation in which it was even remotely possible that il mal occhio was present. Touching iron, a product of the earth, afforded immediate invulnerability, as did spitting through one's fingers and then pointing the sign of the horns (the index finger and little finger extended) at the ground. Such practices were commonly done three times in rapid order, the number three being especially powerful in both pagan and Christian folklore. At birth, babies were given an immediate protective baptism by midwives, a vigilance that was often accompanied by the use of amulets, potions, and incantations involving demonic words and/or nonsense syllables. In a custom that is still followed infants were kissed only on the feet, never on the face or head, to avoid raising a suspicion in the parents that the admiring adult was attempting to cast a spell on the child by means of a Judas kiss.

Mere accidents of birth were thought to have special significance. A child born in his father's old age was thought to be blessed and destined for a fortunate life. Hunchbacks were thought to have magical powers. In a bow to chivalry, the powers of a female hunchback were thought to be benevolent, while those of her male counterpart were regarded as malevolent. The presence of the females was sought, except by pregnant women, and that of the males avoided, except by those calculating to solicit their occult services against their foes.

In a custom probably originating in an all too human thirst for justice, it was believed that a person who was morally offended thereby attained extraordinary power, particularly to cast a *maledizione*, or curse, on those responsible for the ill treatment. It was common practice for enemies to hurl curses at each other and for each to take preventive measures against the maledictions of the other.

Because of their innocence, children were thought to be especially vulnerable to the ever present mal occhio. They were given maximum protection in the form of incantations, chants, amulets, etc. The protection, at first total, was gradually peeled off as the child learned to protect himself. This last metaphor is meant literally in regard to infants. Babies were swaddled from head to toes during the first year of life. The layers upon layers of swaddling cloth strips (fasce) not only held amulets but were popularly regarded as amulets in themselves. The fasce were removed only for brief periods of time and under guarded conditions, conditions which included the presence of a protective maga or stregone if there was any suspicion that anyone or anything was attempting to enchant the infant.

Most women were regarded to be under a mild curse during their menstrual periods and were generally exempted, if not forbidden, from handling food or touching infants. Yet other women, especially those who felt a heightened sense of well-being and enjoyed increased energy during their periods, were thought to have extraordinary power for good and were well entertained by others. In this regard the contadino inclination to link a person's inner feelings and moods with whatever the individual produced served a sensible function. It shifted social burdens from women who were at low points in their capacity to cope with them and onto those at their peak capacity.

In the family-centered Mezzogiorno one of the most desired occult experiences was to communicate with the souls of dead beloved relatives who had led long and happy lives. And one of the most dreaded fates was to confront the souls of the aggrieved dead. Strangely enough these included one's enemies only if a person was guilty about his behavior toward them. Guilt was an essential element in the contadino morality and did not end at the frontier of death. Generally it was thought that the souls of the contented dead did not often walk the earth. They appeared only occasionally to their surviving kin, usually in dreams or less frequently through the medium of a sorcerer, to offer advice and support during periods of stress in the lives of the living. Only the restless spirits of the aggrieved dead stalked the earth to torment the living, and contadini swore that these could be heard at daybreak wailing and

shrieking their protests at having to return to their discon-
solate graves.

Accordingly, the most fearful night of the year for the
contadini was that of All Souls' Day, or, as it was popularly
called, *la Notte dei Morti*, the Night of the Dead. Many
families spent the night uttering prayers and incantations
and performing a mixture of sacred and sacrilegious rites
to keep away from their doors the souls of those dead intent on doing harm. Hapless shepherds whose occupation
kept them in the fields during this dreaded night used to
send word of their survival to their families at daybreak,
often along with promises to relate the unspeakable sights
they had seen in the night's gloom. The visions and dreams
experienced during la Notte dei Morti were thought to
have critical importance as omens and portents and thus
were scrupulously analyzed and interpreted.

The most pathetic of the restless spirits were the souls of
unbaptized infants, whom the contadini believed were
doomed to a worldly limbo, condemned to walk the earth
forever. These poor souls were mischievous rather than
truly evil, and were regarded more with pity than with
fright. The Holy Ghost was invoked more to console these
shadows than to repress them.

To the contadini the Holy Ghost or Spirit meant more
than the third figure of the Christian Trinity. The term
Spirito Santo, in dialect Spiritu Santu, was used as a generic one to cover all those forces which could oppose, cancel, or abate the forces of il mal occhio. In the contadino
mind the world was divided into two large groups of opposed powers akin to the ancient Manichaean division between the Kingdom of Light and the Kingdom of
Darkness. All human emotions and intents, and all natural
and supernatural forces and events, that served to benefit
a person and his kin belonged to the first kingdom. All of
the passions, motives, events, and powers which endangered la famiglia belonged to the second. The war between
the two, between good and evil, was regarded as always
present and unending—without even so much as a truce.
In a world of spite, greed, envy, malice, and undeserved

suffering only a fool would relax his vigilance and thereby expose all he loved to the hateful winds that blow through the human estate. More than two thousand years of experience taught the Meridionale that whatever powers of evil operate here on earth are close if not equal in power to those of the Creator. Until very recently modern Catholics saw this as one of the quasi-heretical conclusions that made enlightened elements in the Church wince in their confrontations with the Southern Italian mind. Then on November 15, 1972, Pope Paul VI gave an address which startled not only progressives within the Church but also good neo-Scholastics whose point of view for centuries had put evil not as a positive force but as a "privation," i.e., as merely the absence of good. In his speech the Pope repudiated this view and echoed the ancient description of the universe held by the contadini of his native Italy. He said that evil is a real and active force. Specifically, he said it is composed of Satan and his entire kingdom of demons. The Pope ended his remarkable statement with a plea to theologians to take seriously this view of the spiritual universe.

During special times in the calendar, e.g., on special saints' days, virtually all stops were pulled out in magical-religious behavior in the Mezzogiorno. Frenzied dancing, chanting in trances, and wild processions were the rule, these rites sometimes lasting for days. The Italian novelist Corrado Alvaro (1895–1954) presented vivid images of his native Calabria in his writings. In his novel *Revolt in Aspromonte* (originally called in Italian *Gente in Aspromonte, People in Aspromonte*), Alvaro presented a scene of a religious procession in the Calabria of the first decade of our century, the period of the heaviest Italian immigration to the United States. It is seen through the eyes of Antonello, a shepherd boy whose character is probably based on Alvaro's own boyhood, and his father. He is spellbound by the procession of people shouting *"Viva Maria,"* firing guns, banging drums, playing bagpipes, and dancing wildly. The pilgrims are heedless of their appearance, and one girl uncaring about a wounded foot which is bleeding.

If the contadini were sometimes feverish in honoring saints and other spirits, they were also harsh in their treatment of spirits who had lost their respect. Statues and pictures of saints and even Madonnas who failed to fulfill their roles despite their being properly worshiped were humiliated and scourged. Only the figures of Jesus were above reproach. All others could be punished, and were. Statues and icons of saints were submitted to public ridicule. Some were bound in chains and others were spat upon or stoned in the piazza. Some were even imprisoned or left out in bad weather until events demonstrated that they had come around and were providing the services expected of them. Conversely, the representations of saints who performed well were privately and publicly rewarded. Rewards included not only votive offerings like prayers, candles, and flowers, money and food, but also love songs and other acts of public tribute and affection.

Norman Douglas spent most of his life studying the ways of the Mezzogiorno. In his *Old Calabria*, published in 1913, he recorded that after the catastrophic eruption of Vesuvius in 1906, many statues and icons of saints and Madonnas were given the ultimate punishment. They were thrown into ditches, literally discarded in favor of new patrons. During the volcanic eruption when a stream of white hot lava headed toward Naples, residents of the city placed statues of the city's patron, San Gennaro, directly in the path of the threatening flow, shouting to the saint, "Save our city or perish!" Giuseppe Pitre in 1913 wrote that when Sicily's patron saint of fishing, San Francesco di Paola, did not provide his hungry worshipers with a successful catch, the fishermen took a statue of him to the edge of the sea and intimidated him with the oath, *"Icca vi abbuddamu"* ("We will throw you in here!").

Mount Allegro (1942) is Jerre Mangione's delightful autobiographical account of his childhood in Rochester, New York, with his Sicilian parents and other relatives. He tells the story of an Italian immigrant who prayed to a statue of St. Anthony in a church to grant him luck in playing the numbers. After losing repeatedly, the man swore to smash the saint if his luck did not improve. Overhearing this, a priest hid the statue and put one of the infant Jesus in its place. When the luckless gambler returned the next day, he eyed the infant and said, "Hey, boy, where's your father?"

Some of the educated people in the Mezzogiorno of modern times sought to enlighten the contadini and thereby erase what was to them mere ignorance, superstition, error, or heresy. Unfortunately others who lived by the subjugation and oppression of the contadini exploited the fantastic elements of the contadino world view for their own ends. These included landowners, of course, but also many government bureaucrats, physicians, pharmacists, teachers, and other professionals. They also included some members of the clergy. For every progressive priest who sought to enlighten the people and improve their condition there were other priests, bishops, and cardinals who cynically manipulated the old beliefs to preserve the social status quo and the privileged position afforded to them and their churches in that scheme.

This brings us to an inescapable truth, the historic bitter animosity between the Church and the people of the Mezzogiorno, an antipathy which is far from resolved in today's relations between the Catholic Church in America and Italian-Americans. The ill-understood paradox is that, although a majority of Italian-Americans consider themselves to be true Catholics, to a large extent they retain the anticlerical views of their forefathers, stubborn individualism concerning doctrinal interpretation, and also intense distrust and scorn for the Church as an institution. This is not to mention the large proportion of Italian-Americans who have left the Church in favor of private religious postures or completely secular ones. One study leads to the conclusion that two-thirds of the Italian-Americans were either only nominal Catholics or had left the Church entirely.

In the Mezzogiorno the major force of the Church was for centuries allied with the exploitive landowning class. In fact the Church was itself the largest single landowner,

owning fabulous acreages of land until the government of
the newly unified nation of Italy forcibly confiscated them
in 1873. The clergy more often than not regarded its interests as identical with those of the propertied class. In
addition, many of the clergy, especially the upper hierarchy, actually were the scions of latifondo and galantuomo families. It was common practice for a landowning
family to send one or more of its sons into the priesthood.
This served two purposes. First, in the days when a father's
land went to his first son, it provided a living for the
younger sons. And with the growing practice of dividing
the lands among the sons of a family, sending one or more
into the priesthood saved the family estate from the disastrous consequences of being slivered with each new generation into ever tinier sections.

The class identification of the Church was the main
reason why the contadini supported the measures stripping
the Church of its lands during the national unification of
Italy. This pro-government attitude was soon changed when
the agents of the new government sold or virtually gave
the confiscated Church lands to the latifondisti. This betrayal merely caused hatred of the new government without lessening enmity toward the Church. Except for the
discarded landlord-tenant aspect, the relationship between
Church and contadini remained mostly the same after 1873
as it had been for generations. The relationship involved
compromise on both sides. The enlightened priesthood was
forced to compromise with the peculiar contadino magico-
religion because of the people's unshakable tenacity and
unchanging conditions in the land that time forgot. The
cynical priesthood, on the other hand, was all too eager to
compromise with contadino folklore and turn it to their
own advantage. On the one hand they exploited the powerlessness of the unschooled contadini and at the same time
hypocritically pointed to their superstitious way of life to
justify clerical resistance to all attempts to give more power
to the people, whom they portrayed as children needing
the paternalistic authority of the clergy and landowners.

The contadino side of the historic compromise was more

complicated. The heart of it was to regard the Church as any other worldly power, to deal with it as such, and to separate religious belief from attitudes toward the Church as much as possible without causing a complete break with the sacraments of the institution. In this way the institutional and doctrinal power of the Church over the family was minimized, leaving la famiglia and its ordine as always the supreme authorities of life.

It was politically and, as has been noted, economically advantageous for a contadino family in the Mezzogiorno to give one of its sons to the priesthood. As long as care had been taken that the chosen young man remained loyal to l'ordine della famiglia, his vocation not only provided him with a living but also provided his family with an ally in the powerful institution's camp. Protection by the Church's power and other advantages could flow to the blood relatives of the parish priest, or even better of a man who managed to climb to the higher ranks of the Church. The typical motivation for sending daughters into the sisterhood was predominantly to provide them with a secure living, especially those who could not be given a dowry or were otherwise unmarriageable. Also the giving of a daughter or son to the Church was a form of tribute, the giving of labor by which contadino families expected to place the local Church in a position to return a favor—remember that a prime maxim of life was as much as possible to place the rich and powerful in your family's debt.

Italian-Americans learned that it is not a financial or political asset to have children enter the religious orders of the American Church. In the American scheme these children could better serve the family and themselves by building economic and political roles in the secular world, the primary site of power in American society. As a result Italian-Americans, even relatively religious ones, have for some time regarded a clerical career for their relatives as wasteful. Rare among them indeed is the sense of joy in a son's or daughter's holy calling so common among their neighbors in the Church, the Irish-Americans. The announcement of a calling by a young person in an Italian-

American family is usually met with attempts to dissuade
the would-be priest or nun or by a silent, stony, grudging
acceptance of the choice of career.

Thus evidence of disproportionately low numbers of
Italian-American clergy comes as no surprise and under-
mines the American stereotype of Italian-Americans as Hibernianized Catholics. According to figures obtained from
the Office of the Italian Apostolate at the Archdiocese of
New York, as of January 1973 there were 58,161 American priests. Of these, six to seven thousand, or about 12
per cent, were Italian-Americans. Of 153,645 nuns, about
10,000 were Italian-Americans, about 7 per cent. Of 10,156
brothers, about 700 or 7 per cent were Italian-Americans.
These figures include clerics born in Italy, thus raising what
would have been an even smaller representation of Italian-
Americans if only the American born were counted.

The Italian-American religious stance was summed up
in a survey's conclusion of American Catholics reported on
page 68 of Father Greeley's book: "Italians are the least
pious of all Catholic groups." Greeley's study confirms the
consistent findings on Italian-Americans in the last six decades. It found that only 13 per cent of Italian-Americans
"scored high on piety," compared to 32 per cent of Irish,
31 per cent of German, 30 per cent of Polish, and 22 per
cent of French-Americans. Greeley also found that, while
46 per cent of Irish and 50 per cent of German-American
Catholics belong to at least one religious organization, only
22 per cent of Italian-Americans were affiliated with any
such organizations. Furthermore, only 30 per cent of
Italian-American Catholics considered church attendance
important, while 72 per cent of Irish-American and 56 per
cent of German-American Catholics consider it important.

To state it bluntly, the Old World contadini regarded
religious observances, churchgoing, and other sacred habits as *cose femminile*, women's things. In fact a certain
degree of sincere religious fervor was regarded as a desirable sign of the *serietà* of *una buona femmina*. But in light
of the ideal of manliness discussed previously, such fervor
in a man was regarded as softheadedness. In his *Father*, a

semiautobiographical novel set in a turn-of-the-century
Mezzogiorno village of Montefumo, the Italian-American
Charles Calitri has his father express the contadino attitude in an outburst at his wife who was chiefly responsible
for guiding their son into the priesthood.

> A devil! That is all! It is the devil which brings tears to my
> eyes because my son walks around this house in his black
> dress like a woman, and cannot find happiness. It is the devil
> which eats at my heart because I have allowed you to feed
> such a man to the black wolves. . . . It is a devil which puts
> fire in my mouth because there was the strongest body and the
> finest shot and the most brilliant brain in all of Montefumo;
> a piece of a man that should have fathered a hundred sons,
> each of whom would have been a giant like his grandfather.
> Instead, he is becoming a dried shell, losing weight and turn-
> ing gray, a face that was filled with the color of the sun! Oh,
> woman, what have you made me do?

From childhood, females were schooled in proper religious attitudes. These included prayer, regular church attendance, and, of course, learning the not so underground
occult beliefs and practices which were also left predominantly to women. The typical contadino male practiced
only the elementary precautions in the magical realm and
limited his Catholic observances to pro forma church
attendance and participation in the frequent Church-
sponsored processions and *feste* of the Mezzogiorno.

We need to be careful in interpreting this assignment of
the major part of the family's religious role to women. Current interpreters have stressed the motive of keeping the
women subjugated in a male-dominated society. I think
this is a gross distortion of the truth, based on the mistaken
stereotype of the Mezzogiorno family as a simple patriarchy. In the more accurate picture of the family as a careful
division of powers, a hybrid between patriarchy and matri-
archy, it is consistent that women should shoulder the major
religious concerns of the family. As the center of the family, the mother, assisted by zie, commare, and daughters,
was responsible for most core concerns, including the fam-

ily budget, education of children, everyday relations with other families—in short, everything that directly affected the internal welfare and morale of la famiglia. Those affairs where the family dealt with more remote powers, such as the economic structure, the state, and the Church as a worldly institution, were male responsibilities. Thus the division of duties regarding religion followed the over-all family pattern. The women attended to daily belief and practice, the men to political and economic relations with the institution. Or to use a medieval distinction, the women attended to the Church invisible, the spiritual force that is the Church beyond particularities of time and place. The men were responsible for relations with the Church visible, the Church as a political, economic, and societal entity here and now.

Visitors to the churches in the Mezzogiorno will find that the traditional pattern still holds. Daily Mass is attended regularly mostly by females, children, for whose religious instruction the women are responsible, and elderly men, who have retired from the male responsibilities to become auxiliaries to the female role and tenders of their own souls as death approaches. This arrangement was the rule in my childhood neighborhood. Males stopped even regular Sunday church attendance and cultivated a Realpolitik attitude toward the Church visible, beginning at puberty.

The traditional male and female religious roles have begun to change only among some of the more well-to-do suburban Italian-Americans. Specifically, this relatively small segment of the ethnic group has adopted some of the ways of the other Catholics in their class and their communities, including more regular church responsibilities for males. The most significant change in Italian-American behavior regarding the Church has been the substantially increased enrollment of their children in parochial schools and Catholic colleges, a change which will be explained later.

The continuing Italian-American aloofness from Catholicism cannot be explained by the experience of the Mezzogiorno alone. To this we need to add the history of the

Italian experience with the Church in the United States.

The masses of Italian immigrants presented themselves to an American Church that was overwhelmingly Irish and German in its membership and all but solidly Irish in its hierarchy. For all intents and purposes the American Church was an Irish-American Church. Almost everything about the beliefs and practices of the Italian immigrants puzzled, shocked, or scandalized the Irish, and the rift between the still Irish-dominated Church and Italian-American Catholics is very wide today.

Both the rationalistic, Thomist-oriented elite among the Irish and the Irish majority who followed their own unique religious folkways found the Italian practices at best superstitious and alien and at worst pagan and sacrilegious. The Irish regarded the religion of the new immigrants as hardly Catholicism, and many said so. The strong creedal orthodoxy, institutional loyalty, and pro clerical feelings of the Irish were jolted by the Italians' chaotic individualism about doctrinal matters, obvious anticlericalism and scorn for the "Mother Church," a popular Irish expression that was rare indeed among the contadini who suddenly confronted the churches of America's major cities. Perhaps above all, the Italians' pragmatic attitude toward the Church and all things sacred outraged the intense piety common to Irish Catholicism. To complete the picture, the everyday religious manners of the two ethnic groups differed, capping the more essential differences.

An Irish-American colleague of mine told me of his experience as a child as Italian-Americans moved into his Irish neighborhood and began to attend the local churches in the early 1950's. The story represents similar encounters over the years. My friend relates that the people of his ethnic group were aghast at the behavior of the newcomers. The old women touched, kissed, and fondled the statues and paintings in his church in their expression of closeness to the spirits represented. Moreover, the younger Italians insisted on talking to each other, usually about decidedly non-religious topics, during the Mass, especially during the parts in Latin. Both old and young Italians showed obvious indifference to the sermons they found uninteresting or unrealistic, and clearly displayed impatience with the priests who delivered them. Unlike their Irish co-parishioners, the Italians made no habit of speaking of the peccadilloes of the local priests in hushed tones. They spoke openly, seemingly gleefully, about every real or imagined fault or act of improper behavior among those who wore what the Irish termed the Roman collar. Many of the Irish finally ended their encounter with their strange Catholic brethren by switching parishes, often accomplished by moving out of the neighborhood.

The story brings to mind the early clash between the Irish and the Italian immigrants over the question of the proper way to make offerings to the Church. Following Irish custom, Catholics in the United States gave money to their church as they entered it for a Mass or other service. The Italian immigrants ignored this custom and continued to give their offerings at or near the conclusion of the rite. They laughed at the notion that one should pay in advance of the service rendered. How, they argued with the Irish, could a person tell how much to give if he has not yet seen the value of what he will be given? The Irish regarded the Italian attitude as irreligious. The Italians responded by terming the Irish custom with the pejorative "American," "like paying at the movies," as some put it, and as *troppo buono*, the disdainful epithet meaning naïve, excessively pious, thin-blooded, prissy, and most of all the attribute of him who is thereby easily taken for a fool.

If the Irish considered the Italian immigrants as less than true Catholics, the Italians considered the Irish as merely one more group of stranieri who had no more in common with them than the various outsiders they had encountered on both sides of the Atlantic. The fact that the Irish stranieri were Catholic and had priests among them changed things not at all. In historical times many of the stranieri in the Mezzogiorno were Catholics and brought their priests with them. Thus a paradox: the only long-standing ethnic antagonism Italian-Americans developed was not against Jews, Protestant Scandinavians, Chinese, or other non-Catholics with whom they were crowded together in America's cities. The antagonism developed against their co-religionist Irish-Americans.

I remember that in Red Hook, Brooklyn, the handful of Jews who lived and worked among us, chiefly as store owners, was accepted. A small pocket of the Protestant Norwegian-Americans found there, because of a famous Norwegian church and seaman's home located in the area, was also accepted. This despite the Norwegian sailors' liberal drinking habits, which the Italian-Americans disapproved but ignored. But the Irish-Americans who lived in nearby neighborhoods were considered anathema. Except for priests, rarely did the adults of the Irish community have anything to do with those of the Italian section. And on those infrequent occasions when boys of one group entered the territory of the other, both sides prepared for trouble.

One of the most painful incidents of my boyhood happened when a friend and I decided to take a short cut and walk through an Irish section. We passed a group of boys our age who glared at us. The tension suddenly broke when I caught a brick in the kidney from one of the Irish kids, who then chased us to the border of our neighborhood—and no farther. My companion, a bull of a boy who is today a policeman, stopped two or three times to trade punches with the closest of our pursuers. On the other hand I never broke my stride, driven by the sharp pain in my back even more than by fear of my chasers. Although the word *segreto* (secret) was not part of our vocabulary at the time, the tradition had been incorporated into our personalities. My friend and I said nothing of this to our parents, but sent the word out to the other boys of our blocks. News of a similar incident when I was about eleven years old caused dozens of us to descend on a small park on Smith Street, not far from the Gowanus Canal, a border between Irish and Italian sections, where Irish boys used to gather. If any of them had been there that evening, they disappeared. We found only an empty playground. After holding it for a while, we walked home with as provocatively casual a manner as we could effect.

My experiences were carryovers of the antagonism established years before, an antagonism that led immigrant generation Italian-Americans to send their children to public rather than parochial schools. By tradition loath to surrender their children to the Church, the immigrants' attitude was buttressed by the new enmity against the American Church. Quite correctly, the Italians saw this Church's schools as institutions organized around the ethnic traditions of an alien group and operating to further those traditions. Although they had great distrust of public schools, the Italian immigrants chose to send their children to these secular schools where often they soon became an ethnic majority rather than to send them to parochial schools to "become Irish." The public schools were simply the lesser of two evils.

The early Italian-American disdain for the Church was reciprocated. The Irish-American hierarchy, very sensitive to the anti-clerical and anti-institutional attitudes of the Mezzogiorno, refused to make concessions to the immigrants. For the pro-state attitude held by them in the Italian church-state conflict and because of their "sacrilegious" and strange ways, the Italian-Americans were punished. Parochial schools in the United States refused to teach the Italian language until 1929, when Mussolini finally formally ended the Italian church-state hostility by negotiating the Lateran Treaty with the Vatican.

But even after 1929 the Irish-American hierarchy attempted to educate Italian-Americans in their brand of Catholicism, and succeeded only in antagonizing this substantial portion of the Church's membership. Finding that Southern Italian priests accommodated themselves to the religious attitudes of their paesani, the cardinals and bishops sent non-Italian or Northern Italian priests to staff Italian-American parishes. To be sure, there were individuals among these priests who learned the customs of the people they served, empathized with their lives, and succeeded in ministering to their needs. But it is safe to say that the majority of these priests merely reflected and perpetuated the distance between Italian-Americans and the American Catholic hierarchy.

Because of this and the other reasons accounting for the unique and aloof stance of Italian-Americans toward the Church, the ethnic group has been and remains scandalously underrepresented in the Church hierarchy. There is not now nor has there ever been an Italian-American cardinal. As of January 1973 there were thirty-four American archbishops. *One* was Italian-American. Of 253 American bishops, only *five* are Italian-Americans.

Of course, these figures reflect the experience of immigrants and their children with the Church, the result being a second generation of Italian-Americans who have now lived into their middle age apart from the Church or on the periphery of its influence. This second generation inherited its predecessors' alienated relations with the Church and became in some ways even more secular than their parents, whose magical and occult beliefs and rites they altogether discarded. But what of their children and grandchildren? Are changes perceptible in the religious positions of the young adults and children in the third and fourth generations?

The pattern into which these young people will eventually settle is unclear. But the circumstances which will influence their direction are discernible. They are the products of homes that are in fact secular although most are nominally Catholic, and their fiber is spun from the values which semiconsciously sustain those homes, those of la famiglia. On the other hand many attend or have attended Catholic schools, a trend begun in the 1950's, when appreciable numbers of their parents at last had enough money to fulfill an impulse inherited from their immigrant parents, the drive to own their homes and land. In the past two decades homes and land in the United States have meant the suburbs, and this is where the old dream was pursued. A substantial portion of the third and fourth generations has been raised in suburbs where the influence of other ethnic groups is felt more closely and persistently

than it had been in the homogeneous Little Italies of the
center cities. In this, I believe, lies the clue to the rise in
Italian-American enrollment in parochial schools in the last
twenty years.

The second-generation parents were instinctively aware
of the threat to la via vecchia presented by the suburbs.
In almost a reflex action they looked for forces in the new
communities that might preserve the values dear to them.
There were three types of institutions that affected the lives
of suburban children in the 1950's and 1960's: public
schools, community recreational facilities, and parochial
schools. The public schools and community programs were
ethnically mixed and usually were dominated by non-
Italians. Unlike the case in the city public schools attended
in the 1920's, 1930's, and 1940's by the second generation,
Italian-American children did not constitute a majority in
the public schools of the suburbs. Thus these public institutions were hardly suitable to the perpetuation of traditional Italian-American values. The second-generation parents thus had no alternative but to look to parochial
schools.

In an uncanny reversal of the experience of their own
childhood years, the second generation found the new
parochial schools more serviceable to la via vecchia, or at
least less threatening to it, than public schools. Many of
the parochial schools of the suburbs were new, having developed with their communities. They did not have the
stigma of Irish domination of the cities' church schools in
years past. Second, Italian-American parents were afforded
a share in founding the new parochial schools and thus
could shape them as *their* ethnic institutions. In this last
goal they sought as natural allies the younger Italian-
American priests, nuns, and brothers sent to staff the new
parishes and schools by the older hierarchy who remained
comfortably settled in their established churches and
schools. Just as the first generation of Italian-Americans
had rejected parochial schools as antithetical to la via
vecchia and l'ordine della famiglia, so the next generation
of parents in larger numbers adopted them to support this

value structure. Desire to maintain ethnic integrity, and not any sudden religious fervor as some have supposed, was the cause of the turn toward parochial schools. And in considering the rise in enrollment in parochial schools by Italian-Americans in the last two decades, we should not lose sight of the fact that even in the suburbs most Italian-Americans still send their children to public schools.

There is much speculation about whether the young third- and fourth-generation Italian-Americans will become Hibernianized in their own religious attitudes as they mature. Those who say yes cite several reasons. First, the unprecedented numbers of Italian-Americans being influenced by parochial school educations. Second, the fading of anti-clerical and anti-institutional feelings, attributed both to time as well as to the general ignorance of their history among the younger people. Third, the desire on the part of these young people to seek out roots as distinct from their parents, who in *their* youth struggled to gain enough freedom from those roots to forge an American identity. Also, the younger people are more secure as Americans and do not need to reject a Catholicism which in former times in the United States was stigmatized as un-American. Last, those young Italian-Americans who do marry outside their ethnic group usually marry other Catholics, whose religious beliefs and practices are stronger and more in the American Catholic pattern. The non-Italian partners to these marriages are likely to assert their religious attitudes in their homes and establish them as dominant even to the point of making their Italian-American spouses more Catholic.

The alternative scenario foresees the youngest generations of Italian-Americans continuing or even increasing the de facto secularism of their parents. The general trend of all young people in the United States against involvement with organized religion in favor of privately religious or secular life styles is claimed as one reason for this prediction. The momentum of the secular traditions of the childhood homes of Italian-American youth is another reason. These forces might overcome the influence of paro-

chial schools on those attending them and place religion
in its traditional position of subordination to l'ordine della
famiglia. The old inheritance's strong pragmatic preoccupation with this world combines with a similar American attitude in the young people, making a turn toward organized
religion even less likely. Thus, young Italian-Americans
might give their energies to the secular values which function in place of orthodox religious lives—education and
work, recreation and family. In short, this view sees the
young people evolving new forms of the old preoccupations
of their grandparents with a distinctly American twist, an
emphasis on education.

It is impossible to conclude which pattern will be followed as the youths mature. For the moment a cross-
section of religious behavior in the Italian-American population reveals a continuity running from the old religious
festivals in the Little Italies, on one side, to the attitudes
of Italian-American middle-aged people and youngsters
who travel to these center-city feste, on the other. The second generation enjoys the food, sights, and smells of the
festivals and indulges itself in memories of its youth, while
its children gawk at the strange goings-on and wonder what
it is all about. As is true of every aspect of Italian-
American life, the old sustaining values run throughout the
continuity, but the consciousness of them and their rich
roots steadily diminishes as we cross the spectrum of generations from old immigrants through second, third, and
fourth generations. A small landmark change that occurred
in 1972 summarizes this part of the Italian-American dilemma.

In September 1972, the forty-sixth annual San Gennaro
Festival was held in Manhattan's Little Italy. This festival
is the largest of the old feste—or as the second generation
translated the word, "feasts"—that are still held. Not long
ago there were many such street feste. Their aromas of
food, the sight of burly men swaying from side to side and
lurching forward under the weight of enormous statues of
exotic Madonnas and saints laden with money and gifts,
the music of the Italian bands in uniforms with dark-

peaked caps, white shirts, and black ties, and the bright arches of colored lights spanning the city streets are essential memories of my childhood, as they are of many second-generation Italian-Americans. True to the spirit of campanilismo, each group of paesani in New York had its festa. People from Catania celebrated Sant' Agata, who according to legend saved that ancient city from destruction by lava during one of Mount Etna's more violent outbursts. The people from Palermo honored their saint, Santa Rosalia, who saved Palermo from pestilence.

Three feste were larger than the others. Sicilians, especially from the region of Agrigento, went all out for the huge September festival of San Gandolfo. In July, thousands turned out to honor the Madonna del Carmine. And in the fall, Neapolitans paid their respect to the patron of their mother city, San Gennaro. San Gennaro, who was named after the powerful Roman god Janus, was martyred by the Romans at Pozzuoli in A.D. 306 and later canonized by the Church. Because he saved Naples from numerous natural and manmade catastrophes, he was especially honored by the proud Neapolitans, who jealously guarded their privileged relationship to the powerful Christian saint who bears the name of an even more awesome Roman god. The San Gennaro festa is today the largest of the surviving Italian religious festivals in the United States. For that matter, it is one of the largest in the world.

As I slowly bumped and jostled my way through thousands of people jammed shoulder to shoulder for blocks at that San Gennaro festival on a cool September evening in 1972, my emotions, memories, and musings about the future of Italian-Americans spun round and round, all about one vortex. I had just read that for the first time since its founding more than a half century ago, New York's Società San Gennaro, which sponsors the festa, had changed its membership rules. No longer was the Società limited to men born in Naples or whose parents were born in that city. For the first time any male of Italian origin may apply for membership. The news brought to mind a passage of Corrado Alvaro, one that haunts me with the past and at the same time excites me about the future of my people. "We have here a disappearing civilization. Let us not weep over its eclipse, but, if we were born into it, let us store up in our memory as much of it as we can." As my grandparents used to say, *"Speriamo"*—Let us hope so!

Childhood and Education

The statistics of formal education of Italian-Americans are both appalling and hopeful, appalling up to the present but indicating a change that may bode well for the future. In a 1969 survey of Americans who were asked to identify their ethnic origin, the U. S. Bureau of the Census compiled a composite of the educational achievements of major ethnic groups. In every category of accomplishment Italian-Americans were the lowest or near lowest of all groups of European origin. Of those thirty-five years old or over only 5.9 per cent of Italian-Americans completed four years of college. This is substantially lower than the average for all groups (9.8 per cent) and considerably lower than the figure for each group except that which identified itself as Spanish (4.5 per cent), a group including an unspecified number of people of Mexican or Puerto Rican origin. The figures for other groups are: Russian, including Jewish Russian (18.4 per cent), English (13.6 per cent), Irish (9.3 per cent), and Polish (7.2 per cent). Of this age group, Italian-Americans had the second lowest median number of school years completed, 10.3 years compared with 12.4 for Russian, 12.2 years for English, 12 each for German and Irish, 10.9 for Polish, and 8.5 for Hispanic-Americans. Again Italian-Americans were second only to Hispanic-Americans among those with the highest percentage (23.5 per cent) of people who completed only seven years of schooling or less, and the second lowest percentage (27.6 per cent) of those who completed high school.

An altered pattern was found among the younger adults, aged twenty-five to thirty-four. Italian-Americans still had the second lowest percentage of those completing four years of college, 11.9 per cent, compared with 52.5 per cent for Russian (Jewish), 17.6 per cent for English, 17.5 per cent for German, 16.2 per cent for Polish, 13.9 per cent for Irish, and 5.3 per cent for Hispanic-Americans. This group of Italian-Americans is again second highest in percentage of those with less than seven years of schooling, 5.3 per cent. They also show the second lowest percentage of those completing one to three years of college, 12.7 per cent. However, the picture of the younger group shows some change. The next figure shows where it has changed most—among those who completed high school. The figure for Italian-Americans is 50.4 per cent, the second *highest* percentage of all groups.

What is clear from this study is that there is a dramatic change in formal education between second- and third-generation Italian-Americans. What is also evident is that the progress shown by the younger generation stops at high school graduation, so that the actual progress of the younger generation beyond the older is only an additional 2.2 school years completed. The generation from twenty-five to thirty-four years of age lagged behind other ethnic groups in college education, keeping the over-all percentage of all Italian-Americans over twenty-five who are college graduates at a low 7 per cent, a figure below the 11 per cent average for all groups and higher only than the Mexican and Puerto Rican figures, respectively 1.6 per cent and 2.4 per cent.

What were the reasons for stopping with a high school diploma among those from twenty-five to thirty-four years of age? Will the generation of Italian-Americans now younger than twenty-five break the high school limit and go on to college education?

To deal with these questions, we must look at the attitudes toward education of each generation of Italian-Americans and their attitudes toward childhood in general. Paradoxically, it is because the essential attitudes have remained the same from generation to generation that change has occurred, and occurred specifically as it has. And I predict the even more paradoxical. Because the attitudes still persist, another dramatic change in achievement will be seen in the group now under twenty-five years of age.

The generation of mass Italian immigration to the United States lived out all or much of its childhood in the Mezzogiorno about or before the turn of the century. The ideal of child rearing then among the contadini, as it remains today among Italian-Americans, was to cultivate young people who were in the old phrase *ben educati*. The simple—and deceptive—translation of this means "well educated." Ben educato meant raised with the core of one's personality woven of those values and attitudes, habits and skills that perpetuated l'ordine della famiglia, and thus one was attuned to the welfare of the family. In the Mezzogiorno the means to accomplish this aim decidedly did not include formal schooling. Pragmatists that they were, the Meridionali did not confuse schooling and sound education. As a matter of fact they regarded formal schooling as a natural enemy of the ideal of being ben educato. Historically they had good reason to feel this way.

One of the landmark laws in the history of modern Italy is the Coppino law of 1877. Considered radical at the time, this legislation made formal education compulsory for all Italian children between the ages of six and nine. Moreover, the law also contained another innovation: the three years of compulsory schooling were to be provided by the state free of charge. It startles students new to Italian affairs to learn that the Coppino law was so widely resisted in the Mezzogiorno that it went all but unenforced. When contadini massively ignored attempts to enforce the statute, and even resisted it in some cases by rioting and the burning of schoolhouses, the new national government did not press the issue. As a result la via vecchia successfully withstood the potential disruptions of formal schooling. But a great price was to be paid.

In 1931 it was estimated that 48 per cent of all the citizens of Calabria were illiterate, a legacy of the fact that in the years 1901 and 1902, according to earlier reports, of the six- to nine-year-olds legally required to be in school only 65 per cent attended school at all. School attendance figures in other areas of the Mezzogiorno were even lower, in some towns approaching 0 per cent.

The intensity of contadino hostility to schools is difficult to appreciate from our perspective of the United States in the 1970's. No instrument of the various stranieri who oppressed la famiglia was more ominous than that of the state school, for only the school dared to reach directly into the family. Moreover it intruded into the family at its most vulnerable point, seeking to influence its youngest and tenderest members with doctrines alien to l'ordine della famiglia. The new Italian state dominated by Northern nationalists and romantics was determined to turn out a generation of new Italians. This intent collided head on with the Mezzogiorno tradition in which the most dreadful curse a parent could hurl at his or her child was *si possa perdere il nome mio in casa tua*—may my name be lost in your home. The schools of the new Italy were hated because they cultivated in their pupils values that were useless to or, worse, at odds with l'ordine della famiglia and la via vecchia.

Under the Bourbons, university professors, the men who controlled the tone of all educational efforts, were political appointees. They were sworn to the king and served at the pleasure of political authorities. The heavy-handed control of education seems superfluous when one considers that there were no state schools. Virtually all contadini were illiterate, a situation that well suited the latifondo and galantuomo classes. In fact the landowners themselves were largely an illiterate lot. When they chose to send their children to schools, which was not often, the little rich ones, *i ricchi*, attended church schools. The religious schools for boys were known as seminaries and those for girls as convent schools. They were institutions which enforced a moribund religious discipline and accomplished little literate education. Often their prize graduates, those selected for religious vocations, emerged from school as illiterate as when they entered.

As a result in 1860 virtually all of the population of the Mezzogiorno, galantuomini and contadini alike, were illiterate. This fact contributed to the 78 per cent illiteracy figure for all of Italy at the time. The Mezzogiorno was in fact living in feudal times. Its government had no educational mission and la via vecchia of the Meridionali was completely untouched by modern schooling.

The nationalists who governed Italy after the Risorgimento were Northern *letterati* fired by the view that they were to create not merely a new Italian nation but a new Italian civilization. Their inspiration came from Giuseppe Mazzini, who had pronounced the mission of the Risorgimento in elevated terms. The new Italy should be a spiritual entity, which Mazzini outlined by contrasting it to America. The latter, he said, "is the embodiment, if compared to our own ideal, of the philosophy of mere *rights:* the collective thought is forgotten: the *educational* mission of the state overlooked."

The Northern nationalists were determined to fulfill a radical educational mission, and not surprisingly compulsory schooling was their first step. And, true to their ideal, their announced aims were to eradicate the illiteracy of the Mezzogiorno, of which they were profoundly aware, and to erase its via vecchia, about which they were just as profoundly ignorant and insensitive. Thus the Meridionali easily perceived a threat to their system of values in the grandiose rhetoric that accompanied the Coppino law of 1877. They clearly and correctly perceived that compulsory education meant more than mere literacy. The educational effort of the new state was to replace traditional values with the new collective thought.

Far from regarding the new Italian who was to be molded in the state schools as an improvement over the time honored ideals, the Meridionali regarded the new Italian as an aberration. The new Italian was the antithesis of all they held dear. He was to value mumbo-jumbo ideals of noble spirituality instead of the worldly ideals of being

furbo and scaltro, foxy and clever. And he was to place
the interest of Italy above all, even above that of la
famiglia! Obviously the rhetorical ideals in which the Coppino law was imbedded were those of scoundrels and fools.
Only a madman would expose his children to them. The
new state schools were downright immoral.

Apart from their revulsion at the philosophical foundations of the schools, the Meridionali were also opposed to
them on more practical grounds. What of real value could
they possibly teach children that was not better taught by
the family in its constant cultivation of children who were
ben educati? Literacy? But knowing how to read and write
was of no use at all in contadino life. Moreover, the old
life was a demanding one with little margin for frivolities,
one in which the time spent learning to read could better
be used in learning the precious lessons of manhood and
womanhood and in working for the family's daily bread
and its vital competitive position. To cap it off, the new
schools, immoral and useless as they were, meant that the
destitute contadini would have to pay more taxes to support them.

The opposition to the schools was further aggravated by
corrupt local authorities who in their traditional manner
pocketed government education funds while school buildings remained unbuilt or in disrepair and schoolmasters
lived in demoralizing poverty. The occasional government
inspector usually gave a cursory examination and moved
on.

Scemenza (foolishness) covering una pazzia vergognosa
(a shameful madness) was the verdict the contadini gave
the new system of secular state education.

If anything the existence of state schools caused the
contadini to intensify their efforts to turn out children who
were ben educati nel buon costume, well educated in
proper behavior. This ideal was seen as not only different
but contrary to being ben istruito, well schooled. The family stepped up its influence on its children and la via
vecchia fought a successful battle against la via nuova of
the new Italy. Children continued to work at early ages,

whether or not they attended school, as part of their character training as well as for economic necessity. As late as 1911, one and one half million of Italy's two and one half million children between the ages of ten and fifteen were employed. A disproportionately high percentage of these working children were in the Mezzogiorno. Of the age group of children required to attend school, 40 per cent were found to be chronic truants in the southern region of Basilicata as late as 1903.

Moreover, the lessons learned by those who did attend school were belittled in the home where they were disparagingly contrasted to the wisdom of *gli anziani*, the wise old people. The family even discouraged their children from learning to read and write, thus further weakening what was a fragile effort at best in three years of schooling. The reason for the resistance to the children even becoming literate is summed up in much-quoted contadino sayings to the effect that only a fool makes his children different from himself. The attitude lies behind a poignant conversation in Calitri's novel *Father*, between the boy, Giunio, and his father. Giunio is one of the children who has learned to read. As a result his father insists that the boy must now attend a seminary school. When Giunio protests that he wishes to remain in his home, his father says to him:

"That is what I would wish, but you cannot stay, Giunio. You have learned how to read, and now you can no longer be a farmer . . . It is not like a pipe," he said. "You cannot spit out the taste of knowledge as you can spit out a piece of tobacco or a drop of juice that finds its way to your mouth. It is more like the smoke, Giunio, some of which must stick to the lungs." He bent down and coughed a sardonic cough. "You will be coughing for the rest of your life with the things you have already learned, and you will need the fresh air of new books to keep you healthy."

Thus the Coppino law accomplished little in a full generation, as witnessed by the figures for illiteracy in Southern Italy in 1867 and in 1900. Campania, the region of

Naples, was 88 per cent illiterate in 1867 and 70 per cent
illiterate in 1900. Sicily was 89 per cent illiterate in 1867
and 70 per cent illiterate in 1900. Apulia, the region of
Bari, was 95 per cent illiterate in 1867 and remained 79
per cent illiterate thirty-three years later.

In 1900 the total population of the Mezzogiorno was
more than 70 per cent illiterate. The import of this is
heightened by comparison with other European populations. In that same year, the figures for illiteracy in Europe
were given in a Report of the United States Commissioner
of Education as follows:

	per cent
Germany	0.11
Sweden and Norway	0.11
Switzerland	0.30
The Netherlands	4
England	5.8
France	4.9
Austria	24
Greece	30
Spain	68
Czarist Russia	62

The Coppino law did little more than expose some of
the contadino children for up to three years to the spoken
and written forms of the new standard Italian language,
a strange Northern dialect most of them seldom heard
spoken from when they left school to the day they died.
In their minds this fact alone justified their parents' antipathy to schooling.

Thus the immigrants to the United States brought an
enormous antischool bias with them. Their notion of successful child rearing, producing young people who were
ben rather than *mal educati,* is summed up in one of their
favorite sayings: *Una mazza, lavoro e pane fanno i figli
belli*—A cane, work, and bread make for beautiful children.
They applied the cane to their children, found work for
them, and provided them with bread, as any second-

generation Italian-American can attest. But they could not be as completely uncompromising in their confrontation with that most distinctly American institution, the powerful public school.

The census figures on the low educational achievements of Italian-Americans over thirty-five years of age, predominantly the children of immigrants, instantly fall into perspective when we note that in 1914 *Century* magazine lamented that of the offspring of all immigrants, Italian-American children were found to have "the lowest in proportion of children in school, and highest in proportion of children at work . . ." Given the antischool bias and poverty of the immigrant parents, the perspective becomes still more defined when Andrew M. Greeley reports in *Why Can't They Be Like Us?* that of four groups of tradition-oriented Americans (Irish, German, Polish, Italian) surveyed in the late 1960's, Italian-Americans scored highest in percentage (48 per cent) of those who agreed with the flat statement that children "shouldn't doubt parents' ideas." They also scored the highest percentage, an astonishing 75 per cent, of those who agreed that there is "nothing worse than hearing criticism of [one's] mother." Among a people whose tradition stipulated that the education of young children was the responsibility primarily of the mother and her female relatives and commare, it is easy to carry the implications of this attitude back to the education of the children of Italian immigrants.

Second-generation children were caught between the conflicting educational forces of family and school. Their immigrant parents became convinced that many American institutions were *contra la famiglia*. Public schools were foremost among these. The schools taught *i costume americani*, and many of these ways were obviously subversive of *la via vecchia*. The schools insisted on impressing a wider identity upon the children than that of family membership. Membership in the larger society and citizenship responsibilities were depicted as transcending family obligations. L'ordine della famiglia was made to seem small-minded and parochial to the children. The ideals of pazienza and serictà were made to appear old-fashioned, quaint, and un-American. The schools either ignored the language the children spoke at home or deprecated it in Italian language courses which made it clear that the Southern dialects were substandard and hence those who spoke them were inferior.

To this day the New York City public school system represents an exception rather than the rule among those in cities with substantial Italian-American populations which offer courses in the Italian language. San Francisco, for example, continues to be typical in that French and Latin are stressed in foreign-language programs. I experienced this bias in my own school career. No foreign languages were offered in my grade school. When I entered a high school in Brooklyn, I learned that foreign language courses offered included Italian. But those of us who were deemed to be bound for college were advised to study French. We were told that colleges preferred it and it was the second language of educated Americans. I attended two other high schools, one in Manhattan and one in Nassau County. Neither offered studies in Italian and both offered the preferred French.

The Francophile snobbism of educated Americans is a remarkable phenomenon. Recently I had a common encounter with it in a well-known New York restaurant, one whose ambiance is of no particular European nationality and whose dishes are predominantly American. The menu offerings included "Spaghetti Italien," as if the French spelling would somehow upgrade an Italian dish. And an Italian-American maître d' in New York's fashionable Hamptons is compelled to use François instead of his real name, Francesco.

When I entered college, I received similar counsel to that I heard in high school, and added German to my studies on the advice that graduate schools looked favorably upon French and German and not at all favorably upon Italian. As a result I studied French for a total of five years and German for one year. I have never regretted these studies but do regret that my studies of the Italian language have been on my own, leaving me with a poor degree of literacy in the language I spoke as a child. Despite my being a graduate of three universities I remain typical of second- and third-generation Italian-Americans. We have not mastered a literate command of the old tongue.

In addition to these cultural shocks, second-generation children were forcefully impressed in public schools with the doctrine of assimilation in American ways, a program that made them feel odd and guilty about everything in their own identities from their mannerisms, clothes, and food to their operatic, vowel-filled names. Little wonder that the immigrants perceived the schools as a new form of an old immorality and adopted a mocking attitude toward their efforts. Any manner, idea, or value the second-generation child carried home from the school was slapped down with the pejorative "American."

The immigrants regarded the Irish-dominated parochial schools as even more American and kept their children away from these, preferring to do battle with the public schools for the identity of their children. In 1910 only one out of six Italian-American children attended parochial schools.

The immigrants permitted their children as little formal education as the law would allow. Typically boys and girls went to school only until the minimum legal age required, and then went to work. Often they quit school, or were removed from school by their parents, before the legal age and were protected against the actions of truant officers by bribery. Although the immigrants learned that there was some pragmatic job value for their children, especially boys, to be schooled, they preferred the old system of having the children enter the labor force and support the family. Thus schooling for boys seldom exceeded high school. Girls had little vocational need for schooling in the eyes of their parents and were less often permitted to attain a high school education.

Of course, higher education was out of the question. In 1910 only ninety-four (eighty-three male and eleven female) second-generation Italian-Americans were attending college. Poverty alone cannot account for this low number, for although the Eastern and Central European Jewish-American population at that time was no larger than the Italian, had arrived here at about the same time, and was equally as poor, 1243 Jewish children were attending colleges, a figure exclusive of children of the earlier-arrived German Jews. As Rudolf Glanz cites in his book *Jew and Italian*, 4.2 per cent of Jewish-American children at the time attended college while only 0.4 per cent of Italian-American children attended college. (These figures include both foreign-born and American-born children.) Moreover, a report of the United States Immigrant Commission showed that in 1910 while 1639 second-generation Jewish-Americans had already become elementary schoolteachers, only seventy-seven second-generation Italian-Americans had done so, and only fourteen of these were children of Southern Italians!

In regard to the impact of other educative institutions which supplemented the schools, such as Catholic, Jewish, and Protestant summer camps, Jacob Riis summed up the unique status of Italian-Americans in one phrase in his *Children of the Poor*, published in 1892. He noted that, while the children of all other immigrant groups were served by these programs, "no one asks for Italian children." This was partly the result of discrimination, but also a result of the extreme reluctance of Italian immigrants to turn their children over to any institution outside the family.

The effects upon the second generation of being caught between two opposed cultures, the one represented by the family and the other by the school, stand out in sharp relief in statistical terms like the census figures at the beginning of this chapter. Indeed, Leonard Covello years ago pointed out that while in 1926 42.2 per cent of all high school students in New York City graduated, in 1931 only 11.1 per cent of New York's Italian-American high school students obtained a diploma. He also pointed out that in this same period Italian-American pupils in New York City had a rate of truancy more than twice as high as that of non-

Italian pupils, a rate of school absences four and a half times as high, and a record of disciplinary cases more than twice the proportional rate of non-Italians. Regarding those children who did not enter high school (common among Italian-Americans, many of whom began working about the age of eleven or twelve), we have Bernard E. Segal's reminder in his *Racial and Ethnic Relations* (1966) that "the children who could not learn English forty years ago got out [of school] before their problems became too noticeable."

The second-generation children faced a torturous quandary. To do well in school was equivalent in emotional terms to a betrayal of the family. The guilt of such a position was unbearable. On the other hand the attempts of the school to capture their loyalties were backed by the entire panoply of American society, and the children soon became aware of the realistic necessity of being Americans in language, manners, and general modes of behavior. As has been indicated this generation eventually made the soundest possible compromise. They rejected the Italian language and the larger Italian culture while adopting the family system and related values of la via vecchia. On the other hand they accepted only limited involvement in American society. Usually schools, jobs, and the military were their only institutional involvements.

The earliest form of this compromise was developed while the second generation were children. They developed an entire subculture of Italian-American children, made possible by the fact that most lived in Italian ghettos and attended schools in which they were numerous and often predominant. Applying the inherited principle of *pari con pari*, peers with peers, second-generation children formed a society of their own, a buffer between the forces of school and family. The nature and importance of Italian-American children's groups have been poorly understood and underestimated. To second-generation and many third-generation children the society of the street corner and the hallway became a cohesive family reflecting the values of la famiglia and hence impervious to the outside world. The relations with one's friends took priority over the demands of the school. In fact the peer group superseded everything except basic demands by the family.

Thus as late as the 1940's and early 1950's, the period of my childhood, the most important influence apart from our families on the children in my grade school came from the groups we formed among ourselves. They were typical of Italian-American youth cliques or gangs. They were composed only of members of the same sex, the boys' cliques beginning at a very early age because we were allowed to play freely on the streets. Girls were kept indoors after school until they managed to steal some daylight time away from home, something virtually impossible in my mother's day but possible for teen-age girls by my time.

In the Mezzogiorno children did not visit and play in the homes of their friends. The pattern held here. We met on street corners, schoolyards, lots, occasionally in abandoned buildings, and often in hallways. Thus, I remember standing on the corner of Clinton Street and Second Place in Red Hook, Brooklyn, in the coldest weather for hours with my friends.

The values of these street corner groups took precedence over the demands of the public school, and the things we valued did not include high achievement in school. In fact any child who achieved high grades was suspect, a fact that tormented me in my earliest years in school because I did well in studies without much effort. I even tried to play down my ability to excel in classroom exercises. I finally was accepted by my peers despite my successes on the report card.

The values that dominated boys' groups in my childhood and that of the previous generation were loyalty to the group, a closemouthed and distrustful attitude toward all outside the group (except blood family), a cynicism about our school and teachers (no doubt a defense on our part against our conflicted situation), and concern with our physical powers expressed in athletics (organized by us but not those organized by school or other institutions) and fighting. Contrary to the stereotype of Italian gangs, fighting in earnest (as opposed to rough but restrained "fooling around") was infrequent. We did not spoil for fights, and really had worked out a system of relations and ritualized behavior that minimized real fights. In a word, we grafted the ways of the tradition onto the streets of Brooklyn.

My mother's second-generation insistence that I do well in school and my ability to do so created special problems for me, for it defined my personal situation in third-generation terms while my social environment was still functioning in second-generation terms. Thus I shared the feeling of the second generation that we did not fit into American institutions, that we were freaks. But the feeling was in conflict with my ability to make my way in the school, and my mother's pressure that I do so. (My father, Italian born, was content if I merely did all right in school.) Thus I was in greater self-conflict than my peers, most of whom developed the attributes typical of the second generation: diffidence and scorn toward and minimal involvement with larger American institutions.

I recall two incidents above others at P. S. 142, which was still staffed mostly by the same teachers who had taught there when my mother, aunts, and uncles attended the school. One occurred when I was in the eighth grade, my last year at the school. My teacher was a dedicated man who kept emphasizing to me that I had the highest I.Q. in the district, a remark that only served to confuse me since I only poorly understood its meaning and could not cope with its implications. Despite his years of experience with Italian-American children, the teacher did not understand the conflict we had about academic achievements, and reacted to our behavior only with an impatience born of frustration.

At the time the Board of Education used to award a medal to the eighth grader who scored highest on a special American-history examination given to children selected to compete by their schools. My teacher was determined that I take the exam and proceeded to coach me in American history. He knew that I had already been reading on my own because of my interest in the subject. I seldom dis-

cussed this interest with my friends. Although they had
long ago accepted my school achievements as an insignifi-
cant eccentricity—Richie was just good in schoolwork—they
were indifferent to my larger interests and unequal to discussions of them. As the exam date approached I became
more and more apprehensive, for despite my peer acceptance the prospect of becoming an academic celebrity raised
too many uncertainties. Typical of my peer training, I did
not even mention the project in my home.

Because my mother left for work in the mornings before
I arose, I relied on an alarm clock to wake me. On the
morning of the examination I slept through the alarm,
something I don't remember having done before. In this
way I resolved my conflict. As it turned out, my school's
alternate, a boy named Fred (Alfredo), won the medal, a
fact that tempered my teacher's anger toward me but increased his sense of frustration. He told me of Fred's success and never said another word of the incident to me.

As already indicated, I was sensitive to the cultural
expectation for a boy to work and found a job after school.
I did this because it increased my status with my friends
even though my parents did not push the expectation to
work on me. In that regard they were second generation.
The immigrants often insisted that their children work, as
did my grandparents with their children. This even when
the children showed obvious talent in school. In *Love and
Pasta* (1968), an account by Joe Vergara of his childhood
with his immigrant Italian parents, the author records a
characteristic conversation with his father, who had been
pressing the boy to learn a practical trade. In the face of
Joe's insistence to further his own schooling, his father, a
shoemaker, compromises and tells him, "OK, my son . . .
I hope you get-a you' wish. I hope some-a day you even
be Presidente, so you never dirty you' hands. But mean-a
time, Sattaday you come and you learn-a the business."

The other incident outstanding in my memory of grade
school occurred when I was in the seventh grade. My
homeroom teacher, another man with experience in the
school, found live .22-caliber bullets in my and a friend's

pockets. He took us into a large walk-in closet and asked us what we were doing with the ammunition. We remained silent. The rest took place with no words uttered. The teacher closed the door and beat us—hard. Punches to our bodies and slaps to our faces. The incident was closed. We were not reported, nor did we report the event to our families. Impudence toward teachers was a vergogna which shamed the family by clearly indicating that its children were mal educati in their behavior toward their elders. As any teachers of second-generation Italian children will attest, a report of such behavior sent home was greeted by physical punishment. Fathers used belts, and mothers used whatever was handy. My mother preferred a stout wooden spoon while her mother had employed one of her heavy high-button shoes. As was true of every Italian-American boy I knew, I preferred a teacher's punches to the ire that would greet me at home if I reported any clash with a teacher.

Of course, the children in my school punished those teachers who were weak in retribution for the respect they were forced to pay to teachers in general. Unfortunately many of the teachers at P. S. 142 when I was there were elderly women, ripe targets of childishly cruel vengeance. Much of my school days was spent in boredom as a few children in my classes tormented these poor creatures with disruptive behavior. One teacher in particular was senile and quickly dissolved in tears, a fact that ended her harassment except from an occasional pathologically sadistic child.

The defenselessness of this woman was more than compensated for by another woman teacher, a small, wiry, and tough old German lady who would crash out of her room and pounce upon any noisy child in the corridors. We feared this slight woman more than any other teacher in the school, even more than the men, except for a certain male assistant principal who had been the school's ultimate enforcer of discipline since my mother's school days. One day my class was passing the German lady's room and the noise irritated her. She flew out and lunged toward the back

of the boys' line—we were always lined up apart from the
girls and by size. It being assembly day (Wednesday) we
were wearing ties—any boy not wearing a white shirt and tie
on a Wednesday had his parents summoned. It was easier
to wear the detested tie. She grabbed four of the biggest
of us, two ties in each hand, and hauled us toward her
room. But the five of us became jammed in the doorway.
She tugged on us, each of whom towered over her. The
scene gave the appearance of her hanging by our ties and
my class laughed itself into an uproar. Finally the woman
stopped, abruptly and coolly slapped each of us in the face,
and ordered us back into line. It was the only time I ever
saw or heard of Mrs. K. being defeated in a school that was
known to house some of the roughest kids in Brooklyn.

The aforementioned bullets were in my coat because we
were experimenting with zip guns. In our case it was because of a fascination with guns rather than any intent to
use them as weapons, although other cliques in the school
did use the guns in gang fights. Our guns were crude con-
trivances made by taping a particular section of an automobile aerial (the gun barrel) to a wooden corner brace of
a fruit crate (the gun grip and stock) with band upon band
of heavy black electrician's tape. We fastened a hammer
from a toy pistol into position at the back end of the barrel
with heavy rubber bands. When pulled back and released,
the toy hammer functioned as a real one, striking the rim-
fire .22 bullet and causing it to fire—sometimes. More often
nothing happened. Occasionally the whole thing exploded.
We used to test the devices near the entrance to the Brooklyn Battery Tunnel, then still fresh from construction immediately below the schoolyard of P. S. 142. We would
tape a gun to a steel fence post, pointed toward one of the
huge mounds of earth at the construction site, pull the
hammer back, let go, jump away, and cheer an occasional
successful firing. Once a gun blew apart so badly that all
we could find in the darkness were remnants of the tape
and splintered wood on the post.

My group, six of us, soon grew tired of this dangerous
activity and graduated to store-bought .22 rifles which we

used in a friend's basement against a homemade backstop
of cardboard, wood, bricks, and steel sheets obtained from
dockside junk yards. We learned how to construct the backstop and also rules of gun safety from literature sent to us
upon request by gun manufacturers who never questioned
the age of those who wrote to them. Our gun club—we
called ourselves "The Snipers"—fired away from the time
I was eleven to when I was sixteen years old, and no one,
not even the other boys on the block, knew of it. We had
learned well to observe the closed behavior of la famiglia.
Apart from my five friends, only my family knew I owned
the target rifle, and they trusted my sense of responsibility
with it, a trust I never violated. All my father required before he would purchase the rifle for me at a Brooklyn department store was my word that I would never do anything wrong with it. Our ammunition was purchased for
us at a discount by the father of one of my friends, a U. S.
Customs officer on the Brooklyn waterfront. Whatever else
may be said for the child-rearing practices of Italian-
Americans, they resulted in children who enjoyed their
parents' trust.

My most serious offense against my parents' confidence
in me occurred also when I was in the seventh grade, and
involved something quite different. In the course of my job
one Saturday I was in an apartment with another boy
hanging venetian blinds. I saw a man's wrist watch lying
on a dresser. It had a black face with luminous numerals
and sweep-second hand, the very kind I had been wanting
badly ever since I could remember. On an impulse I quickly
took the watch and jammed it into my pocket. Then I pan-
icked, too scared to put it back. My fear peaked later when
I discovered that the owner's name was engraved on the
back of the timepiece. I looked to my parents for rescue
by allowing them to find the watch the next day and telling
them the truth about it. My father was angry and my
mother cried. They consulted with neighbors who were
compare and commare to them. It turned out that the compare had served in the Navy with the watch's owner, so it
was returned with apologies, which the owner brushed

aside, assuring my family that the matter was forgotten.

The sense of shame I felt at having publicly humiliated my parents is indescribable even after these many years. I swore to myself never again. Although my parents never berated me with the incident once it was closed, I have never forgotten it. It was the one time when I had violated a primary moral law of la via vecchia and caused public disgrace to my family.

Second-generation children went to work at unionized blue collar or service white collar jobs, the earlier females and males at the minimum legal age or before, the later ones after high school graduation. The relative few who completed college usually studied for a utilitarian vocation. Males chose medicine, law, and pharmacology; the even fewer college females chose teaching and nursing. In their jobs or careers the second generation learned the price of their compromise in disadvantage and became determined that their children go further in school. Thus they urged their third-generation children to get an education. They adopted this part of the American dream while still insisting that their children remain close to the family. Time and again I see the same pattern in my students in college. Their clear understanding of their identity is limited to the fact that their last names are Italian. All else is murky, poorly understood, confusing, and at times agony-causing.

They are bewildered by the seemingly conflicting desires their parents communicate to them. Get an education but don't change. Enter the larger world but don't become part of it. Grow but remain within the mode of the tradition. Go to church, even though we are lacking in religious enthusiasm. In short, maintain that difficult balance of conflicts which is the life style of the second generation.

The problem has become an enormous one as third- and fourth-generation youngsters are entering college in large numbers in the 1970's. The dilemma faced by these young people is staggering. They are unable on their own to perceive their roots or resolve the inevitable questions of their identity. They have little useful guidance to which they can relate. Their parents' guidance is poorly verbalized and merely feeds their sense of conflict. There are very few American-born Italian-American college teachers, few models whom they can emulate or turn to for help. The students are victims of biases on campus because of their Italian working-class backgrounds. The institutions they attend are unaware of their special needs and problems and do not respond to them, while making a great show of their responsiveness to the needs and concerns of other ethnic groups.

Italian-American students are hard working but feel isolated and lack self-confidence. They are determined to do well but are ill equipped to deal with their undermined condition. Taught to respect authority, behave decently, and rely on themselves, they are reluctant to seek help as individuals or organize to demand it as a group. So far, like the few Italian-Americans who preceded them on America's campuses, they are truly among America's most neglected students.

I recall similar loneliness and uncertainties in my own student years. I entered Queens College of the City University of New York as a freshman in 1957. Although C.U.N.Y. was a municipal university in a city whose white population was then about 24 per cent Italian-American, I was one of but a handful of my ethnic group in the student body. Moreover I had only one course in which the instructor was an Italian-American, a physical education course. The counselors provided by the college showed no indication that they understood anything of Italian-Americans beyond stereotypes.

The same set of conditions greeted me in the graduate schools of the University of Illinois and New York University. Although the education I received at the three schools was good and many faculty members and counselors were helpful in quite meaningful ways, the entire experience was unrelated to the ethnic center in my emerging personal identity. All questions of my status and meaning as an Italian-American—intellectual, cultural, and psychological questions—were simply, as it were, deferred to my private life.

When I was a college student there were relatively few Italian-Americans attending colleges. This situation is changing rapidly as the children of second-generation Italian-Americans enter colleges today in unprecedented numbers. For example, 50 per cent of Fordham University's student body is Italian-American. In addition, about 34,000 of the 169,000 matriculated undergraduate students at the City University of New York in 1972 were Italian-Americans. Of 38,256 freshmen entering the university in the fall of 1972, 9,564 were Italian-Americans. The pattern of substantial Italian-American enrollment began in the late 1960's. In the C.U.N.Y. freshman class of fall 1971, 9,803 of 39,211 students were Italian-Americans. The figure in the fall 1970 class was 8,877 out of a total of 35,511, and in the fall of 1969 it was 4,989 out of 19,959. In 1973 there was not one Italian-American among the one chancellor, one deputy chancellor, four vice-chancellors, four university-wide deans, and twenty college presidents in C.U.N.Y. Of C.U.N.Y.'s 165 deans, only fourteen are Italian-Americans.

Despite the fact that their numbers have increased, Italian-American students at C.U.N.Y. face the same institutional situation of their predecessors. They are still unguided and virtually unnoticed as a group, while other ethnic groups have large academic and support programs servicing their special needs. It has been estimated that only 3 to 6 per cent of the C.U.N.Y. faculty are Italian-Americans, and most of these are in the relatively powerless junior academic ranks. At Brooklyn College, a large four-year college serving the borough of New York with the largest Italian-American population, only fifty-nine of a total of 1,700 faculty were Italian-Americans in 1973. Queensborough College, a community college with a large Italian-American enrollment, has 503 faculty members. Of these only forty-six were Italian-Americans, and of these only two were full professors and six were associate professors in 1973. As far as I can determine, no one has compiled statistics of Italian-Americans at other colleges and universities today. My impression from conversations with professors across the nation is that Italian-American enrollment is up dramatically in every state with a substantial population of the group.

The SEEK program, College Discovery Program, Urban Centers, and other programs of the City University which are designed to provide special assistance to students whose circumstances make a successful college career difficult serve about 17,600 students. Of these only two hundred are Italian-Americans. And the number of Italian-American counselors in these programs is proportionately as low. This does not reflect the needs of Italian-American students at C.U.N.Y. It reflects neglect of them and their own diffidence, disorganization, and powerlessness.

In a 1970 study of C.U.N.Y.'s community colleges sponsored by Hostos Community College of C.U.N.Y., Professor Richard M. Bossone found that 8.5 per cent of the students at these colleges reported Italian as a language spoken in their homes besides English. (Other figures were Spanish 15.7 per cent; French 2.6 per cent; German 2.2 per cent; other 11.7 per cent). Of the Italian group 52 per cent were found to have comprehension study problems. (Other figures: Spanish 49 per cent; all others 39 per cent.) Thirty-three per cent of the Italian group had critical reading problems, 22 per cent had vocabulary problems, and 36 per cent had difficulty following directions integral to academic study.

The situation at C.U.N.Y. can be summed up by noting that in the spring of 1973 the university had several programs designed to meet the needs of other ethnic groups, notably Jewish, black, and Puerto Rican studies programs, and several programs which in fact serve needs of other ethnic groups, for example, the SEEK program, which in fact serves black and Puerto Rican students almost exclusively. Yet in a city which the 1970 census reported as having a white population more than 20 per cent of which is Italian-American, not one C.U.N.Y. program was designed to meet the specific needs of this group, nor did any C.U.N.Y. program give attention to these specific needs in their actual practices. To my knowledge, no college in the country has special programs or services for Italian-Americans. At C.U.N.Y. as on all American college campuses the third-generation Italian-American student finds himself precisely as the fewer second-generation students found themselves before him—isolated, alone, disoriented, conflicted, and neglected.

It is not surprising then that every study of Americans by ethnic background has found Italian-Americans among the worst equipped for success in American society. Writing in the *American Sociological Review* in April 1971, David L. Featherman reported a study of males of five ethnic backgrounds over the decade from 1957 to 1967. The groups were Anglo-Saxon Protestant, other Protestants, Jewish, Roman Catholics other than Italian and Mexican Americans, and Italian and Mexican Americans. The results of the study were summed up as follows:

> Jews, regardless of ethnic ancestry, attain higher levels of education, occupation and income than all other subgroups, while Roman Catholics of Italian and Mexican heritage achieve the lowest levels. . . . There is no evidence of occupational and income discrimination on purely religious or ethnic grounds. Contrary to current emphasis in the social psychology of religio-ethnic achievement, achievement-related work values and motivations of adults are neither key intervening variables nor do they influence the process of stratification to a substantial degree. *The most important variable in explaining the differential socioeconomic achievement of the religio-ethnic subgroups is education,* after the variation owing to the handicaps and benefits of social origins has been removed statistically. [Emphasis added.]

Another study, by B. C. Rosen, reported in the same journal in February 1959, found that Italian-American schoolboys scored very low on tests designed to measure "achievement aspirations" and "achievement-related values." The author concludes that "motivational orientations" account for the achievement showings of the different groups and specifically for the poor achievement of Italian-American boys in school. In *Racial and Ethnic*

Relations (1966), Bernard E. Segal reported the results of complicated studies of six ethnic groups in the U.S.—Negroes, Jews, white Protestants, Greeks, French-Canadians, and Italians. The author's summation of the detailed findings of complex research is in terms that clearly indicate the unfavorable condition of Italian-Americans.

> Achievement motivation is more characteristic of Greeks, Jews and white Protestants than of Italians, French-Canadians and Negroes. The data also indicate that Jews, Greeks and Protestants are more likely to possess achievement values and higher educational and vocational aspirations than Italians and French-Canadians. The values and educational aspirations of the Negroes are higher than expected, being comparable to those of Jews, Greeks and white Protestants, and higher than those of the Italians and French-Canadians. . . . Social class and ethnicity interact in influencing motivation, values and aspirations. . . .

Thus sociologists argue whether Italian-Americans do poorly in school because they are poorly motivated, and whether they do poorly in American society because they are poorly schooled or because of their class background. An understanding of the cultural history of Italian-Americans should reveal that each of the insights is accurate. More important, this understanding explains how the achievement record and class of the group are related to its particular, complicated motivational patterns regarding education.

The second generation entered the blue collar union labor force and did better financially than its levels of formal education would seem to indicate. The median income of Italian-Americans reported by the 1970 Census was $8,808. This is higher than the median of all ethnic groups ($7,894) and higher than the better educated English ($8,324), German ($8,607), and Irish-Americans ($8,127). In the 1970 edition of *Beyond the Melting Pot*, Glazer and Moynihan report that only 8.1 per cent of Italian-American men in New York City are employed in professional or managerial roles. This figure is far lower than that for the city's white Protestant males (22 per cent) and Jewish males (21.5 per cent). In fact it is even lower than that for New York City's black males (8.5 per cent), an ethnic group that deservedly has had its problems widely publicized and its needs supported.

Blue collar union labor, the route of Italian-Americans in the past is not indicated as an expanding labor force of the future. Future well-paying jobs will be more and more in the service industries and vocations. Many of these jobs require some level of college education. If the third generation *is merely to maintain* the Italian-American economic position, it must be the first generation to succeed in college in significant numbers. Of course to improve the economic position and the general class condition of Italian-Americans, higher education is an imperative for today's Italian-American young. The struggle for educational achievement is one in which young Italian-Americans cannot afford to fail. To succeed, they will have to overcome the paralyzing feeling of the previous generation of Italian-American youth, for example as reported by Joe Vergara in his account of his own youth. "My contemporaries had labelled me Italian. . . . I didn't want to be Italian. Or Swedish. Or Irish. Or anything 'different.' Like countless bewildered young people before me—and to come—I just wanted to be myself. 'Why can't I just be Joe?' I thought."

Because of the lack of educational achievement of the immigrant and second generations, there is a relative dearth of literature about Italian-Americans by Italian-American authors. In addition, Italian-Americans up to now have been a group that did not read. Therefore, the literature about them that was produced did not directly benefit them. Greeley reports the reading habits of Italian-American college graduates of June 1961, my own college class, to be very low. In fact they are lower than almost every other ethnic group of that year's graduates who were studied. Italian-Americans scored lower than graduates whose ethnic backgrounds were Jewish, Irish, Scandinavian, English, Polish, and black. Moreover, they scored lowest among eleven ethnic groups studied in the 1961 college class in percentage of those who entered the academic profession, the profession that does much of the writing in America. Only 5 per cent of the Italian-American graduates entered the academic realm, compared with 23 per cent of Catholic Polish graduates, 17 per cent of German-Jewish graduates, and 14 per cent of black graduates. This is reflected in New York City's public school system. In 1973, less than 10 per cent of the system's sixty thousand schoolteachers were Italian-American. Only one of the system's ninety high school principals was Italian-American. The scarcity of teachers of their own ethnic group simply adds to the strong temptation of Italian-American teen-agers to drop out of school. Their dropout rate is the second highest of the city's white ethnic groups.

Ninety-three per cent of the Italian-American population is not college educated, and this group reads little. Moreover they tend to view writings about Italian-Americans with distrust and even hostility, particularly those written by non-Italians. From the perspective of la via vecchia, any such efforts, no matter how sympathetic the feelings of those writing, are regarded as unwelcome exposure to the outside world. Whereas most other ethnic groups lionize their members who write of them, Italian-Americans often disdain even their own writers as people who have violated one of the principal codes of la via vecchia: to guard against all intrusions by the outside world. The effect of the scorn on the morale of Italian-American authors and scholars has been devastating. Many writers have either been frustrated in their efforts to succeed specifically as Italian-Americans or have turned their talents upon topics other than Italian-American experiences. Once again the very codes which have permitted the ethnic group to maintain its identity have functioned to minimize its own understanding and celebration of its identity. As has been true since the earliest second-generation children, today's Italian-American youngster is left to struggle to achieve a satisfactory sense of identity largely on his own.

The uneven struggle of the third generation is thus compounded. Not enough help comes to them by literature produced by their predecessors, just as it does not adequately exist from parental guidance, faculty awareness, or institutional programs.

The gap between Italian-American writings by Italian-Americans and the dearth of impact of these writings could be closed if today's Italian-American college student would read some of the fictional and non-fictional works about his group. But in my experience the typical third-generation student doesn't know of the existence of the literature and is inhibited from seeking it by the paralysis of his identity confusion and conflict. To compound it, much of the writings are not easily found, being absent from libraries and bookstores or out of print. All the young Italian-American finds about his group in the world of print is a flood of sensational writings about the Mafia, hardly something of use to him in the resolution of his problem.

The blind cycle of the dilemma of Italian-American youth must be broken. It must be opened by useful reading, institutional services, academic courses, parental communication, and discussions among the young themselves. But the cycle whirls by a powerful concurrence of forces. The young person is caught in its center. Its circular momentum forces him to use all his energies to hang on like a child on a playground go-around. He fears being flung into the void either by his home throwing him entirely away from outside world or his outside world throwing him entirely away from home. Labor, and especially union labor, gave the second generation the handholds to keep from being flung too far into the world while enabling working-class Italian-Americans to reach out and draw enough economic sustenance from the world to support the home. Few of this generation did better than a minimum education; few sacrificed secure low-level jobs to gain more upward social mobility. However, the road taken by the second generation did provide them with economic and social mobility beyond the status of their parents, despite the fact that the degree of advance was limited.

Yet this type of compromise by the large majority in the future will place the third generation not in higher but in lower economic and social positions than their parents, at the very time when their aspirations are to move up. The third generation cannot even remain at the status in which they have been raised if they follow the course of their parents. Their realities dictate that they will be socially mobile, moving either up or down. If it is to be up, they must be given assistance so that they can succeed in the task indirectly set for them in an article by Peter L. and Brigitte Berger called "The Blueing of America." The Bergers write, "As the newly greened sons of the affluent deny the power of work, blue collar class youth quietly prepare to assume power within the technocracy."

For Italian-American youth the alternative to assuming in the future the place of which the Bergers write is to slide from the lower-middle class into the lower class of society. Educational failure by Italian-Americans today means nothing less than their becoming the poor underclass of tomorrow's America. The educational part of the dilemma of Italian-Americans has become critical and urgent. Unless effective attention is devoted to it in the near future it will become desperate, and the third and fourth generations may find themselves where their immigrant forebears started—at the bottom of American society. On the other hand great hopes are possible for the young generations. No group of young people surpasses Italian-American youth in its sense of the power of work. It remains for them to root their sense of work in an enriched and integrated identity to take their proportionate share of what America has to offer. An education that serves all their needs as hyphenated Italian-Americans is an absolute necessity in the forging of such an identity. In this regard Italian-American youth and those who purport to educate them must become sensitive to Dante's warning in the *Divine Comedy: Vassene il tempo e l'uom non se n'avvede* —Time passes while man remains unaware.

The Problem of the Mafia Image

"Badi che, infamità, come non voglio farne io a nessuno, così non voglio che ne facciano gli altri, servendosi di me." (Look, I wouldn't like to commit an outrage, but I also wouldn't like others to commit an outrage and make use of me.)

—Pirandello

One of the television programs most popular while I attended college was the series called "The Untouchables." Week after week the program regaled the American public with the thrills of Elliot Ness and his team of G-men cracking down on an endless army of gangsters, practically all of whom had Italian names. I remember having to clench my teeth in anger and humiliation when I overheard some students casually refer to the program as "Cops and Wops."

I wanted to strike back. Yet I did not. I did not even attempt to argue against the insult. This was so partly because I was too emotional to trust my capacity to argue effectively. But it was so also because I had seen others go through the familiar argument that very-few-Italian-Americans-are-criminals. And I had seen the controlled but perceptible indulgent, supercilious smirks that answered this defense.

Isolated as I was on a campus with few other Italian-Americans, I did not believe I stood a chance of reversing the prejudice. Instead I responded in a typical student mode. I decided to study the topic of how Italian-Americans have come to be associated in the American mind with crime. My research led me back decades to the time when Southern Italians began to arrive in this country in significant numbers.

In the course of my study I discovered how the Mafia image was born and how it came to be used as a smear against Italian-Americans in general. More specifically I discovered two early incidents that explain why, of all the terms in the Italian and English languages for illegal and criminal societies, the word "Mafia" has become dominant. I also came to understand how the Mafia image has become so confused with the Italian-American life style in the minds of Americans. The explanations are quite different from those which Americans might expect. The explanations are far more complex and interesting than would be accounted for by the mere existence of Italian-American gangsters or the fact that "Mafia" is an Italian word.

The Mafia image of Italian-Americans is an older one than is commonly understood. It has been a cross laid across the shoulders of every Italian-American for upwards of a full century. It is a burden which has become heavier with time. A succession of events has steadily added to its weight. The most dramatic of these began long before names like Al Capone and Lucky Luciano became symbols upon which ignorance, anti-Italian fear, sensationalism, and bigotry could fasten.

The month of March is a turning point in the Mezzogiorno. The fall rains and winter coolness come to an end and the already hot sun predestines the fiery sirocco air of spring and summer. Memories of the Southern Italian spring must have occupied the mind of Lieutenant Joseph Petrosino as he stepped off a ship at Palermo, Sicily, in March 1909. A detective in the New York City Police Department, Lieutenant Petrosino was on one of the strangest missions ever attempted by an American policeman. It was to end abruptly a short time after the police officer landed in Sicily. As the detective walked in the Piazza Marina in front of Palermo's courthouse, he was killed by gunfire.

Credit for his murder was claimed by Don Vito Cascio Ferro, who let it be known that he had personally fired the gun that killed the New York plainclothes officer. The leaking of this revelation was sensational, for the don was the most powerful leader of the Mafia in Sicily and one of the most powerful in the history of the island. His career spanned a generation until 1926, when he was imprisoned by Mussolini's ruthless police chief Cesare Mori. Prefetto Mori was a tough hand. Fascist rule permitted him to act regardless of the ethics and law of a democratic state, and in 1928 Don Vito died in prison, where legend has it he carved on a wall the credo *vicaria maladia e nicisitati, si vidi lu cori di l'amicu*—prison, sickness and necessity reveal the heart of a "friend," a word having double meanings since it also meant a mafioso.

Whatever the heart of his self-proclaimed assassin, if there was time for Lieutenant Petrosino to think during the attack upon him, he must have been astonished. He was born in Salerno, an area far away from Sicily lying midway between the cities of Naples and Potenza. Migrating to the United States when he was thirteen years old, Giuseppe Petrosino joined the New York police when he grew up, and became a crack detective.

Years of investigation of crimes in the city's Italian community had convinced Petrosino that there was no organized crime syndicate in New York at that time. His findings told him that the criminals in the Italian immigrant culture were petty hoodlums who victimized their own people and that the thugs acted as common criminals either alone or with a few accomplices and not as members of an organized and disciplined illegal society. Yet he was in Palermo to investigate stories that these small-time thugs whom the Italian immigrants referred to by the insulting term *lazzaroni* (good for nothing, "bums") were somehow linked to the mysterious and fearful Mafia in Sicily, stories the detective was convinced were nonsense. In fact Petrosino was checking on the activities of hoodlums who had returned to Italy and the records of Italian born criminals active in the United States. The sad death of the man is overlaid with ironies. He was said by the press to be in Palermo seeking links (he was convinced did not exist) be-

tween the Sicilian Mafia and a counterpart American organization (which he did not believe existed).

Moreover subsequent research confirms that he was correct. No evidence was ever found that linked Don Vito or
any other criminal leaders in Sicily at the time with crimes
by Italians in the United States, crimes which consisted
mostly of petty extortion and which were committed almost
exclusively against other Italians. What brought Lieutenant
Petrosino to Sicily on such a strange mission? Why was he
murdered?

Answers to these questions bring to the surface the history of the Mafia image in America and the problems it
has created for Italian-Americans for decades. In the past
few years the mafioso rivals the cowboy as the chief figure
in American folklore, and the Mafia rivals the old American frontier as a resource for popular entertainment. The
problems presented by the image of a monolithic, criminal
Italian subculture called the Mafia, among the most severe
and persistent difficulties which Italian-Americans have
had to face, now overshadow all other obstacles to Italian-
Americans in overcoming their predicament in the United
States.

Detective Petrosino undertook his fateful trip to Palermo
in part to assuage a public hysteria about Italian crime that
was as irrational as it was widespread. By 1909 it had been
building for over twenty years. The hysteria had been simmering ever since Southern Italians began to come to the
United States in significant numbers after 1875. Fueled by
slanders about Southern inferiority and violence acquired
from the talk and writings of Northern Italians, and fed
by the strange ways of the immigrants who kept to themselves and resisted any intrusion by outsiders into their affairs, a bigoted paranoia took hold regarding the "innate
criminal ways" of the strange immigrants.

The facts about crime in the early Italian-American
ghettos did not support the bigotry. In their book *The
Italian in America,* published in 1905, Lord, Trevor, and
Barrows cite official records of arrests in cities with large
Italian-American populations in the year 1903. They show

that the record of Italian-American crime was no higher than that of other foreign-born Americans in the same cities. As a matter of fact the rate of crime among Italian-Americans was usually lower than that among other foreign-born groups. For example, the percentage of Italian-Americans among the foreign born arrested in Boston was 6.1 per cent at a time when Italians constituted 7 per cent of Boston's foreign-born population, according to the census of 1900, a percentage which, given the heavy immigration from Italy from 1900 to 1903, was surely lower than the reality. In Providence, where Italians made up at least 11.2 per cent of the foreign-born population (by the 1900 Census), their arrests constituted only 10.8 per cent of those of that population in 1903. In New York, where Italians constituted at least 11.5 per cent (1900 figure) of the foreign born, their arrests accounted for 12.3 per cent of the total among foreign born. And as James W. Vander Zanden points out in his *American Minority Relations* (1963), the rate of criminal convictions among Italian immigrants was less than that among the American-born white population.

Facts do not often dispel bigotry. They certainly did not in the early years of Italian immigration. An incident in 1890 caused the simmering prejudice about Italian criminality to erupt into the full-blown hysteria that eventually sent Detective Petrosino to Palermo, a hysteria that fed itself even more with his killing.

As indicated, crime in the early Little Italies was almost exclusively an affair of Italian criminals against Italian victims. In addition to common crimes like theft, robbery, and assault, Italian thugs practiced extortion against their poor brethren, a commonplace crime among all immigrant peoples whose status as impoverished aliens made them vulnerable to such victimization. However, the Italian victims of these and other crimes were loath to go to the police for help. In la via vecchia the authorities were oppressors and certainly no source of relief or protection. The immigrants preferred to suffer extortion rather than co-operate with the police of the stranieri. When on occasion presented with the means and opportunity, the victims retaliated against the extortionists by violence, frequently committed either by their own hand or by their kin in the tradition of the vendetta. Less frequently thugs were hired for the purpose, an extension of the traditional vendetta.

The misunderstood refusal to talk about crimes and the mysterious practices of vendetta alarmed Americans who insisted that they be investigated. Of course, investigations met a wall of nonco-operation and thus nourished the Americans' fear. The pattern was self-propelled, self-fueled, and grew on its own momentum. Italian secrecy based on mistrust of official authorities brought American alarm, in turn bringing American investigation, in turn bringing on more Italian mistrust and fear of outsiders and thus more evidence of secrecy, which in turn caused more alarm and investigation—and so went the cycle.

The cycle of fear was whirling at high speed in New Orleans in 1890. The city's superintendent of police had made a name for himself by investigating cases of extortion within the city's mostly Sicilian Little Italy around Decatur Street. In the process the mutual fear between Italian-Americans and the other residents of New Orleans was escalated to a frightening level. When Superintendent Hennessey was shot to death on October 15, 1890, a crime that still remains unsolved, the natural—and bigoted—response was to blame it on the Italian immigrants. The long-simmering anti-Italian hysteria burst into an ugly frenzy. The police embarked upon a wholesale roundup of Italians while the then prevalent yellow press in America screamed for vengeance. An article in the *Popular Science Monthly* of December 1890 was typical. Entitled "What Shall We Do with the Dago?" the article went on to allege a grave threat to all decent Americans posed by Italian immigrants who, according to the bigotry of the time, were cast as stiletto-carrying dagos. As the article described them, Italians delighted in using their knives "to lop off another dago's finger or ear, or to slash another's cheek."

The extent of the fear of Italian immigrants and its lack of justification cannot be exaggerated. It is indicated in an event that took place two years earlier in Buffalo, New York, on March 4, 1888. On the following day the *Buffalo Daily Courier* reported on the activities of the city's police that night. "Captain Kilroy of the first precinct sent consternation into the Italian colony last night in the persons of forty-two stalwart bluecoats who were ordered to bring in all the male Dago [*sic*] that looked as if they carried knives." The paper reported that 325 "swarthy-looking, jibbering foreigners were taken to the stationhouse." The raid led to the confiscation of two knives. To the bigots the disappointing catch only indicated just how insidious were the ways of the Italian immigrants.

Such was the state of affairs when Hennessey was murdered. Fourteen of the hundreds of Italians who were arrested after the murder were indicted, including a fourteen-year-old boy. Nine of the indicted were tried. Six were acquitted by a jury which could not reach a verdict regarding the three others. This outcome did not satisfy the hate-filled mood of much of the country. All fourteen accused were kept in jail, including the six already acquitted.

On March 14, 1891, some of the leading citizens of New Orleans openly led a mob of six to eight thousand people which stormed the jail holding the prisoners. As the police looked on and made no attempt to intervene, the mob savagely beat the Italians, hanged one or two of them, and blasted the others into bloody heaps with an arsenal of guns. Despite the fact that the leaders and many members of the mob were identified, no one was ever held accountable for the slaughter of the eleven prisoners. The outrage caused the Italian government to recall its ambassador from Washington in angry protest. (Three of the victims were Italian subjects, the eight others being naturalized American citizens or in process of becoming American citizens.)

While some Americans and newspapers condemned the lynching and other assaults against Italian-Americans in New Orleans, many condoned it, including Theodore Roosevelt. The tone of those who approved illustrates the first major manifestation of the Mafia image and the problems it presents to Italian-Americans. Ignorant rumors of an Italian secret society of criminals circulated, and all Italian-Americans were accused either directly or by implication of being somehow responsible. For example, the New York *Times* editorials of March 16 and 17, 1891, justified the New Orleans lynchings. "These sneaking and cowardly Sicilians," said the first editorial, "the descendants of bandits and assassins, who have transported to this country the lawless passions, the cut-throat practices, and the oath-bound societies of their native country, are to us a pest without mitigation." On the following day the paper said, "Lynch law was the only course open to the people of New Orleans to stay the issue of a new license to the Mafia to continue its bloody practices."

The Rochester *Union Advertiser* on March 17, 1891, wrote that it found "the whole affair deplorable." However it went on to say, "We are not unfriendly to the men of any foreign land who come here to be Americanized, and all we ask is that they shall not bring murderous plots and vendetta along with them or the readiness to establish such against Americans who may incur their displeasure."

As Professors Salvatore Mondello and Luciano I. Iorizzo have documented in a well-researched essay in a small volume published by the American Italian Historical Association (*An Inquiry into Organized Crime*, 1970), a debate now began among Americans about whether there existed among Italian-Americans a society or societies of criminals referred to as the Black Hand or Mafia. Americans debated whether Italian-Americans were somehow all disposed to criminality by their genetic endowment or cultural inheritance.

Writing in the *Chautauquan* in November 1892, one writer concluded that America was "draining off the criminals and defectives of Europe." An article in *Public Opinion* in May 1893 warned that America must determine whether "the desperadoes of Italy shall steal peacefully into the heart of our democracy." An essay in *Charities Review* in 1894 asserted that a criminal society called the Mafia existed in the United States. An article in *Arena* in 1897 said that Southern Italians were "especially licentious and passionate."

Some Americans took contrary positions. In the *South Atlantic Quarterly* in July 1905 an article by Emily F. Meade entitled "Are the Italians a Dangerous Class?" concluded that "Italians never burglarized houses, even when known to be empty," and "Americans are never afraid to meet them alone, day or night." In an article in the February 24, 1906, issue of *The Outlook*, John F. Carr waxed poetic in his defense of Italian immigrants. "So far from being a scum of Italy's paupers and criminals, our Italian immigrants are the very flower of her peasantry." The Rochester *Democrat and Chronicle* on November 29, 1908, reported that the Sicilian-Americans there had produced a religious play in the city to plead their case against the allegations that, as the paper put it, "they were all members of a Black Hand society and had no religion or respect for the law."

But the defenses of Italian-Americans were overwhelmed by the fear with which Americans regarded them. When the New York *Times* called for a special police force to combat what it termed organized crime among the low-class Italians of New York, the proposal was acted upon. In December 1906 a special squad was established to investigate crime among Italian-Americans, and Detective Joseph Petrosino was named as its head. Petrosino and his men repeatedly announced their findings. They found that, while Italian thugs did victimize other Italians, the hoodlums acted either alone or in small independent, unconnected groups.

The Italian Consulate investigated thirty cases of crimes which newspapers attributed to the Black Hand, and found that all but one were explainable by events and reasons not involving Black Hand criminals. Nonetheless the scare continued and grew upon every report, no matter how absurd. Thus, when an Italian anarchist killed a Catholic priest on February 24, 1908, in Denver, Colorado, the Binghamton *Republican* across the country in New York State jumped to an obviously groundless conclusion. "That the mind of this Denver murderer was illy [sic] balanced," the paper wrote, "and he was partly irresponsible for what he did, cannot be doubted, neither can it be doubted that we are having more exhibitions of Black Handism than is good for the country and we must enforce the laws in a manner to make less of it."

The debate continued nationwide until Petrosino's murder in 1909. This act was decisive in the minds of many. In a leap beyond logic they concluded that his killing proved despite all evidence that the dreaded society did exist, that it was responsible for many if not all unsolved crimes in American cities, and further that all Italian-Americans were to blame. In Chicago in 1913, the police said that forty-five unsolved murders that year were the work of the Black Hand—and offered no evidence to back the assertion. At one point the Chicago police arrested fifty Italians at random. A court fined them each one dollar and court expenses on trumped-up charges of disorderly conduct, and released them. As Professor Alexander De Conde observed in his *Half Bitter, Half Sweet* (1971), "The inspector who imposed the punishment assumed that the entire Italian community in Chicago was somehow implicated in the crimes and that the fines would frighten the Italians into good behavior. Actually, the arrest and conviction of men known to be innocent stimulated distrust rather than respect for law."

The cycle of mutual fear and distrust between Italian immigrants and the larger American community was out of control. The New York *Times* echoed hundreds of similar editorials when it wrote on March 14, 1909, of the Camorra (a name that Americans had recently begun to use), the Mafia, and the Black Hand that their "bloodthirsty operations must be stopped in this country, even if it is necessary to exclude immigration from Sicily or from any part of Italy."

Thus began a confused but incessant and widespread maligning of Italian-Americans that continues to this day. Petrosino's murder remains shrouded in mystery. Even if we accept the claim which the Sicilian Mafia leader is said to have made for his murder—a claim of which some were skeptical, suspecting that the don may have falsely boasted of responsibility for a notorious murder merely to publicize his power in Sicily and thereby increase it—we have no knowledge of the reasons why Petrosino was killed. Among the many speculations about the incident I have read and heard, those I heard from my grandfather seem most likely.

My grandfather was a young man about twenty years old living in Palermo when Petrosino was shot. For years afterward he and his Palermitano friends discussed the affair and came to what appear to be reasonable conclusions. They did not know, as today we still do not know, whether crimes in America at the time were linked to the Mafia in Sicily. All we may say with certainty is that despite many investigations made at the time no evidence was brought forth indicating a transatlantic criminal conspiracy. But my grandfather and his friends concluded that it isn't likely that Petrosino was killed to prevent him from uncovering ties between the Sicilian Mafia and American crime even if in fact they existed. Petrosino had not uncovered any such connections in the United States, where he had considerable authority and power to operate, much more than he would have had in Sicily. At the time the Italian government with all its power was unable to find much real information about the Mafia in Sicily. It is highly improbable that the leaders of the Mafia there would be afraid that a single New York policeman, born in faraway Salerno and unfamiliar with Sicily, would be able to do better. If Petrosino was assassinated by the Sicilian Mafia rather than criminals unconnected with it, the killers must have acted from different motives.

My grandfather and his friends conjectured that the detective was murdered for some or all of the following reasons. As indicated, the Mafia in Sicily may have seen his murder as an easy way to intensify its reign of terror in its homeland. Petrosino was a high-ranking police officer from the United States, a land which many Sicilians at the time regarded with awe. To them it was an imagined place of fabulous wealth and power, a land to which one could go to escape the poverty and oppression of the Mezzogiorno. The Sicilian mafiosi may have been unable to resist the golden opportunity afforded them to cut down a symbol of this power and riches and thereby emerge as giant killers. The fact that the policeman was alone in their own backyard and very vulnerable to successful assault may have made the temptation to exploit the opportunity irresistible. If this was in the minds of the mafiosi their assumption was correct. The American's murder catapulted their terrorist prestige to new heights.

My grandfather's group believed that Petrosino was murdered also because his very presence in Sicily was an insult to all Sicilians, indeed to all people of the entire Mezzogiorno. Giuseppe Petrosino was contadino-born. He was raised in the Mezzogiorno until the age of thirteen, the age of manhood as reckoned by the old contadini. They regarded his return to the Mezzogiorno to investigate their affairs in the historically-despised role of a police official of a remote government as an extreme and deliberate affront. Just as their attitude is difficult for Americans to appreciate, the contadini could not begin to understand the American cultural phenomenon in which a young man could be assimilated in the American moral and legal system and serve these with a sense of honor. To them Petrosino's behavior constituted a very offensive immorality, nothing less than an *infamia* that demanded punishment. As they saw it, Petrosino violated a kind of extended *ordine della famiglia* by publicly taking the side of strangers against his own kind and thus advancing his own individual position in life. The mafioso who claimed credit for his punishment—for his execution, as it were—no doubt sought to gain himself the reputation of a hero by his disclosure. Through his boast he sought the status of a defender of the venerated *via vecchia*. The fact that most Sicilians regarded this punishment as excessive dovetailed well with the desire of the mafioso to strike terror in the hearts of their countrymen.

Whatever we may surmise about the motives of

Petrosino's killers, and however much we may understand how the killing was regarded from the perspective of the contadini living in the Mezzogiorno, the effects of the news of the murder were calamitous for Italian-Americans. Petrosino's death brought a plague of vilification and persecution upon them. The edition of the New York *Times* that reported the murder makes fascinating reading. In addition to the story, the paper ran column upon column speculating about Italian crime and a list of alleged Black Hand crimes committed that year in New York City. Most were bombings, but the list also included one body found dead of "stiletto wounds." The killers were unknown, but evidently the *Times* could distinguish between wounds caused by Italian knives and those caused by other knives. Another case involved twelve Italians who attacked three revenue officers on a street corner who were taking two of their countrymen to a post office to be arraigned. A third case, one of murder of a butcher, was linked to the criminal society because "the cartridge that held the bullet that killed him came from [was manufactured in] Italy."

The Brooklyn *Daily Eagle* represented the mood of many Americans when on March 15, 1909, it declared that "the fight against the Black Hand in the city will now be undertaken in earnest." Because officials were unable to identify members of Italian criminal societies the major thrust of their fight was frequently directed against the Italian-American population as such. Mass police raids against Italians became common in America's major cities. For example, in a typical raid 194 Italian-Americans were jailed in Chicago. The police charged en masse into Little Italy and collared anyone who appeared to be suspicious according to the feverish criteria of the time. When the authorities were unable to produce any link whatsoever between the prisoners and crimes, the police reluctantly released all 194 men seized in the raid.

In many cities these tactics designed to keep the Italian immigrants in line created a state of open hostility between police and Italian-Americans. In May 1909 the police were greeted with a riot when they entered the Italian section of Hoboken, New Jersey. According to the New York *Times* of May 6, Italian residents exchanged gunshots with police from tenement windows during the disorder.

Meanwhile, the police persecution of Italian-Americans was accompanied by the more damaging and lasting persecution by the press and public opinion. The American mentality was so pervaded by bigotry that even E. A. Ross, a man who held a reputation as a progressive in his time, wrote an article about Italians in 1914 in *Century* magazine in which he asserted, "That the Mediterranean peoples are morally below the races of northern Europe is as certain as any social fact. Nothing less than venomous is the readiness of the southern Europeans to prey upon their fellows."

The theme of innate criminality has become so entangled with the American picture of Italian-Americans that it continues today stronger and more confused than ever. Even those who would defend Italian-Americans from this slander unintentionally contribute to the confusion by contrasting the legitimate status and decent lives of today's Italian-Americans with vague references to their cultural heritage. The implication is that the historical background of Italian-Americans is shameful and that they become acceptable only as they renounce their roots. Writing in the New York *Times* on August 1, 1972, William V. Shannon of the newspaper's editorial board seems to set this theme in motion when he links his defense of Italian-Americans against the gangster stereotype with an ambiguous reference to the necessity for Italian-Americans to overcome their "dark legacy." In an angry denunciation of the film *The Godfather* he wrote:

No one denies that a few Italian-Americans are gangsters. To that extent, "The Godfather" rests on a substratum of fact. But for the millions of Italian-Americans who are not gangsters, the success of this film raises an enormous cultural obstacle. It retards their efforts to overcome this dark legacy from the past and to establish positive heroes for their children to emulate.

While Shannon's words are equivocal about whether the
dark legacy is the history of Italian-American gangsters or
a historical culture which is itself criminal, the insinuation
that Italian-Americans have a special cultural heritage of
crime and thus a propensity to become criminals is common. For example, the implication that the only gangsters
on the scene today are Italian-Americans is unmistakable in
a piece by another influential writer. Writing in *Life* magazine on June 23, 1972, Richard Schickel tore apart a film
called *Prime Cut*. The film had nothing to do with Italian-
Americans, criminal or law-respecting. It concerned what
Schickel scores as nonsensical goings-on among absurdly
fictional gangs controlling today's meat industry in the
Midwest. Yet Schickel saw fit to write, "The mobs at war
[in the film], incidentally, are Wasp and Irish, which
should please the Italian Defense League, if not the realists
among us." The implication is that it is inconceivable that
gangsters who are not Italian-Americans operate in the
United States. Even when wholly fictional mobsters are
portrayed on the screen they must be made to be Italian-
Americans. They must conform to the long history of such
Hollywood slanders, including such famous films as *Little
Caesar*, in which Edward G. Robinson played an Italian-
American mobster, and *Detective Story*, in which virtually
every criminal shown in the movie's presentation of police
life in New York from ordinary thug to wealthy gangster
was depicted in the crudest, most insulting stereotypes of
Italian-Americans. These films, including one which was
a sensational, highly fictionalized movie of the Petrosino
murder, were seen by millions of Americans. Little wonder
that Jerre Mangione in his autobiographical novel, *Mount
Allegro* (1942), recounts that his Sicilian father forbade
him and his brother to carry boy scout knives when they
were children in Rochester, New York, "because of the
unpleasant association they had in the public mind with
Sicilians."

It is time to look into the hoary distortion that Italian-
Americans inherit a legacy of crime. In doing this once

again it is wise to heed Justice Holmes's belief that a page of history is worth a volume of logic.

In the nineteenth century the world became aware that a number of outlaw groups were operating throughout the Mezzogiorno. News of them became especially frequent after the 1860's, when the new Italian government publicized its conclusions about them. Although various kinds of illegal bands operated throughout the South, attention became focused on activities in three areas—Calabria, Naples, and western Sicily.

In Calabria, as elsewhere in the Mezzogiorno, bands of brigands operated in the rough terrain. These bands engaged chiefly in smuggling and banditry. The victims of their robberies often were members of the galantuomo class, the very wealthy, government officials, and those occasional outsiders who traveled in the hills of Calabria. The ranks of these groups were filled with the sons of local contadini who could not survive the extreme poverty, unemployment, and exploitation of the landowners, the old Bourbon government, and the new Italian government.

In 1861 the new Italian government sent troops to police Calabria. The old economic order had collapsed under the strains of national unification, and the numbers of gangs had increased. Because of the government's deliberate policy of favoring the North over the South of Italy in its programs of economic development, and because of its ignorant and arrogant insensitivity to the customs of the South, the Calabrians soon grew to hate the new government in the North. They naturally turned to the gangs which they had traditionally called brotherhoods and *fibbie* (buckles). They began to call gangs *onorate società* (honored societies), as illegal bands became called throughout the Mezzogiorno.

These groups, collectively called in Calabria 'Ndrangheta (the Brotherhood) as well as *Onorata Società,* now took on the role of guerrilla units against political oppression. The older *'ndrine,* who to some degree had always mixed political insurrection with outright banditry, and the members of the newer and predominantly political bands were forced into a war with the Italian army. The Italian government viewed them plainly and simply as *briganti* and began a massive effort to wipe them out.

Complaining that *invece che del pane ci si dà il piombo* —instead of bread they send us lead (bullets)—the members of the bands fought back against the government, which had attempted to destroy la via vecchia, had brought starvation to the villages of Calabria, and now was engaged in a military effort to kill them. Because they were thrust into the role of the region's defenders against political oppression and military aggression, these brigands became known to their paesani as *giovanotti onorati*. To this day the contadini of Calabria still remember them as honored or honorable young men. They became martyrs as the government troops carried out its campaign of extermination with an earnest ferocity. In just two years from March 1861 to April 1863 the Italian troops from the North killed or wounded 7,151 of the giovanotti onorati while suffering only 307 casualties.

The army's campaign against *il brigantaggio* was seen by the Calabrians as a massacre of their sons. Brigandage became associated with legitimate and heroic self-defense. This attitude was broadcast to the rest of the world by the Italian government. The report served to convince the outside world that the Northern Italians were right in their assertions that the Southern contadini were violent underdeveloped people whose primitive culture was inseparably interlaced with criminality.

In the past the various old 'ndrine had been founded, died out, and replaced by others. There is no evidence that they were unified. Nor is there any evidence that the honored societies of the period after 1860 were anything but unassociated bands, each operating in its own locality. Yet Calabrians referred to the bands in the singular as the brotherhood and the honored society. The manner of speaking represented nothing but semantic custom, a custom which we also follow in the English language. For example, we speak of "municipal government in New York State" as if it were of one piece, when in fact we mean a class of unconnected local governments in many cities and towns. The semantic practice lent credence to the allegation that there was a vast monolithic outlaw society in Calabria.

Many Calabrian families were related to individual giovanotti onorati. This led to the identification of a vast criminal society with the contadino family structure as such. The well-publicized, often exaggerated and romanticized activities of the Calabrian Onorata Società continued throughout and beyond the period of Italian immigration to the United States. In fact news stories still appear of the brigandage in the mountains of Calabria. This stream of news, legends, and propaganda preceded and accompanied the Italians who arrived in the United States.

Meanwhile sensational news coming out of Naples also seemed to confirm the confused identification of Meridionale customs with those of a monstrous criminal society. Stories emerged of a highly organized secret society in Naples called the Camorra. The outside world learned that the Camorra specialized in extortion, blackmail, kidnaping, and smuggling. It enforced its will through a bloodcurdling terrorism that included torture, horrible disfiguring of victims, and murder. The news reports often exaggerated the numbers of camorristi, and once again depicted a single unit, whereas in reality the Camorra was composed of several unconnected bands of hoodlums. Yet the reports of the Camorra's criminal activities were essentially accurate. The camorre of Naples were secret gangs which engaged solely in terroristic crime. At no point did they play any social or political role.

The beginnings of the Camorra go back to the late seventeenth century or early eighteenth century. The name is thought to be a derivative of the Spanish words for "cloak" and "gang," respectively chamarra and morra. The gangs first came to public attention early in the nineteenth century in the Neapolitan prisons run by the Spanish Bourbons. These camorre were organizations of prisoners which ruled other prisoners through a reign of terror. The situation was similar to the "barn boss" system in some American prisons today. The Neapolitan gangs moved outside prison walls as their members were released from prison. The former convicts either transported the prison gangs to Naples and its surrounding villages, or more likely they established new groups modeled on those they had known in prison.

Fantastic legends grew about the camorristi. It was said that they swore oaths of loyalty, obedience, and secrecy in rituals in which the initiates smeared themselves with their own blood. People believed the legends as they saw the results of the thugs' violence. The camorristi sometimes slashed their victims' faces and painted the wounds to impede healing, so that they left hideous scars. At times they killed people and left their mutilated corpses where they would easily be found as calling cards of their terror.

The terror in Naples became widely known in the world in the years following 1877. In that year the Italian government launched an all-out, highly publicized, but unsuccessful campaign to eliminate the several camorre which it claimed constituted one centrally controlled Camorra. Scholars still dispute whether there ever was such a single Camorra, but no one disputes the fact that the camorre were at a peak of their power in the years between 1880 and 1900. The chronology meant that stories of the Camorra also accompanied Italian immigrants in their voyages to the United States.

In 1877 the Italian government also began a public effort to eliminate certain *associazioni* in western Sicily known as *mafie*. The Sicilians referred to these groups collectively as the Mafia, and the Italian government insisted that the singular designation reflected more than semantic custom.

The origins of the word "mafia" and of the organizations it designated are obscure. A fanciful legend has it that the word is an acronym for the expression *Morte alla Francia Italia anela* (Italy desires or strives for France's death) or *Morte ai Francesi gl'Italiani anelano* (Death to the French as Italians wish, or for which they strive). Those who explain the word in this way refer to a famous historical incident which took place in Sicily in the year 1282. On

Easter Sunday of that year the residents of Palermo began a bloody rebellion against the despised French who ruled and oppressed them. The rebellion quickly spread throughout Sicily and almost all of the French on the island were killed. With characteristic sarcasm Sicilians dubbed the violent Easter rebellion with a term that history books have used now for seven centuries—"Sicilian Vespers." However, it is most unlikely that this is the origin of "mafia," since there is no evidence that the word was used before the nineteenth century.

Others believed the word "mafia" is an acronym for another battle motto. It is said that in 1860 a Sicilian society loyal to Mazzini was organized to conduct a campaign of sabotage against Bourbon officials. Its motto is supposed to have been *Mazzini Autorizza Furti, Incendi, Avvelenamenti* (Mazzini authorizes—or calls for—theft, arson, and poisoning). Still others trace the origins of the word to Arab words meaning "cave" and "place of refuge." Sicilians who rebelled against the authorities during the days of Arab rule often took refuge in caves.

Whatever the origins of the word, it is clear that Sicilians have long used the adjective "mafia" with a small *m* to refer to an ideal. It is an ideal of courage, strength, agility, quickness, endurance, and intelligence. Use of the word in context of this ideal has nothing to do with crime or outlaw societies. In this custom the Sicilian immigrants who lived in Brooklyn when I was a boy would use the adjective *"mafioso"* (pronounced by Sicilians *"mafiusu"*) to mean "good," "fine," or "admirable." For example, they would say of a good example of a man, *"che mafioso (mafiusu),"* just as they would refer to a courageous spirited animal, e.g., a dog, as *uno cane mafiusu*. Used in this sense "mafioso" has no connotations of a criminal group or person.

However, the word was also used by Sicilians to refer to criminal organizations in Sicily, and Americans learned only this meaning of the word from news reports from Italy. The twofold usage of the word by immigrants in America's Little Italies caused great confusion and fed suspicions around the turn of the century. Every time Americans heard "mafioso," they thought the Sicilians were speaking of a member of a secret society.

As a matter of fact immigrants did not use "Mafia" to refer to the gangs of extortionists operating in America's Little Italies in the period before 1920. They called these gangs collectively *la Mano Nera*, the Black Hand. The term originated in the fact that the extortionists used an old symbolic threat to their victims. The thugs would send a picture which resembled the mark obtained by pressing an open hand covered with black ink against a flat surface, usually a sheet of paper. Immigrants rarely referred to the members of these Black Hand gangs as mafiosi, and only when intending to mean that a certain member was courageous, spirited, or displayed some other quality of the old ideal.

In the custom of the old land the immigrants referred to members of the Black Hand gangs with terms that indicated the status and power of the individuals as such. One who had little status or power was called simply a *delinquente* (criminal), a *lazzarone* (bum), *carogna* (scoundrel, "louse"), or a *disgraziato* (evil wretch or "slob"). A powerful criminal was a *uomo rispettato*, a man who commands respect. Throughout the Mezzogiorno this last term was a morally neutral one that referred to any person who had position or power regardless of the legal status of what he did. It was a Realpolitik term used to refer to lawyers, professors, priests, politicians, businessmen, doctors, landlords, farmers, and criminals. In fact, all who succeeded in acquiring status or power in any vocation, legal or illegal, were *uomini rispettati*.

In medieval times a person would *mostrare il suo rispetto* (show his respect) by kissing the hands of very powerful uomini rispettati. The immigrants to America still followed the custom on occasion. Sicilians in the Brooklyn of my childhood commonly used an expression I have since heard used in Sicily. When a relationship of mutual respect was formed between two people (not necessarily a relationship of affection of any kind), they would say to each other, *Baciamu li mani*—dialect for "Let us kiss hands,"

Because reports from Italy placed the custom of *baciare le mani* only in the context of tribute paid to criminals, Americans were further alarmed when they heard residents of Little Italies frequently use the expression and occasionally actually kiss hands.

The Mafia in Sicily is very likely a very old institution, although the word was not used much before 1860. Prior to that it had existed in the form of local secret bands which later became known as "mafie." By definition these were ideally (if not in fact) composed of men who possessed the mafioso qualities mentioned. Although mafie existed in large cities like Palermo, Trapani, and Agrigento, most of the mafie operated in the rural villages of western Sicily. Over the centuries such groups had functioned in different areas and at different times as 1) brigands and extortionists, 2) as local private armies employed by government agents or absentee landowners to repress the contadini, especially as the feudal system of Sicily became moribund after Napoleon's Italian victories, and 3) sometimes as quasi-political guerrilla bands on the side of the landowners and/or contadini as *vendicatori* (avengers) against government oppression.

Because their members were contadini, the early mafie naturally appropriated old contadino institutions, three in particular. They adopted as their own structure an organization analogous to l'ordine della famiglia. Their members carried the ideal into the mafie with them and made altered forms of it the organizations' code. The mafie also employed the old practice of vendetta, a custom of revenge against enemies by deadly violence, seen as an impersonal family duty.

The appropriation of traditional contadino behavior by the early mafie accounts for the terms used by Sicilians to refer to the bands and their members. A local band was sometimes called *la santa mamma* (the holy mother). Later it was called an onorata società as such groups were called in Calabria and throughout the Mezzogiorno. It was also known as a *società degli amici*, society of friends, "friends" here meaning associates. (Recall that the contadini distinguished among three types of friends. Compare were very close friends, almost kin. Amici were companions or co-workers. And paesani, which literally meant fellow townsmen, also was used to mean "friend" in the most casual sense, an acquaintance.)

The leader of a mafia group was called a padrino (god-father) and mafiosi to this day are called *gli uomini qualificati* (qualified men; specialists), and *gli amici degli amici* (friends of friends in the sense of co-collaborators). Sicilians seldom colloquially referred to the bands as mafie or Mafia or called their members mafiosi.

This practice continues. On a recent trip to Sicily I heard a song sung in public on the coast of eastern Sicily, an area where the Mafia has never taken hold as an institution. The theme of the song was that the Mafia was a *sanguisuga*, a blood leech. Such a song probably would have not been sung in western Sicily, where there is little casual use of the word Mafia as it refers to an organization.

After the Italian unification upheaval of 1860 the mafie enlarged their role as political forces, filling the power vacuum created in the social turmoil. Local military units called *squadre della mafia* fought with Garibaldi against Bourbon troops. Some of these squadre were made up of men who had been members of the old mafie. In fact some of Garibaldi's squadre were nothing more than old mafia bands who temporarily set aside their normal activities to become guerrilla fighters for a political movement.

Later as the mafie increased their political power, they took the side of the large landowners, who had turned most of the government's reform efforts to their own interest, and repressed contadino pressures for genuine social reform. As a matter of fact, in many regions mafie, government agents, and great landowners formed corrupt alliances against the contadini. By 1894, when populist contadino groups known as Fasci Siciliani revolted against the government in the name of reform, the mafie collaborated with government troops in the armed repression of the Fasci (*fasci* simply means "bands").

By the latter half of the nineteenth century the mafie had

lost their sometime role of defender of the Sicilian people and the via vecchia. They totally corrupted and perverted traditional codes of la famiglia and vendetta. As their power and greed grew and their corruption spread, the mafie also began to collaborate with each other. Thus, the Mafia became a federation of gangs controlling western Sicily for its own profit and power. It is not known exactly when one leader or *capo* became *capo di tutti capi*, or supreme head of the federation, but by the late nineteenth century it was clear that the Mafia had reached some degree of federation. News of it spread to the world through the reports of the Italian government and press.

So it came to be that when the immigrants from the Mezzogiorno settled in the United States, Americans were aware of the existence of outlaw bands and societies in Calabria, Naples, and Sicily. Aside from this, however, Americans had little knowledge of the nature of the Calabrian Onorata Società, the Neapolitan Camorra, or the Sicilian Mafia. The term Mafia rather than other terms came to be dominantly associated with Italian-American crime by the historical accident that the two earliest notorious incidents that took place on the American scene were the murders of Hennessey and Petrosino. Both crimes were in Sicilian contexts. Americans came to label the Black Hand activity of the time as Mafia crime. Despite lack of evidence Americans also came to suspect that the Sicilian Mafia had transplanted itself to the United States or had formed itself anew here. And they came to suspect that all crimes by Italian-Americans were linked to the Mafia and that the Mafia controlled all organized crime. Again, all of the evidence collected about the period before 1920 indicates that there was no basis in fact for these views. The year 1920 marks another critical point in the cancerous growth of the Mafia image of Italian-Americans.

Every group living in poverty in the United States or elsewhere has spawned crime. The poor Italian-American ghettos produced criminals who quite naturally combined their heritage of the ideal of the *uomo segreto* or *uomo di panza* (a man who kept things in his guts), the comparaggio custom of kinship extended to nonrelatives, and in some cases of la famiglia itself with their criminal activities. As time passed some of these criminals looked beyond the Black Hand activities in their quest for expanded profit and power. In the 1920's they joined rapidly expanding gangs which operated outside as well as within the Italian ghettos. The gangs were getting rich meeting the demand for bootleg liquor created in 1920, when the Volstead Act went into effect.

Italian-American criminals did not form these early Prohibition gangs, but joined them as low-ranking members. The gangs were most often controlled and led by Jewish and Irish-American gangsters. Rothstein, Bouchalter ("Lepke"), Shapiro, Diamond, Lansky, Kastel, Siegal, Weiss, Madden, Zwillman, Farrell, Schultz, Connolly, O'Bannion, Moran, and O'Donnell were names of some of the most notorious of these mob leaders. Nativists slandered the Jews and Irish in this country by attributing criminal tendencies to their ethnic groups per se. But there were no legends of secret criminal societies in the European roots of these groups, and no Gaelic or Yiddish word equivalent to "Mafia" enjoyed the notoriety the press had given that term since the Hennessey and Petrosino cases.

The avarice of low-level gang members grew with the profits and power of the gangs. Eventually young Italian-American hoodlums in a series of gang wars seized control of much of the bootlegging and other rackets financed with the profits of bootlegging. One of the most publicized of these was between an alliance of Jewish and non-Sicilian Italian gangsters which included the notorious names of Joseph Masseria, Vito Genovese, Joe Adonis, and Frank Costello on one side, and a group of Sicilian-Americans on the other side, including Joseph Bonanno, Stefano Magadinno, Joseph Profaci, Salvatore Maranzano, and Gaetano Gagliano. Because some of the Sicilians had come from the town of Castellamare del Golfo in Sicily, the 1930 fight was dubbed by the press "the Castellamarese War." After a series of murders, betrayals, and counterbetrayals, a group of Italian gangsters emerged as leading figures in organized crime.

As other Italian-Americans emerged as gang leaders, the press began once again to use the term Mafia, which had become dormant as the frenzy following Petrosino's murder in 1909 abated. Many of the most infamous of these men in the 1930's and after were not of Sicilian background. For example, in addition to those mentioned, Al Capone, the era's most infamous gangster, was of Neapolitan background. Some of the leading gangsters in the 1930's were not Italians at all, notably Dutch Schultz and Meyer Lansky. Yet the growing use of the word Mafia by the media led to the widespread belief that gang crime was a matter of one organization, composed of Italian-Americans, and that they were of Sicilian origin. The film industry was quick to exploit the sensationalism of the Mafia myth and greatly added to it.

Several incidents in subsequent years lent credence to the belief. Chief among these were the Kefauver Hearings in 1950, the Apalachin Meeting on November 14, 1957, and the Valachi Hearings in 1963.

After a series of hearings broadcast on television, Senator Estes Kefauver's Senate committee reported its disputed conclusion that "the Mafia . . . has an important part in binding together into a loose association the two major crime syndicates as well as many minor gangs and individual hoodlums throughout the country." The Kefauver hearings lent credibility to a belief in the existence of a group of Italian and Jewish gangsters uncovered just before World War II which was dubbed by the press "Murder Incorporated." In addition, Lucky Luciano had revived suspicions of a link between American and Sicilian mafiosi by appealing to the patriotic sentiments of Americans to prevent the efforts of the U. S. Government to deport him. Luciano claimed that on behalf of the American government he had contacted friends in Sicily who aided the Allied invasion there during World War II. American authorities termed the claim ridiculous.

Seven years after the Kefauver hearings, the New York State Police stumbled across a meeting of over sixty Italian-Americans, most of whom had criminal records, at a home in Apalachin, New York. Most of the men were from a radius of two hundred miles of New York City, a fact leading to the conclusion that the meeting was one of the New York Mafia.

In 1963 Joseph Valachi, a confessed low-echelon gangster, described a criminal organization which he said was called by its members by the up to then unheard term of "Cosa Nostra," Italian for "Our Thing." The precise conclusions to be drawn from Valachi's testimony and of the Apalachin meeting are disputed by law officials and other experts on crime.

But in a sense these disputes are irrelevant. From the perspective of the vast majority of Italian-Americans the problem of the Mafia image is severe whether there is one centralized or federated Mafia or merely unconnected groups of Italian-American criminals. The fantastic sensationalism in all the media has identified Italian-American life with the Mafia in a self-locking stereotype. When Italian-Americans are depicted on television, in films, and in fictional literature, they are almost always cast as vicious hoodlums, childish buffoons, or both. Before the 1930's the stereotype justified itself by pointing to the garbled reports of Black Hand activity. Thus the unfair depiction of an ethnic group almost exclusively in a stereotyped image has been given spurious credibility in each of three generations.

Actual Italian-American gangsters, like all members of the ethnic group, live according to many customs of la via vecchia, adopting some of these to their criminality. Because Americans have never understood these customs except in crude and shallow caricatures, the media's confusion of Italian-American customs with the criminal behavior of Italian-American gangsters is once again given a false but effective guise of truth. Because of prevalent American ignorance of la via vecchia and long exposure to the Mafia image it has been impossible to communicate a basic truth. The truth is that the common characteristic of the at most five to six thousand Italian-American gangsters claimed by federal governmental agencies and the upwards of twenty million other Italian-Americans is the morality of la famiglia, a noncriminal morality. The distinguishing characteristic therein that separates the relatively few gangsters from the millions of law-abiding Italian-Americans is that the gangsters have turned that morality to serve criminal ends.

This may seem a gloss to those who might see in my explanation of the Mezzogiorno ideal of manliness a system of values that is easily perverted into criminality. Certainly the characteristics of the uomo segreto are among the most important influences molding the character of Italian-American men. Some of these characteristics clash with conventional American ideals. For example, the ideal of being wily, artful, and cunning (furbo) runs against the grain of the American ideals of honesty and trust. The prescription to make opportunistic use of people who block one's will clashes with the ideal venerated in American folklore of being a straight shooter who gives his opponents in life a fair deal. In addition, the characteristics of being furbo are in America popularly associated with the characteristics of con-men.

These clashes produce confusion and conflict in the minds of later generation Italian-Americans, as I indicated in an earlier chapter. The clashes between some Italian manliness characteristics and American ideals also produce suspicion and resentment against Italian-Americans by other Americans. Does the Southern Italian ideal and the disapproval of the ideal by American tradition make Italian-American men more prone to embrace a criminal career than other Americans? For several reasons I think the answer is no.

First, there is no statistical evidence that Italian-Americans enter crime in higher numbers in proportion to their total numbers than other ethnic groups under similar social conditions. Poverty and other social deprivations are the correlates of crime in the United States. When Irish, Jewish, Italian, and other immigrant groups suffered these deprivations they sometimes produced higher per-capita ratios of crime than some groups long established in the

American social and economic framework. As these immigrant groups moved up in the American structure, they spawned fewer common criminals and gangsters. Similarly, black, Chicano, and Puerto Rican populations have high crime ratios today because of the deprivations they suffer. If we can believe accounts in today's press, criminals from these groups are edging Italian-American hoodlums out of the rackets. For example, news reports have it that blacks are in effect buying out Italian and other white control of rackets in Brooklyn. White gangsters there have given blacks crime franchises in the borough's large black and Puerto Rican neighborhoods. The press has repeatedly indicated that black hoodlums are forcibly pushing Italian-American gangsters from control of organized crime in Harlem and in areas of other cities like Chicago and Newark.

Second, we should note that much of Americans' criticism of themselves has always involved the charge that the ideals of honesty, trust, a fair deal, etc., are much professed but have never been much practiced. Press reports tell us daily of rife corruption and of deceitful and devious practices in almost every area of American life. Lest anyone think this is but a recent criticism against the Americans in the time of the Watergate affairs, let him recall the charges of the muckrakers of the turn of the century. Let him also attend to words written earlier by Walt Whitman, a man justly famous for his eloquent celebrations of what is best in American life. In fact, the most frequent criticism leveled at Whitman today is that he was excessive in his praise of America. Yet Whitman wrote a scathing critique of behavior which he saw prevalent among every group of Americans in his time. The criticism was included in an essay called "Democratic Vistas." It is worth quoting at length.

> I say we had best look our times and lands searchingly in the face, like a physician diagnosing some deep disease. Never was there, perhaps, more hollowness at heart than at present, and here in the United States. Genuine belief seems to have

left us. The underlying principles of the States are not honestly believed in, (for all this hectic glow, and these melodramatic screamings,) nor is humanity itself believed in. What penetrating eye does not everywhere see through the mask? The spectacle is appalling. We live in an atmosphere of hypocrisy throughout. The men believe not in the women, nor the women in the men. A scornful superciliousness rules in literature. The aim of all *litterateurs* is to find something to make fun of. A lot of churches, sects, etc. the most dismal phantasms I know, usurp the name of religion. Conversation is a mass of badinage. From deceit in the spirit, the mother of all false deeds, the offspring is already incalculable. An acute and candid person, in the revenue department in Washington, who is led by the course of his employment to regularly visit the cities, north, south and west to investigate frauds, has talked much with me about his discoveries. The depravity of the business classes of our country is not less than has been supposed, but infinitely greater. The official services of America, national, state and municipal, in all their branches and departments, except the judiciary, are saturated in corruption, bribery, falsehood, mal-administration; and the judiciary is tainted. The great cities reek with respectable as much as non-respectable robbery and scoundrelism. In fashionable life, flippancy, tepid amours, weak infidelism, small aims, or no aims at all, only to kill time. In business, (this all-devouring modern word, business,) the one sole object is, by any means, pecuniary gain. The magician's serpent in the fable ate up the other serpents; and money-making is our magician's serpent, remaining to-day sole master of the field. The best class we show, is but a mob of fashionably dressed speculators and vulgarians. True, indeed, behind this fantastic farce, enacted on the visible stage of society, solid things and stupendous labors are to be discovered, existing crudely and going on in the background, to advance and tell themselves in time. Yet the truths are none the less terrible. I say that our New World democracy, however great a success in uplifting the masses out of their sloughs, in materialistic development, products, and in certain highly deceptive superficial popular intellectuality, is, so far, an almost complete failure in its social aspects, and in really grand religious, moral, literary, and esthetic results . . . It is as if we were somehow being endowed with a vast and more and more thoroughly-appointed body, and then left with little or no soul.

Judged in contrast to such behavior, even the most questioned aspects of the uomo segreto seem superior. Do not misunderstand. I am not spouting any hate-America nonsense that Americans are worse than other peoples. But their behavior as a whole is not superior to that of others, and such things must be judged on the whole. Marlon Brando evaded the issue when pressed on how he could be totally silent on the criminal stereotyping of Italian-Americans while sensitive to Hollywood's depiction of American Indians. He rationalized:

> I think [*The Godfather*] is about the corporate mind. In a way, the Mafia is the best example of capitalists we have. Don Corleone is just any ordinary American business magnate who is trying to do the best he can for the group he represents and for his family.

One does not have to endorse Brando's nonsense to say that the values actually lived by the large majority of Americans are on the whole not superior to those of the millions of law-abiding Americans of Italian origin. The immigrant Italians perceived this and held their own ideals without apology, including those of manliness. However, beginning with the second generation, Italian-Americans have felt diffident about asserting their traditional value scheme in the face of what Whitman termed the "hectic glow" of professed American values. Taught to shun hypocrisy and disposed by their heritage to limit their involvement with the world outside la famiglia, American born Italian-Americans have withdrawn from ill-informed attacks upon their values.

Southern Italian characteristics do not dispose men to criminal behavior. However, where the mode of life has been impressed onto organized crime, it has made it difficult to combat effectively the criminal activity. Italian-American criminal groups have been difficult to root out, and this has fed Americans' fear of and hostility to Italian-American ways. In this fear anyone in competition with an Italian-American finds a ready weapon. For example, Italian-American politicians, businessmen, and career men are frequent targets of whispering attacks initiated by their non-Italian rivals. Insinuations or brazen lies about Mafia connections are enough to rouse the know-nothing fears of Americans and torpedo the career of an Italian-American.

The absence of a sizable Italian-American corps in the media and in the academic world, coupled with the diffidence of the masses of Italian-Americans, leaves fear of Italian-Americans unallayed; and bias, slander, and hatred against them unchallenged. But there are other reasons why bigotry against Italian-Americans remains virulent today.

Unlike the crude bigotry of the old American nativists, the more recent discrimination against Italian-Americans has become respectable. It is no longer the bigotry of redneck types, although this brand still exists. The more damaging bigotry today is that shown by educated middle- and upper-class Americans. This prejudice is by no means confined to reactionaries, the popular villains on whom many of America's ills are blamed. Respectable bigotry is probably more widespread among liberals in the United States. Writing in the autumn 1969 issue of *The American Scholar*, Michael Lerner examined the bigotry toward Italian-Americans fashionable among upper-class liberals. His points are telling.

An extraordinary amount of bigotry on the part of elite, liberal students goes unexamined at Yale and elsewhere. Directed at the lower middle class, it feeds on the unexamined biases of class perspective, the personality predilections of elite radicals and academic disciplines that support their views. . . . The radical may object that he dislikes the lower middle class purely because of its racism and its politics. But that is not sufficient explanation: Polish jokes are devoid of political content. . . . Hip radicals are often amused by the Italian defamation league bumper sticker: "A.I.D.-Americans

of Italian descent." Poles, Italians, Mayor Daley and the
police are safe objects for amusement, derision or hatred.

Lerner's observations bring to mind comments that
greeted me in response to an experience of mine in 1972.
During a trip to Sicily, thieves in the city of Catania broke
into the trunk of my automobile and stole my luggage.
Upon hearing of this, a college-educated engineer in New
York commented, "There are no criminals in Sicily, only
the natives." Another educated middle-class New Yorker
said, "Catania? That's where crime was invented, wasn't
it? No, it was Palermo." Yet three years before, when my
car was burglarized on the very street where I live in New
York City, the incident elicited no comments at all. The
widespread crime in American cities is simply regarded as
a fact of life. But crimes committed by Italians or
Italian-Americans are cause for sensation-mongering.

The fact is that Italian-Americans have become the
scapegoat of comfortable, educated, influential Americans. In the 1970 edition of *Beyond the Melting Pot*
(M.I.T. Press), Nathan Glazer and Daniel Moynihan commented:

> During the 1960's the mass media, and the *non-Italian poli-*
> *ticians*, combined to make the Mafia a household symbol of
> evil and wrong-doing. Television ran endless crime series,
> such as *The Untouchables*, in which the criminals were, for
> all purposes, exclusively Italian. Attorneys General, of whom
> Robert F. Kennedy was the archetype, made the "war against
> organized crime" a staple of national politics. . . . This is
> rather an incredible set of facts. Ethnic sensitivities in New
> York, in the nation, have never been higher than during the
> 1960s. To accuse a major portion of the population of per-
> sistent criminality would seem a certain course of political
> or commercial disaster. But it was not. The contrast with the
> general "elite" response to Negro crime is instructive. Typi-
> cally, the latter was blamed on white society. Black problems
> were muted, while Italian problems were emphasized, even
> exaggerated. Why?
> We do not know. There may have been some displacement

of anti-black feeling to Italians, possibly as a consequence of the association of the Mafia with drug traffic, and the latter's association with high rates of black crime. It may be that society needs an unpopular group around, and the Italians were for many reasons available. Democratic reformers, in largest number Jews but also including among them political figures who had come from Irish Catholic and white Protestant groups, were able to use the Italian association with crime to topple any number of Italian political leaders and, perhaps more important, to prevent others from acquiring any ascendancy. Many political figures thus gained advantage.

Similarly, Lerner observed:

In general, the bigotry of a lower-middle-class policeman toward a ghetto black or of a lower-middle-class mayor toward a rioter is not viewed in the same perspective as the bigotry of an upper-middle-class peace matron toward a lower-middle-class mayor; or of an upper-class university student toward an Italian, a Pole or a National Guardsman from Cicero, Illinois—that is, if the latter two cases are called bigotry at all.

The long-standing bigotry against Italian-Americans has in recent years become respectable also because many white Americans find in the Italian-American a scapegoat for their own guilt about the sufferings of blacks. The constant association of the Mafia with ghetto crime, especially crime involving drugs, affords the guilt-laden liberal villains with whom to relieve his overwrought conscience. The Mafia, linked with or supported by their racist ethnic kin, is to blame and not the white upper middle class whose historic unconcern for blacks now pricks their conscience. The ballyhoo about Mafia drug suppliers permits the liberal anti-Italian bigots to repress in their own minds, or rationalize away, the fact that in many cases their ancestors owned slaves or exploited blacks after their legal emancipation, as Italian-Americans did not. It is very easy, and certainly less painful, simply to see the Mafia—and by extension all Italian-Americans—as the cause of the black problem.

The adoption of the words "Mafia" and "Cosa Nostra"
as linguistic synonyms for all confederated crime has the
psychological effect of conditioning people to believe that
organized crime is an Italian-American invention based on
the culture of their ancestors, and an Italian-American
monopoly. For example, on May 14, 1973, an article in
the New York *Times* by Everett R. Holles reported a savage struggle for power by two Mexican-American gangs of
prisoners in California's Soledad prison, which call themselves by Spanish names. Although the writer explicitly
states that the situation *in no way involves any Italian-
Americans or Italian-American criminal organizations,* he
goes on to refer to the Chicano gangs and prisoners as
"Mexican Mafia," "Mafia," and "Mafiosi" at least eighteen
times in the course of his article.

Incidentally, the American media have totally ignored
the fact that in other countries with large populations derived from the Mezzogiorno there is no Italian organized
crime. For example, Argentina and Brazil have old Italian
communities and Australia and Germany more recent ones.
The absence of Italian criminal organizations in these
countries gives the lie to the suspicion that Mafia-type activities are inherent in and inextricable from the culture of
ordinary Southern Italians. Also ignored is the fact that
the per capita rate of violent crime in Sicily today, the so-
called home of crime, is far lower than that of American
cities. According to the report of the *Chronache Parla-
mentari Siciliane* of 1968, in the year 1965 only twelve
homicides, four forcible rapes, and 13,254 aggravated robberies were committed in Sicily, where the population totals
almost five million. Compare this to New York City, where
in 1972 there were over 1600 homicides among a population of almost eight million. And the per capita rates of murder, rape, and other violent crimes are higher in many
other American cities than they are in New York.

The maligning of Italian-Americans continues unabated.
Recent responses to this by Italian-Americans fall into four
categories. Some have adopted as the lesser of two evils the
Uncle Giovanni buffoon image. Better to be a clown than

a thug. Interestingly Italian-Americans use a contemptuous Italian word for this kind of vulgar fool, *cafone*. The cafone has never been well tolerated among Italian-Americans. Today's younger Italian-Americans do not tolerate him at all.

Some Italian-Americans have sought to get public relations mileage out of today's Mafia chic by half jokingly adopting the Mafia myth. For example, I arrived at a posh New York restaurant recently and gave my name to the maître d' in charge of reservations. He said hello in Italian and we exchanged a few words in the language. Then, searching for something else in common in our background, he said, jokingly, "I expected somebody from *The Godfather*."

At least the mafioso is taken seriously, an improvement over being considered a buffoon or being ignored entirely. Moreover, the myth of an extrasocietal, almost omnipotent power has great appeal in a complicated American society in which people are exasperated by feelings of confusion, impotence, and defeat. Americans are experiencing the breakdown of their family tradition and yearn for a sense of security that comes from belonging. As a result the ordine della famiglia of Italian-Americans is most appealing to them, even though they see it almost exclusively in its corrupted form in the media splashings of Mafia stories. The temptation felt by some Italian-Americans to exploit the appeal of the myth is great. It is a way to gain the respect and even envy of their non-Italian neighbors.

Other Italian-Americans patiently repeat, "We are not criminals. The percentage of racketeers among us is small. Etc." But such voices of reason are all but lost in the scream of the Mafia craze excited by the media. Even in Florence, Italy, I was casually asked if I, my family, or my friends knew or were involved with the Mafia in New York. Recently, a (non-Italian) resident of the large building in which I live was murdered in his apartment, and the police sought clues by interviewing residents in the neighborhood. One of the detectives when he learned my name repeatedly asked me if I was associated with the Mafia despite his knowledge that I am a college professor. He expressed puzzlement when I finally told him that the question was angering me. The irrational Mafia mania has grown to fantastic proportions. It brings to mind a word I have heard used in Italy—*americanata*. The word means something wildly excessive, something exaggerated beyond all reality. In the midst of all the americanata about the Mafia and its confusion of the Italian-American life style with the behavior of criminals, rational defenses of the ethnic group so far have been but whispers against a hurricane.

In recent years some Italian-Americans have taken to denying that the Mafia exists at all in this country. This hyperdefensive reaction is in reality an expression of rage, a reaction to years of abuse. This response lends itself to even more americanata based upon the Mafia and buffoon images of Italian-Americans. The media have had a field day with the opportunity. When Mafia boss Joseph Colombo founded the Italian Civil Rights League and attracted fifty thousand Italian-Americans to a protest rally in New York's Columbus Circle on June 29, 1970, all the worst biases against Italian-Americans were confirmed in the minds of Americans. The media turned the event into a circus without attempting to distinguish the legitimacy of the feelings of the protesters from the tainted reputation of the league's early leaders.

The fact that some racketeers attempt to exploit for their own purposes the outrage felt by Italian-Americans is unfortunate. But it is also beside the point. There is opportunism in every social expression. Instead of responsible treatment of this issue, newspapers, magazines, TV newscasts, and talk shows outdid themselves in transforming a difficult social problem of organized crime into a raucous round of forced hilarity. Just as many media people for years found that exploitation of the Mafia myth was lucrative, so they now discovered that ridiculing overstated denials of the myth is also lucrative. The americanata becomes ever more out of control.

The Mafia issue must be kept in perspective while the spurious Mafia image is expurged. In the preoccupation with these questions, we are in danger of focusing only on a side show which diverts attention from the larger issues involving Italian-Americans in American society. So far none of the responses of Italian-Americans to the old Mafia myth and the new Mafia chic have been effective either in improving our image or solving our other real, complex problems. We desperately need to develop other responses. While we focus on our other needs, we should not once again adopt the old attitude of withdrawal. Quiet anger, resentment, and retreat into insularity were ineffective in the past and would be worse than useless in the future.

As indicated in the last chapter, we need to educate our young so that some of them may enter vocations of influence and power, including those that deal with the spoken and written word. They will then be in a position to prevent the repeated portrayal of Italian-Americans exclusively within the criminal and clown stereotypes. At the same time we need aggressively to protest the slurs against us by adopting those means of protest which are effective in today's society—economic and political pressure. These types of behavior seem to go against the grain of traditional Italian-American responses to the outside world. Yet part of that tradition included pushing back against stranieri when their incursions became too obnoxious. We now must learn to alter our techniques of pushing back. Building upon the strengths of our tradition, we must update our relations to the outside world.

This brings us to the subject of the next chapter. For the difficult nature of the Italian-American dilemma is that it is an integrated whole. All of its elements must be resolved at the same time or the Italian-American saga will falter in its entirety. Although it may seem melodramatic to state it in these terms, we are forced to confront the slander of us as criminals and clowns with the old vendetta attitude. We must hurl at the Mafia image the vow of the ancient code. As Sicilians expressed it in a rhyme in their dialect it was: *Si moru mi vorricunu; si campu t'allampu—* If you kill me I will be buried; if I live, I will kill you. The days when we could or should ignore or compromise with Mafia slurs, insults, slanders, and indignities thrown at us by the outside world are over.

Attitudes Toward Outsiders,
Authority, and Politics

My mother's three brothers experienced combat during World War II, two in the army and one in the navy. In their service, two of them visited Italy for the first time. My uncle Joe took part in the invasion of Italy. Because he had grown up speaking the difficult Southern Italian dialects, he was pressed into service as a translator as the Allied army fought hard to defeat the Germans occupying Italy. Again and again Meridionali said to him, "But you are Italian, what are you doing in an American uniform?" Civilians in every way like his parents, living in homes which mirrored theirs, pleaded with him to remain with and protect them.

The ordeal was torturing for the twenty-two-year-old corporal whose parents had christened him Giuseppe Rossolino. The only response he could give merely served to heighten the tragic madness of the situation: *"Ma sono Italo-AMERICANO"*—But I am Italian-*American!*

Because my uncle's division, the Thirty-fourth, was one of the first American units to enter the war and be engaged in hard fighting to its end, the *Saturday Evening Post* dubbed it the "champion hard luck division." There was special meaning in this nickname for Italian-American soldiers. It came to a climax for my uncle when he was injured during the bitter fighting at Monte Cassino. In violation of army regulations, my uncle kept a diary during eighteen months of combat. The entry of Friday, January

21, 1944, describes how the war ended for him. It ended—
as it had begun—enveloped in conflicted relations with his
parents' paesani.

About eight o'clock this evening as I was writing to my
family and sweetheart we received a phone call from agent
Don Funk telling us that G-2 wanted us to go up to the for-
ward command post of the 133rd Infantry to pick up two
Italian civilians with information concerning German fortifi-
cations in Cassino. Lou Coniglia and I were up there last
night so we knew just where to go in the pitch black night.
We got to the 133 Inf. C.P. which was just past the town of
Cevaro and about two or three miles from Cassino. At the
C.P. we found an Italian, aged 52, and his wife who had
previously lived in Cassino and had recently passed our lines.
I questioned them, and Lou and I started taking them back to
our Prisoner of War enclosure in San Vittore for further
questioning in the morning. Lou was driving and since artillery shells were going over our heads from both directions
he must have been a little nervous. When we were between
Cervaro and San Vittore, we very faintly saw a GI truck coming towards us. Lou pulled to one side of the road in order
to let the truck by, but in the pitch darkness he went too far
and our jeep rolled over a four foot embankment. Lou was
thrown clear but the Italians and I remained pinned under it.
It sounded like the League of Nations as the Italians called
"aiuto" and Lou and I shouted "help." Some nearby soldiers
raised the jeep and the Italians and I managed to creep out.
Fortunately the Italians had no weight on them, but I had
the weight of the hood on my left arm. I crawled out with a
broken arm and bruised foot. An ambulance soon came and
the medic put a splint on my arm in the dark, for it was too
dangerous to use any light whatsoever. I couldn't walk so
they put me in a litter and drove me to the 109 Clearing Station in San Vittore where I spent the night. This was in the
cellar of an old school building which was about the only
building not badly damaged.

Lou and the Italians went to the P.W. enclosure in San
Vittore.

Joe's younger brother, my uncle Sam (Santo Vin-
cenzo), was a naval officer attached to the Merchant Ma-

rine fleet. His ship called at Palermo after that city was
captured by the Allies. Sam took the opportunity to look
up his maternal aunts. He found their home still standing in
the heavily bombed port area of Acqua Santa, knocked on
their door, and called out his name. He also announced
that he was one of their nephews from America. When
the women opened the door and saw the uniform of an
alien officer, they were terrified. The war had confirmed
the traditional Sicilian distrust of outsiders and of uniforms
that represent authority. He identified himself again,
speaking in particular to his mother's sister, who bore an
unnerving resemblance to his mother. But in vain. They
stared at him with fear and distrust and seemed not to understand what he was saying despite his fluency in Sicilian dialect. They were calmed only when he pointed to a
photograph of his parents he noticed on the wall and said,
"My mother and father, Cassia and Giuseppe."

The children of Italian immigrants were not merely
bilingual. They were bicultural. Their upbringing in
l'ordine della famiglia made them as Italian as they were
American. They could almost be described as English-
speaking American Meridionali. World War II came during the young adulthood of this generation. Whether they
actually attacked the homeland of their parents, as many
did, or merely read of the fighting in Italy, for them it was
a special kind of war. It was a civil war. They had struggled throughout their childhoods with the conflicting demands of Mezzogiorno and American cultures. The outbreak of war represented a cruel peak in this generation's
extreme culture conflict. Characteristically the group remained true to essentials of both cultures. Its members
maintained the values and loyalties of l'ordine della famiglia and also loyally served the United States Government
against the Fascist government of Italy. This choice was possible first because their parents had little use for any Italian
government. The second generation had assimilated the
values of loyalty to the United States Government. When
they clearly demonstrated their loyalty by enlisting in the
struggle to destroy fascism in Italy, their parents supported

them. The older generation supported their blood rather than the new political authority in the old land. Given the character of the immigrants and the character of the second generation, the choice of the loyalty of both to the United States in the war was inevitable.

But also characteristic of their resolutions of their problems, both generations were forced to pay an agonizing price for their choice. They participated in the killing of their paesani and even their relatives in the old country. And they helped devastate the ancient land. For both generations of Italian-Americans World War II was one of fratricide. The way they chose America's side in the war reveals an important part of the value system of Italian-Americans. It reveals first the attitudes of immigrant Italians toward outsiders, toward authority, and toward politics. Second, it reveals how those attitudes evolved in their second-generation children. It is only by understanding this evolution and tracing it further that we may understand the attitudes of Italian-Americans today toward outsiders, authority, and politics.

The predicament presented by World War II is often said to represent the final, conclusive, and positive test of Italian-Americans' American identity. In an important sense it was. Although when the war first broke out the American government arrested four thousand Italian-Americans, it detained only two hundred of them. At the onset of the war, some war industries restricted the Italian-Americans who worked in them. For example, Italian-Americans, who comprised a large proportion of New York City's longshoremen, were not permitted to work on "sensitive" ships. But all such restrictions were soon abolished. It is one of the most remarkable facts of American history that a people whose recent roots are in a land where no governmental authority was respected overwhelmingly supported the authority of America with their labor, sacrifice, and blood.

It is also ironic that today's Italian-Americans are stereotyped as superpatriotic Americans who automatically back governmental authority in any controversial situation while their ethnic brothers in the Mezzogiorno continue their overt struggles with political authority. For example, on March 22, 1973, the New York *Times* ran a news story entitled, "Reggio Calabria Goes Back to the Barricades." The story reported widespread antigovernment rioting in the city of Reggio di Calabria, located at the very toe of the Italian boot across the Strait of Messina from Sicily. The account demonstrates that the classic Mezzogiorno wariness toward outsiders and hostility toward political authority are very much alive. Tanks were called in to quell the disorder in the city where walls were freshly painted with the slogan, "Reggio Calabria will not yield!"

The news story reminded me that in 1945 a movement was organized by Sicilians to have their island secede from Italy. They were disgusted with Italian authority. At one point the Sicilian secessionists actually proposed that Sicily apply for membership in the United States of America!

How strange that Italian-Americans, only one or two generations removed from the Mezzogiorno and still steeped in its values, are seen by their countrymen as law and order patriots. What happened in the American experience that transformed a system of values totally opposed to authority outside the family to one that is strongly loyal to the authority of the American nation? What is it in the Italian-American experience that even made some Sicilians, usually among the most fiercely independent people on earth, propose that their homeland become one of the United States?

Italian immigrants in America established neighborhoods modeled upon the campanilismo of the Mezzogiorno. These areas were socially so self-sufficient that many immigrants never bothered to learn English. As already indicated, it simply was not necessary. A study printed by O. D. Duncan and S. Lieberson in the January 1959 issue of the *Journal of Sociology* indicates that of foreign-born Americans in Chicago from ten European countries, the Italian groups had the lowest percentage among them during the years from 1930 to 1950 of those who could speak English.

The immigrant generation transformed many English words and adapted them to their dialects. For example, they called an automobile a *carra*, a store a *storo*, a bar a *barra*, a job a *giobba*. In my neighborhood a toilet was called a *baccausa* after the backhouses of early tenements. The immigrants' children learned these words as Italian. Those who later studied the Italian language in high school were embarrassed to have their naïveté exposed in classes.

In addition the immigrants ignored many attitudes, habits, and social conventions of their fellow-Americans. Their intercourse with the surrounding community consisted mostly of labor in its economic structure. Their simple economic desires were satisfied by saving the cash they earned. They resolved among themselves most antagonisms that emerged between them. They regarded their life style as one of healthy campanilismo. Other Americans called it parochial.

The second-generation children compromised between the Italian and American perspectives. They accepted each in part. And they rebelled against each in part. Both generations regarded the political activities of the world outside as irrelevant. The political world of Italy raised few feelings among them. The attitudes of the *prominenti* on both sides of the Atlantic had little influence on the consciousness of Italian-Americans.

True, many Italian-Americans had served in the American army during World War I, when both the old country and the new one were allied. Michael Musmanno estimates that 400,000 Italian-Americans were in the American uniform during that war. Eighty-three Distinguished Service Crosses, the nation's second highest military citation, were awarded to Italian-born Americans, and another twenty to American-born Italian-Americans, during World War I. In his book *The Story of the Italians in America* (1965), Musmanno quotes George Creel, head of the public relations section of the Department of War during World War I. Creel said, "The Italians in the United States are about four percent of the whole population but the list of casualties shows a full ten percent of Italian names."

But this wartime participation in the larger world was regarded as a disruption of normal life. Instead of parading their service before their countrymen, Italian-American soldiers came back to the United States in 1918 eager to resume the life of l'ordine della famiglia. The Great War was cast aside, relegated to the status of earthquakes, pestilence, drought, and other upheavals that proved inevitable in centuries of Mezzogiorno history.

Between the World Wars, immigrant and second generations continued to cultivate their in-group life style. The immigrants maintained a sentimental interest in their homeland. When Mussolini embarked upon widely publicized campaigns of aid to and development of the Mezzogiorno, many Italian-born Americans looked on approvingly. Some even supported Italy's invasion of Ethiopia. But this support—which incidentally was not shared by most who continued to live in the Mezzogiorno—was superficial. In fact it was less enthusiastic than the pro-Italian Fascist sentiments of other Americans who exaggerated the degree of Italian-American feeling for Mussolini.

Many prominent Americans were lavish in their praise of Il Duce. They were captivated by his personal flamboyance and the supposed efficiency of his government, which, according to the popular phrase of the time, made the trains run on time. The original version of Cole Porter's song "You're the Top" contained the line "You're the top/ you're Mussolini!" In 1934, Henry Luce's *Fortune* magazine in one issue both endorsed Mussolini and insulted Italians and Italian-Americans. The entire issue was devoted to Fascist Italy. The magazine declared Mussolini to be "brilliant" and concluded:

> Other nations falter or reel hysterically in search of unity. Italy is calm and united under the emblem of common strength and effort which is Fascism . . . With uplifted hearts and Augustan pride the wops are unwopping themselves.

The large number of Italian-Americans regarded the political opinions of Luce and other *pezzi grossi* ("big

pieces," meaning "big wheels") in both America and Italy
with indifference. This must be kept in mind when we note
that some of the more than one hundred and fifty Italian-
language newspapers in the United States during the 1930's
either supported Mussolini's actions or denounced President Roosevelt's efforts limiting the supply of exports of
war matériel to Italy during the Ethiopian War. The larger
Italian-American newspapers were owned by the prominenti. In their traditional role, these men tried to influence
Italian-American opinion rather than reflect it.

The Ethiopian War aroused ethnic sensibilities of Italian-
Americans rather than true pro-Fascist feelings. It provoked their ethnic pride. Sensitive to decades of slander
about supposed Italian knife-wielding treachery, Italian-
Americans finally were stung by President Roosevelt's
choice of the "knife in the back" phrase he used in 1940
to characterize Italy's attack on France.

As it became clear in the late 1930's that war between
Italy and the United States was very probable, the spirit
of campanilismo colored a serious weighing of loyalties by
Italian-Americans. In the end it was decisive despite ill feelings about anti-Italian bias. The now older immigrants regarded their Italian-American communities as their paesi.
These areas sustained their families. Their children shared
this loyalty and joined it with the loyalty they had toward
the United States, their native land.

Because it was of military age, the second generation
bore the heat and burden of the problem. At the end of
Joseph Vergara's novel *Love and Pasta*, Joe enters the
army at the start of World War II. His loyalty is clear.
Yet his conflict is great:

During those first days, I wondered how I would react if I
was sent to Italy. Could I treat Italians as enemies—men just
like Il Lungo, The Gink, Compa' Francesco? Would I be able
to pull the trigger if I saw one of Pop's compa's through the
gun sight? When the time came, I told myself, I would do
what I had to. But, all the same, I wondered . . .

Joe's dilemma was shared by many Italian-American men, and resolved by service in the American military. We do not know precisely how many Italian-Americans were in uniform during World War II. The War Department did not classify most personnel by ethnic background. Michael Musmanno claims "there can be little doubt that the number considerably surpassed a million." On August 25, 1961, Governor Nelson Rockefeller of New York delivered a speech to Italian-American war veterans in which he said, "Throughout America, the services mustered over one million five hundred thousand of Italian descent—over ten percent of the might of America" during World War II.

During the war Americans had mixed feelings toward Italians. They reflected the American government's statements that the war was against the Fascist Italian government and not against the Italian people. In order to strengthen this attitude, American propaganda fixed upon the old childlike stereotype of Italians. In an effort to remove guilt from them, America's propaganda machines portrayed Italians merely as naïve simpletons misled by the Fascists. The stereotype spilled over onto Italian-Americans. When they genuinely professed indifference to the Italian government and loyalty to America, Americans saw it as confirming the view that the Italian nature is childlike and easily influenced in politics and other serious affairs. The old slur of Italians as sunny but irresponsible people was mobilized for the war effort. Italian-Americans still suffer from the successful war service of the image.

Paul Barone, the second-generation central character of Michael De Capite's *No Bright Banner* (1944), also joined the army. He did not enlist because his character was simple and easily swayed. He decided to fight, as he put it, because he hated "the life of fascism more than the half truths of our lives in the United States." Previously, Paul had explored various political philosophies. He rejected all of them. True to his Meridionale heritage he found all political ideology to be false to life. Political schemes are too neatly defined, too clear in their divisions of right and wrong, too removed from the flesh and blood realities of people, and too sanguine in their proposals to deal with complicated problems. Thus Paul entered the war carrying no bright banner.

"No bright banner." No phrase could better sum up Italian-American attitudes toward politics. Like their predecessors in World War I, the Italian-American veterans of World War II returned home convinced of the wisdom of the traditional Mezzogiorno cynical aloofness toward political affairs and political movements. True, a small number of the second generation became actively involved in American politics. Through their efforts over the years some succeeded in achieving outstanding firsts. John Pastore in 1946 became the first Italian-American elected governor of a state—Rhode Island. In 1950 he became the first Italian-American elected to the United States Senate. In 1962, President Kennedy appointed Anthony J. Celebrezze as Secretary of the Department of Health, Education and Welfare. Celebrezze was the first Italian-American to hold cabinet rank in the federal government. Only one other has since served at that level. John A. Volpe, a former governor of Massachusetts, was appointed Secretary of Transportation by President Nixon. In 1973 Volpe, the son of immigrants from Abruzzi, became the first Italian-American ambassador to Italy.

But political activists represent the exception rather than the rule among Italian-Americans, who have a predominant pattern of attitudes toward political questions. If an issue is perceived as unconnected with the well being of la via vecchia, it is regarded apathetically. If a question is seen as a reflection upon la via vecchia, it is regarded with interest. If it confirms the values of the old way, a political phenomenon is approved. If it is inconsistent with some critical element of the old way, it is disapproved. These attitudes are relatively passive. It is only when a political, social, or economic issue directly threatens the key values of the old way that Italian-Americans become truly active politically.

A dispute that lasted for seven years in the Corona section of Queens, New York, is illustrative. The area in question is typically working-class Italian-American. Its residents are normally inactive politically. In 1965 New York City announced it would tear down some seventy homes owned by Italian-Americans to build a high school, a school which would have served youngsters from other neighborhoods. The community's residents became incensed. The plan would have had a doubly destructive effect on la via vecchia. It would have destroyed a substantial number of homes and moved their families, thereby decimating a community Italian-Americans had spent two generations in building. Second, it would have meant a daily influx of hundreds of high school students—in New York City a frequently disorderly and disruptive group—into the neighborhood. Corona's homeowners organized themselves. For seven years the politically inexperienced residents doggedly fought City Hall and finally won.

The repercussions of the success of Corona's Italian-Americans are being felt around the country. New appreciation of the stability that carefully cultivated ethnic communities lend to our crisis-ridden cities is emerging. In addition, new sympathies are developing in our turbulent times for the humanistic values lived by Italian-Americans and others that Michael Novak has appreciatively called the unmeltables of America's melting pot in his book *The Rise of the Unmeltable Ethnics* (1971). New respect is also growing for the potential political power of white ethnic groups.

Italian-Americans as a group are neither liberal nor conservative, radical nor reactionary. They are reactive. They ignore politics until and unless their ethnically originated values are accosted. For these reasons, they are not consistently loyal to either Republicans or Democrats. They have a generally poor voting turnout except for elections concerning events which are critical to la via vecchia. Often they are unpredictable regarding questions not perceived as related to la via vecchia.

Writing in the spring 1971 issue of *Social Problems*, Nathan Glazer reported that New York City's Italians had the second poorest voting record in state elections of all the city's white ethnic groups. A survey indicated that only 56.2 per cent of Italian-Americans vote. Jews have the highest turnout (over 80 per cent), followed by Irish (73.9 per cent), Protestants (64 per cent), blacks (43.4 per cent), and Puerto Ricans (32.5 per cent). Greeley reported in 1971 that Italian-Americans scored lower than the average of all Americans who approve of political militancy by anyone, including themselves. On a scale from 0 to 18, the national average was 9.5, while the score for Italian-Americans was 8.3. Other scores reported were Jews (11.9), Irish (10.6), Polish (10.5) and German (9.2). Greeley also found that Italian-American college graduates of the class of 1961 had the least number approving of student militancy, only 24 per cent. The 1961 percentages in other ethnic groups ten years after graduation who approve of student militancy were: German Jews (50 per cent), Polish Jews (45 per cent), blacks (39 per cent), Protestant Scandinavians (33 per cent), Catholic Irish (29 per cent), Protestant Irish (28 per cent), Catholic Poles (28 per cent), Protestant English (23 per cent), Protestant Germans (21 per cent), and Catholic Germans (20 per cent).

In Greeley's studies Italian-Americans scored high in percentage of those who do not belong to any organization, 62 per cent. Other scores were Scandinavian (40 per cent), Jewish (45 per cent), German (53 per cent), English (56 per cent), Irish (57 per cent), Polish (66 per cent), and French (83 per cent). Yet Italian-Americans scored significantly higher than other nonjoiners in percentage of those who belong to local PTA groups. This affiliation is directly connected with their children and l'ordine della famiglia. Thus 62 per cent of Italian-Americans belong to PTA organizations, while only 30 per cent of French and 44 per cent of Polish-Americans belong to PTA groups.

J. Spiegel, in the book *Transactions: The Interplay Between Individual Family and Society* (1972), reports very interesting differences in attitudes found among Italian-Americans and Anglo-Americans. Although not in themselves conclusive, when cast in the perspective of other findings they corroborate the notion that Italian-Americans are either apathetic or reactive in relation to the outside world. Italian-Americans see themselves as subordinate to nature; Anglo-Americans see themselves as mastering nature. Italian-Americans are oriented in the present and regard enjoyment of everyday pleasures as the most important life goal. Anglo-Americans see future-oriented activity and productivity as the most important efforts of life. Italian-Americans identify themselves with their relatives and behave collaterally with them. Anglo-Americans are more individualistic in self-image and behavior.

A study of Americans by Bernard C. Rosen in *Racial and Ethnic Relations* (1966, edited by Bernard E. Segal) reported that "the cultures of white Protestants, Jews and Greeks stand out as considerably more individualistic, activistic and future-oriented than those of the Southern Italians, French-Canadians and Negroes." As the main reason for the characteristics of Italian-Americans, Rosen says "there is the Southern Italian saying, 'the family against all others'."

Preservation of la via vecchia constitutes the main drive behind Italian-American politics. It explains why 62 per cent of Italian-American voters went for conservative Richard Nixon in 1972, while in 1968 57 per cent of them voted for liberal Hubert Humphrey and only 37 per cent for Nixon. Liberal Humphrey in 1962 was sensitive to their ethnic sensibilities. Liberal McGovern in 1972 was not. It also explains why in 1968 Newark's Italian-Americans, perceiving la via vecchia endangered in their city, gave 20 per cent of their vote to George Wallace while Italian-Americans elsewhere, not feeling such a proximate threat, gave few votes to him. In 1970 Nelson Rockefeller hired Arthur Massolo to woo ethnic sensibilities in New York State. Arthur Goldberg, his opponent in the gubernatorial race, told an Italian-American audience, "I don't like ethnic campaigning. I think it is kind of cheap." Goldberg's overwhelming defeat was in part a result of this attitude.

Over the years Italian-American political power has been in an important sense accidental. It has been directly related to whether or not the group's reactive politics happened to coincide with other currents in the American community. Italian-Americans had little political power in New York City during the mayoralty of its first Italian mayor, Fiorello La Guardia. Despite his Italian heritage on his father's side, La Guardia's brand of progressivism was regarded by Italian-Americans as a threat to la via vecchia. In 1932 57 per cent of Italian-American voters in New York City voted against him and for O'Dwyer, a quintessential Irish politician. In the 1930's any Italian-American working class pro-Democrat tendency was canceled by Italian-American sentiment for Italy and anger at President Roosevelt's anti-Italian posture. In the 1940's Italian-American power suffered from the enormous shock of a major war against Italy. After the war, the power was gradually rebuilt as America searched for stable community life and preoccupied itself with Cold War international concerns. The result was the success of Pastore, Volpe, Celebrezze, and others.

In the 1960's Italian-American political interests were swept aside by the overriding preoccupations of the country. The concern with civil rights made Italian-American support of their communities seem reactionary. The nation's concern with crime together with the Mafia image delivered another hard blow to Italian-Americans. Joseph Alioto lost in his bid to become governor of California when *Look* mazagine alleged links between him and the Mafia, an allegation which a court later declared libelous.

In 1965, New York City's Republican Party failed to run an Italian-American for any significant city office for the first time in more than thirty years. The 1960's also saw Italian-Americans pushed out of their dominant position in the politics of Newark, New Jersey. In the 1950's and '60's Irish and Jewish populations fled Newark while Italians and blacks remained. Riding the crest of the civil rights momentum of the period, blacks were able to elect one of their own as mayor, Kenneth Gibson. The political defeat of Newark's Italian-Americans was applauded by a nation preoccupied by sympathies with the problems of blacks. When the administration of former Mayor Addonizio was exposed as heavily corrupt, any hope that attention would be paid to the problems of Newark's working class and poor Italian-Americans was crushed. Offered a choice by propagandists between stereotypes of oppressed blacks struggling with new dignity and courage, on one side, and Mafia-ridden Italian-American reactionaries on the other, the nation's sympathies swung overwhelmingly to the blacks.

In the 1960's militant blacks enjoyed an uncritically good press. Italian-Americans suffered a thoughtless and careless press. As a result, Italian-Americans were badly hurt and have not yet recovered. Responsible leaders of Newark's Italian-American community, especially Steve Adubato, pleaded in vain with the federal government's Model Cities Agency to help Newark's large number of poor whites as well as blacks. Virtually all Model Cities funds and jobs went to blacks. In an article by David Shipler entitled "The White Niggers of Newark" (*Harper's*, summer 1972), an embittered Adubato was quoted in uncharacteristically cynical terms. "We're the niggers now, that's what's happened," he said. "It just is who's on top. The group that's second's gonna catch shit—they're gonna be niggers. This is what this country's really all about."

The nation is now reacting against the domestic turbulence of the 1960's and is coming around 180 degrees in its appreciation of the Italian-American attitudes. There are Italian-American mayors in Philadelphia and San Francisco. Other Italian-American politicians show rapidly growing strength in New York City.

Decade after decade Italian-Americans' basic values remain the same. Their political positions at particular times and places are determined by these. At different times Italian-Americans appear to be liberal (pro-Roosevelt in 1932, pro-Kennedy in 1960, pro-Humphrey in 1968), radical right (anti-Roosevelt in 1944) and reactionary (anti-Lindsay in 1969). They remained predominantly Democrats *during their quarrel with Roosevelt and during their* support of John Kennedy's election on a plank of strong domestic liberalism. Now they are shifting their votes to the Republican Party. In 1971, Greeley found that 51 per cent of the youngest and best educated group of Italian-Americans, third-generation high school graduates, still belonged to the Democratic Party. Yet this middle-class segment was the strongest of all for Nixon in 1972. In the suburban Long Island town of Elmont, 78 per cent of Italian-Americans voted for Nixon. In Deer Park, Long Island, 79 per cent voted for Nixon, Italian-Americans align themselves politically according to their own ethnic values rather than to political parties or ideologies.

The political success of the steady Italian-American underlying position which supports la via vecchia depends not so much on the shifts of Italian-Americans as on the shifts of other Americans. Herbert Gans's conclusion about Boston's lower-class Italian-Americans (*The Urban Villagers*, 1962) during the 1950's still holds true. He found that the Italian-American is decisively influenced by his family and by other Italian-Americans his own age. The influence upon him by the outside world and its political currents is secondary and weak. The politics of Italian-Americans have always been and continue to be the apolitical politics of la via vecchia. Their only bright banner is that of the old way. Italian-Americans hoist up political banners to fly beneath that of la via vecchia when these enhance the supreme allegiance, and pull them down as soon as they no longer serve this purpose. But the colors of la via vecchia, the essential ethnic values, remain nailed to the mast.

The essentially apolitical politics of Italian-Americans leaves them relatively powerless. Their poor voting record and lack of party enthusiasms cause them to suffer. In a system where massive bloc voting and party loyalties are decisive, Italian-Americans enjoy power disproportionately below their numbers. They are easily played cheap even by political machines dominated by other ethnic groups. Political candidates on the stump enter their communities and deliver symbolic flatteries to their life style. Once elected, the pizza-munching politicians ignore their problems and needs. The paucity of Italian-American commu-

nity leaders, their ineffectiveness, and the group's lack of
political organization leave Italian-Americans frustrated
even in publicizing their demands, let alone gaining them.
In New York State, where some 40 per cent of the State
Legislature is Italian-American, the political power of the
group is comparatively weak. For years it has been easily
manipulated by others. Italian-American power is weak
even in New York City, where one out of every five white
residents is Italian. In the 1970 edition of *Beyond the Melting Pot,* Glazer and Moynihan describe how in the 1960's
Jews with black support pushed Irish-Americans out of political predominance and at the same time kept Italian-
Americans even further from the centers of political power
in New York. In the opinion of these scholars, non-Italian
politicians effectively used the Mafia and antiblack images
of Italian-Americans to keep them out of power.

In the last years Italian-Americans have become increasingly restless about their lack of power as the values of
la via vecchia have become directly threatened. While concerned with other changes which confront their value system, Italian-American alarm has been most strongly
aroused by one fact above all. Blacks are now their neighbors in inner cities and even in suburbs, competing with
them for jobs and power. Left by other white groups who
fled as masses of Southern blacks moved to Northern cities
since 1950, Italian-Americans now find themselves neighbors of a people whose value system is perceived as dia-
metrically opposed to la via vecchia.

The cultural roots of the impasse between blacks and
Italian-Americans run deep. It is difficult to think of two
groups of Americans whose ways of life differ more. The
two cultures are at odds with each other in superficial styles
and in critical values. The groups clash more and more
as ghetto blacks confront lower-middle-class whites in inner
cities over efforts to integrate schools and housing and in
competition for jobs and political power. The dispute in
Newark, New Jersey, over the building of high-rise housing
for blacks in the predominantly Italian North Ward, the
conflict in Brooklyn's Canarsie regarding the bussing of

black children into schools heavily populated by Italian-Americans, and the animosities in Philadelphia over the law-and-order policies of Mayor Rizzo are conspicuous eruptions of a cultural conflict that began to boil a few years ago. Conflicts between blacks and Italian-Americans are likely to occur in other cities such as Boston, Chicago, New Haven, San Francisco, St. Louis, Buffalo, Providence, and Cleveland, where the pressures of urban crises are pushing the two peoples against each other.

Conflict between the two groups is more likely because in a sense Italian-Americans are far more integrated with blacks than other whites. In their book *Side By Side: Integrated Neighborhoods in America* (1971), Bradburn, Ludman, and Gockel report that for "the Italians, French, Poles, Russians and other Eastern Europeans, the percentage of households is higher in integrated than in segregated neighborhoods. Conversely, there is a higher percentage of WASPs in segregated than in integrated neighborhoods."

The Bureau of the Census reports that since 1960, Italian-Americans have the highest percentage (88.2 per cent) of all white groups living in highly populated areas designated Standard Metropolitan Statistical Area (SMSAs). Of this group, 84.4 per cent live in the racially troubled SMSAs of the North, the second highest percentage among all white groups in the North.

There is no doubt that racism plays a role in the relations between the two groups, and the media have emphasized this as if it were all that needs to be understood. But it is a serious mistake to think that mere racism is the determining factor in the frictions between them. The painful truth is that there are enormous differences throughout the cultures of blacks and Italian-Americans which determine their attitudes toward each other. So far the media have been all but blind to these differences. The press reports clashes with words like "militancy," "race," "radical," and "conservative," terms which are so simplified that the resulting picture is superficial. Not surprisingly the attitudes of each ethnic group toward the other remain based upon great misunderstandings. Blacks and Italian-Americans need perspective and depth in their knowledge of one another, and the rest of the country needs a clearer view of what is involved if relations between the two groups are to improve from their present condition of explosive tension.

As we have seen, the culture of Italian-Americans is based on a centuries-old pattern inherited from the land of their immigrant fathers and grandfathers. A code of behavior developed centered around a family-based small town social web. The influence of outsiders was sealed out and the demands made upon insiders were severe. Whereas, the culture of American blacks is rooted in tribal traditions of the west coast of Africa which were tempered in the crucible of slavery followed by Jim Crow racism.

At first glance the two routes seem similar. The network of families that was the African tribe seems a parallel to the network of clans that formed the towns and cities of the Mezzogiorno. In each case the family struggled against oppression, the Africans against slavery in the New World and the Italians against alien power in the Old World and Know-Nothing hatred against immigrants in the new. Each group knows the bitter experience of what Shakespeare called ". . . the law's delay / The insolence of office . . ."

Yet these are only surface parallels. The two groups are greatly dissimilar in both their Old World traditions and in their present pattern of life, which in each case is the result of the struggles of old ways in the circumstances of the new land. The shape of the origins of each group, the type of struggles waged on behalf of those origins, and the resulting culture of each group are not only different but are also in marked contrast to each other. The subject of these differences is an extremely sensitive one. Perhaps headway can best be made by beginning with superficials and gradually uncovering deeper layers of differences.

We have grown accustomed to thinking that the soul of a people is exposed in its music. Recently we have learned to read the character of people by scrutinizing their body language, the way they stand and move. In each case external expressions are keys to deep-seated realities. A look at the music and body languages of blacks and Italian-Americans is revealing.

The music of American blacks continues to echo its rich African origins. African music emphasizes intricate vibrant rhythms which are perhaps unmatched anywhere in the world. Melodic patterns in African music are subordinate to rhythm. By comparison to African rhythms, African melody is less developed and less prominent. When the voice is used in African music, it is most frequently employed in rhythmic chant rather than flowing melody. This has its upshot in America's pop music today, music that is greatly influenced by contributions by generations of black Americans. Much of American pop music is rock music or soul music. In each case its heart is its compelling beat. Melodies are often crude and words are slighted, often even unintelligible. True to its African roots, it is the music of dance more than of song.

On the other hand when one thinks of the music of Southern Italy it is song which comes to mind. Just as rhythm and dance were rich cultural expressions in West Africa, so melody and song were the mode of the Mezzogiorno. These were expressed in the everyday folk songs of the people as well as in the most stylized development of folk song, the opera of the nineteenth century. Words and melodies were all-important. The parts of Italian opera that are strictly dramatic or theatrical are stiff and unimaginative compared to its soaring, exquisite arias. Even the spoken parts of opera were channeled into melody and became recitative. The folk songs of the old Mezzogiorno were either arias—for example the Neapolitan song *"O Sole Mio"*—or recitatives, like Sicily's *"La Luna Mezzu o Mari,"* the afore-mentioned song familiar to Americans from the wedding scene of the movie version of *The Godfather.* Even the most rhythmic of all Southern Italian music, the tarantella, is a rhythmic melody, a dance which has as its core a melodic line.

The body languages of the two groups are also plainly in contrast to each other. The movement of blacks mirrors that of their Ashanti, Ibo, and Yoruba ancestors. It is fluid, agile, graceful, easy, and seemingly relaxed and uninhibited. Black nationalists have fixed upon the cat as their symbol, and the image that blacks are a catlike people is a motif of many recent Afro-American expressions in art as well as in speech. Even the lingo of the black ghetto has long used the slang "cat" to refer to a man. In contrast the Italian-American stands and moves in a controlled, guarded way. He reflects the demeanor of the people of Naples, Apulia, Calabria, Abruzzi, and Sicily. His shoulders are kept back even when he is sitting. His shoulders and hips remain locked even during the fastest dancing, in contrast to the focus on pelvic movement of black dance. It is a code of a self-contained rocklike body punctuated by deliberate staccato movements.

In themselves these observations about music and body languages are trivial. But there are cultural realities behind these clichés in the histories of black and Italian-Americans which flow into and pervade the psychologies of the people of both ethnic groups.

The great tribes of West Africa traversed, hunted in, and tended animals on great expanses of land. The land was not enclosed physically, legally, or psychologically. It was the communal property of a tribe. The experience of slavery reinforced this sense of community property. Paradoxically, slavery's cruel destruction of the family served to extend the notion of communal responsibility among blacks. Children became the children of all, the realities of slavery necessitating their being cared for regardless of questions of family relationship. Wrenched from their parents by the slave system, children were nurtured by whatever black community into which they were sent. Coming to grips with the torment of generations of slavery, blacks developed their sense of community rooted only partially in family and not at all in land as private property. The ethnicity of the group itself became the foundation of its sense of community. This has culminated in today's strong expressions of black solidarity, which cut across and cancel all differences of class, region, or individual preferences in favor of brotherhood among blacks.

The April 1973 issue of *Intellectual Digest* contained an interview with Huey Newton and Erik Erikson. In response to Erikson's mention of the importance of the family to children, Newton replied:

> You are saying that the family is the traditional method for bringing up children. I would say that the family has always been a traditional way of keeping people children.

When asked if "the [Black Panther] party will be your family," Newton agreed. He said of the party, "I am willing to make any sacrifice, not because of a suicidal tendency on my part, as some psychologists and sociologists have concluded, but because the sacrifice is compensated for by the fraternity." That brotherhood, a community of ethnicity in itself, should emerge from the horrors of racist oppression is a tribute to the viability of African culture and the strength of Afro-Americans. Yet the contrast between this scheme of values and l'ordine della famiglia is extreme.

The recent ancestors of Italian-Americans also faced severe problems of surviving and developing a culture in the face of generations of oppression, an oppression less familiar to Americans than that suffered by blacks. There are important differences in the manner the two ethnic groups coped with crisis. Unlike blacks who were surrounded by an oppressive alien group in a foreign land, America, the people of the Mezzogiorno struggled in their own land against aliens. Although the aliens in Southern Italy were sometimes numerous, they were always in the minority. (Keep in mind that the struggles of blacks in America and Italians in the Mezzogiorno were simultaneous in history.) Because their struggle took place on their own familiar, harsh land, Southern Italians were able to develop two major responses that enabled them to prevail. One was a unique family system. The other was a distinct community pattern. It involved a ceaseless struggle to control the homes and towns and the land on which the town dwellers worked. (In the Mezzogiorno there are few isolated farmhouses as in America. Almost all people lived in towns and went out each day into the surrounding fields to work the land and returned to their homes each evening.) As we have discussed, this system of campanilismo was transported to the United States and re-established in Italian-American communities.

The structure of the Southern Italian family has also been described in detail. We need only recall that it was based upon several principles. First in importance was the authority of the parents, the father as the head and the mother as the center of the family. Second were the strict demands upon each family member to work within the family code and for the family's good as a whole. And third were relations with members of the larger family, aunts, uncles, cousins, etc., and also with special friends and their families carefully selected in the system of comparatico or comparaggio. Each town formed a solid unit difficult to penetrate. All codes of behavior were strict and they all served to strengthen the solidarity of the family and the community. Family relationships and towns became interwoven, a pattern which the immigrants continued by setting up Little Italies in the first decades of this century and which their children and grandchildren perpetuate in the myriad Italian-American neighborhoods of our cities and suburbs.

Landless, propertyless, and surrounded by a merciless majority, blacks fought against the oppressions of slavery and Jim Crow using means of direct confrontation culminating in today's political militancy. As they must, blacks strike out to tear down the thick fibers of oppression in white society that suppress them. In the past they struck at slaveowners, at Jim Crow laws, and now they strike at discriminatory patterns of behavior. Significant as they are, the movements for black liberation have dominated our attention in the last twenty years, and it is unnecessary to review them in greater detail here. Theirs is a determined drive toward true and equal membership in American society. Even if no other factors were present, the blacks' irrepressible frontal assault upon white society and the

Italian-Americans' stubborn determination to maintain the
stability of their ways and their communities would lead
to conflict, misunderstanding, anger, bitterness, fear, distrust, and hatred. Unfortunately these ugly consequences
are nurtured even more by other important cultural differences that aggravate the conflict between the ethnic
groups.

Because they were denied other opportunities of life style
as well as means of livelihood, blacks have become heavily
dependent upon a monstrous welfare system which they
hate more than whites hate it. Moreover, because they perceive that their poverty has been forced upon them, they
feel that American society owes them compensation, sub-
sistence, or both. They feel no guilt at accepting public
aid, only anger. A disproportionately high percentage of
people chronically on welfare are blacks. Many of the
black people on welfare are members of families in which
there is no male head. Black literature has raged at the
oppression of the black male which has left him unemployed or underemployed and suffering a host of other social ills imposed on him. In New York City one out of
every three black families is not headed by a male figure.
According to a study made public by the U. S. Bureau
of the Census in August 1972, 32.4 per cent of the city's
black families have female household heads.

Welfare dependence and fatherless families understand-
ably are the objects of black rage. From the perspective
of a different background, Italian-Americans view them
with another set of values and emotions. In the strict code
of Southern Italy it is considered shameful to accept *carità*
or *pietà*—any aid from someone not a member of the extended family. The person who accepts such aid is considered to disgrace himself and his family. His acceptance of
aid is equivalent to an admission that his family is failing
in the traditional strict morality of taking care of its own.
Following a long history in which the state had been for
centuries the instrument of the worst threats to the family
system absolutely critical to culture and life, Italian immigrants brought with them an enormous distrust of the state.

All associations with agencies of the state were shunned. The New York *Times* on September 29, 1972, published an article entitled "The City's Italian-American Needy: Too Proud to Take Aid They 'Earned'." The piece detailed the refusal of impoverished Italian-Americans to seek or accept welfare aid or other state aid. The report showed that immigrant, second, and third generations continue to regard such assistance as anathema. Even elderly individuals who worked and paid taxes for decades, thus entitling them to aid in the moral view of most Americans, refuse state aid. In the old code which is still very much alive, to be poor is a misfortune, but to be the object of carità is shameful. The viability of the old code is illustrated by the 1970 Census reports, which show that only 1.7 per cent of Italian-American males in the labor pool are unemployed and that only 0.8 per cent of whole Italian-American families with dependent children had unemployed fathers.

A survey of major white ethnic groups published in Greeley's *Why Can't They Be Like Us?* found that by large percentage differences over members of other ethnic groups adult Italian-Americans "most often live in the same neighborhood as their parents and siblings and visit them every week." The 1970 Census found that of all major ethnic groups *American-born* Italian-Americans between the ages of twenty-five and forty-four had the highest percentage (37.1 per cent) of those who spoke a foreign language as their current language. In August 1972 the Council on the Teaching of Foreign Languages reported that only the Spanish and Italian languages show absolute gains in the numbers of Americans studying them while the study of all other foreign languages declines. Greeley's surveys found that by a wide margin Italian-Americans have the highest percentage (63 per cent) of adults of all white ethnic groups who "followed old world customs as children." As already indicated, of all white ethnic groups Italian-Americans had the least sympathy with political or social militant behavior by anyone, themselves included.

One of the most sensitive differences between the two

ethnic groups is in regard to sexual attitudes. On November 26, 1972, the New York *Times* reported the results of a study by two sociologists at Johns Hopkins University.

> An analysis of sexual experiences among unmarried young women in the United States indicates that poverty by itself does not account for the fact that black women are more likely than whites to have premarital sexual intercourse in their teen years . . . In fact, among young white women, if there is any link between socioeconomic status and sexual activity, it appears to be in the reverse direction: unmarried whites near or below poverty level were found to be less likely to be sexually experienced than those clearly above poverty level.

Among lower-middle-class and middle-class whites, as we have seen, Italian-Americans have the most conservative attitudes toward sex.

The Italian-American community has one of the lowest records of all ethnic groups in terms of formal education. The 1970 Census reported that only 7 per cent of Italian-Americans over the age of twenty-five are college graduates. Only 6 per cent of the white population over twenty-five years old of Canarsie, Brooklyn (Italian and Jewish), are college graduates. These figures are only slightly higher than the 1970 Census figure for college graduates among blacks in New York City—4 per cent. As noted, Glazer and Moynihan report in the 1970 edition of *Beyond the Melting Pot* that the percentage of Italian-American men in New York City employed as professionals or managers (8.1 per cent) is actually lower than the percentage of the city's black men who are employed as professionals or managers (8.5 per cent). Compare these figures to those of the city's white Protestant men who are employed in professional or managerial roles (22 per cent) and Jewish men so employed (21.5 per cent). Yet while the median family income of blacks ($6,156) is far below the national average ($8,632), that of Italian-Americans is at the national average ($8,808). Another element of the family code inherited from the Mezzogiorno accounts for the fact that Italians have done better economically than educationally—their severe work ethic.

Their inherited work ethic has been effective for Italian-Americans. Patterning their lives in it, they have achieved economic progress since the days of immigrant landings. The family-neighborhood-labor pattern has led to slow but steady progress from the time when Italian labor was on the bottom. The U. S. Immigration Commission found that in 1910 Italian-Americans had a considerably lower income than other whites and that of blacks. Of males eighteen years or older, the national average for whites was $666. For blacks it was $445. For American-born Italian-Americans the figure was $408 and for the Italian-born it was $396. It took sixty years for Italian-Americans to catch up with the white average and pass that of blacks. How they did it can be indicated in two sets of figures. As already said, 60 per cent of Italian-American families in 1910 had more than one working member. The U. S. Bureau of Labor in that year estimated also that 95 per cent of Italian-American laborers saved twenty-eight dollars to thirty dollars a month. At a time when they averaged only forty dollars a month in income, the sacrifice was incredible. At the time almost all Italian-Americans were laborers. Even if they had not faced intense discrimination they were not equipped to live any other way. From 1890 to 1914 the immigrants arriving from the Mezzogiorno had the highest percentage of unskilled labor of all immigrant groups coming into Ellis Island. A study there in 1901 showed that they also had the highest percentage of illiteracy. Among Italian men 62 per cent could not read or write in any language or dialect, and 74 per cent of the women were similarly handicapped. Italian-Americans have survived economically only through their discipline of work and saving.

Blacks on the other hand are impatient with mention of any work ethic. Historically they have been lectured to work harder in a system that consistently exploited their labor and discriminated against any economic progress by them. The work ethic has not worked for blacks because

its rewards have been deliberately blocked from them or
canceled. Thus blacks regard the work ethic as a smoke
screen used to hide economic injustice by rationalizing it,
while Italian-Americans regard it as a tried-and-true, inescapable truth. Blacks have good historical reasons to
be cynical about the work ethic. Italian-Americans have
equally valid reasons to believe that it and it alone spells
economic survival.

The details of Italian-American economic survival also
lead to a present source of conflict between them and
blacks. The 1970 Census reports that 44.7 per cent of
Italian-Americans are either skilled or semiskilled laborers,
a figure that has remained stubbornly unchanging with
each census report every decade. Italians have kept to the
only social device apart from the family that has served
them economically, their labor unions. In the days when
labor was struggling to unionize, employers played ethnic
groups against each other, blacks vs. whites and whites vs.
whites. Thomas R. Brooks gives an authoritative account
of this in his *Toil and Trouble* (Dell, 1964), a history of
the American labor movement. He says of the ethnic character of the unions in the early years of this century:

> Needless to say, each group protected its own as it organized
> its trade. The process—and results—were markedly different
> in industry where employers followed a deliberate policy of
> pitting one immigrant group against another as a means of
> forestalling unionization. In a report made by John R. Com-
> mons in 1904, he notes that he "saw seated around the
> benches of the company's employment office a sturdy group
> of Nordics. I asked the employment agent, "how comes it you
> are employing only Swedes?" he answered, "Well you see, it
> is only for this week. Last week we employed Slovaks. We
> change about the different nationalities and languages. It pre-
> vents them from getting together. We have the thing system-
> atized. We have a luncheon each week of the employment
> managers of the large firms of the Chicago district. There
> we discuss our problems and exchange information. We have
> a number of men in the field who keep us informed. . . . If
> agitators are coming or expected and there is considerable

unrest among the labor population, we raise the wages all around. . . . It is wonderful to watch the effect. The unrest stops and the agitators leave. Then when things quiet down we reduce the wages to where they were." This deliberate policy is one reason that unions failed to secure an early foothold in industrial plants. Among the skilled trades, ethnic lines reinforced craft solidarity. But among the unskilled in factories, worker solidarity was defeated by the babel of tongues.

As did other white ethnic groups, Italian-Americans formed *ethnic* unions and since then have sought to keep out all other ethnics, both whites and blacks. Italian-Americans have invested their unions with the cohesive closed-to-the-outside structure of their two basic units—the family and neighborhood. Thus their unions have been compared to guilds.

Blacks were systematically excluded from the American labor movement and are now striving to enter it. Quite naturally they regard the exclusionary practices of Italian-American unions in the light of the same discrimination. From their perspective it is cold consolation that Italian-Americans exclude other whites as well in their effort to protect their only economically successful institution. Again it is more a tragic clash of two positions well justified by disparate histories rather than a case of clear-cut right vs. wrong. Having used their efforts to build the labor unions rather than other organized means of economic progress, for example an educated class or mass political or social movements, Italian-Americans have no choice at present but to protect that in which they have invested their survival. Suffering widespread poverty, blacks have no choice but to break into all of society's economically gainful institutions, including Italian labor unions.

Because they have concentrated on semiskilled and skilled labor rather than formal education, Italian-Americans have achieved less social and political mobility than they might have. An even more significant reason for this is their cultural pattern of rooting themselves not in political ideologies or social class identification but in the neighborhoods they have worked to build. The inherited dream was to own a plot of land no matter how small and a home no matter how humble. Canarsie is typical. Italian-Americans bought cheap undeveloped land there because they could afford no better and no one else wanted it. Canarsie was the butt of jokes—marsh land enhanced by the mammoth New York City garbage dump. As has been often noted, Italian-Americans are neighborhood builders. Over the years they turned Canarsie from a joke into a community of extraordinary stability, as they have done with many other neighborhoods in different cities and suburbs. More than any other sizable white ethnic group, Italians have stuck with the neighborhoods they built over two or three generations. In August 1972 the U. S. Bureau of the Census reported that in contrast to other white groups Italian-Americans had not deserted New York City in the decade from 1960 to 1970. In 1960 they composed 22.7 per cent of the city's white population, and in 1970 they accounted for 20.7 per cent. In fact, the ratio of Italian-Americans to other whites in New York City is higher today than it was in 1930. The Italian-Americans who have moved from the city have set up a much-overlooked phenomenon—suburban Little Italies. They still cherish the family-neighborhood life. The 1970 Census shows that the Italians who moved to Long Island have clustered together in large areas of towns like Valley Stream, Franklin Square, Elmont, North Babylon, and Levittown rather than dispersing into the non-Italian population.

It is interesting to note that Mayor Rizzo turned down an early proposal to have Philadelphia host the bicentennial celebration of the founding of the United States in 1976. Philadelphia had welcomed being host of the sesquicentennial celebration in 1926. Yet according to reports in the press, Mayor Rizzo turned down the proposal to play host in 1976 because the proposed celebration would upset the integrity of an Italian neighborhood near the proposed ceremonial site. Philadelphia's Italian-Americans saw the proposal almost in terms paralleling the World War II Allied invasion of Italy. Yielding to this feeling, Philadelphia was willing to give up the money and prestige of being the host at America's birthday party to preserve the inviolability of its Italian neighborhood.

The pattern of Italian-American life is continuous with that of their ancestors. Its verities continue to demonstrate that family, community, and work mean survival and that outsiders are threats to the neighborhood stability which is necessary to the close-knit life and culture of the people.

In the cities and suburbs of the North, Midwest, and West, blacks live in neighborhoods not of their choice. As they moved from the South they were forced into neighborhoods by discriminatory laws and patterns. Thus we call them ghettos. Blacks were denied the opportunity to own the houses in which they lived and the means to improve them whether or not they owned them. Blacks identify with each other and not with their physical surroundings, which are for the most part owned not by them but by whites. This was demonstrated in the riots of the 1960's, when they tore up their own neighborhood buildings (except for the few owned by soul brothers and marked as such). The buildings in which they live and shop are symbols of the remote white power structure which has oppressed and exploited them for generations. Again for very good reasons which are poorly understood by each group when it regards the other, blacks and Italian-Americans have very different definitions of neighborhood values. The Italian-Americans' impatience with being branded reactionaries for their community values is indicated by one who said to sociologist Joseph Fitzpatrick, "Why do you criticize us for trying to preserve the very thing you are trying to help the Blacks and Puerto Ricans create?" (Reported in a paper Rev. Fitzpatrick delivered in 1969 to the Chicago Consultation on Ethnicity.)

Only recently having moved beyond the dire poverty of their immigrant fathers and grandfathers, and some remaining still in poverty, Italian-Americans are for the first time turning toward education and overcoming their historic distrust of state schools. They have awakened to the possibilities of social mobility in formal education. As blacks also now view the schools as a source of mobility for their children, something which was impossible until the breakdown of segregation, which began with the effort following the famous Supreme Court decision of 1954, they find themselves in direct competition with their Italian-American neighbors in the inner cities. As has been noted, till now Italian-Americans have done little better than blacks in higher education, and they intensely resent any hint that they should pay the price of past discrimination against blacks. Second, even apart from the inherent problems in the ethic of collective responsibility, Italian-Americans, whose ancestors arrived here in largest numbers in this century, feel no responsibility for American slavery. Nor do they feel responsible for Jim Crow discrimination against blacks, since their immigrant forebears did not benefit from it. Their resentment is not directed against blacks as much as it is against the white upper classes and their media.

The white elite has shown little understanding of Italian-American history, culture, or problems and less empathy with them. In the past fifteen or twenty years, the liberal segment of this elite, which is especially powerful in its control of media, has gone to great lengths to develop empathy for blacks and understanding of the objective conditions of their plight. Italian-Americans receive little attention except for the incessant bad press of the Mafia, and the white working-class image which is currently out of favor with the white elite. White liberals are closer to blacks in attitudes running from radical political ideology to liberated sexual values than they are to Italian-Americans. The white upper class goes so far as to admire qualities in other ethnic groups which it scorns among Italian-Americans. For example, today's liberals admire Chinese-Americans whose life style is square and family-centered. Yet the liberals see this life style as vulgar and reactionary in Italian-Americans. The reason is simple.

Chinese-Americans are self-segregating, while Italian-Americans in recent years have asserted their life style in the open. Italian-Americans embarrass white liberals by insisting that their working-class, square, uneducated, unpolished values deserve a place in the American mainstream. They even put Italian flag decals on their cars! Italian-Americans have become easy scapegoats for the racial guilt and political turmoil of the country.

The result of the disparity in how influential whites view them is that in any conflict between blacks and Italian-Americans the conflict is depicted merely in the gross distortion of white racism vs. black militancy. The image projected helps to create the reality as hotheads in each group who confirm the image become the focus of media attention. Scenes of whites yelling racist remarks at black children in Canarsie and black militants raging against "Ku Klux Klan" racism in Newark dominate television and popular print media. These media are the ones on which the entire nation most depends and the ones upon which the poorly educated black and Italian-American populations entirely depend for their picture of the world beyond their own lives. Lacking the sophistication to do justice to the reality beyond the distorted pictures, people from both ethnic groups fall into coded clichés to articulate their feelings. For example, Italian-Americans talk of property values, and blacks inveigh against the same old racism they have faced for three hundred years. At the same time a part of the white upper-middle class which has escaped the problems of inner cities by moving to wealthier suburbs or sending their children to private schools is only too glad to hold the coats of blacks and Italian-Americans while they exhaust their energies fighting each other. The cycle of media simplicity, mutual misunderstanding between the two groups, and stereotyped or hypocritical responses by the larger public becomes ever accelerated.

We come to the present situation. Blacks view the small home, stable neighborhood, hard work and thrift, law-and-order values of Italian-Americans as square, paranoid, and racist. Italian-Americans view the hip street life, and politically militant style of blacks as irresponsible, wild, and careless. The same attitudes become expressed over differences perceived in music, body language, attitudes toward welfare, in family patterns, sexual behavior, and neighborhood characteristics.

In one final culmination these differences are expressed in political stances. The black vote in New York City in 1972 was 85 per cent for McGovern. The predominately Democratic Italian-American vote was 65 per cent for Nixon. Mayor Rizzo of Philadelphia is lauded by the city's Italian-Americans for his law-and-order efforts and blasted for them by blacks and the media. Mayor Gibson of Newark is praised by blacks for his rhetorical and practical efforts to improve their lot and scored for race chauvinism at their expense by Italian-Americans. Mayor Lindsay of New York City was elected in 1968 with heavy support of blacks only because his two Italian-American opponents, John Marchi and Mario Procaccino, split the majority of the city's vote. Uncomprehending polarization everywhere is the rule.

Blacks and Italian-Americans are each strong in their ethnicity and have each contributed much to the nation because of it. This strength could be the foundation for the strongest of ethnicities, the kind that is so vital and confident that it can reach out to another ethnic group to understand its roots and structure and appreciate its values. So far the extent of understanding has been limited. Italian-Americans respect black rage and blacks respect Italian-American determination. In recent confrontations the leaders and people of both groups have taken pains not to aggravate antagonisms. Both sides have pulled back from the brink.

No one can ever do complete justice to all the complexities and nuances of emotion-filled realities. My thoughts about blacks and Italian-Americans will leave members of both groups dissatisfied, as they should be. I hope the dissatisfaction leads to further expressions of the cultures of both groups which will serve greater mutual understanding and better relations. My thoughts here are intended as an invitation to others to make that effort. The effort must be continued and must succeed.

In addition to problems resulting from the powerlessness of their traditional apolitical stance, their tenacity in staying with their old communities, and their being made shock troops and scapegoats for America's racial problem, Italian-Americans have other dilemmas on their agenda of relations with the outside world. Just as they let previous social revolutions pass them by, Italian-Americans remained largely impervious to the 1960's revolution in social welfare. With their classic distrust of outside authority and power, Italian-Americans underutilize social benefits available to them from government and private sources. For the same reason, Italian-Americans have mostly failed to develop self-help organizations like the old societies organized by the early Italian immigrants.

Conversations with Italian-Americans who are active in founding and supporting Italian-American philanthropies, charities, and institutions provoke a consistent story. Italian-Americans do not contribute to charity. In fact their typical response is icily cold. About a year ago I listened as an Italian-American millionaire told me of his experience soliciting funds from Italian-American businessmen to support a hospital in a wealthy Florida community which is divided among Italian, Jewish, and WASP populations. Italian-Americans contributed least of all. The WASPs contributed some, and Jews contributed the majority of funds. The man confessed to me the shame he felt when his community became aware that wealthy Italian-Americans refused to contribute to the hospital which serves them.

Of course, middle-aged people like those my friend approached in Florida normally are the greatest contributors to charity. This generation was studied in its youth by Leonard Covello. In his *Social Background of the Italo-American School Child* (1944), he reported a study conducted of Italian-American boys then attending New York City schools. Most were second generation and about an eighth of them third generation. They and other boys were asked, "If you came suddenly into money, whom would you help first?" The boys were given twelve choices: 1) club or team, 2) charity organization, 3) friend, 4) church, 5) grandmother, 6) cousin, 7) relative, 8) whole family, 9) sister, 10) brother, 11) father, 12) mother. Italian-American boys overwhelmingly listed some family member or the entire family as their first choice. Very few mentioned any of the choices beyond the family. These responses were in marked contrast to non-Italian boys, who scored much higher among them in those who would give to nonfamily recipients. Almost fifteen times as many Negro boys listed nonfamily recipients. Four times as many Spanish-speaking and eight times as many of other ethnic groups listed charity organizations as did Italian boys. Similar figures represent the responses to giving to a church, club, or friend. On the other hand, only Italian boys listed cousins as those with whom they would share their wealth.

Italian-Americans are frozen in their current political relations with the larger community. Unable to put their old values aside, they have yet to make them work in terms of contemporary rules of American power. The American political, social, and economic system continues operating in effect to exclude incipients from entry into its areas. In the book *Better than You: Social Discrimination Against Minorities in America* (1971), Terry Morris explains that social discrimination hits hardest against those who begin to move up the economic ladder than it does the very poor. The author lists Italian-Americans as among those in this category. Several examples are detailed. In the wealthy suburb of Grosse Point, Michigan, a realty board devised an elaborate questionnaire to screen prospective home buyers. Key points were ways of life ("typically American" or not), name ("American" or not), occupation ("typical of applicant's ethnic group"), applicant's accent, and education. Polish-Americans had to score a difficult fifty-five points. Italian-Americans had to score a very hard seventy-five points, and Jews eighty-five points.

In Buffalo, New York, County Court Judge Joseph S. Mattina has collected data to support his charge that the top business clubs of the city systematically exclude Italian-Americans or keep their numbers at a token level in their memberships.

Historically, groups have broken into systems of power and status by one of two means. Some have entered by mastering the game's rules. Irish- and Jewish-Americans are outstanding examples. Other groups have entered only after demonstrating their willingness to violate the rules and resort to illegitimate conflict. The labor movement in our century's early decades and blacks in the last decade provide illustrations. Because of la via vecchia's code of remaining uninvolved in political activity, Italian-Americans have made poor progress along the first, legitimate route. Paradoxically, the respect Italian-Americans feel for their own communities and their live-and-let-live attitude toward others also prevent them from following the second, disruptive road with any deliberation, determination, or consistency. Italian-Americans remain mostly odd men out in American political, social, and economic competition.

Comparatively little reliable information is available about Italian-Americans in the political sphere. Lumped together with other large groups on studies as "others," they are usually disregarded. The controversy on whether they vote as a bloc feeds on this ignorance. One of the most popular textbooks used for years in political science college courses, V. O. Key's *Politics, Parties and Pressure Groups*, deals with the entire question of ethnic voting in one general paragraph.

Even the basic question of how many Americans are of Italian origin is difficult to answer. The census survey lists only those born in Italy or who have at least one parent born there. It excludes the largest group, third and fourth generations. The Bureau of the Census lists seven million Italian-Americans. Other sources calculate the number as from thirteen to twenty-three million. Starting with the five million Italian immigrants to land in the United States before 1924 and whose numbers peaked in the years 1900–14, and using a conservative birth rate figure, it is reasonable to conclude that there are upwards of twenty million Italian-Americans.

Whatever total figure one uses, it is clear that Italian-Americans are underrepresented among holders of political power. Lawrence H. Fuchs studied the question in his *American Ethnic Politics* (1968). He confirmed findings generally agreed upon by social scientists. For example, he found that in Providence, Rhode Island, Italian-Americans are now the largest single ethnic group in the Republican Party but enjoy disproportionately few positions of power within it. He also found that in 1960, only 11 per cent of New York City's Democratic assembly district leaders were Italian-American. Fuchs concludes, "True to what one knows about their situation in other cities, the Italians appear to be underrepresented."

Jerre Mangione's *Night Search* (1965) is a novel set in the early 1950's. Its hero, Michael, sets about investigating the murder of his Italian-American father, Paolo, some twelve years before. Paolo was a politically active journalist deeply involved in combating both Fascist and Communist attempts to influence Italian-Americans. His murder was purely a political act. Michael learns that his father refused the advice of friends to seek police protection when he learned that political enemies had hired a professional killer to gun him down. His answer was, "You t'ink I'm sick in head? . . . Police all sonofabeetch fascisti." Instead Paolo bought a pistol, relying on himself rather than the authorities. At one point he was approached by a racketeer who explained he had learned of Paolo's problem. The apolitical gangster offered his help (and of course made Paolo indebted to him), an offer whose import Paolo immediately understood. Matters of life and death—in fact all significant questions—transcended politics and called for personal actions and alliances, non-political solutions in the patterns of la via vecchia.

Hearing this story was a turning point for Paolo's son. His reaction aptly symbolizes the dimension of the Italian-

American dilemma which concerns relations with the outside world, authority, and politics.

> Of all the stories about his father . . . this one haunted him the most. It suggested an approach to life, a method of dealing with problems, that was entirely outside his ken. More than his eccentric English and the Garibaldi scarf, it made him aware that Paolo was a Latin with an innate distrust of the obvious, a blood brother of Pirandello, another Sicilian who operated beyond the boundaries of conventional logic. For all his bull-in-the-china-shop tactics, Paolo loomed as a mountain of elusive subtleties, a person Michael could never fully understand.

Italian-Americans must recapture full command of the elusive subtleties of our cultural heritage to develop fully our new identity. Other Americans need to understand these subtleties if they are to appreciate what it means to be Italian-American.

What It Means to Be Italian-American in Today's United States

Alack the heavy day,
That I have worn so many winters out
And know not now what name to call myself!
Shakespeare, *Richard II*

In the past months I have asked people not of Italian background what comes to mind when they think of Italian-Americans. The responses have been standard ones to which we are all accustomed. The same words are repeated with remarkable uniformity—the Mafia; pizza and other food; hard hats; blue collar; emotional, jealous people; dusky, sexy girls; overweight mammas; frightening, rough, tough men; pop singers; law and order; pastel-colored houses; racists; nice, quiet people. I told a group of Italian-American college students of these views. As I recited the litany of familiar pictures, the group's responses ranged from sounds of exasperation (Mafia, pizza and hard hats) to titters (law and order, unchic homes, and jealous passions), to outright laughter (sexy girls, fat mammas, frightening men). They reacted to the other images with interest and bemusement.

When I asked the group whether the composite picture accurately reflected their sense of Italian-American identity, they answered strongly and unanimously in the negative. Upon my asking them what it means to be Italian-American, an initial period of silence was followed by an increasingly intense but confused discussion which produced no consensus or even any clear directions.

Trying another approach, I asked a different group of Italian-American students whether they thought of themselves as Italian. Their response was decidedly affirmative. Then I listed five questions on a blackboard and suggested they respond to them:

1. Do you instinctively think of yourself as Italian, American, or Italian-American?

2. Have you ever felt conflict between the Italian part of you and American demands on your nature?

3. What particular insights, nerve endings, advantages, do you have from your Italian background?

4. If there is one thing that you think you as an Italian-American do not share with others, what is it?

5. Name some Italian-Americans of whom you are privately most proud.

The questions left the students in absorbed thought. They tentatively offered only a few vaguely formulated answers. After a period of mostly silence, I asked them whether they thought the five questions were significant. The answer was a quick and firm yes. When I next repeated my question of whether they identified themselves as Italian, the response was even more assertively affirmative than the first time. I then asked why they thought they had difficulty forming answers to the five questions. The group again fell into silence, until one girl said, "The questions are too complicated," a response to which the others instantly gave accord. When I suggested that they were too complicated because we had a deep identity problem, they quickly agreed. They relaxed. Their paralyzing puzzlement turned into eagerness to discuss the question of their identity.

If this was consciousness-raising, it was easily accomplished because their consciousness wanted to be raised. Additional evidence that Italian-Americans are concerned with their ethnicity is found in a flood of mail I received in response to an article I wrote about Italian-Americans in the New York *Times Magazine* in 1972 which was reprinted in papers across the country. Many writers said that they were at a loss in knowing how to begin solving the urgently felt problem, as one letter put it, "of the enigma of being Italian-American."

In this book I have suggested that the core of Italian-American ethnicity consists of a distinct and rich familial culture combined with a complicated psychology. I have repeated that this identity is dilemma-producing, generating both strengths and problems. The strengths are such that Americans now envy them, albeit that they perceive them usually in distorted ways. For example, the key to Americans' fascination with the Mafia is not merely that violence thrills. Many less popular books, movies, and TV programs are more bloody and brutal than those depicting the Mafia. The key to the Mafia mania is that Americans yearn for the aura of l'ordine della famiglia that emerges from Mafia stories. Values of belonging, loyalty, control of one's life, canny ability to assess people and events, and palpable rather than abstract human relations radiate through the criminal sensationalism of the tales.

I was struck by this when I read an excellent article (in the New York *Times Magazine* of February 18, 1973) by novelist Anne Roiphe. Miss Roiphe keenly and touchingly discusses a television series that fascinated Americans, the thirteen-part production of WNET entitled "An American Family." Week after week Americans watched despair-inspiring relationships in the affluent California family of Mr. and Mrs. Bill Loud and their five children. As shown on TV, the Louds are likable people but beset by their lack of insight into themselves, by self-deceptions, by inability to talk with each other in other than a nonengaged style in which any insights that surface are instantly deflected, and by a community environment that is all surface and utterly bereft of any cultural, psychological, or spiritual depths. This America, and these Americans, are mere thinly attractive exteriors with undeveloped substance. Most tragically, we feel for them because we recognize the monstrous life style as uncomfortably familiar. This sterile culture is ours. It leaves us—underneath the material fat of American culture—like Giacometti's emaciated statues, spiritually undernourished, gaunt, stick figures in pathetic search of our own humanity. It is significant that Miss Roiphe concludes her humane, telling discussion of the devastation of American families and the people they produce by suddenly invoking Italian-American culture. She does so in the form of a reference to the fictional Corleone family of Puzo's *The Godfather*. Her closing words about the Louds are almost painfully sensitive.

> I was shaken with a particularly searing kind of sadness . . . Each new family holds out a brazen kind of hope—'Not us, no, not us, we can love one another forever, raise our children, make good our home, find our way'—and in the newness there is such a touching bravery.
>
> . . . Sentimentally speaking, I wish we could return to an earlier America when society surrounded its members with a tight sense of belonging, of being needed. Maybe the melting-pot idea was a bad one. Maybe it's better to be a Corleone than a Loud, better to be tribal and ethnocentric than urbane and adrift. We are like jelly fish in the vast ocean, dropping our young into the waves and immediately losing them because we are all merely transparent. If great social change is coming today, we don't hear it or see it. For now there is nothing to be done. We should set young girls to work restitching the familiar sampler: "Be it ever so hollow, there's no place like home."

Miss Roiphe's sentiments resonate in the discovery by two researchers at the American Jewish Committee, Irving M. Levine and Judith Herman, that college students and other young Americans in large Northern and Midwestern cities are attracted to Italian neighborhoods because of the quality of "peoplehood" they find in them. ("Search for Identity in Blue-Collar America," *Civil Rights Digest*, Winter 1972.)

Italian-Americans in their parochial aloofness have resisted post-industrial urban American currents that trivialize and undermine the family and the person and make life impersonal and empty. In their archaism Italian-Americans cleave to a life that gives dimension to emotions and spirit. Some Americans have made a virtue out of our society's "necessity" to wipe out structured and ongoing meanings in love, family, loyalty, interdependence, community, sex, work, and recreation. To these people, pathetically whistling in the dark as every element of the human soul evaporates in the heat of modern America's pressures, the Italian-American seems quaint or reactionary in his determination to protect la via vecchia. Yet our new chicness, with its enlightened liberation, provides nothing to replace the corny old values. To the extent that we are still capable of introspection and examination of life, the empty people of our brave new world yearn for what Italian-Americans have not yet lost.

This is the setting in which young Italian-Americans need to view their quest for identity. They are still plugged into a humanistic life. But critical questions need to be resolved. Are these young people capable of using their ethnic current to animate their lives? Are their ethnic values vital enough to withstand the crunch of modern American life? Are Italian-Americans capable of revitalizing la via vecchia, transforming it into modern terms, and thereby perhaps even helping to give new America a better soul? Or will they lose hold of their inherited meanings and be swept into the riptide of today's America and become more of Miss Roiphe's jellyfish people?

If these questions are to be deliberately and not accidentally settled, we need to fix exactly the latitude and longitude of the Italian-American dilemma this book has attempted to describe. To use today's slang, where are Italian-Americans at?

Ethnic groups go through different regions in their inevitable journey toward new self-identity and changed relationship to the larger society. Broadly, we may identify three regions, three stages of the journey. First there is the stage in which a group almost totally lacks access to the larger society. This stage characterized the immigrant period of Italians and other European ethnic groups, and most of the history of blacks in America. Second there is a stage in which a group blames itself. It feels guilty about its differentness, shies away from contact, and deferentially subordinates itself to the larger society. This stage was typical of second-generation European ethnics, especially Italian-Americans. It was also typical of blacks after the Civil War and until the 1960's, when the "black is beautiful" spirit took hold. The overwhelming majority of Hispanic-Americans is still locked in this stage.

Only Jews seem to have skipped the second stage, jumping directly from the first to the third stage. Jews developed two cultural values in response to centuries of life in the European Diaspora. They succeeded in keeping their culture alive by reinforcing the value attached to learning. Without a homeland, for Jews written words became the center of their ethnicity. The People of the Book developed a high priority value on learning and literacy. Second, Jews were excluded from the guild economic system of the late Middle Ages. They were pushed into the role of proto-commercial people at a time when the Church regarded financial business as sinful usury and the guilds resisted the rise of capitalism. By happy coincidence, the strong Jewish value on literacy and experience with commerce met a most propitious environment in the rapidly expanding industrial society of early twentieth-century America, when Jewish immigrants came here. By contrast, other ethnic groups lacked either the regard for literacy or the experience of modern commerce. Italian immigrants lacked both.

In the third stage, a group faces two possible paths. Its members may let old values die and become jellyfish Americans, transparent souls in surface pursuits. Or they may revitalize their traditions and contribute them in new form to an enriched American culture. Most Jews are in this third stage, some choosing the empty first path, some the admirable second. Those who revitalized their culture have had enormous influence on the United States in the last thirty years. Only a handful of elite blacks have entered this stage. They too have divided between the two paths. WASPs and Irish long ago entered this stage, some taking the arid path, others the culturally vital one. The *contributions* of the WASPs and Irish are commonly thought of as constituting mainstream America.

Third- and fourth-generation Italian-Americans are just beginning to enter this stage. It remains to be seen which path they will travel. At this point we can only chart their apparent inclinations as they arrive at the juncture. In doing this, it would be helpful to look at that seemingly simple but actually intricate complex of facts, myths, and emotions known as "ethnicity." Ultimately, these lie behind what it means to be Italian-American—or for that matter black, WASP, Jewish, Polish-American, or any other type of American, hyphenated or not. It is only by resolving what we mean by ethnicity that we can resolve whether America is to be a melting pot (and if so, what kind?) or a pluralistic society (and if so, what kind?).

Myths are among the strongest determinants of people's behavior. Contrary to a popular corruption of the term, a myth is not a mere fiction. A rich myth is a mixture of facts, insights, and ideals. An ethnic myth is made of the facts and wisdom of a people's life, and their outreach toward certain ideals. The energies thus expended by people define the values they live. Myths are born, grow, die, and replace each other in a complicated process. It is difficult to invent a myth deliberately and get people to believe in it. And it is equally hard to stamp out a myth which enjoys popular credence.

American culture is vast and complex. Americans hold many myths. Some are vital. Others are on the wane. One of the dying myths is the old melting pot ideal. In fact, we may question whether this was ever a myth truly commanding popular belief. More probably it was fully believed by only the relative handful of people in all ethnic groups who wished to replace ethnic characteristics with their alternative artificial myth of a uniform culture purely American in nature. Attempts to impose this myth on the American people met only limited success. We now discover that ethnic characteristics persist during generation after generation of American life. To be sure, these characteristics evolve. To be Italian-American, Afro-American, or Anglo-American is different from being Italian, African, or English. Yet the distinctions among Italian-, Afro-, and Anglo-Americans are just as important as the elements of Americanism they hold in common. In a real sense, we are all unmeltable ethnics, to use Michael Novak's apt phrase—even Mayflower descendants. Walt Whitman said it long ago when he called the United States "a teeming nation of nations."

The stubbornness of ethnicity is as strong as human psychology and culture, for it is woven of these. Even brutal totalitarian attempts to eradicate ethnicity fail. On July 31, 1972, the New York *Times* ran two revealing stories. The first reported new affirmations of ethnic identities among the one hundred ethnic groups in the Soviet Union. More significantly, a major shift of official policy was reported. The Soviet government has for the last fifty years vigorously and ruthlessly pressed a campaign to achieve a melted pot of Soviet culture, a homogeneous culture rooted in international socialist ideology. It tried to obliterate popular ethnic myths and impose in their place an artificial exclusive myth, using all the formidable means of a totalitarian state in the effort.

Now, in evident recognition that the attempt failed, the official policy of the Soviet government has turned to compromise with the realities of ethnicity, rather than attempts to destroy them. Speaking of the new policy, the story reported:

> Within the limits of its republic, region or other autonomous area, each ethnic group was given the right to foster an education and culture in its own language, but under the over-all umbrella of a Communist ideology. In terms of a widespread slogan, ethnic cultural development became "national in form and socialist in content."

On the same day, a second article reported a similar effort by the Chinese government regarding the fifty-four major ethnic groups that constitute most of that nation's seven hundred and fifty million people. The Central Institute for Nationalities in Peking is attempting to cultivate, among carefully selected young leaders, both Maoist ideology and different ethnic identities.

It is now clear that Americans in large numbers are reasserting myths of ethnicity contrary to the classic melting pot. These ethnic myths remained alive but submerged throughout the onslaught of the melting pot ideal that attended mass European immigration. Today it is no longer in doubt that ethnicity is a powerful force on the American scene and is likely to remain in the open rather than resubmerging. The likelihood derives from the very meaning of ethnicity.

Ethnicity is an identity of a person with himself and his experience. For as long as the history of humanity has been recorded, people have identified themselves by their membership in groups. Among the most frequent criteria for group definition have been common languages, common culture, common psychology, common history, and common morality. In a phrase, ethnic characteristics.

Today, gigantic forces of urban industrial life create feelings of rootlessness, anonymity, impotence, and hence meaninglessness. People try to resolve their crises of meaning by turning in a number of directions—for example, toward personal achievement, political ideology, and religion. Ethnicity is outstanding in several ways among the paths to meaningful identity available to people. First, it is immediately available. One is already a member of one or more ethnic groups by birth and/or upbringing. Personal achievement, to cite one other criterion of identity, is an uncertain and long-term affair. Second, events of recent history have demonstrated ethnicity's effectiveness in providing identity at a time when other criteria, such as political ideology, have proven to be of dubious reliability. Given the overwhelming need for meaningful identity, ethnicity has a powerful psychological appeal, perhaps unmatched by any other criteria.

Ethnicity, however, is a vague word. Each of its different meanings carries with it different possibilities for America. We may distinguish between two types of ethnicity. The first is tribalistic or chauvinistic ethnocentrism. The second is creative ethnicity.

Tribalism and chauvinism begin by distinguishing *us* from *them*. Bases for distinguishing between members of the tribe or group and outsiders have been innumerable in history. They include virtually every real or fictional criterion one could imagine, including religion, age, sex, class, interests, the cut of one's clothes or hair, etc. Of course, ethnicity has been one of the most often used defining characteristics in creating tribalistic, chauvinistic ethnocentrism.

From the initial division of humanity according to the criterion of ethnicity, all other meanings follow in the mind of the ethnic chauvinist. The very framework for all his thoughts, feelings, and actions follows. A statement by a New York City woman comes to mind. Several years ago, *Time* magazine conducted a survey among New Yorkers asking them if ethnic factors influenced their choice of a political candidate. One woman went to the point by repeating an old joke. "Ethnic, schmetnic," she said, "as long as he's Jewish."

Less humorously, we may say of the ethnic tribalist what George Orwell said of the chauvinistic nationalist, merely reading "ethnic group" where Orwell used "nation or other unit":

> I mean first of all the habit of assuming that human beings can be classified like insects and that whole blocks of millions or tens of millions of people can be confidently labeled 'good' or 'bad.' But secondly—and this is much more important—I mean the habit of identifying oneself with a single nation or other unit, placing it beyond good and evil and recognizing no other duty than that of advancing its interests.

Tribalistic, chauvinistic ethnocentrism provides a strong sense of identity and security. Moreover, it provides answers, or at least the directions for solutions of problems. And it provides a clear guide for all relations with those outside the group.

But it is a stunted identity, a false security, and a poten-

tially *disastrous guide* for human relations. For ethnic tribalism stifles the very psychological characteristics needed
for genuine identity, well-grounded security, and constructive intergroup relations. These include active intelligence,
sensitivity to the tragic aspect of life (all is not clear cut),
and positive appreciation and utilization of differences between groups. Instead the ethnic chauvinist is conformist,
obstreperous, uncritical of himself or his group, overwrought, pugnacious, prejudicially critical of those outside
the group, paranoid, and enormously energetic and determined. In short, he is potentially very destructive.

The creative ethnicist, on the other hand, uses his ethnic
background as a point of departure for growth rather than
as proof of his worth. By inquiry and reflection, he shapes
his identity by building upon inherited ethnic characteristics he judges to be valuable. (He neither rejects his
ethnicity—the transparent American—nor sets it and himself
in solid unchanging rock—the chauvinistic ethnocentrist.)
In shaping a true identity, he gains insight into himself that
gives a sense of meaningful, realistic self-control of one's
own life. In the process he also learns to appreciate how
the identities of other groups are formed and to respect
their different inheritances.

Educated ethnic awareness provides the creative ethnicist
with identity, energy, and direction. And it cultivates in
him respect for others (rather than contempt or obsequious
deference), with possibilities of genuine communication
and interchange of what may become valuable to all from
each ethnic group. It is creative ethnicity, for one learns
to live not only as a rooted person, but also to live beyond
one's roots and shape the emerging synthesis of contributions coming from various ethnic groups.

Italian-Americans, among others, desperately need educated ethnic awareness. The young of the group are just
leaving the guilt, conflict, and diffidence of the second generation and entering the stage where they must turn toward
either transparent nonidentity, or chauvinistic ethnocentrism, or creative ethnicity. They are confused, uneducated,

and uninsightful about their background. Thus it is *unlikely* that they are in danger of chauvinistic ethnocentrism.

I was struck by this recently in an incident involving the president of a large college. I had been invited to speak to a group of Italian-American students about our ethnicity. I was welcomed to the meeting by the college's president, who took the opportunity afforded him in making opening remarks to warn the students about the dangers of ethnocentrism, or as he put it, about developing attitudes of being better than other groups. The warning was totally misdirected. Italian-American youngsters are so confused about their ethnicity and tend to lie low to such an extreme that it was rare and significant that they had come to such a meeting in the first place. The college president, no doubt conditioned by dealing with aggressive students of other ethnic groups, completely misjudged the condition and needs of his audience.

Italian-American youngsters are not at all in danger of becoming ethnic chauvinists. They are very much in danger of becoming paralyzed, confused, aimless people because they are unable to communicate with their own ethnic personality centers. They are in no position to make real choices about identity, for such choices require knowledge and insight. The youngster who resists being identified as Italian-American because he is only vaguely aware of his roots and ashamed of them in his confusion is not making a real identity choice. He is not equipped to do so. Nor is the person who aggressively boasts an identity he does not understand.

Sadly, many Italian-American youngsters are in the shame-born-of-confusion condition. It is my impression that the great majority of them suffer from it at least to the extent that they avoid and resist public discussion of their background. In their insistence that such discussion is not needed because they are "just Americans," the heartbreaking truth is they protesteth too much.

When the third-generation youngster leaves his parents' home for school or work, he finds himself in a peculiar situation. A member of one of the largest ethnic groups in the country, he feels isolated, with no affiliation with or affinity for other Italian-Americans. He often wants and needs to go beyond the minimum security his parents sought in the world. In a word, he is more ambitious about life. But he has not been given family or cultural guidance upon which this ambition can be defined and pursued. Ironically, this descendant of immigrants despised by much of the old American establishment tries to live by one of the latter's cherished myths. He sees himself as purely American, a blank slate upon which his individual experiences in American culture (washed clean of all ethnic elements) will inscribe what is to be his personality and his destiny. He regards himself as an empty vessel waiting to be filled by the pure waters of American experience. The myth was imposed by one of the greatest propaganda efforts in American history. In his essay "Evil and the American Ethos" (in *Sanctions for Evil*, edited by N. Sanford and C. Comstock, 1971), Robert Bellah makes the point with a fantastic example.

> For a festival sponsored by Henry Ford during the early 1920's a giant pot was built outside the gates of his factory. Into this pot danced groups of gaily dressed immigrants dancing and singing their native songs. From the other side of the pot emerged a single stream of Americans dressed alike in the contemporary standard dress and singing the national anthem. As the tarantellas and the polkas at last faded away only the rising strains of the national anthem could be heard as all the immigrants finally emerged. The enormous pressures which created this vast transformation amounted almost to a forced conversion.

The myth of being "purely American" is untenable logically, psychologically, and sociologically.

Although the young Italian-American is diligent and highly responsible, other elements needed for a powerful personality are frozen in a nondeveloped state by his pervasive identity crisis. His ability for sustained action with autonomy, initiative, self-confidence, and assertiveness is undermined by his lack of integrated personality. In addition, the youngsters' false view of themselves as atomistic individuals leaves them unorganized, isolated, diffident, and thus powerless in a society of power blocs. In a turn of the vicious cycle, feelings of powerlessness lead to more feelings of shame, confusion, etc.

Joe Ponzi is a young playwright who wrote a play (*Union Street*) about Italian-Americans, set in and performed on the streets of my boyhood neighborhood in Brooklyn in May 1973. His purpose, in his words, is "to give people pride in being Italian." In a newspaper interview, Mr. Ponzi said, "There's almost an inferiority feeling among Italian kids in the city. The street bravado is a cover-up. It's like we can't admit we're afraid."

The reporter's description of the play's first performance before a youthful audience bears out Mr. Ponzi's feelings:

The Sunday premiere in Carroll Gardens, a few blocks from the scene of the play, was a case of life imitating art. An unruly crowd of several hundred, unable to hear because of a faulty sound system, began heckling and whistling from the first scene. In it, a candy store owner is reading newspaper headlines to show that nothing changes. When he got to "Mother Kills Son," a youth in the crowd, wearing the kind of turned-up hat made famous by Heintz Hall of the Dead End Kids, yelled "They shoulda killed you!" By the end of the play the audience was stealing props from the set.

The dilemma of young Italian-Americans is a lonely, quiet crisis, so it has escaped public attention. But it is a major ethnic group crisis. As it grows, it will be more readily recognized as such and not viewed merely as the personal problems of individuals. If this is to be realized sooner rather than later, these young people must learn whence they came and why they are as they are. Until then their behavior will alternate between sterile diffidence punctuated by equally ineffective overdefensive outbursts.

In a recent book called *The Hidden Injuries of Class* (1972), Jonathan Cobb and Richard Sennett report their findings about working-class people, many of them specified as Italian-Americans. They found that they seldom say "I,"

but prefer to use the passive voice. Instead of speaking of
real accomplishments as their own, these people talk of
themselves always as objects of other agents. "They gave
me a pay raise." "It was straightened out," instead of "I
did it." The authors conclude that self-alienation from one's
own power and competence is a defense that wards off
humiliation. By separating one's inner, real self from the
social roles played (despite the fact that these roles are
frequently real, challenging, and socially useful), one pro-
tects himself. Working-class people separate their self-
worth from society's picture of them, thereby preserving
their self-esteem even at the expense of willfully demean-
ing society's image of them. In effect they neutralize the
degrading picture society paints of them by accepting it
as true but at the same time holding it at arm's length from
their real self-esteem.

It is the Uncle Tom syndrome with a special schizoid
twist of double realities. This twist is easy for Italian-
Americans. At the heart of their heritage is a view of life,
made famous by Pirandello, in which there are several
distinct layers of reality and several distinct layers of appearance. All of the Meridionale's *savoir-faire* is concerned
with maneuvering in and out of these multiple layers. In
a psychology that is all but incomprehensible to most Americans, Italian-Americans don't care about certain layers of
their public appearance which they separate without strain
from other strata of appearance and reality.

The American mind insists that Pirandello must either be
a jokester or a cynical relativist when he names one of his
plays *Right You Are, If You Think You Are* (*Così è, se vi
pare!*). In fact he is neither merely punning nor acting the
sophomoric relativist. He is expressing the Southern Italian
psychological sophistication into which he was born and
raised, a scheme more complicated and subtle than the
American no-nonsense approach. For example, in American common sense, "you either love something or you
don't." Meridionali and their Italian-American descendants
intuitively understand what good psychologists work to discover and analyze. Namely, that it is not only possible but

common both to love and not love something, and that in addition there are an infinite number of possible variations to the ambivalence.

But truth is more than split in the old Mezzogiorno view of reality. The ancient view is above all one of extreme skepticism. Di Lampedusa writes of it in *The Leopard:*

> Nowhere has truth so short a life as in Sicily: a fact has scarcely happened five minutes before its genuine kernel has vanished, been camouflaged, embellished, disfigured, squashed, annihilated by imagination and self interest; shame, fear, generosity, malice, opportunism, charity, all the passions, good as well as evil, fling themselves onto the fact and tear it to pieces; very soon it has vanished altogether.

At a recent conference on ethnicity, I heard a Ph.D. candidate in anthropology tell of his findings about working-class Polish-Americans in Detroit he is living among and studying. He described an interview with a married couple he has come to know and admire. They talked about the TV show "All in the Family." The couple liked the program. The husband said, "Archie is like me. He doesn't come home from the office wearing a tie. He comes home in a jacket like me." But the graduate student was astounded at what was next said. "Archie is a bigot," the man said, "and I'm a bigot." "That's right," said the wife cheerfully, "Archie is just like my husband." Having come to know the couple over months of living close to them, the graduate student knew that the husband in fact was not a bigot, nor close-minded, nor of dim intelligence.

The student was startled also by the wife's next offering that she was just like Mrs. Bunker. The couple, married twenty-seven years, sat holding hands and the graduate student was stunned by the discrepancy between their self-description and what they are in fact. Far from being a mindless dingbat, the wife is highly intelligent, holds real responsibility in community organizations in which she is active, and expresses herself well. Moreover, the couple show respect for each other. Their relationship in no way resembles Archie's sadistic treatment of his witless wife.

Only a deliberate successful effort at educated self-awareness can break Italian-Americans' willingness to accept a false and humiliated public image of themselves while holding themselves aloof from it. The paralysis of this stance will disappear and its suffering with it. The social price paid in this attitude has been already described, the psychological price outlined. If anyone still clings to the image of Italian-Americans as sunny and content, he should note more of Greeley's findings. One is that only 33 per cent of Italian-Americans in the Eastern United States consider themselves very happy, and only 37 per cent in the Midwest. Moreover, 59 per cent in the East score high on anomie (feelings of being rootless and directionless), while 41 per cent in the Midwest confided that they suffer from anomie. Twenty-six per cent across the nation said they worry all the time, a figure higher than those of Irish, German, Polish, French, English, Scandinavian, and Jewish-American groups.

It is only by communicating with their background that Italian-Americans can create whole lives for themselves. The shape of the identity they could then create is an open question. They may opt for one of the several models that have served other ethnic groups. For example, they may choose to cultivate their Italian culture, pursue personal careers, and somehow fuse the two into an energetic and confident relationship—an approach that has been characteristic of Jewish-Americans. They may also turn toward the church, revive it, and build political clout and group morale upon its power base, as Irish-Americans did. Or, they may feel it necessary to form strictly nationalistic power blocs, as some blacks are doing.

On the other hand, they may forge their own models of individual and group identity out of an imaginative use of their unique inheritance. In my opinion, the greatest possibilities lie in this approach. The unique values and approaches to life of Italian-Americans, if cultivated and updated, could contribute sorely needed perspectives and purposes to American life. Italian-Americans would then become truly full participants in American society, not merely assimilated in it as in a melting pot, nor standing half outside it as they have so far.

Assuming Italian-Americans can fulfill this challenge, the question of America's receptivity to their offerings remains. The chief obstacles to America's acceptance of Italian-Americans are vestiges of the melting pot ideal, paradoxically existent even in the minds of young Italian-Americans; the buffoon and Mafia stereotypes; and a new type of American society whose outlines have become clear in recent years. The new society results from the combined effect of ethnic groups all behaving as tribalistic chauvinists.

As the revolution of rising expectations of the 1960's became one of rising nonnegotiable demands by ethnocentric groups, America entered a severe social crisis that further complicates the dilemma of Italian-Americans who stood mostly outside the decade's social drama.

As noted, it became clear in the 1960's that the melting pot myth is no longer viable as a basis of common culture. However, two other essential foundations of America's common culture were also rocked in the period—the myths of fairness and merit. Put simply, the American beliefs that all ethnic groups should be treated equally by the majority society and that contributions coming from each group be evaluated on the sole basis of merit were badly shaken. The myths are fundamental to our culture. Their weakening signals an acute social pathology. The very roots of the authority around which Americans center their lives, plans, and hopes disintegrate as fairness and meritocracy crumble. Without the strong center provided by these two myths, centrifugal forces of ethnicity could cause American society to fly into fragments. Restoration of a common culture would be difficult.

Unfortunately, the '60's moved us in this direction. This is widely recognized as shown by "A View of American Public Opinion," printed in a paper of the Department of Health, Education and Welfare, dated November 26, 1971. Of five hopes and eight fears of Americans surveyed over twelve years, the sharpest increase occurred in the fear of "national disunity," jumping eighteen percentage points from 1964 to 1971, and twenty-three percentage points from 1959 to 1971.

One of the key causes of the rise of both creative ethnicity and chauvinistic ethnocentrism was the civil rights movement. At first impelled by the Supreme Court's 1954 school desegregation decision, the movement demanded equal rights for individuals, and therefore sought to tear down the walls of racial segregation that impeded enjoyment of equal rights. At this stage, the movement raised the ethnic consciousness of blacks, and raised corresponding awareness of their own ethnicity among whites. In the middle '60's, however, a concurrence of forces moved the across-the-board ethnic awareness toward tribalistic, chauvinistic ethnocentricity.

Although it did not cause the shift in direction, the slogan of "black power" stands as the first symbol of the change from ethnic awareness to ethnocentric chauvinism. Since the middle '60's, the swing by members of all ethnic groups away from fairness and merit to their chauvinistic interests has become pronounced. Each of large segments of various ethnic groups now thinks exclusively of its own interest, in Orwell's phrase "placing it beyond good and evil and recognizing no other duty than that of advancing its interest."

When challenged on the socially divisive results of this, chauvinists of various ethnic groups answer with one or more of the following responses:

1. America was always divided. It has always been each group for itself. This answer ignores the fact that the common culture myths of fairness and merit have until now had considerable vitality. Although less than perfect, and denied to some groups of Americans, the myths have been operative. Responding to the limitations of the myths by wanting to scrap them altogether is an understandable result of rage. Understandable yet ill considered. There is far more compelling logic to the response that seeks to increase in fact the effectiveness of the myths.

2. Citing the constructive aspects of ethnicity. Those who do this are either confused themselves regarding the differences between chauvinistic ethnocentrism and creative ethnicity, or are consciously manipulating and exploiting the confusion in the minds of others.

3. Asserting that tribalistic, chauvinistic ethnocentrism is a necessary, temporary step toward creative ethnicity. The dynamics of how one would lead to the other are explained, if at all, in terms of a dangerously inadequate understanding of the self-perpetuating nature of chauvinistic ethnocentrism.

These three apologies are used to legitimize violations of fairness and merit. Various whipping boys are advanced. They are said to deserve to suffer from unfairness and violation of respect for merit. WASPs are a favorite group. For example, Peter Schrag in his *Decline of the Wasp* (1972) lays virtually everything wrong with America on this one ethnic group. In the process, he slurs WASPs in a way that American sensibilities would no longer accept if such slurs were aimed at some other ethnic groups.

Viciously, violations of fairness and merit are legitimized not only when aimed against the hitherto dominant ethnic groups but also when directed against Italian-Americans, who are among those who have all along suffered from the shortcomings of the actual application of fairness and merit! Reasons for this have been discussed in previous chapters. Italian-Americans are convenient scapegoats for spurious explanations and drastic remedies of America's social ills. Double standards abound. Great sympathetic attention is given to objective conditions determining social ills among favored ethnic groups. But social ills among Italian-Americans are dismissed without recognition, sympathy, or understanding. Often they are approached with hostility, ridicule, and malice.

In the high schools of the suburbs surrounding New York City, students now commonly refer to those students who are placed by school authorities on "tracks" leading to dropping out or vocational training (rather than preparation for college) as "greasers." Sol Stein in his novel,

The Magician, records this practice. Of course, the epithet "greasers" in the Eastern United States originally referred to Italian-Americans. It is no accident that it is now used there to cover all those of whatever ethnic group are regarded as destined for failure. (The greaser in Stein's novel has a Polish name.)

Americans, including many who pride themselves on their social consciousness vis-à-vis certain oppressed groups, have made an equation of being a failure with being Italian-American or being like Italian-Americans. Further, the emotional thrust of the prejudice is that Italian-Americans "and their ilk" deserve to fail. Their culture, characteristics, and aspirations are inferior. Therefore failures are, *ipso facto,* greasers. Failures are by their very nature Italian-Americans and vice versa. The dilemma of Italian-Americans is cruelly compounded by this prejudice common to both parties of the 1960's alliance between non-whites and upper-class, self-styled liberal whites.

Despite generations of contributions to America, the Italian-American today is in fresh danger of being cast by his countrymen into the oldest role they imposed on him, the inferior wop. Richard H. Huber in his *American Idea of Success* (1971) described another classic American myth. It holds that individuals and groups should gain status, as he puts it, by "achievement rather than ascription." Italian immigrants were denied full human status by ascription. Despite immigrant achievements and those of their second-generation children, today's youthful third- and fourth-generation Italian-Americans are in real danger of failing in this country, not by their merits, but by self-fulfilling ascriptions of failure to them by their fellow-Americans. If, as is so often true, things Italian-American are regarded as inferior, cheap, ridiculous, or criminal, then the achievements of Italian-Americans will be inhibited and their actual accomplishments will not count. It will be impossible for Italian-American achievements to become contributions to the larger society.

The type of society that results from a combination of chauvinistic ethnocentrisms and abandonment of fairness and merit is a parody of genuine pluralism. It is a mosaic society. This is a fitting metaphor, for it connotes the static quality of such a society, each ethnic piece in the mosaic unmoving and isolated from the others. And the Italian-American part of the mosaic is being fixed once more at the outside edges of the mosaic, out in the cold.

A genuinely pluralistic society is one of creative ethnicities. In it, each ethnic group is treated with equal fairness and respect according to the merit of its contributions. It is not a melting pot, for the characteristics of each group are cultivated and contributed to the whole rather than diluted or erased. America's common culture in pluralism would evolve from its examination of its peoples' lives and not from some hollow sense of an enlightened life to which all must become assimilated as in the melting pot ideal. The Socratic ideal of the *examined* life is more substantial and realistic than that of the enlightened life. In the latter, the form of enlightenment must be either some utopian ideal which ignores human realities, or composed of the characteristics of one dominant group or combination of groups which masquerade as universal ideals.

It is the responsibility of Italian-Americans to turn their ethnic awareness into creative ethnicity. It is the responsibility of American society as a whole to turn away from its mosaic direction and toward real pluralism. The two responsibilities are interdependent, but because of the disproportion of power between a minority group and the whole society, the bulk of responsibility lies with the larger American society.

A group is more likely to develop creative ethnicity when the larger culture acts fairly toward it. It is more likely to spawn chauvinistic ethnocentrism when it is abused. Therefore, it is no surprise that John Goering found third-generation Italian-Americans in Providence, Rhode Island, to be both much more conscious of their ethnicity than their parents and much less convinced that America is a land of equal opportunity. "The third generation," writes Goering, "returns to the seclusiveness of ethnicity in resentment against unattained promises." ("The Emergence of Ethnic Interests," *Social Forces,* March 1971.)

In the end, a group achieves real identity with its larger society by cultivating its own characteristics to levels of strong, contributing sophistication. Attempts by it to assimilate without this development, or pressures upon it from outside to do so, bring on personal disaster for its members and aridness in the larger culture. Italian-Americans, then, must foster their ethnic awareness and shun temptations and pressures to become transparent people, without substance, or to drop out altogether. The dangers in the first type of pressure are dramatically highlighted by the story of Roseto, Pennsylvania, a town of 1,600, 95 per cent of whom are Italian-American descendants of immigrants who founded the town in 1882. Until recently, the townspeople successfully held to Old World life patterns. On May 8, 1973, *Newsday* carried a story by Bill Richards. His findings are chilling.

> In the early 1960's researchers found that Rosetans ritually sat down to meals that would send most doctors reaching for their blood pressure gauges, yet not one person under 47 ever had had a recorded heart attack. Rosetans seemed to eat more and live 10 to 20 years longer than everyone else.
>
> But the so-called miracle of Roseto is over. Last year, the town's heart attack rates soared to three times the national average. The blame, according to those who have sought to explain the phenomenon, lies in the fact that Rosetans are becoming "Americanized."
>
> A medical research team from the University of Texas has been studying Rosetans since 1961. The opinion of its head, Dr. John G. Bruhn, is definite. "In Roseto," he said, "family and community support is disappearing. Most of the men who have had heart attacks here were living under stress and really had nowhere to turn to relieve that pressure. These people have given up something to get something and it's killing them."

Hopefully Italian-Americans will have the strength to build creative ethnicity and not chauvinistic ethnocentrism.

The fact that fewer Italian-Americans live in Italian neighborhoods than in past times is irrelevant, for ethnicity is made of a community that is cultural and psychological, not necessarily geographic. And hopefully, America will give them, by its fairness and respect, the minimum social requirements to make this possible.

Italian ethnicity comes with the blood if not through it. Its components are unique and strong—family, work, pragmatism, pazienza, serietà, humanistic life orientation, and a Realpolitic stance toward authority and power. Future success for Italian-Americans depends on whether we can develop these and adapt them to present and future American needs and realities. It is a psychological cliché that adaptability depends on intelligence. But fully successful adaptability depends on more than mere intelligence. It depends on insight and wisdom—on the old Socratic maxim of knowing oneself. It is my faith that Italian-Americans have all other requirements for greatness, their own and their country's. To set their destiny in motion, they need only to know themselves. With self-knowledge and the imagination it stimulates, added to the legacies of courage and fortitude inherited from the earlier generations, young Italian-Americans can realize dreams denied their immigrant grandparents and sacrificed by their culture-conflicted parents. And in doing so, Italian-Americans are perhaps uniquely equipped by their tradition to help restore America to the verity that full humanity lies only in continuity with our traditions, with what comes with our blood. In our eagerness to adjust to the demands of modern life we have become victims of those Frankensteinian social structures originally developed to serve life—commercial, educational, governmental, entertainment, and religious structures. Italian-Americans are specially outfitted by the values of their old culture and its state of high preservation to help heal the lassitude, uncertainties, ennui, paralysis, and doubt that are the result of America's having lost itself in the means of life. Italian-Americans can help their country to place itself once again in touch with human ends. The point can be put succinctly. As Professor Robert Di

Pietro is fond of pointing out, Americans typically say that a person is "good as gold." The standard Italian expression carries a fundamentally different, more humanistic meaning. In Italian, a person is said to be *buono come il pane*—as good as *bread*.

Index